WITHIN THE PALE

The Story of Sheriff Hutton Park

By the Sheriff Hutton Women's Institute
Community Pale Project

Edited by Ed Dennison

William Sessions Limited
York, England

ISBN 1 85072 332 X

Printed in 12 point Times Typeface
By Sessions of York
The Ebor Press
York, England

WITHIN THE PALE: THE STORY OF SHERIFF HUTTON PARK

CONTENTS

ACKNOWLEDGEMENTS

It is inevitable that a book of this size and scope relies on a lot of contributions, not only from the individual authors of the various chapters but also from a large number of people who have worked behind the scenes.

The Sheriff Hutton Women's Institute Community Pale Project gratefully acknowledge all the help and encouragement they have received from the Sheriff Hutton community, especially the farmers, landowners and tenants who have allowed access to their land. Thanks are also due to those local residents who have provided documentary and pictorial sources which appear in the book, as well as oral history. Without their help and co-operation, the book would not have been completed. In particular, individual authors would like to thank the following:

Reminiscences and oral history:
Pauline Boullier, Robert Brumby, Sheila Clark, Edwin Cooke, Alan Coverdale (deceased), Claud Coverdale, Jean Farnaby, Barbara Foreman, Barbara Grinham, Wendy Haste, Barbara Helliwell, Myrtle and George Hull, Phyllis Hull, Yvonne Jack, Tessa Mitchell, Viv Nelson, Margaret Nicholson, Nora Ward (deceased), Nancy Wright, Tony Wright and Mrs Sarah Sherwin (nee Ledgard).

Archaeology and history:
Jim Halliday, NYCC Sites and Monuments Record, Chris Chandler (English Heritage), Vivien Swan, Dr Bridgett Jones, Ed Dennison Archaeological Services Ltd, Nick Pearson (On Site Archaeology), Marjorie Dandy, Anne Hodgson, GSB Prospection Ltd, Margaret Boustead (NYCC Record Office), Chris Taylor, and the late Christopher Gilbert.

Buildings:
David and Sheila Armitage, Michael Armitage, John Armitage, Robin Barker, Georgina Ratcliff, Mike and Dorothy Rickatson, June Wood, Kevin Grinham, Richard and Jenny Howarth, and Pamela Palmer.

Ecology:
Ted Green, Jill Butler, Luke Steer and the Coxwold Botanical Group.

The research for this book was carried out at a variety of libraries and record offices, and thanks are also due to staff at the British Library, Temple Newsam, York Central Library, York City Archives, the North Yorkshire County Record Office, the Borthwick Institute of Historical Research, and the Public Record Office (National Archives).

The majority of the photographs in the book were taken by Keith Roberts, with others being provided by Ed Dennison, Alan Pitman (figure 7/11 and plates 16, 28, 45, and 77 to 81) and BM Photographics of Hull (plates 29 to 31, 34 and 35). The maps, plans and survey drawings were produced by Ed Dennison, Shaun Richardson generated the line drawings, and the original watercolours, reproduced throughout the text, is by Jean Farnaby. Anne Hodgson drew the various archaeological artefacts in Chapter 4. The following organisations are also acknowledged for permission to reproduce specific photographs: Cambridge University Collection of Air Photographs (figures 1/4, 4/2, 4/7, 6/5 and 7/18); Aeroscene Ltd (figure 7/1 and plate 17); English Heritage NMR (figure 4/6); York City Art Gallery (figure 7/17); Ryedale Folk Museum (figure 8/4); National Archives (figure 11/4); National Portrait

Gallery, London (figures 11/2, 11/3, 11/5, 17/3 and 17/4); Temple Newsam, Leeds (figures 12/2 and 12/3); the Company of Merchant Adventurers of York (figure 13/2); North Yorkshire County Record Office (figure 17/2); British Library (plates 37 and 38); and the West Yorkshire Archive Service (figures 12/1, and 15/1 to 15/4); Bibliothèque Nationale de France (BnF) (figures 3/1 to 3/8 and plates 21 to 26). Plates 70 and 71 are reproduced with the acknowledgement of Mrs Sarah Sherwin (nee Ledgard). Other sources and individual copyrights are acknowledged in the captions.

Readers should note that many of the areas and places described in the book, including much of the park and the second castle site, are on private land. Permission to enter these areas should be sought from the relevant landowners.

INTRODUCTION
By Barbara Foreman
Co-ordinator, Sheriff Hutton Women's Institute Community Pale Project

Sheriff Hutton, in the North Riding of Yorkshire, is best known for the gaunt remains of its medieval castle, which tower over the centre of the village, and for the 12th century church which contains the famous alabaster tomb, attributed by some as a memorial to Edward of Middleham, Prince of Wales and son of Richard III.

Fewer people know that there was once also a medieval deer park, which covered the countryside below the castle and which provided food, entertainment, wood, grazing and other resources to both aristocracy and peasants. It is known that kings and princes hunted and hawked here, that lords held parties, that peasants were arrested for stealing deer, and that there was at least one Civil War skirmish in the park. Elizabeth of York (mother of Henry VIII), Thomas Howard (Earl of Surrey and the victor of the Battle of Flodden) and Edward, the unfortunate Earl of Warwick, all grazed their horses in the park. The core of the medieval park still survives around the 18th century Hall, itself a Queen Anne conversion of a substantial mansion built here in the reign of James I.

The Sheriff Hutton Women's Institute started their community Pale Project in 2003 with the object of creating a pictorial map of the park pale, the boundary which kept the deer in and the predators out. However, with the aid of a grant from the Local Heritage Initiative, the project has grown and reaches its culmination in this book. It tells the fascinating story of the park, from its creation in medieval times right up to the present day.

The book has been produced with the help of numerous individuals who are mentioned in the acknowledgments. However, this always was a community project, and especial thanks must go to the local villagers and farmers of Sheriff Hutton who have been so generous with their time and information. Inevitably, many questions remain unanswered, and it is hoped that this book will encourage others to investigate and contribute to future publications!

In the meantime, enjoy the book, and keep up to date with new discoveries on our website: http://www.lhi.org.uk/projects_directory/projects_by_region/yorkshire_the_humber_/north_y orkshire/sheriff_hutton_wi_pale_project/index.html).

CHAPTER 1: BACKGROUND TO SHERIFF HUTTON AND THE PARK

Introduction by Ed Dennison

Although the title of this book is 'Within the Pale', the park does not, and never did, exist in isolation, and it can only be properly understood and appreciated in association with other elements of the surrounding landscape. The purpose of this initial chapter is to provide a background to some of these elements, and to set the scene for the subsequent chapters which discuss the history, development and characteristics of the park.

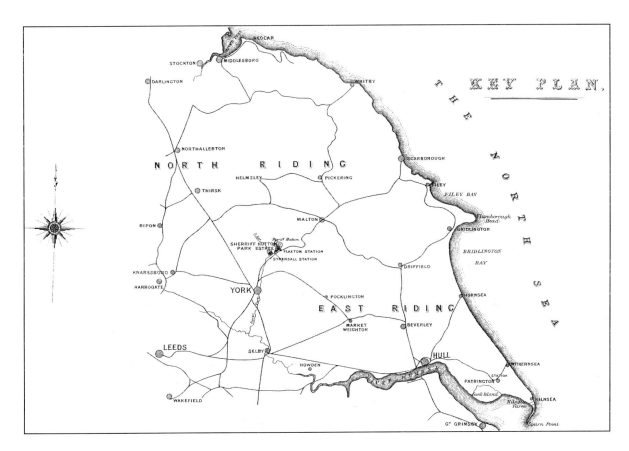

Fig. 1/1: General location of Sheriff Hutton (taken from the 1880 Sale Catalogue).

Sheriff Hutton village lies some 16km north-east of York, in North Yorkshire, on the southern edge of the Howardian Hills. The village is located on a prominent east-west aligned ridge of Lower Jurassic 'mudrocks' and sands, which rises to a height of c.65m (213 feet) above sea level half way along Main Street, the principal east-west thoroughfare;[1] the name 'Hutton' stems from the Old English *hoh* (a projecting piece of land) and *tun* (a farmstead), while the 'Sheriff' prefix stems from the association with the Bulmer family, Bertram (de) Bulmer being Sheriff of Yorkshire in 1115.[2] The village is characterised by its two castles, the first lying adjacent to the church at the east end, while the more impressive stone ruins of the second dominate the west end of the village. The former medieval deer park occupied some 750 acres (c.300 hectares) to the south of the two castles, within what is now a broadly flat agricultural landscape. The local topography is such that the second castle can be seen from almost everywhere within the boundary of the park (see for example plate 27).

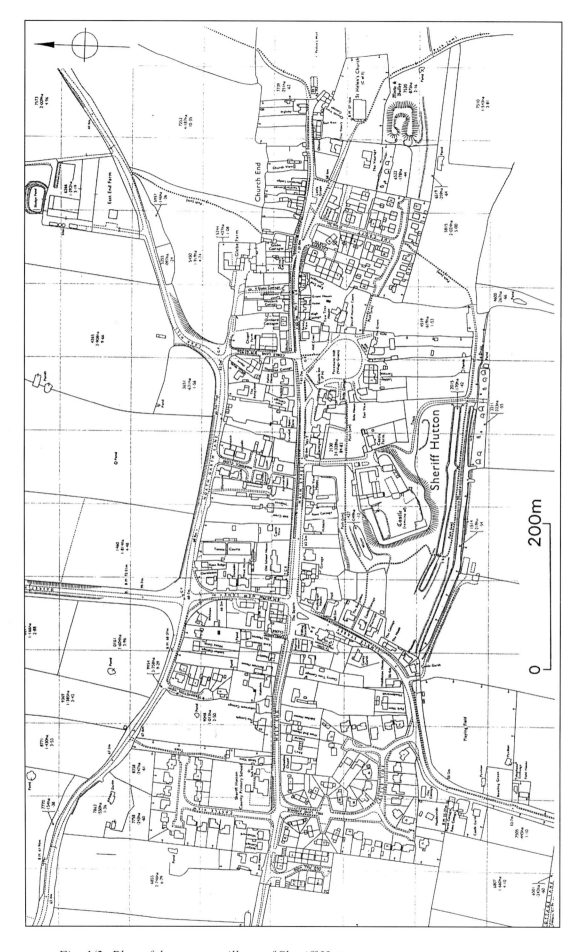

Fig. 1/2: Plan of the present village of Sheriff Hutton.

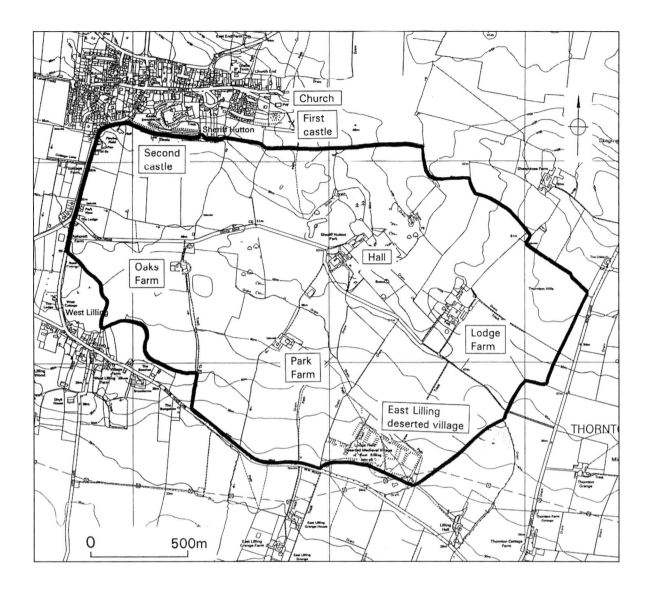

Fig. 1/3: Extent of Sheriff Hutton park, as depicted by Norden in 1624.

The village, castles and park are overlooked from the north and north-east by settlements such as Terrington and High Stittenham which lie on the steep south-facing scarps of the Howardian Hills. Sheriff Hutton's ridge location means that both the village and in particular the ruins of the second castle stand out in sharp relief against York Minster and the Vale of York beyond. The area to the north of the village comprises a low lying, flat and featureless valley formerly occupied by a post-glacial lake; this area remains prone to winter flooding even today, a factor which may have played an important part in the transportation of stone from Mowthorpe when constructing the second castle (see Chapter 7).

Like any other Yorkshire village, the development of Sheriff Hutton has been influenced by the complex interaction of many factors, including geology, topography and climate. These latter were perhaps most important during the earliest days of settlement, and the fragmentary evidence for prehistoric activity in and around the village and park are discussed in Chapter 4. There are good reasons to believe that the Romans also had a presence in the park and the traces they have left behind are outlined in Chapter 4. It is likely that the earliest part of the present village has Saxon origins (see below), but it was in the later medieval period in

3

particular that it assumed greater significance. This came about for a number of reasons. Sheriff Hutton was inextricably linked with two major families, the Bulmers and Nevilles, both of whom became key players on the regional and national stage. The village also occupies an important strategic position close to York, England's second city during this period and home of the institutions of royal government for much of the first half of the 14th century.[3] In addition, Sheriff Hutton was on a major transport route, running between Crayke, Easingwold and other centres to the west and the east.[4]

The village was therefore ideally placed to become a centre within the Bulmer and Neville estates, and the Nevilles in particular, especially Ralph (d.1367) and his son John (d.1388), undertook a systematic and co-ordinated programme of development in the mid to late 14th century which included the expansion of the village, the creation of a market, the construction of the impressive stone castle and a significant expansion of the deer park. It seemed that they valued the existing hunting facilities and perceived there to be good economic opportunities for the development of the village and market. We should also not forget the role of an individual's choice or whim, and perhaps John and Ralph Neville personally preferred Sheriff Hutton to their other estates. A combination of all of the above is probably closer to the truth.

The Manor and Lordship of Sheriff Hutton by Tony Wright

The growing importance of Sheriff Hutton during the later medieval period can be traced through the surviving documents which detail the complex pattern of land ownership and tenure within the village. A detailed consideration of these would fill a book in itself, and the general reader might find their eyelids growing heavy after a few pages! Therefore only a summary is given here; as with any of the other chapters, those wishing to pursue the subject in more detail should refer to the accompanying footnotes or the bibliography at the end of the book.

At the time of the Domesday Survey, completed in 1086, the land comprising Sheriff Hutton was held jointly by the Crown (4 carucates of land or c.480 acres) and the Count of Mortain (11 carucates or c.1,320 acres).[5] The Crown land had been held as three separate 'manors' before the Conquest by three Saxon nobles, Turchil, Turolf and Turstanby. Mortain's land, which was held by his chief tenant, Neil Fossard, also included 5 carucates (c.600 acres) in Welburn and Ganthorpe, and 3 carucates and 5 bovates (c.430 acres) in Terrington. Fossard held most of the other manors which later became the lordship of Sheriff Hutton, but there is no evidence to suggest that 'Hotun' (Sheriff Hutton) was pre-eminent among them at this time. The presence of the first castle site and the acquisition of the prefix 'Sheriff' to the village name between 1154 and 1163[6] has been taken to indicate that the manor had some importance in the mid 12th century, but this is probably not so. Although the lordships of the manors of West Lilling, Cornbrough and Farlington followed that of Sheriff Hutton,[7] as do the lordships of other parts of the Fossard and later the Bulmer landholdings,[8] there are again no signs that Sheriff Hutton was pre-eminent amongst them before the mid 13th century; indeed, both West Lilling and Cornbrough have sizeable moated sites which may be indicative of important alternative manorial organisations.[9] One possible exception might relate to the organisation of the church of Sheriff Hutton, which had dependant chapelries at Farlington and Stittenham.[10]

However, from 1277, documents start to refer to 'Sheriff Hutton and its members',[11] assigning it six knights' fees (a feudal tenure which obliged the holder to provide military assistance to the Crown). Although the Nevilles had already been present in the manor for some time, they received the overlordship of Sheriff Hutton from the de Mauleys in 1331, when the 5th Peter de Mauley released all his rights to service on it to Ralph Neville.[12] The way was then clear for the Nevilles to commence their re-development of the village, which may itself have been recovering from Scottish incursions; these reduced the value of many Yorkshire manors dramatically, including Sheriff Hutton, between 1291 and 1319.[13] Any planned re-development was probably also delayed by the frequent absences of the Nevilles and the Thwengs (who may have acted as their stewards) in the Scottish and French wars of the period (see below).

Fig. 1/4: Aerial view of Sheriff Hutton village, taken July 1951 prior to recent housing developments (Cambridge University Collection of Air Photographs, GU82).

At the Sheriff's inquiry into Robert Neville's lands at his death in 1282 (*inquisition post mortem*),[14] it was stated that he held the manor of Sheriff Hutton from Peter de Mauley by service of one knight's fee; at that time the manor comprised 350 acres of arable and 300 acres of meadow, and a windmill and fulling mill are both mentioned. The later *inquisition* of Ralph Neville in 1331 noted that there were 40 bovates (c.600 acres) of land worth £10 per annum, 32 bovates (c.480 acres) of waste and 120 acres of meadow. Another plot of land called 'Le Cotegarth' is specifically mentioned, as well as a wood called 'Le Laghwode'.[15] By the time of Ralph Neville's death in 1367, the manor included 4 carucates (perhaps c.480 acres) of land in demesne, two thirds of which was sown, with one third lying fallow, as well as 300 acres of meadow of which 280 acres had been mown.[16]

By 1367, the larger lordship of Sheriff Hutton comprised lands in several groups of manors. One group was centred on Sheriff Hutton itself, and comprised Sheriff Hutton, West Lilling,

Cornbrough, Farlington, Flaxton, Whenby, Terrington, Ganthorpe, Thornton-le-Clay and Earswick. Another lay on the East Yorkshire wolds (Towthorpe, Fimber and Burdale) and there was a looser group in North Yorkshire and Cleveland (Helmsley, Kepwick, Pinchingthorpe, Stainton, Thornton and Wilton). There were also some outlying manors such as Habton, 'Thornton under Risebergh', 'Bolleby in Whitbystrand', 'Thorntonfield', 'Hemlington' and Stainsby.[17] At John Neville's death in 1388, by which time he had acquired licenses for a fair and market (in 1378) and a new stone castle (in 1382) in the village,[18] further estates had been added to the lordship, including Sutton on the Forest, Stearsby and Tholthorpe.[19] Ralph Neville, 1st Earl of Westmoreland, then separated Sheriff Hutton lordship from the rest of his lands between 1396 and 1404,[20] and gave it to his second wife, Joan Beaufort and her heirs. Although the estates were re-joined partly after his death, their eldest son, Richard, Earl of Salisbury, leased the lordship separately to Cardinal Beaufort and some retainers for three years at 1,000 marcs per year from 1441.[21]

The changes to the lordship during the early and mid 15th century are as yet unclear, as are the roles played by it and the other northern lordships in the life of Richard, Duke of Gloucester, later to be Richard III. However, in 1486 the lands are described as being in the king's hands 'by ... the nonage of Edward, son and heir of Edward, late Duke of Clarence'.[22] The accounts for this year show that the lordship of Sheriff Hutton now included land in Sheriff Hutton itself, East Lilling, West Lilling, Scoreby (Scawby?), Stamford Bridge, Busby, Faceby, Carlton (in Cleveland?), Terrington, Wilberfoss, Calton (Catton, Carlton or Cawton?), Easthorpe, Appleton-le-Street, Hook, Towthorpe, Askham Bryan, Wilton, Hotham, Wetherby, York, Hundburton, Sutton on the Forest, Sherburn, Knapton, Cropton, Skirpenbeck, Rise, Elvington and Sutton on Derwent.[23] Easingwold and Huby were added between 1487 and 1509[24] and Raskelf and Kirkstall in 1488,[25] Kirkstall being separated in 1518.[26] From 1525 to 1530, the lands were granted to Henry Fitzroy[27] and a fishery in the River Foss appears amongst them in 1545.[28]

Increasingly during the later 16th century, the lordship's lands were granted in groups of small parcels on long leases to 'contractors'.[29] Successive Tudor monarchs were wary of any attempts to recreate the powerful northern lordships and, as we shall see in Chapter 7, the castle at Sheriff Hutton was allowed to decay. In 1609 the lordship's lands were granted to Charles, then Prince of Wales,[30] but by 1624, his remote and disinterested management had resulted in their deterioration. From 1627, they were again contracted out, many to the Ingram family (later Lords Irwin) (see Chapter 12). However, some trace of the onetime lordship of Sheriff Hutton may still be found in the estates of the Irwins' successor, the present Earl of Halifax.[31]

It is important to appreciate that not all the land within the manor of Sheriff Hutton was held by the Neville family. The other great landowners of the medieval period were the monastic or ecclesiastical organisations. One such was Marton Priory, which is located some 7km to the north-west of Sheriff Hutton. The priory was founded by Bertram de Bulmer in the mid 12th century, and the 3rd Peter de Mauley confirmed grants of land in Sheriff Hutton to the priory in the latter years of Henry III, probably between 1282 and 1296;[32] this land was known to have been in the hands of the priory since before 1227.[33] These lands included 8 bovates (c.120 acres), a close called 'le Frith' and the attached crofts and tofts (small plots and houses), and 2 acres in the marsh.[34] In 1543 this land was granted to the Archbishop of York.[35]

In 1310 the priory also held a messuage and 1 acre of land which Thomas Fresyng held 'lying by the churchyard on the south side' and one acre in West Toftes.[36] A capital messuage (a large house) was mentioned in 1535,[37] and this building was still standing in 1608 when the tenant was Edmund Bennet.[38] The leases of monastic lands in c.1532[39] note that their holding extended to a farm of two messuages and 8 bovates of land in the lordship of Sheriff Hutton, a close next to the park, a small croft next to Northerngate, and a waste called Castlehill. The priory also held land in East Lilling and, as will be noted in Chapter 4, the final desertion of this village between 1471 and 1485 was sealed by an agreement between the prior and Richard III.

Other monastic landowners included St Mary's Abbey in York, who held half a carucate in Sheriff Hutton in 1245,[40] and three carucates (c.360 acres) in East Lilling.[41] In 1294 St Peter's Hospital in York was given 36 acres in 'Sutthon' by Robert de Neville;[42] 23 acres of this lay on the south side of the grange of the hospital while the other 13 acres lay on the "west side of the close which the poor men [of the Hospital] have of the gift of Henry de Neville, ancestor of Robert". In c.1343-44 Ralph Neville gave 200 acres of marsh in Sheriff Hutton to Kirkham Priory, but this was deemed not be harmful to the king's interests because "owing to the depth of the marsh on-one is able to enter it, and that the free tenants of Sheriff Hutton already have sufficient pasture in the town".[43] Mention is also made of the Prior of Bridlington holding 3 carucates (c.360 acres) in Sheriff Hutton in 1275.[44]

As yet, few of these ecclesiastical holdings have been located precisely within the manor. However, in 1282 it was noted that Marton Priory had granges situated in the rectory court for the laying up of their fruits, one with a garden and a dovecote;[45] in this instance, the word 'grange' may not necessarily mean an outlying monastic farm, as is usually the case, but probably refers to a barn.[46] A wall is also mentioned in this 1282 document, as running around the middle court and down to the low gate or postern. This latter name might be perpetuated by the 1848 tithe map,[47] which notes a field called 'The Postern' just within the north boundary of the park (field 28 on figure 5/7 in Chapter 5). The 1765 survey of Sheriff Hutton[48] also notes that several of the fields between the village and the later deer park are called 'Kirk Lands', perhaps a reference to the Marton Priory land. As will be suggested in Chapter 4 below, this land lies within the area of the first deer park, which was located to the south and east of the church. The 'Kirk' names may therefore be a reference to land given back to the priory in compensation for the creation of the second, larger, deer park to the south of the village in c.1334. Another part of the priory landholding might be located on the north side of the 'Church End' part of the village, where the 1765 plan names a 33 acre plot of ground as 'Gleab Old Inclosures' with several barns shown as well as a 'tythe barn'. Perhaps this is the core of the priory estate, located between the village and Carr Hill. The 1765 plan shows that access into this area was through a gap between the plots on the north side of Main Street, with another building at the end of the passage, as if suggesting a gatehouse or forebuilding.

Other monastic land in the village might be represented by a narrow east-west aligned field behind the house plots on the south side of Main Street, in the area between the market place and the Rectory. An aerial photograph taken in March 1956[49] shows two co-joined square enclosures at the west end of this plot (see figure 6/5) and the 1765 plan depicts a small ruined structure here named as 'stable'. Unfortunately, much of this area was developed for housing in the 1970s, although there are reports of foundations being uncovered during construction work. This 1956 aerial photograph also shows an area of earthworks just to the north-east of the churchyard, subsequently overploughed with ridge and furrow, which might also be connected to another monastic landholding. Clearly, the areas and extents of the ecclesiastical estates within the village and manor is an interesting subject meriting further documentary and archaeological research.

The Neville Family in the later Medieval Period by Shaun Richardson

As has been stated above, two families, the Bulmers and the Nevilles, played pivotal roles in the development of Sheriff Hutton during the later medieval period. However, it is the Nevilles who were largely responsible for the growth of the village and park, as well as Sheriff Hutton's most instantly recognisable feature, the second, now ruined, castle. Given their impact therefore, it is appropriate to briefly consider their family history.

The marriage of Geoffrey Neville, a minor Lincolnshire landowner, to the Bulmer heiress of Brancepeth (County Durham) in c.1176 set the family on the road to national importance. They subsequently acquired the lordship of Raby (County Durham) and Middleham (North Yorkshire) through marriage, and eventually developed a series of holdings which formed the core of the lordship of Sheriff Hutton (see above).[50] During the 14th century, the family continued to improve their standing through a variety of different means. For example, they played prominent roles in the contemporary French and Scottish wars. Ralph Neville (d.1367), Lord of Raby, was a prominent solider and took part in the sieges of Dunbar in 1337 and Tournai in 1340. On 17th October 1346, he commanded the first division of the victorious English army against the Scottish at the Battle of Neville's Cross, near Durham.[51] His eldest son, John Neville, was awarded 24,000 marks for his role in securing the release of the Scottish king, David II, captured at this battle, and he was still collecting instalments of this some 40 years later.[52] John Neville also became a paid retainer of John of Gaunt, Duke of Lancaster (d.1399), son of Edward III and uncle of the future King Richard II (see below), and he saw active military service with Gaunt in Spain and soldiered as far afield as Turkey.[53] In 1378 he was appointed Seneschal of Gascony and by the time he returned from his service as the king's Lieutenant in Aquitaine in 1381, he was reputed to have recovered 83 castles in France,[54] thus providing ample opportunity to make fortunes from ransoms and booty. As a result, by the latter part of the 14th century, John Neville had sufficient wealth to maintain the estates of an earl - Richard II actually granted him an earldom in 1384 but the title was never confirmed.[55]

Richard's grant of an earldom was made for political reasons, to gain the support of the Neville family in the sphere of northern English politics and particularly in his control of the Anglo-Scottish border, which was divided into several areas known as the Marches. By the later 14th century, the governance and security of the Marches was dominated by a small number of English and Scottish magnates, who were at times effectively beyond royal control. Most prominent amongst the English were the Percy family, Earls of Northumberland after 1377, who acted as wardens of the Marches often in conjunction with the Nevilles;[56] for example, Ralph Neville (d.1367) was Warden of the West March, and was at various times keeper of Bamburgh castle and keeper of the castle and town of Berwick.[57] In 1379, John of Gaunt was appointed by Richard II as Lieutenant of the Marches with all other wardens, including Northumberland, subordinate to him. The earl resented Gaunt's powers and was further antagonised when Gaunt appointed John Neville as warden of the East March in 1381 in Northumberland's place.[58] However, it was not possible to exclude the earl completely and, following the outbreak of open warfare between England and Scotland again in 1384, he again returned to the fore.

The resurgent power of the Percy family led Richard II to cultivate and promote Ralph Neville (d.1425) as a balancing force. In 1397, Ralph was created Earl of Westmoreland. This earldom was accompanied by the lordships of Penrith and Sowerby, and also many other manors and estates; as a result, Ralph held an estimated 80 manors in six different counties at this time. However, Richard's appointment of his favourite courtiers to the Marcher wardenships from 1396 onwards appealed neither to Ralph Neville nor the Earl of Northumberland. Consequently, when Henry Bolingbroke, John of Gaunt's son, landed in England in 1399, both great northern magnates gave him their backing.[59] The new king Henry IV continued to favour the Nevilles over the Percys and, a few days after his accession, he granted the honour of Richmond to Ralph Neville for the term of his life; this important estate provided Ralph with an additional annual income of £1,700 and it formed a geographical link between his castles of Raby, Middleham and Sheriff Hutton. Ralph's prominent role in border affairs continued and in 1402 he was elevated to the Order of the Garter, also briefly holding the office of Earl Marshall. He also played a pivotal role in securing Henry IV against revolts in 1403 and 1405 and he profited from the eclipse of the Percys.[60] By the turn of the 15th century therefore, Ralph Neville was the richest and most influential lord in the northern counties.[61]

Fig. 1/5: Effigy of Ralph Neville (d.1425), 1st Earl of Westmoreland, and one of his wives, in Staindrop church, County Durham.

The great fertility of the Neville family also contributed to their success. For example, Ralph Neville (d.1425) had nine children by his first wife and 13 by his second, Joan Beaufort. Ralph's second marriage was particularly well chosen, as Joan was one of the four legitimised bastards of the aforementioned John of Gaunt. This royal connection proved important following Richard II's deposition, as Joan was to become the half-sister of Henry IV, the aunt of Henry V and great-aunt of Henry VI.[62] The dynastic links that Ralph secured for his children were no less successful; in the words of an admiring herald, Ralph "maried his children gretly",[63] and he was the grandfather of Richard Neville (1428-71), the famous Warwick the Kingmaker. The Nevilles expressed their power, wealth and status in the same way as many of their contemporaries, for example by founding abbeys, friaries, hospitals, chantries and a college.[64] At the 2003 *Gothic* exhibition held at the Victoria and Albert

Museum, a whole section of the catalogue was devoted to the artistic patronage of the Neville family and their Beauchamp relations.[65] In addition to their ecclesiastical and artistic patronage, John and later Ralph Neville embarked on an extensive scheme of improvements to their residences in the late 14th and early 15th centuries - work commenced at Raby in 1379, at Brancepeth it was carried out between c.1369 and 1388, and the Neville reconstruction of Middleham castle started in c.1400.[66]

When Ralph Neville died in 1425, his second wife, Joan Beaufort, is said to have preferred Sheriff Hutton to the other Neville residences and she continued to live at the castle.[67] Ralph had taken steps, as soon as he had a surviving family by Joan, to ensure that the lordship of Sheriff Hutton would go to them, rather than to the children of his first marriage, including the eldest heir. Not surprisingly, the older branch felt somewhat aggrieved by this,[68] and the resulting dispute was not settled until after Joan's death in 1440.

The pivotal role that the Neville family played during the Wars of the Roses is well known,[69] and it need not be repeated here. Edward IV placed Richard, Duke of Gloucester (the future Richard III) into the household of Richard Neville, Earl of Warwick. After the Earl of Warwick was killed at the Battle of Barnet in 1471, his estates were divided and Sheriff Hutton passed to the duke.[70] Little is known of Sheriff Hutton during these years, although much has been surmised and written as fact.[71] It is probable that Richard visited Sheriff Hutton frequently, both for business and to hunt in the park. For example, he was there on 21st September 1476, and was certainly believed to be at the castle in October 1480, when York City Council agreed that an alderman should ride out to meet him.[72]

In 1485, Richard III created a council to run the north of England and a household in which its head and members could live. The absence of any building work by Richard at Sheriff Hutton, in contrast to almost all of his other castles in his northern Lordships, suggests that the council usually stayed at York when in the area, although they were at Sheriff Hutton in May 1485.[73] During the summer of the same year, when Richard III was at Nottingham awaiting Henry Tudor's invasion, he moved his niece, Elizabeth of York, to the castle to be far from the conspiracies resulting from Henry's oath to marry her. Her presence generated stories of imprisonment by her 'wicked uncle', unlikely in view of the fact that she was granted certain grazing rights within the park, suggesting that Richard was taking the same steps he took with other members of his family to provide them with a means of support. The post-1485 ownership of Sheriff Hutton park and castle is described in Chapters 11 to 13 below.

The Plan Form of the Village by Ed Dennison

What then remains of the influence of the Nevilles, the Bulmers and others on the village's development? More than might at first be expected.

The layout of many of the settlements in Yorkshire and the Vale of York suggest that they originated as planned villages with streets often set out around a green. To date, there are no firm conclusions as to when these plans originated, but it is generally assumed that they represent the post-Conquest re-ordering of earlier, probably Saxon, settlements, usually by landowners undertaking a deliberate policy of estate re-organisation in the late 11th or 12th century.[74] As can be seen from figure 1/2, Sheriff Hutton village is linear in plan with the stone castle located towards the west end, and the church and an early earthwork castle at the east end. There is a former market place, now a grass green (Pavement Hill), in the centre of the south side of Main Street (see plate 20). There is a back lane (now North Garth Lane but previously named as Back Lane), running to the north of and parallel to the Main Street, which is now the through route between Stillington and Bulmer. The other main route between York, Strensall and Hovingham runs north-south through the west end of the village (Finkle Street and New Lane).

An examination of the morphology of the village, based on a detailed 1765 plan[75] and the Ordnance Survey 1855-56 1st edition 6" maps,[76] which depict the village before modern housing estates, shows it to have developed in several stages, as originally suggested elsewhere.[77] The following hypothesis builds on this work.

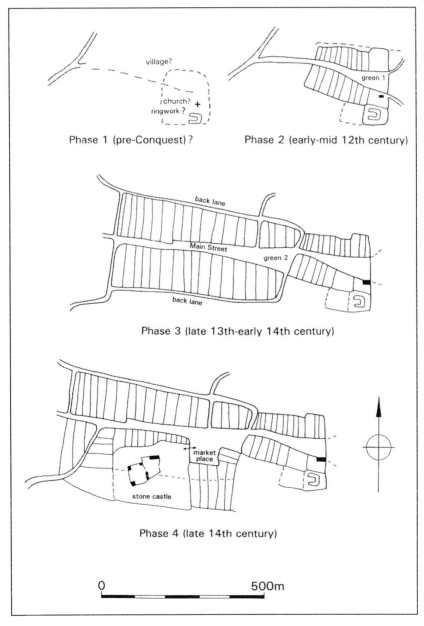

Fig. 1/6: Suggested phases of development for Sheriff Hutton village (after Dennison 1998a).

11

Phases 1 and 2

The east or Church End part of the village, which contains the church and the first castle site, appears to be the earliest part of the settlement (phase 1). This area lies just to the east of the present Strensall to Bulmer road which runs in a south-west/north-east direction around the north edge of the Foss Marshes; it is assumed that this route has early origins and that the straight section to the south of the Sheriff Hutton was re-aligned at a later date when the deer park was created (see Chapter 4).[78] Although there is no archaeological evidence (as yet), it is presumed that the Saxon settlement was in the general area of Church End, possibly representing one of the three manors or estates recorded as existing before the Domesday Book. Chapter 6 notes that the earthworks at the castle site may have earlier origins, and so it is possible that this settlement may have been centred on a Saxon ringwork and possibly a small aisleless church with a west tower; the earliest fabric of the present church is generally considered to be 11th century in date,[79] although it might be slightly later.[80] Perhaps this was an example of what is termed a 'magnate core', formed by church, castle and settlement, which is commonly seen in early villages throughout Yorkshire and elsewhere.[81]

A new and planned village appears to have been subsequently added to this complex (phase 2), possibly in the early-mid 12th century when the manor became associated with the lords of Bulmer, perhaps by Ansketill de Bulmer who was enfeoffed (granted) [Sheriff] Hutton by Nigel Fossard in 1106 or 1115.[82] Both the castle and the church are first documented in 1100-1115,[83] and the castle appears to have a 'courtyard' plan typical of 12th century structures. This plan is clearly hampered by having to re-use and remodel an existing site (see Chapter 6), and so perhaps the addition of a bailey on the west side may also belong to this period. As will be seen in Chapter 4, this period is also when the adjacent deer park might be first recorded and when the nearby village of East Lilling, a much smaller hamlet, was established.[84]

The new village, with its 'Sheriff' prefix to reflect the status of the new lord, comprised two rows of crofts (rectangular plots of land) and tofts (house sites on the street frontage), located either side of a triangular green (the present 'Little Green') (see plate 19). The church was located in the south-east corner plot and it is possible that the single larger property in the north-east corner (now sub-divided into several separate plots) represents a complex belonging to the main sub-tenant; it is noticeable that this block of land extends further to the north than the rest of the village (see figure 6/5). The village would have been surrounded by open fields, represented by the ridge and furrow which characterises medieval and early post-medieval arable cultivation, and it possible that the two footpaths extending north-east and south-east from the east end of the green may have originated as droveways.

Despite some infilling and recent development, some elements of the phase 2 planned village layout remain. The majority of the crofts on the north side of the green survive, although the western end has been disturbed. However, the southern row is now almost completely gone, mostly lost through the development of 'The Croft' and 'Calverts Garth'. Nevertheless, the alignment of the rear boundary has been partially preserved behind the vicarage and through the modern housing development.

Based primarily on aerial photographic evidence, Swan has noted that the first castle site, the church and the early village were enclosed by a substantial boundary.[85] To the north of Church End, this boundary is clearly visible as a ditch on aerial photographs taken in the 1960s and 1970s.[86] The line of this ditch runs east from the post-1765 Glebe Farm towards the back line of the extended property in the north-east corner of the north row, and it survives on the ground as a spread double bank with ditches, now no more than 0.4m high but c.10m-11m wide. The ridge and furrow runs up to this boundary, and there are further earthworks just to the north, perhaps representing a barn and another building depicted here on the 1765 plan.[87] The line of the boundary appears to have run between two trackways shown in 1765, Back Lane (now North Garth Lane) to the west and Riddings Lane to the east. Was this therefore another back lane which ran around the north side of the phase 2 planned village? The apparent fore-shortening of most of the plots before this boundary is, at present, unexplained. As noted above, the area to the north of this back lane may have been occupied by Marton Priory.

The east side of Swan's early boundary coincides with a sharp break of slope to the east of the now extended churchyard, where the ground falls away steeply to the east, but no earthworks can be seen in arable fields today. However, an aerial photograph taken in 1956[88] does show a bank here, overlain by ridge and furrow which extends right up to and presumably originally under the extended churchyard wall (see figure 6/5). The south side of the early boundary is now covered by 'The Croft', although a slightly wider 'ridge' can be seen in the ridge and furrow shown here in the aerial photograph. This boundary probably coincides with the flat-topped bank which lies on the south side of the first castle site, separating the castle from the adjacent ridge and furrow (see figure 6/3).

Fig. 1/7: View of the first green, looking east towards the church.

Phase 3

A new and substantial settlement was subsequently established to the west of the existing small village. This development appears to have taken the classic two row plan type seen in numerous villages in this part of Yorkshire, with crofts and tofts extending north and south in a regular fashion to two parallel back lanes.

The new east-west main street was essentially a re-alignment of the old Strensall to Bulmer road, and it opened out into a new triangular-shaped green which butted up to the edge of the earlier village. A new side road was also possibly added at this time, allowing travellers to rejoin the Bulmer road after having passed down the main street; the 1765 plan shows that these two lanes are directly aligned. The main street was at least twice as wide than at present, as the 1765 plan shows that the houses on both sides were on the street frontage. The northern back lane extended further west beyond the present New Lane before turning south along what was 'Martin's Lane'. The southern back lane ran west through what was to become the Castle Garth (see below), across the present Finkle Street, and north to meet up with the Main Street. This phase of expansion might have been accompanied by the enlargement or remodelling of the first castle site, perhaps by the addition of the western bailey, although the latter could well date to an earlier period (see above). The adjacent church was also enlarged during the 13th and 14th centuries, with wide north and south aisles being added and the tower being extended upwards.[89]

The process of adding new planned settlements to existing ones is already well known in many parts of the country, for example, in north-west Lincolnshire (e.g. Cold Hanworth and Coates),[90] and it is often attributed to the re-organisation of estates by a dominant landowner. The phase 3 expansion of Sheriff Hutton is most likely to be associated with the Nevilles, the increasingly powerful tenants and by 1331 the overlords of the manor. This phase of development is therefore tentatively suggested to be around the late 13th/early 14th century, and the new village may be the work of Ralph Neville (d.1331), who was created the 1st Lord Raby in 1300, or his son Ralph (d.1367) who gained the lordship of the manor in 1331 and extended the deer park in 1334-45.

Today, the northern back lane remains, although many of the original plots have been infilled or re-developed (see figure 1/2). Martin's Lane is represented by an elongated strip shown on the Ordnance Survey 1856 1st edition 6" map, running through and behind (north) 'Bertram House'. The south side of the green can be seen in the alignment of the buildings from 'Castlegate', the 'Castle Inn', and 'Sheriff Hutton Court'. Little remains of the southern back lane, although its alignment can be traced through a number of boundaries, particularly that between 'Westways' and 'The Cottage' on the east side of Finkle Street.

Phase 4

This phase is dominated by the construction of the stone castle towards the west end of the village, on land presumably owned or commandeered by John Neville (d.1388); as will be noted in Chapter 7, construction started in 1382 and so this is the only securely datable phase of the sequence. This act had a major effect on the morphology of this end of the village. As can be seen from figure 1/6 above, the southern back lane was removed and the south ends of those crofts which ran back from the Main Street were truncated; the houses on the street frontage were not affected, which meant that the number of tenants (and therefore Neville's income) would not have been significantly reduced. It is also possible that Finkle Lane (called 'Forest Lane' on the 1765 plan) was added to the plan at this stage, resulting in the re-alignment of some of the crofts on the east side (see below).

It is also documented that in 1378 John de Neville obtained a grant to hold a market in the village on Mondays and a fair on the vigil and feast of the Exaltation of the Holy Cross (14th September).[91] It has been suggested that in some parts of England the acquisition of a market grant in the 12th to 14th centuries led to the deliberate creation of market places within or attached to a settlement,[92] and this also appears to have occurred at Sheriff Hutton. The south-west part of the new village green was extended south to accommodate the square market place, and the place name of 'Pavement Hill' might actually refer to the area being paved for stalls.[93] There had been some properties originally fronting the south side of the green and, as a consequence of this expansion, they were relocated slightly to the south and their crofts were extended south, almost as far as the park boundary.

Fig. 1/8: View of the market place, looking west towards the entrance into the castle complex.

Fig. 1/9: Painting of houses built on the green in 1856 (Source: Sheriff Hutton WI 1975).

It is noticeable that only four years separate the date of the market grant and the licence for the building of the stone castle. As mentioned above, it is therefore suggested that these two events, as well as a second expansion of the deer park, were conceived as part of an overall re-development scheme undertaken by the Neville family. Both the 1765 plan and the Ordnance Survey 1855/56 1st edition 6" maps show that there were relatively few houses on the west side of the new rectangular green, and is it thought that there was a gatehouse here, allowing access into the castle's outer garth (see Chapter 7). This theory is given added weight by the fact that one of the manorial customs in the mid 1500s allowed farmers and tenants to drive their cattle and horses to the village and hold them there 'upon the pavement before the castle gates'.[94] The green actually remained under the control of the castle until 1910, when it was presented to the village at the coronation of George V.[95]

Finally, it is interesting to note that the 1765 plan shows that both the market place and the earlier green at Church End are depicted as containing houses that have been 'built upon the waste'. There are also documents relating to a forge 'new built on the green' from 1525-26.[96] From 1677 to 1757, rents of 6d. per annum were also collected from the cottages built on the waste.[97] The last houses on the main green were only demolished in 1900.[98]

Late Medieval Life in Sheriff Hutton by Barbara Walker

As has been shown, the major medieval landowners left their mark on the village and its surroundings. But what about its ordinary inhabitants, the successive generations who inhabited its houses and worked the surrounding fields? They are more elusive but a good source of information for this period are the lay subsidies of 1301 and 1327.[99] The lay subsidy was quite literally a tax levied on the lay population, usually for a specific purpose such as financing a foreign military expedition; the taxes were originally assessed at one-tenth of the value of a person's moveable goods.[100] For the 1327 subsidy, half the tax was paid on February 3rd 1327 and the rest paid on the 3rd June 1328.

The lists are written in Latin and are arranged neither alphabetically nor financially. The people mentioned are the wealthier individuals within the community, who had a greater number of moveable goods (including sheep, cattle and other beasts) whilst the poorer villagers of servile status, the serfs, bondsmen or villeins do not appear. As can be seen from the adjacent table, there were 28 people in the lay subsidy for 1301 and only 15 in the one for 1327. Swan cites this as evidence of the national decline in the rural population from the early 14th century,[101] although it might also reflect the changing economic circumstances of those being taxed. A truer reflection of the village's population might be found in the late 14th century poll tax returns of 1377 and 1381, which taxed everyone aged 14 years and older. The unpopularity of the tax apparently led to widespread evasion, making the returns somewhat unreliable, but that being said, the Sheriff Hutton returns show 110 people altogether.[102]

The surnames listed in the lay subsidies are an important source of information, as they can be derived from local place names or be related to a person's trade or occupation. However, some caution is needed in their use and interpretation. For example, a person with a trade or occupational surname might not have carried out that job themselves, but could have come from a family that did.

Domina Ida de Neville (Lady Neville) is one of the wealthiest of those listed in 1301. She undoubtedly belonged to the Neville family who had such an influence on the development of the village (see above), and she may have been living at the first castle site at this date. The wealthiest individual shown in 1301 is Johanne Bercario, worth slightly more than even Lady Neville. The surname *Bercario* is interesting and it may derive from either *bercarius* (shepherd) or possibly a *bercary* (a medieval sheep farm); perhaps Johanne had a sheep farm in the vicinity of the village? The same might apply to the less heavily taxed Nicholae Vacario, the surname possibly derived from *vacary*, the medieval term for a cattle farm. Willelmo Carectario (in Latin *carectum* means a sedge plot) may possibly have been a thatcher and could have owned land in the flat marshy area of ground to the north of Sheriff Hutton known as 'the Nabbes' and described by Norden in 1624 as being 'two wett boggis and marshie grounds, not passable'.[103] Most dwellings in the village would have been thatched during the later medieval period, some no doubt with used rushes from this area. In the 1537 accounts for the repair of the castle, there is a reference for monies 'payed to thomas shayre John Grynside John henryson John Cobbe and Robert marshal of Sheriff Hutton for mowing cokking of xxvj lode of Rushes in the nabbes at ijd a loode'.[104] The rushes were then used to thatch the newly-built castle slaughterhouse.

Lay subsidies for

1301	s	d	1327	s	d
Petro de Raby	3	3¼	De Willelmo filio Christopheri	2	2
Ada Molindinario		16¼	Johanne filio Nicholai		22½
Roberto le Tanure		17	Simone filio Michaelis		9
Avota relicta Tropinell	2	7	Ada Scanlouman	2	6
Thoma de Stanlau	7	2	Hugone Fyn		23½
Roberto Wreyde	4	0¼	Alano filio Nicholai	2	9
Henrico Emermare	6	6	Willelmo Codling		7
Willelmo Russell	2	8	Willelmo Sturdy		7
Michaelo filio Rodulphi	3	2	Willelmo Patre		6
Willelmo Syffewryth		16¼	Richardo de Cestria	6	6
Nicholae Vacario	3	5	Ranulpho de Nevil	6	0
Rogero de Ingelton	3	9¼	Johanne Stabler		13½
Richardo de Brandsby	3	4¼	Roberto de Holderness	2	9½
Thoma Bercario	2	1	Roberto filio Willelmi	2	1
Radulpho Coco	2	10	Roberto Clerico		9
Domina Ida de Neville	13	3¼			
Simone filio Stephani		9			
Johanne de Waldo		8			
Willelmo Carectario		8			
Hugone Nutel		11			
Roberto le Seure		6			
Willelmo Falcatore		8			
Radalpho Tunnock		9			
Domino Philippo de Ely	5	6			
Johanne Bercario	13	4			
Johanne le Stabler	4	5			
Willelmo filio Ivette	3	11			
Richardo Crake	4	6			

Ada Molindinario was a miller. As noted above, Sheriff Hutton had both a watermill and a windmill in 1282.[105] The watermill stood at the bottom of Carr Hill on the north side of Bulmer Road. The windmill would probably have been at Windmill Hill next to Mill Lane just north of Mill House at the west end of the village, but the first definite records of a mill being located here that we have found are on the 1765 plan and the 1774 Enclosure map,[106] and so the medieval mill might have stood elsewhere. A mill was repaired using the timbers taken from the great barn in the castle's outer court in 1598,[107] although no specific location is given. The timbers could have gone to one of the mills in Sheriff Hutton or to another local mill, of which there were once numerous examples; for example, a Johanne Molindenario also appears in the 1301 lay subsidy for Stittenham.[108]

Johanne le Stabler may well have been a local official employed by the Nevilles and this is the only name appearing in both 1301 and 1327. Could he perhaps have been in charge of the stables located around the first castle site? The Stablers were an important family for generations in Sheriff Hutton and were wealthy enough to leave wills which named several sons and daughters and other relatives. Some junior sons became priests in the late 15th and early 16th centuries, but there are no Stablers living in the village at present. Willelmo Falcatore could have taken his name from *falcarius* meaning a sickle or scythe maker.

As well as the possible occupations inferred by the surnames, the lay subsidies give some idea of where the people living in Sheriff Hutton had come from. As might be expected, these are dominated by Yorkshire locations, such as Ingleton, Brandsby and Holderness. Raby is interesting, as the Neville family had a long-standing association with this place and so some villagers may have come to Sheriff Hutton through this connection. The expansion of the deer park by the Nevilles during the 14th century and the completion of the second castle in c.1400 would have generated significant local and regional demand for labour and skilled workmen of all kinds. Many of the castle servants would have been recruited at a relatively young age from the village. The majority of children did not go to school, and those recruited learnt on the job, perhaps eventually earning promotion. Boys from the gentry were employed in jobs such as servers or cup bearers, their families even paying for them to enjoy the benefits of serving in a noble household. Each department in the castle had a 'boy' from the lower orders, working in the kitchen, scullery, kennels, stable, coach-house, bakehouse, butchery and armoury. Documents show that the boys might receive board, lodging and wages of 13s. 4d. per year.[109]

Adults would also have found work in the castle if they had a special skill to offer, with agreements drawn up between employer and employee; for example, in 1465 John Howard, later Duke of Norfolk, engaged 'yonge Copdoke' as a carpenter for six months. He was to receive meat, drink, a gown and 36s. 8d. per annum, but he had to find his own bedding![110] The only female servants employed at the castle were attendants or companions for the lady and nurses for the children, usually taken from wealthier families. From the lower orders came the laundresses and dairy workers who were not usually resident in the castle. This working relationship between the village and the major landowner did not end with the demise of the castle in the early 17th century, as the occupants of Sheriff Hutton Hall drew many of their servants from the village until well into the 20th century, as described in Chapter 16.

Footnotes

1   Myerscough 2005; Myerscough 2003.
2   Gelling 1984, p.167; Smith 1928, p.31; National Archives Lists of Sheriffs.
3   Ormrod 2000.
4   Harrison 1984.
5   Faull & Stinson 1986, 1N87 & 5N54.
6   Usually expressed as the suffix 'Vicecomitis' or 'Viscount' etc in written sources, e.g. Farrer 1915b, p.364.
7   Calthrop 1923, pp.179 & 181-3.
8   Farrer 1915b, pp.325 on; ibid., pp.122 on.
9   Le Patourel 1978, pp.118 & 120.
10   Calendar Charter Rolls, 1300-26, p.135; Robinson 1978, p.153.
11   Cal. IPM vol 2 (Edward I), pp.172, 249 & 293.
12   Catalogue of Ancient Deeds vol 2, p.384; Swan *et al* 1990, p.94 note 15.
13   e.g. Robinson 1970, pp.3, map, 5, 15, 16, 18, 19 & 43.
14   National Archives C133/35/1 Robert de Neville IPM 10th February 1282/83.
15   National Archives C135/27/19 Ranulph de Neville IPM 22nd April 1331.

16   National Archives C135/195/1 Ralph de Neville IPM 28th August 1367.
17   Cal. IPM vol 12, pp.133 on.
18   Calendar Charter Rolls, 1341-1417, m13, 9; Calendar Patent Rolls, 1381-85, p.108.
19   Cal. IPM (1384-1392), p.280 &c.
20   National Archives Lists & Indexes vol 113, Catalogue of Ancient Deeds, B4517; Calendar Patent Rolls,
      1401-05, p.470, m.24.
21   T. Madox 1702 *Formulare Anglicarum*, pp.146-7 quoted by Storey 1966, p.114.
22   Calthrop 1923, p.178.
23   National Archives Lists and Indexes vol 34, Ministers' Accounts vol 2, pp.186 on; National Archives
      DL/10510.
24   National Archives DL/10511-10514.
25   National Archives DL/10512.
26   National Archives DL/4178.
27   National Archives DL/4184-4189.
28   National Archives DL/4199.
29   e.g. Calendar Patent Rolls Elizabeth vol 2, 1560-3, no. 991(4); ibid., p.80; ibid., p.152; ibid., p.507; ibid.,
      p.534; ibid., vol 3, p.339; ibid., vol 4, p.116; ibid., p.53; ibid., p.143; ibid., p.178; ibid., p.,387; ibid.,
      p.432; ibid., vol 5, p.8; ibid., p.530; ibid., p.83; ibid., p.466.
30   Calthrop 1923, p.178.
31   Calthrop 1923, p.179 etc.; Debrette's Peerage, "Halifax"; Elvington and Sutton on Derwent for example.
      Sheriff Hutton and its immediate environs were sold off, mainly to the tenants, soon after the Great War.
32   Calthrop 1923, p.176; Fallow 1913.
33   Swan *et al* 1990, p.94 note 13.
34   Calendar Charter Rolls 1300-26, p.155.
35   Letters & Papers, Foreign & Domestic, Henry VIII vol 1, p.266.
36   Calendar Charter Rolls 1300-26, p.135-7.
37   Dugdale, W 1817-30 *Monasticon Anglicanum* vol 6, p.199.
38   Calthrop 1923, p.179.
39   National Archives E315/199.
40   Bodleian Library Dodsworth MSS 156, f.17v.
41   Farrer 1915b, pp.352-3 no. 456.
42   Calendar Charter Rolls 1257-1300, vol 2 p.445-46.
43   National Archives 143/285/13.
44   Calthrop 1923, p.176.
45   Robinson 1978, no. 404.
46   Bridgett Jones, *pers. comm.*
47   Borthwick Institute TA411S.
48   West Yorkshire Archive Service (WYAS) Leeds WYL/100/SH/B4/2.
49   Cambridge University Collection of Air Photographs (CUCAP) RU62 taken 26/3/56.
50   Emery 1996, pp.132-133.
51   Turnbull 1985, pp.38-39; Emery 1996, p.133; Weaver 1998, 23.
52   Pritchett 1887, p.219.
53   Tuck 1968, pp.38-41; Emery 1996, p.133.
54   Matthew & Harrison 2004 vol 40, p.506.
55   Saul 1999, p.382.
56   Neville 1994, p.7.
57   Weaver 1998, p.23.
58   Tuck 1968, pp.34-41.
59   ibid., pp.49-52; Arvanigian 2003, p.125.
60   Arvanigian 2003, pp.124-27; Tuck 1968, p.33; Hicks 2002, pp.13-15.
61   Weaver 1998, p.25.
62   Hicks 2002, pp.14-15.
63   Payne 2003, p.221.
64   Hicks 2003, pp.12-13; Coverham Abbey, Richmond Friary and a college at Staindrop.
65   Payne 2003, pp.219-223.
66   Emery 1996, p.133.
67   Raine & Clay 1854, p.241 note.
68   *Ricardian* vol 5, no. 75 (December 1981), pp.421 & 425 on.
69   see for example Hicks 2002.

70   Calendar Patent Rolls, 1467-77, p.260, m23; ibid, p.266, m18; ibid, p.483, m6; ibid, p.486, m3; Act of Parliament, 23 February 14 Edward IV: Edward's appropriation and grant has been seen as his own method of fulfilling the inheritances of Isabel Neville (wife of George) and Ann (who was to be Richard's wife) complicated by the dispute between these two brothers (e.g. Kendall 1987, pp.107 & 113). Edward, however, certainly bent the accepted rules of inheritance - especially with respect to the rights of the Countess of Warwick (Kendall 1987, p.113; Ross 1981, pp.24, & 26-27).

71   e.g. Kendall 1987, p.128; Markham 1973, pp.84-85: Markham says that Richard built the chapel of St. Mary in Sheriff Hutton church, whereas his evidence says merely that Richard arranged for a priest there to be salaried.

72   Pollet 1971, p.136; Raine 1939, p.36.

73   British Library Harleian MSS no. 433, f. 264b: York is the only named site at which the council was obliged to sit, once per quarter; York Civic Records, f.65; Raine 1939, p.116.

74   Sheppard 1974 & 1976; Muir 1997, pp.131-134.

75   WYAS Leeds WYL/100/SH/B4/2.

76   Ordnance Survey 1856 6" map (sheet 140), surveyed 1851-52; Ordnance Survey 1855 6" map (sheet 141), surveyed 1854.

77   Beresford and St Joseph 1979, pp.154-156; Dennison 1998a & 1998b. Thanks are also due to Chris Taylor for discussing the morphological development of the village.

78   Swan *et al* 1990, p.99.

79   Field Archaeology Specialists 2003, p.62.

80   Pevsner 1966, pp.338-339; Calthrop 1923, p.184.

81   Creighton 2002, p.111.

82   Farrer 1915a, pp.281-85.

83   Tony Wright, *pers. comm.*

84   Swan *et al* 1990.

85   Vivien Swan, *pers. comm.*

86   e.g. CUCAP AQH29 taken 13/12/66 and BBQ taken 4/6/70.

87   WYAS Leeds WYL/100/SH/B4/2.

88   CUCAP RU62 taken 26/3/56.

89   Calthrop 1923, p.184; Field Archaeology Specialists 2003, p.63.

90   Everson, Taylor & Dunn 1991, pp.93-94 & 185-189.

91   Calthrop 1923, p.173 quoting Charter Rolls 1 Richard II, m.13.

92   Taylor 1982.

93   Chris Taylor, *pers. comm.*

94   Bodleian Library Rawlinson MSS 450 ff.144-5.

95   Sheriff Hutton WI 1975, p.26.

96   National Archives Minister's Accounts 17-18 Henry VIII.

97   WYAS Leeds WYL100/SH/B3/2; WYAS Leeds WYL100/SH/A4

98   Sheriff Hutton WI 1975, p.26.

99   Brown 1896, p.77; Parker 1929, p.143.

100   Friar 2001, p.243.

101   Swan *et al* 1990, p.98 note 4.

102   Quoted in Beresford 1957, p.225.

103   British Library Harleian MSS no. 6288.

104   National Archives E101/484/3.

105   National Archives C133/35/1 Robert de Neville IPM 10th February 1282/83.

106   WYAS Leeds WYL100/SH/B4/20; WYAS Leeds Farrer Add. 313.

107   National Archives E178/2792.

108   Brown 1896, p.75.

109   Orme 2003, pp.110-127.

110   Woolgar 1999, pp.37-38.

CHAPTER 2: PARKS IN THE MIDDLE AGES
By Ed Dennison

Introduction

Before considering the details of the Sheriff Hutton deer park, it is perhaps useful to review the wider background to medieval parks, and how they were defined and managed.

Today, the word 'park' conjures up a picture of a heavily managed public landscape of lawns and ornamental planting, often in an urban environment and associated with children's playgrounds, boating lakes and so on. However, parks have meant different things to different people at different times. In the 18th century for example, a park usually meant an area of private landscaped grounds ('parkland') surrounding a large county house. In the medieval period, a park had a more specialised meaning, being a tract of wild, often wooded countryside enclosed as a private game reserve or deer enclosure.

The word 'park' is derived from the Old English *pearroc*, which originally meant an enclosed field or paddock surrounded by a fence, and it is still sometimes found in this sense in surviving field names. It is becoming increasingly clear that parks of some sort existed before the Norman Conquest, and a number of Saxon charters mention a *haga* which has been interpreted as a woodland game enclosure. There are also references to Saxon 'deer-folds' and 37 deer parks are recorded in the Domesday Book, although there were probably many more.[1] Generally however, parks were a product of a feudal society and their creation is traditionally associated with the Norman aristocracy.[2]

Medieval parks have been extensively studied and a vast range of literature is available. Many authors have provided general accounts and summaries,[3] while others have discussed details relating to the management and economies of individual, or groups of, parks.[4] Others have dealt with associated topics such as hunting,[5] poaching,[6] the boundaries of parks,[7] and deer farming,[8] and there are many county-wide or regional surveys.[9] There are also some 19th century publications which contain useful information about the practicalities of deer farming in parks.[10] Some of the these accounts have been used in the following text, while medieval hunting is discussed in more detail in Chapter 3.

Types of Hunting Ground

Four main different types of hunting grounds can be identified in the medieval period.[11]

The Forest

A medieval forest was not necessarily a continuous tract of wood, but it frequently covered large areas of land containing differing types of countryside, such as cultivated fields, pasture, woods, marshes, as well as villages and farmsteads. The key to understanding the medieval 'forest' is to appreciate that this was a legal rather than a descriptive term, and it meant an area which was subject to Forest Law and retained by the king as a large royal hunting reserve. The laws were designed to preserve certain animals and their habitats for the king's hunting and to maintain his income from various rents, for example 'pannage' (the right to pasture pigs), 'firebote' (the right to take wood for burning), 'hedgebote' (the right to take cut foliage from hedges) and 'housebote' (the right to take timber for building and repairing houses). Forest Law was initially very harsh and was strictly enforced by a hierarchy of forest officials, and the fines and punishments for poaching, encroachment (taking land from the park for private use), trespass and other misdemeanours were often heavy and severe.

It is not known precisely how many royal forests there were in Britain because, as they lay outside common law, they are rarely described in any detail. Those that are documented usually date from the 13th century, and their extents are described as boundary perambulations. It must also be remembered that their number did not remain static, as new kings established new forests or increased the areas of existing ones. However, it has been suggested that forests reached their greatest extent under Henry II in the mid 12th century, when some 70 odd forests are thought to have covered approximately one-fifth of the country.[12] Some of the royal forests were extensive, for example the New Forest covered over 30,000 hectares (75,000 acres) and Sherwood Forest extended over 20,000 hectares (50,000 acres). There were nine royal forests in North Yorkshire including Galtres and Knaresborough,[13] and Sheriff Hutton originally lay within the royal Forest of Galtres (see Chapter 4).

The Chase

The chase was an unenclosed hunting ground held normally by a landowner other than the king, in which Civil Law rather than Forest Law applied (unless it lay within a forest). The king gave the right to hunt in these areas to local magnates, both lay and ecclesiastic. At various times in the Middle Ages there were at least 26 chases in existence.[14]

Warrens

Originally, any commoner was allowed to hunt the smaller game outside the forest limits. However, during the 12th and 13th centuries, there are frequent references to the Grant of Free Warren, whereby local lords were given the sole rights by the king to hunt small game over their own manors or estates, and more importantly gave them the right to prosecute any commoner found hunting on their land. Small game was defined as hare, rabbit, woodcock, partridge, and pheasant which were hunted for the table, while fox, wildcat, badger, marten, otter and squirrel were hunted as pests as they damaged crops.[15] By the middle of the 14th century such grants had become so common that the majority of the manorial lords seem to have enjoyed them. In some cases, a grant of free warren was a prelude to the creation of a park.

The hare was the principle beast of the warren, but the right of free warren should not be confused with a warren, which is a term given to an area of ground specifically set aside for the protection and breeding of rabbits. Unlike hares, which are a native species, the rabbit was almost certainly introduced into the country after the Norman Conquest.[16] The rabbits were valued for their fur and flesh, and they could be raised in different environments. However, they remained sensitive to the rigours of the English climate, and so were largely restricted to specially constructed enclosures or 'coneygres', this name coming from the term used for adult rabbits. In these areas, the rabbits could burrow in specially created mounds of soft earth, sometimes even containing artificial stone-lined channels, and were fed from specially grown crops such as dandelions, groundsel and parsley by the warreners; these mounds could have a variety of shapes, being rectangular, round, square or even cruciform.[17]

Deer Park

The deer park differed from the three areas noted above in that it was an area specifically and securely enclosed to retain deer, principally fallow and red deer, for both hunting and as source of fresh meat. Throughout the Middle Ages, deer hunting was the preserve of the king and the aristocracy, and the acquisition of a park was one of the ways a landowner could have been said to have 'arrived'. The creation of deer parks peaked between 1200 and 1350, which was a general period of economic growth, and by the early 14th century there were some 3,200 parks in England occupying 2% of the entire land surface.[18] Deer parks vary in size from a few acres to several hundred, with a concentration in central England. Again, their numbers and distribution vary over time, with new parks being created, others becoming abandoned ('disparked'), and many expanding or contracting in size according to the fortune and standing of their owners. The fact that the parks were held by the major landowners (both lay and ecclesiastical) meant that one owner could have several parks, for example the Earls of Lancaster held 45 separate parks while the Bishop of Winchester had 23 on his estates.[19] Cantor lists some 67 deer parks in North Yorkshire, with six other possible examples, and this number has recently been repeated, although it is probably a severe underestimate.[20]

The Medieval Deer Park

The most distinctive feature of a medieval deer park was its boundary. The most common type of boundary was a fence of tall, cleft oak stakes fastened to a rail and set in a broad high earth bank (together usually known as the pale), with an adjoining ditch on the inside of the park; the latter is a defining characteristic as in most other forms of enclosure the ditch is on the outside. As deer are able to leap up to 6m horizontally and 3m vertically, the boundary had to be substantial and the construction and maintenance of the pale often represented a significant expense for the owner. The accounts of the Bishop of Winchester for 1252-53, for example, record that it cost £31 to make the 12 furlongs (c.2.4km) of pale for a relatively small park at Bishop's Sutton, which equated to some 6,000 man days of work.[21] Some parks had a 'palester' or 'pallister' whose sole duty it was to ensure that the pale was kept in good repair. Sometimes a significant gap was left between the pale and the ditch, or the pale was set back from the boundary of the park, to leave a c.5m wide strip known as the 'freeboard' to facilitate the inspection and repair of the boundary. Instead of an earthwork bank and ditch, some parks had stone walls and/or quickset hedges, or utilised natural features such as watercourses.

Fig. 2/1: Park pale, Westbury-sub-Mendip, Somerset.

Fig. 2/2: Park pale, Raby Castle, County Durham, another Neville castle.

It goes without saying that the optimum shape for a deer park was circular, but this was rarely achieved. Although many are oval, there are numerous parks with elongated or angular shapes, often resulting from specific constraints such as local topography, watercourses or existing boundaries, or due to a desire to funnel or drive deer into specific locations. Parks were not static features in the countryside, and several alignments of the pale, reflecting the expansion or contraction of a park, may be apparent. There are also several examples of deer parks adjoining each other.

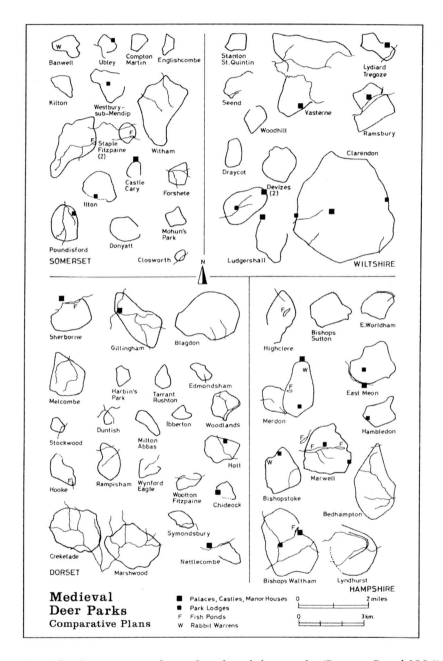

Fig. 2/3: Comparative plans of medieval deer parks (Source: Bond 1994).

The perimeter of a deer park would be broken by gates and occasionally by deer-leaps. The latter was a device which enabled deer to enter a park but not leave it, and it could take a variety of forms. Most simply, a deer-leap could be an earthen ramp leading from the exterior to the top of the pale, but most commonly it appears as a lowering in the paling fence or an arrangement of poles placed across a gap in the pale, coinciding with a pit or ditch on the inside of the park. The deer inside the park belonged to the owner, and the ownership of such a device was a highly prized and expensive privilege, granted only by a royal license. A deer-leap constructed in the Bishop of Durham's park at Crayke in 1229 was 20ft long, while others recorded in Hatfield Forest in 1624 were 16½ft long and 4ft high.[22] In 1389 Ralph de Neville was granted a licence to enclose his wood at Raskelf which adjoined the Forest of Galtres, and to make a park there with three deer-leaps 'adjoining each of length of 100ft'.[23] The medieval term for a deer-leap is *saltatorium*, and it now seems likely that 'salter' field names may provide a clue to sites now removed.[24]

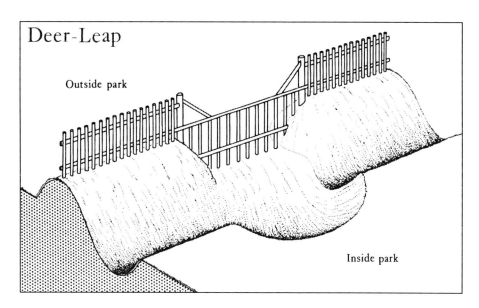

Fig. 2/4: Representation of a deer leap (Source: Woodward 1982).

Although there are references to red deer and roe deer (the native species), and fallow deer (introduced by the Normans), the documentary sources suggest that the fallow deer were the predominant species in deer parks.[25] The fact that they breed at two years old meant that their numbers were always maintained but there are also frequent references to grants of live deer, which could be moved over distances of 20 miles or more, to replenish or stock parks elsewhere; as one example, parks in south-east Oxfordshire were supplied from Windsor Forest.[26] The various types of deer do not always mix well, and there are instances of owners putting different species into different parks.

Deer parks contain a mixture of woodland and grassland, and during their heyday the parks represented carefully managed economic blocks of land. The woodland provided cover for the deer and a forest ambience for the hunters, but a balance had to be struck between the amount of wood and the number of deer. The cultivation and management of this woodland was very important and the areas of young trees and underwood were frequently protected from the deer by additional pales and/or fences, which may in turn contain deer-leaps or gates. At Leconfield Park in East Yorkshire more than 40 acres of underwood were described as being 'greatly spoiled for lack of a good fence' in 1577.[27] Large timber was a valuable commodity in the Middle Ages, and many of the bigger trees were pollarded to put the new growth out of the reach of the deer (see Chapter 10). The grassland provided fodder for the deer in areas called *laundes* (later 'lawns'), and holly was often specifically grown to provide a winter feed.[28] 'Deer browse', cut from either deciduous or evergreen trees, provided a much cheaper alternative to holly. Rackham distinguishes between the wood pasture or non-compartmental park, where trees and grass were intermixed, and the compartmental park where the grassland areas were physically separated from the woodland.[29] *Hayes* or *haies* are also frequently mentioned in connection with parks. This word is derived from the Old English *(ge)haeg*, meaning a fence, hedge or enclosure, and it seems to have been associated with a part of the forest or park fenced off from hunting, or a series of hedges designed to control the movement of deer or to trap them for the hunt.[30]

Fig. 2/5: Deer browsing.

Fig. 2/6: Stag, doe and oak.

The deer provided a source of food, but the degree to which they were also kept purely for sport or entertainment is becoming more evident. The fact that some of the smaller later deer parks appear to have areas of landscape and woodland deliberately created to improve the success of the hunt, with deer being channelled into specific killing grounds or along deliberately constructed 'deer courses', has led some authors to suggest that they should really be considered as 'amenity' parks, which formed part of wider designed landscapes which frequently incorporated planned vistas and water features[31] (see Chapter 3). There has also been some discussion as to whether it was true hunting to kill a deer in a park because the animal was already confined by the park pale.[32]

Venison was a highly prized meat often consumed at celebratory meals, and the gifts of deer (both alive or dead) and the right to hunt deer were powerful royal prerogatives. Large numbers of deer were killed for the royal table, for example the marriage of the Henry III's daughter, Margaret, to Alexander III of Scotland in York in 1251 required the provision, at only one week's notice, of at least 500 stags, as many roe deer as possible and a dozen does from the forests of Yorkshire and Cumberland, while over 900 deer were ordered for the royal household between October 1260 and September 1261.[33] Overall, it has been estimated that the royal household consumed some 500 deer a year from the royal forests.[34] In terms of royal gifts, it is suggested that over 2,000 deer (1,150 dead and 930 live) were given away between 1231-35.[35]

It is a matter of debate as to how many deer any individual park could accommodate, and this will be dependent on a number of other factors such as availability of water and fodder.[36] Numbers could be increased by reducing the woodland cover, improving the quality of the grass, and regularly re-stocking with imported deer. Shirley recommends two bucks and one doe to every 3 acres of parkland, though in practice, ratios of a half to two head per acre were commonly used.[37] Numbers in the seven parks held by the Duchy of Cornwall ranged from 15 in Launceston Park to 300 at Restormel, while the Bishop of Durham had 540 deer in his four main parks in 1457.[38]

As well as venison, deer parks also provided alternative sources of food. Many parks therefore contain fishponds (which often utilise the water supply used for the deer), rabbit warrens and other animal hunting enclosures such as for pheasants, hares and partridges. The provision of a secure boundary also meant that some parks contained horse studs and livestock farms, and a useful income could be generated by letting out specific areas for grazing ('agistment') by cattle or pannage for pigs; sheep were rarely allowed into parks as it was thought that they would compete with the deer for the grass, although they became more widespread from the 16th century. Some areas within parks were also given over to arable cultivation.

Fig. 2/7: Feeding the boars in the park.

Fig: 2/8: Lodge in Hardington Park, Somerset.

A 'parker' or park keeper was usually employed to care for and oversee the running of the park and a house or lodge was often provided for him within the pale. In many cases, these were relatively simple structures, providing the keeper with domestic accommodation or a temporary base for the park official, and they were often sited on the highest point in the park to provide a viewing point. At East Meon in Hampshire, for example, the lodge consisted of a hall and chamber with a stable in 1376-77.[39] These lodges should be differentiated from the grander and more elaborate structures which were built for the owners of the park, either as a base from which hunting could take place or where entertainment took place before or after the hunt. These buildings could, in effect, be small palaces containing a large number of rooms, including kitchens, cellars and even a chapel. Dower houses were also built to provide some seclusion from the hunt, while other structures formed viewing points, especially in the early post-medieval period when the hunt became more of a spectator sport. In many cases, these grander buildings were moated, thus allowing the deer come up to the boundaries of the lodge from where they could be viewed. While these lodges are invariably located within the park, 'detached lodges' positioned on the edge or further away from their parks are also becoming recognised, and they are often associated with gardens – they should be seen as places of private refuge away from the main house or castle.[40] All these various buildings may survive as modern farmsteads, having appropriate 'Park' and 'Lodge' names.

Deer parks can also contain other structures associated with the management and hunting of the deer, for example, kennels for the dogs, mews for hawks, sheds for the storage of fodder such as hay and deer browse, and prisons for poachers.[41] In many cases these buildings would be linked to the park keeper's lodge, but they may form separate complexes.

The creation of a deer park effectively fossilised that part of the landscape on which it was placed, at least during the lifetime of the park. As a result, many deer parks are associated with a wide range of earlier features such as prehistoric and Roman monuments, especially field systems, roads and settlements. Although the deer park was often created on unimproved land on the edge of a medieval manor and estate, in some areas the previously open fields and associated settlements were emparked, especially when individual parks expanded over time. However, the subsequent breaking up of the parks into smaller farming units, which occurred from the 16th century onwards, can mean that these field monuments are reduced or destroyed by subsequent agricultural activity.

Documentary sources provide some information about the creation and management of deer parks, although these are often patchy particularly for the early parts of the Middle Ages. Records that do survive may include details about the construction of the pales and walls, the number of deer hunted and killed, accounts of income and expenditure, details of stocking and transportation of animals, and the accounts of poaching and other illegal activity. As will be seen in subsequent chapters, the available documents have provided a significant amount of information on the Sheriff Hutton deer park.

Footnotes

1   Liddiard 2003.
2   Cantor & Hatherley 1979, p.71.
3   e.g. Cantor & Hatherley 1979; Stamper 1988.
4   e.g. Roberts 1988; Bond 1981.
5   e.g. Almond 2003; Cummins 1988 & 2002.
6   Birrell 1982 & 1996a.
7   Blackett-Ord 1986.
8   Birrell 1992.
9   e.g. Bond 1998, pp.22-31; Bond 1994; Neave 1991; Woodward 1982; Steane 1975 to name but a few.
10   e.g. Whitaker 1892; Shirley 1867.
11   Bond 1994, pp.115-116; Cantor 1982.
12   Cantor 1982, p.61; Young 1979.
13   Dormer 2003, p.79; Cox 1907, pp.501-517.
14   Cantor 1982, p.70.
15   Bond 1994, p.116; Cantor 1982, p.82.
16   Bond 1988; Veale 1957.
17   Dennison 2004, pp.137-139; Bond 1994, pp.144-148.
18   Stamper 1988, p.140; Rackham 1986, p.123.
19   Cantor 1982, p.76.
20   Cantor 1983, pp.89-90; Dormer 2003, p.80 ; Moorhouse 2003a, p.35.
21   Roberts 1988, pp.69-70.
22   Birrell 1992, p.120; Rackham 1989, pp.120-121.
23   Calendar Charter Rolls vol 5 (1341-1417), p.310.
24   Higham 2003.

25   Bond 1994, p.125; see also Chapter 3.
26   Woodward 1982, pp.4-5.
27   Neave 1991, p.9.
28   Spray 1981.
29   Rackham 1986, pp.125-126; Rackham 2004, p.3.
30   Woodward 1982, p.3.
31   e.g. Cummins 2000, p.47; Taylor 1998, pp.18-21; Taylor 2004.
32   Cummins 2002, p.46.
33   Birrell 1996b, pp.440-441.
34   Rackham 1980, p.181.
35   Birrell 1996b, p.442.
36   Birell 1992.
37   Bond 1994, p.142; Shirley 1867.
38   Stamper 1988, p.143; Birrell 1992, p.124.
39   Roberts 1988, p.77.
40   Chris Taylor, *pers. comm.*
41   Bond 1994, p.151.

CHAPTER 3: MEDIEVAL HUNTING
by Barbara Walker
with contributions by Ed Dennison

The Importance and Role of Hunting

Hunting was a central part of medieval culture which permeated the lives of the nobility and peasants alike. Richard Almond in his book 'Medieval Hunting' gives a useful definition: "Hunting is the pursuit and taking of wild quarry, whether animal or bird, using any method or technique."[1] Rather than being a solely male preserve, evidence from medieval writings and illustrations suggests that women, at all levels of society, were also involved in hunting in various ways. Gaston Phoebus was one of these medieval writers. He started to write his highly regarded manual *Le Livre de Chase* in 1387. The miniatures in his book vividly enhance the text which his contemporaries studied to further their knowledge of the art of medieval hunting. Most of the figures in this chapter are taken from the illustrations in his book.[2]

Gaston Phoebus, Counte de Foix and Viscount of the Béarn (a region on south-west France), was born in 1331 and rose to become an important and powerful noble on the Continent. Between 1350 and 1390 he led a band of mercenaries on quests from the Pyrenees to Scandinavia, changing his allegiance as appropriate. He died in 1391 after signing a secret treaty with Charles V of France, in which he sold him all his property.[3] Surprising as it may seem, Sheriff Hutton has a tenuous link with Gaston Phoebus. John Neville, Lord of Sheriff Hutton from 1367 to 1388 and the man who started building the stone castle at the west end of the village, was made King Richard II's Lieutenant in Aquitaine between 1378 and 1380. It was there that John 'treated' with Gaston, who was one of the French negotiators at the time.[4]

The upper classes of society viewed the benefits of hunting as being widespread. Besides providing healthy, exciting exercise, entertainment and pleasure, it required knowledge and skills of horsemanship, tracking and the management of weapons, which was all good training for fighting and war. As was written in the 13th century, "Knightes ougt to hunte at hertes, at bores and other wyld bestes, for in doynge these thynges the knyghtes exercyse them to armes".[5] By the 15th century there were several texts to teach young men the terminology of hunting and the procedures and rituals to be followed – one of the most important of these was written by Edward, Duke of York between 1406 and 1413.[6] Noble boys would be taught to hunt from the age of 14 as it hardened their bodies, accustomed them to blood, and developed their cunning.[7] Those tutoring Henry Fitzroy, Henry VIII's bastard son by Elizabeth Blount, at Sheriff Hutton castle in the 1530s complained that he preferred hunting and hawking to schoolwork.[8]

Hunting also provided a source of fresh meat. Many useful by-products included clothes from the furs and pelts, medicines from parts of the deer, knife handles, sword grips, buttons etc. from the antlers, and glue from the bones. Animal teeth were used for adornment and to protect the wearer from the evil spirits. Feathers were fashioned into writing quills and used to fletch arrows, whilst long decorative feathers trimmed hats and smaller ones were used by artists as brushes.

For the nobility, the hunt provided an important social activity and alliances could be made with visitors who came to hunt. For example, in 1542 the Duke of Norfolk entertained the

Scottish Ambassador to hunting in Sheriff Hutton park.[9] Venison was not generally available on the open market and so gifts of venison cemented prestige and social relationships and, when given to the local parson, paid the lord's tithes. In 1483 the Abbot of St. Mary's in York was to get 'ii bukkes' in summer and 'ii does' in winter from the 'Park of (Myddeham) Sherefhoton'.[10]

As has been noted in Chapter 2, hunting took place in the royal forests, chases and deer parks, while the rights of free warren allowed for the hunting of lesser game, but not red deer, on the king's land. Ralph de Neville was granted the right of free warren in Sheriff Hutton in 1334[11] and in the following year he obtained a licence to 'enclose his woods of Middleham and Sheriff Hutton and make parks there, with a deer leap in the same park of Sheriff Hutton'.[12] As will be explained in Chapter 4, this licence appears to relate to a significant expansion of an existing park which dates from at least 1282-83.

The Quarry

Although the love of hunting was universal, the quarry hunted by the nobility differed from that taken by the lower orders. Most medieval pictorial sources show the nobility hunting red deer, both stag and hind, as well as hare, wild boar, wolf and bear, and sometimes otters and badgers. Common people hunted any bird or mammal that was edible. They also killed wolf and fox because they were predators and had useful pelts, but rabbits were their main target.

Fig. 3/1: The quarry – fallow deer (Source: BnF FR616, fol.20).

Fig. 3/2: The quarry – hares (Source: BnF FR616, fol.24v).

Animals preserved in the parks and forests were mostly red deer and roe deer (the native species), fallow deer and wild boar. All these were regarded as 'noble', to be hunted by the aristocracy. Red deer were the larger and more widespread of the two native species, although their numbers seemed to have declined after the 13th century, perhaps as a result of agricultural enchroachment into the waste and woodland. Roe deer were also becoming scarce by the 15th century, partly because the spread of coppicing restricted access to hazel which formed an important part of their diet, and possibly also because they were excluded from the protection of Forest Law in 1338. Fallow deer are a native of southern Europe, and they seem to have been introduced into England by the Normans. They are particularly well suited to being kept in parks, being gregarious in nature, able to fatten on poor land, they need relatively little attention or management, will breed regularly, and will graze alongside cattle. As a result, they were widespread in deer parks by the mid 13th century.[13] Hinds were considered inferior sport to the stronger stag or hart with its great rack of antlers. The supreme noble quarry was a hart of at least six years old with ten points or tines to its rack of antlers. This was royal game, though sometimes the king granted special licences to favoured courtiers to take red deer.

The wild boar was of lesser importance although it was strong and more dangerous to hunt. Hares were the principal beast of the warren, and were held in high esteem - chasing hares with greyhounds was a more informal and less expensive sport. Hares were believed to be melancholy animals and it was thought that eating the flesh would induce melancholy. Gaston Phoebus recommended that the flesh should not be given to hounds because it was indigestible; he advised that they could eat the tongue and kidneys, and bread soaked in blood.[14] Though the wolf was dangerous and cunning, its strength, speed and strong scent made it a challenging quarry but the flesh was not eaten.

The numbers of deer that were taken were tightly controlled, and hunting had several close seasons. Edward, Duke of York,[15] mentions the 'Fence Month'. This was generally 15 days either side of midsummer when the hinds and does fawned, and another close season occurred during the autumn rut. In both cases, the deer were not to be disturbed and in some cases 'watchers' were employed to ensure that this happened.[16] Recommended hunting seasons coincided with the time when the deer were fit and in prime fat condition or 'in grease'.[17] Various sources on the seasons contradict each other, but generally red deer stag and roe deer buck were hunted from June 24th to September 14th, red deer hind and fallow doe from September 14th to February 2nd, and roe doe from September 9th to February 2nd. Edward, Duke of York, said hare hunting lasted all year but other sources state the season was from September 29th to February 2nd or June 24th.[18]

The close seasons were rigidly observed by the nobles, although perhaps not so carefully by the peasants, particularly if they were out poaching deer. This main purpose of the seasons was, of course, to maintain stocks to ensure the preservation of deer for future hunting. Other measures were also taken, for example by limiting or excluding competing activities in the park; the grazing of domestic animals was restricted so that adequate fodder remained for the deer, and in some forests domestic stock was driven out in the winter months specifically for this purpose. 'Laundes' or hay meadows were created within the parks to provide fodder, and leafy branches ('deer browse') were cut and stacked to be used as winter fodder.[19]

The aristocracy went hunting in splendour on fine horses with packs of well kept hounds or dogs of different breeds and attended by a variety of servants. Although the methods used by the common people were less showy and did not require much equipment, they were no less effective. Their hunting took place on foot using traps, snares and nets of different types.

The Hounds

The nobility took great pride in their hounds and made sure they were well looked after. Greyhounds, in particular, were constant companions of their masters during journeys and at home.

Gaston Phoebus tells us that the kennels were single storey buildings with two doors. The door at the front was only opened for the hunt, while the back door was always open and led straight onto an exercise yard.[20] Edward, Duke of York, advised the huntsman to choose a boy servant as young as seven or eight to care for the hounds. He should be physically active and keen sighted, and beaten until he had a great fear of failing to carry out his duties properly. The hounds were never left on their own, and kennel boys slept in a loft above the hounds to prevent any fighting that might break out in the night.

The duties of the kennel boy, or 'dog boy', are graphically described by T. H. White in his classic story "The Sword in the Stone".[21] One of the first jobs was to learn the name of each hound and recognise it instantly. Cleaning the kennels, replacing straw bedding, watering the hounds and undertaking running repairs such as removing thorns from paws, were daily routines. Every morning and evening the hounds were led out for exercise and to relieve themselves, and they were groomed and wiped down with wisps of straw. In addition, kennel boys learned to spin horse hair and make leads for the hounds. All this was a good apprenticeship for starting on the path of becoming a skilled hunter.

Fig. 3/3: The kennels (Source: BnF FR616, fol.52v).

Fig. 3/4: The hunting dogs. Top L-R: rough coated greyhound, running hound, lymer. Bottom L-R: two alaunts, two smooth coated greyhounds, running hound, mastiff (with spiked collar), greyhound-mastiff cross (Source: BnF FR616, fol.37v).

Different types of hounds performed different functions. The main breeds were greyhound, alaunt, mastiff, running hounds, lymer and spaniel. Greyhounds had great speed and a willingness to pull down running quarry as soon as they reached it. A 'fewterer' was the man who held the dogs in slips or couples until he judged the time right to release them for the chase. The alaunt was similar to the greyhound, but was burlier and stronger, and could seize a running animal and bring it down; Edward, Duke of York, thought they were treacherous and hare-brained! A mastiff was also used to pull game down, and many packs included one or two 'bercelets', which were able to follow the trail of a wounded deer. Running hounds were similar to our foxhounds, some hunting with their noses in the air, others with their noses close to the ground. It was considered best to use a blend of both types of running hounds as the former were useful in cover and woodland, whilst the latter were best in the open ground.

The lymer, a tracking hound, had a specialised role, being used to detect a hart and taught not to bark (see plate 21). They were kept apart from the other hounds and sometimes even lived with the huntsman. The spaniel was used when hawking with falcon, goshawk and sparrowhawk. He was useful for setting up partridge, pheasant and quail, but was not very sociable with other dogs.

Owning a good pack of hounds was expensive. In Edward's time it cost a halfpenny a day to feed a running hound, three farthings a day for a greyhound, and a penny a day for a lymer.[22] The 'dog men' were commonly paid 1½d. or 2d. per day while huntsmen earned 12d. per day; in 1285, one three-week hunting expedition in the Wiltshire forests cost £6 2s. in wages alone.[23]

Hunting establishments consisted of a hierarchy of people each with a special skill necessary for a successful hunt. Some of the specialist royal huntsmen travelled around the country overseeing the hunts, especially if the deer were destined for the royal table; White describes how William Twyti and his team of huntsmen turn up to run the boar hunt for Sir Ector in Forest Sauvage.[24] In contrast, many of the hunt servants came from humble origins. A commoner and his son could rise up the social scale through becoming skilled at some aspect of the hunt. They had to have a sound understanding of the correct terms to use and how to conduct the intricacies of the hunt properly, as well as detailed local knowledge about the park or forest and the lie of the land. Considerable prestige and financial reward came from employment as a professional huntsman or falconer.

Gifts of hounds could be used to further relationships. In February 1527 Henry Fitzroy sent ten couples of hounds to his cousin James V in Scotland along with Nicholas Eton, his yeoman of the hunt and a groom, to demonstrate the correct method of using the trained dogs. Delighted with the gift, James reciprocated with two brace of hounds and a promise to send some red hawks.[25]

Of course a good horse was essential to the nobleman who was expected to have great skill in horsemanship, his status being enhanced by the possession of a good mount. Even a huntsman or senior forester would be mounted. Medieval illustrations indicate that the horses were of medium weight, clean legged, low in height with good strong hind quarters and a broad chest. Manes were usually neatly tied or plaited. In selecting a horse, one with a calm temperament was prized as it had to respond to the bit so it was easily and quickly turned to avoid branches or rocks.

With a fine mount and good hounds, a noble was well equipped for an exciting and rewarding day's hunting, but he relied heavily on the skill of the master of the hunt and his hierarchy of assistants.

The Hunt

The various sources which deal with medieval hunting, and the contemporary tracts mentioned above, provide numerous details about the hunt itself and the various operations and activities that were associated with it.[26]

When a lord wished to go hunting he would order his Master of Game to make the necessary arrangements. The Master of Game was often a lesser nobleman appointed to the post and usually paid. For example, Richard Cholmeley was appointed Master of Game for Sheriff

Hutton park in 1501 and was also granted the income from the 'herbiage' (grazing) in the park for which he had to pay a rent.[27]

Hunting 'par force de chiens'

The most common and classical form of hunting was the hunt *par force de chiens* or 'by strength of hounds', or more accurately with a pack of hounds accompanied by aristocratic hunters on horseback. This was the purest form of medieval hunting, whereby a single beast was selected and pursued to its death in whatever place its strength, speed and willingness enabled it to reach before it was outwitted by the hounds and men. The hunter's pleasure lay in experiencing the contest of instincts and abilities between the hart and the hounds, and it is this type of hunting with which we are most familiar today. In some cases, the hart won and escaped, and the hunters returned empty-handed. Obviously this form of hunting required wide open spaces, and so it was a common feature of the royal forests and chases, and some of the larger enclosed deer parks.

It is important to appreciate that this was hunting in its purest and most complex form which was, in the medieval period, a very symbolic and ritualistic activity. Several clearly defined stages have been identified: the quest; the assembly or gathering; the moving, finding or unharbouring; the chase; the baying, abay or death, the unmaking or undoing; and the *curée*. All of these stages had their own rituals and procedures; Gaston Phoebus for example, provides some ten chapters of instructions for the quest alone.

The evening before the hunt, the Master of Game went to the yeomen and 'lymerer' (the man who looked after the tracking hounds) to decide tracking arrangements for the next day. They would plan to look for a warrantable hart of ten or more tines.

Early the next morning, the lymerers, with their lymers on leash, would track the quarry on foot looking for signs of the hart's size (the 'quest') (see plate 21). They would take account of how high he had reached up the branches in his fraying (rubbing the velvet from his antlers) and examine his lair to see how broad and trampled it was. Tracks would be examined - if the sole was four fingers wide they would know it was a great hart. They would gather the 'fumes' (droppings) to take to the 'assembly' as these would indicate the quality and age of the quarry. Before leaving, they would mark their tracks through the forest or park by snapping branches or leaving other clues so they knew where to return to.

Having been warned the night before, everyone gathered early at a chosen place for the 'assembly' where tables would be set with a substantial hunt breakfast (see plate 22). The Master of Game assessed the reports of the trackers and everyone examined the fumes, and the lord chose which animal they would hunt. The selected hart was not always the biggest or easiest to kill, but the one thought to provide the best sport.

With the blowing of the horn, the assembled field of huntsmen and hounds moved off (see plate 23). The horn was used to control the hunt and denote progress. The selected hart was moved from its refuge (the 'unharbouring') and was pursued by the pack of running hounds, followed by hunters both on horseback and on foot (the 'chase') (see plate 24). The hounds relied on scent to follow the hart, and in some cases relays of dogs were used, with fresh hounds positioned along the route the deer was thought likely to take. After a long chase, the hart would eventually stand at bay to the hounds, and the rest of the hunters would be called for the 'abay' or death. In some cases, a huntsman would creep up behind the hart and sever a sinew in the hind leg. The hart was then killed with a specialised sword or hunting knife as the horn was blown again to mark the death of the animal (see plate 25). Sometimes the beast was killed with a bow or crossbow, but whatever method was used, death was always as quick as possible. Once dead, the hounds were briefly allowed to eat the flesh from the front of the shoulders. This was their reward by right and an integral part of their training to encourage them to recognise the next quarry and to work hard.

Fig. 3/5: 'Par force de chiens' – the quest. The huntsman chooses the quarry (Source: BnF FR616, fol.61v).

Fig. 3/6: 'Par force de chiens' – the curée. The lymer is rewarded separately (Source: BnF FR616, fol.72).

Next came the 'unmaking', a heavily stylised ritual to honour the deer. Firstly the head was cut off and the body cut open and laid out, and then the animal was skinned and finally cut up. Pieces of the carcass were given to the chief guests at the hunt and other portions were reserved for feasting or presents. Convention had it that the hunter who killed the hart received the skin. Finally, came the *curée*, the ritual rewarding of the hounds (see plate 26). Some of the meat was laid out on the hide to feed the hounds, consisting of cleaned and chopped up paunch and intestines mixed with blood and bread. It was the custom to reward the lymer separately by itself, away from the rest of the pack.

Ladies sometimes appear in the medieval illustrations depicting the 'unmaking', but there is some doubt as to whether they joined the *par force* or were summoned later to the unmaking by their lords. However, some illustrations show the *par force* in full cry with ladies sitting on horseback behind their husbands. Both situations may have occurred, but the former would have been more usual. When ladies were present at the unmaking, they might be presented with a foot or exceptionally the head of the deer.

Bow and stable hunting, and coursing

The purest form of hunting described above was evidently too strenuous for some, and another type of hunt, by 'bow and stable' evolved. In essence, this involves the hunters being more or less static, with the quarry being driven towards them; the odds are firmly in favour of the hunters and the point of death is specifically chosen. This type of hunting had an advantage in that it could operate in smaller areas, such as a deer park, and it was the standard method of hunting before the arrival of the Normans. The contemporary writers such as Edward, Duke of York, and Gaston Phoebus generally disapproved of this type of hunting, the latter observing that those who hunted with cords (see below) should have them round their own necks! Nevertheless, he offers advice on, for example, the types of bows and arrows to be used, and how best to shoot.

In bow and stable hunts, there is no preliminary quest and no selection of a preferred beast. The running hounds, beaters and mounted hunters simply pushed or drove as many quarry animals towards or past stationary hunters who were waiting at a pre-arranged location with crossbows or longbows. The quarry were prevented from escaping sideways by lines of beaters or even physical barriers. Few of the animals died immediately, and so they were pulled down by large greyhounds and killed. Raised platforms known as 'stable stands' or 'standings' were sometimes erected to provide individual shooting positions, often at the end of the drives or among the trees along the route, and women were often included within the shooters. A woodcut dating to 1575 shows Elizabeth I standing on such a structure, receiving her huntsman's report.[28] Lines of archers were called 'sets'.

This method of hunting is indiscriminate and involves mass slaughter. It has been compared to the modern pheasant shoot where rich men provide easy sport for their guests 'who commonly include the stout, the idle, the inexperienced and the downright dangerous'.[29] However, it was a relatively quick and efficient way to obtain large amounts of meat, as might be required for large events, ceremonies or the royal table; as noted in Chapter 2 above, for example, over 900 deer were ordered from various forests for the royal household between October 1260 and September 1261.[30]

A variation on this theme might be employed when live deer were required to be caught, for example when they were to be presented as gifts or when they were required to be transported to re-stock adjacent parks or forests. The bowmen and the greyhounds of the bow and stable hunt could then be replaced with nets and snares. However, nets were also used to catch deer which, once caught, would then be killed. Gaston Phoebus provides good illustrations and advice concerning the making and deployment of nets[31] (see figure 3/8 below). Hurdles and fences were also used to channel animals into traps.

The drive was often a labour-intensive and expensive form of hunting, both in the supply of manpower for the drivers and hunters, and the equipment and structures that went with it. Of course, the numbers of people involved could vary. Some 30 named men (including an abbot, a prior and several knights) participated in a hunt in the Forest of Galtres in 1251 to provide venison for the Christmas festivities in York,[32] whereas there are other examples of just a few people taking part and single animals being hunted in this way. When Edward IV was hunting in Epping Forest in 1481, the entertainment was rounded off with a feast in a 'beautiful arbour' erected specifically for the occasion.[33]

The technicalities of the bow and stable hunt are splendidly described in the 14th century *Sir Gawain and the Green Knight*.[34] This shows that the drive frequently took place down a wooded valley, which provided a natural channel, and that rows of stables or 'sets' were positioned along the upper side or along both sides of the route.

Fig. 3/7: Bow and stable hunting (Source: BnF FR616, fol.111v).

Fig. 3/8: Catching live animals in nets (Source: BnF FR616, fol.103).

In areas where the topography was not suitable, artificial drives were created, but these are traditionally thought to date mainly from the 16th century. Several different types of these 'deer courses' are discussed in the contemporary literature and depicted in illustrations. The main difference to the other forms of hunting is that it was designed to be a spectator sport, with people watching from vantage points or specially constructed standings or buildings. This may represent a variant on the more traditional form of bow and stable hunting which seems to have taken place out of the public gaze.

'Purlieu coursing' was essentially hunting *par force* along a defined track, while other sorts involved dogs chasing deer along a course which may or may not have been permanently defined. Courses may be marked by nets or fabric supported on poles but more permanent courses were defined by parallel walls, hedges or palings. These latter courses are frequently associated with paddocks or enclosures in which the deer and/or dogs were carolled before or after the drive, and are referred to as 'paddock courses'; a 'breathing course' allowed the deer to escape, and a 'fleshing course' was where the dogs were allowed to pull down and kill the deer.[35] One particularly fine early 17th century example survives at Sherbourne Lodge in Gloucestershire, where the 1.6km long walled course has a wide funnel entrance at the start and a lodge with flat roof and viewing balcony near the finish.[36]

More recent research shows that these paddock courses have earlier origins, and it seems quite likely that they represent a type of bow and stable hunting. Edward, Duke of York, describes the king on his standing with his bow ready, perhaps with other huntsmen, while 'fair lodges to keep the king and queen .. from the sun' were erected.[37] Other 13th and 14th century French works mention using relays of dogs which set out from marker posts positioned at intervals along the course.[38]

The remains of these courses can be identified in a number of different ways, for example from suspicious-looking parallel or funnel-type field boundaries depicted on later post-medieval maps, from significant field names such as 'The Parrock' or 'Slips' (the latter referring to slipping the dog's leashes so they can chase the deer), from upstanding earthworks such as the banks and ditches defining the courses or platforms representing the viewing or shooting standings, and from the surviving buildings, lodges or other viewing structures.[39] The lengths and widths of the courses can be up to 2km long and c.50m wide, and they need not necessarily be straight – some are curved or sinuous, presumably to give an element of surprise to the huntsmen and spectators. At Ravensdale Park in Derbyshire, for example, a 1.6km long course has a reverse-S alignment and is formed by two parallel hedges set 80m apart, narrowing at one end. A standing from which the other end can be viewed is formed by a revetted bastion, located a short distance from the site of a medieval lodge.[40] This type of paddock coursing or bow and stable hunting is eminently suited to enclosed deer parks, where space was more limited than in the open forest, and in many cases they are associated with grand designed landscapes which incorporate planned vistas, water features, grand houses and/or palace residences and gardens.

In addition to these two main types of hunting, a third more complex and hybrid type is described by Edward, Duke of York, and by Chaucer in his 'Book of the Duchess'.[41] As implied, this type of hunting is a mixture between *par force* and bow and stable, and uses two different packs of hounds with different abilities for two distinct phases. In the first phase one pack of less experienced dogs clears the forest of animals except the hart, and these are driven towards the killing ground. The second pack of dogs, the hart hounds with their more experienced training, seeks out the remaining hart, and this is hunted using the *par force* method.

Hawking

Hawking was an altogether gentler and more leisurely sport than the rigour of *par force* hunting, with its connotations of training for war.[42] It was an aristocratic pastime requiring a relaxed, well dressed and debonair mixed company. Lone hawking was considered to be poor sport. A friendly, flirtatious attitude, tinged with a competitive spirit provided a good day out.

Ladies went hawking on foot with their merlins on their wrists seeking out larks, for lark's tongues were a great delicacy. Mounted men attended by spaniels who quested for birds accompanied them. Edward, Duke of York, claimed that hawking went on from May to August, and outside that time the hawks were 'mewing' and unfit to fly. Often women were hawk keepers.

Hawking was an upper-class sport because the birds were expensive, and they needed a long training period and someone employed to look after them. Nobles prized their hawks highly and a good pair was seen as a status symbol. By the 14th century, different species of hawk were linked to different ranks of society;[43] a peregrine was fit for an earl, a merlin was for a lady, and the male sparrowhawk was suitable for a priest as it hardly eats anything, although officially priests were forbidden to go hunting or hawking! For everyone, a day's sport would provide meat for the table.

There were two main categories of hawk.[44] 'Hawks of the tower' were unhooded, long winged and they would come to the lure. They climbed on thermals and gained altitude over the area where the game was known to be. As the spaniels flushed out the game the hawks swooped down on it. Birds in this category included falcons, such as the peregrine and hobby. The peregrine was trained to catch heron, stork, crane, bustard and wild goose, as well as pheasant and partridge. 'Hawks of the fist' were short winged and trained to come to the fist not the lure. These included the merlin which took smaller birds. The female hawk is larger than the male and altogether more useful. A good hen merlin could catch partridge. Sparrowhawks were cast from the fist taking ground game such as partridge, woodcock, pheasant, blackbird and thrushes. They were carried by ladies during country picnic hunts.

Fig. 3/9: The Hawk.   Fig. 3/10: 'My Lady is to Hawk'.

The falconer held high office in many households. Valued for the many important skills he possessed, he particularly cared for the long winged hawks and directly supervised the mews. The austringer trained and flew short winged hawks such as the goshawk. Sparrowhawks were generally regarded as unpredictable, especially the male; they were trained and reared by the sparviter. Stealing a hawk was a felony and destroying eggs could bring a year's imprisonment.

Extravagant feasts were held after a good day's hunting had provided a full bag. Unlike the feasts held after the *par force* hunting, where the male nobles and servants who had helped them roistered together, the hawking feasts were for male and female royal and noble guests only. Such occasions were gentler and more gracious, where the guests may have enjoyed delicious 'Sparviters Pie'. The recipe is as follows:

> *"Make the centre of your pie three plump partridges, with six fat quails to give them support; around the quails set a dozen larks; then take wheatears and small birds, as many as you have, and scatter them around. Then take fresh smelling fat bacon, cut into dice and strew it over the birds. As an extra improvement, add verjuice grapes and sprinkle with salt for savour. The case should be a rough pastry of pure wheaten flour, with eggs. Add no spices; add no cheese; put it in a good hot oven, well cleared of ashes, and you will find no food to rival it".*[45]

Hunting in Sheriff Hutton park

At present, there are only a few documentary references to hunting in Sheriff Hutton park during the medieval period, although research is still continuing. It would appear that in its early years, the park was overshadowed by the larger royal Forest of Galtres but, as noted in Chapter 4, by 1228-29 its boundaries had been re-drawn so that Sheriff Hutton lay just outside the forest. Some of the references are noted above, namely that the Abbot of St Mary's in York was to get 'ii bukkes' in summer and 'ii does' in winter from the 'Park of

(Myddeham) Sherefhoton' in 1483, that the young Henry Fitzroy preferred to go hunting and hawking rather that doing his school work in the 1530s, and that the Duke of Norfolk took the Scottish Ambassador hunting in the park in 1542.

It is not known, as yet, what sort of hunting took place in the park, but it is assumed that it would have been along the lines described above. Perhaps the park was doubled in size at the end of the 14th century (see Chapter 4) so that there was enough room and the right sort of landscape to undertake the hunting *par force*. There are some records for the number of deer present and the names of the various park officials; for example, John Dawnay, Ralph Bigod and Thomas Hargyll were successive Keepers of the Park in the late 1480s, and in 1500 there were approximately 200 deer in the park and 400 in 1538-39 (see Chapter 11). The distribution of the various woods, lawns and lodges within the park are discussed in detail in Chapters 4 and 10.

Sheriff Hutton park would also have been an ideal candidate for a deer course; it was a designed landscape with a rich and powerful owner who would have wanted to impress guests and visitors alike. As yet, no such feature has been positively identified. However, a presumed avenue runs north-west from the present Hall, which is the site of Ingram's 17th century lodge and possibly on the site of an earlier building, towards a rectangular ditched enclosure which contains a structure of some kind (see figure 4/2). At present, the avenue is considered to be a garden feature associated with the 17th century lodge and the enclosure is thought to be a Roman site (see Chapters 4 and 14), but the fact that it might represent an admittedly very straight deer course cannot, as yet, be totally discounted. In addition, there are a few tantalising references to 'deer walks' in an 1598 inquisition into the state of the park, but these appear to refer to the fact that the deer were being hindered from walking where they wished by the enclosure of some areas of ground.[46]

There are also a few references to a 'coney garth' in the Sheriff Hutton documents, for example in 1487-88 when it is described as being a 'farm of one close iuxta Fosse called Le Coneygarth', worth 6s. 8d.[47] It is also mentioned in 1521,[48] and in 1525-26,[49] the latter noting that it had been formerly enclosed by Richard, Earl of Salisbury. This area, which covered some 11 acres, was adjacent to the River Foss and so was not in the deer park, and it is shown on both the 1765 plan of Sheriff Hutton and the Ordnance Survey 1856 1st edition 6" map adjacent to Foss House, north-west of Sheriff Hutton Bridge.[50] However, from the late 16th century another 'coneygarth' appears, this time in association with the stone castle. In 1579, for example, there is a lease for two closes, 'formerly one called Castlegarth and Coneygarth',[51] while in a 1610-11 grant of the manor of Sheriff Hutton there is a 'parcel [of ground] called a rabbit and coney warren and orchard within the Castle Garth'.[52] The 1618 grant to Thomas Lumsden, in which he is given the ruined castle (see Chapter 7), also includes the phrase 'lands called Castle Garth and the Coney Warren, with the orchards and fish ponds there within the Castle Garth'.[53] It is assumed that, once the castle went out of use, the rabbits were allowed to move in to a small part of the former outer court, where they were presumably harvested in the usual way, with nets and dogs.

Footnotes

1   Almond 2003, p.3.
2   These figures, as well as plates 21 to 26, have been taken from the Bibliotheque Nationale de France's website (*www.bnf.fr/enluminures/themes/t_4/st_4_01/a401_001.htm*), with permission.
3   Bise *no date*, pp.9-10.
4   Matthew & Harrison 2004 vol 40, p.506.
5   Ramon Lull, published by Caxton in early Tudor times, quoted by Williams 2003, 23.

6   Baillie-Grohman 1909.
7   Orme 2003, p.182.
8   Murphy 2003, pp.71-72; see also Chapter 11.
9   Bain 1890 vol 1, p.223 no.176.
10 British Library Harleian MSS no. 433, f.153.
11 Calthrop 1923, p.178 quoting Calendar Charter Rolls, 2 Edw III, m.13, no. 43.
12 ibid., p.173; National Archives Patent Roll CC66/184.
13 Bond 1994, pp.125-126; Birrell 1996b, pp.438-439; Rackham 1986, pp.39-40.
14 Bise *no date.*
15 Baillie-Grohman 1909.
16 Birrell 1996b, p.455.
17 Birrell 1992, pp.122-123.
18 Almond 2003, p.87.
19 Birrell 1992.
20 Bise *no date*, p.42.
21 White 1998, pp.60-62.
22 Baillie-Grohman 1909, p.27.
23 Birrell 1996b, p,444.
24 White 1998, pp.238-240.
25 Murphy 2003, p.81.
26 The following descriptions are mainly taken from Almond 2003, Cummins 1988, Cummins 2002 and Birrell 1996b.
27 Calendar of Patent Rolls, Henry VII vol 2, p.269; see Chapter 11.
28 Almond 2003, p.157.
29 Cummins 2002, p.41.
30 Birrell 1996b, pp.440-441.
31 Bise *no date*, pp.43 & 99.
32 Birrell 1996b, p.452.
33 Taylor 2004, p.52; Ed Dennison is most grateful to Chris Taylor for supplying a pre-publication version of this paper.
34 see, for example, Cummins 1998, pp.53-55.
35 Taylor 2004, p.45.
36 Fretwell 1995.
37 Baillie-Groham 1904, p.188.
38 Thiébaux 1967, pp.267-268.
39 Taylor 2004.
40 ibid., p.42-43.
41 Cummins 2002, pp.41-42; Almond 2003, p.84.
42 Cummins 1988, pp.187-216.
43 Almond 2003, pp.20-21.
44 Cummins 1988, pp.187-194.
45 ibid., p.216, quoting from Gace de la Vigne.
46 National Archives E178/2792, testimony of Stephen Nevison: ".. and this exam[t] haith not Knowne any ground enclosed w[th]in the said Parke frome mR Pollerds Comying thither Savinge onelie one close called the Sev-all Conteyning about Twenty acres Albebyt the deere may have theire Course or walke into the same".
47 National Archives DL29/10510/650 Ministers Accounts, 3-4 Henry VII, Sheriff Hutton.
48 Letter & Papers, Foreign & Domestic, Henry VIII vol 3(1), p.480.
49 National Archives SC6/Henry VIII/4184 Ministers Accounts 1525-26.
50 West Yorkshire Archive Service (WYAS) Leeds WYL100/SH/B4/2; Ordnance Survey 1856 1st edition 6" map sheet 140, surveyed 1851-52.
51 National Archives E310/33/199.
52 National Archives C66/1804 m.25 Patent Roll 9 James I.
53 WYAS Leeds WYL100/SH/A1/3.

CHAPTER 4: THE ARCHAEOLOGY OF THE PARK – 1: UP TO THE 17TH CENTURY

by Ed Dennison and Shaun Richardson
with contributions from Robin Wardell and Tony Wright

Introduction

The extent of the park, and the evidence for how it has been used, changed and evolved over time, survives in both the landscape and the documentary record. Like a book, the landscape can be 'read', and the various layers can be peeled away to provide a series of 'snap-shots' which can illustrate the history and development of the park. It is fitting that one of the first archaeologists to adopt this 'landscape detective' approach was Maurice Beresford, who was also the first to excavate at East Lilling deserted village and to look at Sheriff Hutton deer park in any detail.[1]

At the time of writing, the area formerly occupied by the park is mostly farmed from four centres, the Hall, Oaks Farm, Lodge Farm and Park Farm. The majority of the land is given over to a mixed dairy/arable regime, with arable land being concentrated in the southern half of the park and improved pasture in the north. There are few areas of plantation or woodland, most of which are associated with the Hall; the small remnants of older woodland and individual ancient trees surviving throughout the park are discussed in Chapter 10.

The Pre-Park Landscape

The discovery of numerous prehistoric artefacts from within and around the area of the medieval deer park shows that there has been some occupation or at least activity here from an early time.[2] Several Neolithic (4000-2200 BC) flint scrapers and cores have been recovered from non-systematic fieldwalking in the general area of the park, and there are also records of Bronze Age (2200-700 BC) artefacts, both flints and metal finds (see plates 28 and 30). The latter include a hoard of 16 socketted axes found 'in Sheriff Hutton' in 1823 (possibly at Stittenham), a 'Beaker-type' axe hammer now in Preston Museum, a 'Migdale-type' flat axe hammer now in the Yorkshire Museum, and another axe hammer described as 'destroyed';[3] the Migdale flat axe is an outstanding example of early Bronze Age workmanship and is an exceptional find. A further socketed axe head was found just outside the eastern pale boundary in 1977. The Victoria County History also notes another perforated stone axe of the same period,[4] although this may be a second reference to one of those listed above. Unfortunately, the precise locations of many of these finds are not known, and it is presently unclear whether they represent one or several specific settlement sites or merely a transient population.

Recent aerial photographic survey work, together with excavations and other fieldwalking programmes, has shown that the Vale of York was densely populated in the Romano-British period (800 BC-410 AD) with a landscape full of field systems and farmsteads linked by a network of roads.[5] Many of these sites are revealed as cropmarks, which appear as a result of differential crop growth over buried archaeological deposits, and it is now apparent that occupation extended onto the heavier clays and alluvium of the lower-lying ground as well as on the higher areas. The hinterland of the great northern Roman town of York was especially rich, and recent excavations at places like Naburn, Easingwold, Stockton on the Forest,

Flaxby and Stamford Bridge, amongst others, have uncovered importance evidence relating to the nature of the rural Romano-British settlement and its role within the wider landscape.[6]

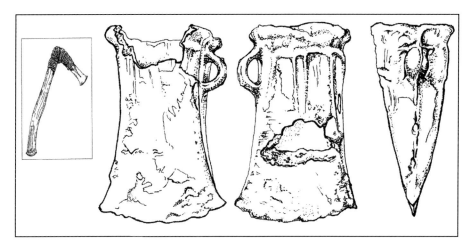

Fig. 4/1: Bronze age socketed axe head, found just outside the east side of the park in 1977.

Cropmarks have indicated the presence of a large Romano-British settlement, made up of a large double-ditched rectilinear enclosure which is divided into smaller compartments and surrounded by a field system and access tracks, on the south side of the River Foss near Lilling Green; limited fieldwalking has recovered a small amount of Roman pottery from the site. It has been suggested that this settlement may have been the centre of an estate associated with a ford across the river.[7] Just to the north, on the other side of the river and on the north side of Lilling Low Lane, parts of another similar site have recently been excavated in advance of the construction of a pipeline.[8] This work revealed dry stone wall foundations, cobbled surfaces, roofing tile and hypocaust material, and the site seems to have been occupied from the 2nd century AD to the early Anglo-Saxon period. Although not strictly a villa, the site was a large and important high-status farmstead complex.

There is also an enclosure within Sheriff Hutton park, to the south of the first castle in the area known as the High Park. The site shows up well on aerial photographs,[9] as a large rectangular enclosure some 94m across, defined on three sides by a bank between ditches and on the southern side by a single ditch (see figure 4/2). Another slightly misaligned ditch continues the north side of the enclosure to the west for approximately 70m. There may be other smaller enclosures attached to the west and south sides of the main enclosure, which are also just visible on the aerial photographs. An earlier photograph taken in c.1949[10] (see figure 4/3) shows the earthworks in sharp relief, with possible structures in the centre of the enclosure. The enclosure is crossed by what appears to be a later avenue leading out from the Hall, which is discussed in Chapter 15.

Unfortunately, the High Park was bulldozed in 1982, and subsequently ploughed, and many of the earthworks are now severely denuded or have been removed completely. However, in a good light and when the grass is short, the east and north sides of the main enclosure are just still visible – the main enclosure sits on a relatively level area of high ground which then slopes away to the south-west where a number of steps, suggestive of broad levelled areas or terraces, may contain further structures (see plate 36). Further to the east, beyond the footpath which bisects the field, there are more levelled areas of ground, and a broad gully curving around to the north-east. The latter appears to have been caused by water action, perhaps by springs located at the head of the gully.

Fig. 4/2: Aerial photograph taken in February 1970 showing the presumed Roman enclosure cut by a later avenue (Copyright reserved Cambridge University Collection of Air Photographs, BAT4).

Fig. 4/3: Oblique aerial photograph taken in c.1949 showing the presumed Roman enclosure.

The enclosure has long been thought to be Romano-British in date, due to its similarities with other nearby sites such as Lilling Green, and the fact that many Roman artefacts were brought to the surface when it was bulldozed and subsequently ploughed. Many of these artefacts have been recovered by Robin Wardell, and they include mortaria (large strong bowls) and pottery sherds (see plate 29), many of which originate from the Crambeck kilns to the north-east, sections of Roman tile, a fragment from a large amphora (wine jar), a pierced whetstone, a bone gaming counter, and the end fragment of a stone sarcophagus. Several Roman coins have also been found in the area of the enclosure by metal detectorists. Despite all this strong circumstantial evidence however, the interpretation of the site as a Romano-British enclosure cannot be positively confirmed without further investigation, such as geophysical survey and/or excavation, and there are other, medieval, possibilities for the site (see below).

Over the years there have been other Roman discoveries in and around the park. In 1999 a Roman Bull Head mount or weight of 1st-2nd century date was found in Skegmer Bottoms just outside the northern park boundary in Stittenham, and several 2nd century brooches have recently been unearthed by metal detectorists on the southern boundary near West Lilling; another trumpet brooch has recently been found close to Sheriff Hutton church in the 'Vineyard' (see plate 31). An intact stone sarcophagus complete with a coped lid was also unearthed when drains were being laid at an unspecified location in the park in the 1860s; it is now kept adjacent to the Hall. Once again, the precise locations of many of these finds are not known, and so it is unclear whether there is just one or several specific Roman sites within the park. Slightly further afield, in Stittenham, a set of five bronze vessels (*paterae*) were discovered during drainage work in the mid 19th century; these are high status objects, complete with the maker's name and a finely engraved rim pattern.[11] Finally, there are two small ornate Roman altar stones in Sheriff Hutton church, which are reputed to have been found somewhere in the parish.

Fig. 4/4: Intact Roman stone sarcophagus found in the park c.1860s, now located at the Hall.

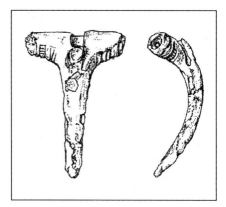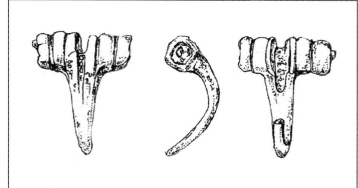

Fig. 4/5: Roman brooches found by metal detectorists at West Lilling.

Several Roman roads pass close to the park. One ran between Stamford Bridge, Thirsk and Northallerton, and its alignment is thought to be represented by an unclassified road running between Sand Hutton and Claxton, and then north-west towards Flaxton. Beyond Flaxton Station, the alignment is less uncertain; it probably went through West Lilling to reappear near Stillington, although an alternative route might have been through the park and along Mill Lane to Cornborough and Farlington.[12] Another road appears to run north-east from York to Stockton on the Forest, and perhaps continuing on to Malton.[13]

These major roads would have been supported by numerous other more local routes, and several have been identified from aerial photographs crossing Sheriff Hutton Moor. One runs on a north-east/south-west alignment past the Lilling Green site, and it has been suggested that it may have crossed the River Foss and continued north along the line of the Howl Beck, and then north towards Terrington.[14] The central section of another road through Sheriff Hutton parish, locally known as 'Braygate', has not been confirmed, but it is thought to be represented by the line of the present Moor Lane running along the eastern edge of the park towards High Stittenham. In addition, the survey of the park carried out for the Pale Project has identified a section of a straight earthwork running on a north-east/south-west alignment through a field just to the north-west of Lodge Farm. It is a raised flat-topped causeway approximately 4m wide and 0.4m high which extends for a distance of some 160m. It continues through the field to the south and can be traced as far as the trackway beyond on aerial photographs, for nearly 400m. This feature has all the characteristics of a section of a Roman road, and it might represent the line of 'Braygate'. However, several early post-medieval boundaries also pass through this same area on a similar alignment, in particular the west side of 'Bushy Lawnd' as depicted by Norden in 1624 (see below), and so this interpretation remains to be confirmed.

It was noted in Chapter 1 that it is quite possible, if not probable, that the present village of Sheriff Hutton has Saxon origins, like the neighbouring settlements of Terrington and Bulmer. Several authors have commented that its excellent defensive and prominent ridge-top position makes it a prime settlement site overlooking the Vale of York, while the 'ton' suffix to Hutton traditionally implies an Anglian settlement.[15] However, there is, as yet, no record of any Saxon material having been found in the park, the village or the immediate vicinity, apart from the excavated site on the north side of the River Foss mentioned above and some parts of Sheriff Hutton church.

The Royal Forest of Galtres

Before looking at the successive Sheriff Hutton deer parks, we should consider two other aspects of the medieval landscape of the area, the much larger royal Forest of Galtres and the deserted medieval village of East Lilling, both of which have a bearing on the parks.

The relationship between the deer parks and the royal forest is complex and has not, as yet, been satisfactorily resolved. Originally the forest covered a huge area stretching from the gates of the City of York as far north as Aldborough and Crayke, representing most of the Wapentake of Bulmer.[16] However, the boundaries were redefined by Henry III to exclude some vills or parts of vills, and a perambulation of 1316[17] shows that the eastern boundary then followed the River Foss; nevertheless, the forest still comprised about 60 townships and some 100,000 acres (4,050 hectares) at this time.[18]

According to this 1316 perambulation, Sheriff Hutton lay just outside the forest, and it has been suggested that it had been removed by 1228-29,[19] or possibly by 1274.[20] However, it still lay within a peripheral disafforested area called the 'purlieus' or 'outer grounds', where the forest laws were less restrictive and the inhabitants had some obligations, such as not to disturb deer grazing in their crops; in compensation, they had gained some grazing rights in the forest.[21] The forest laws were finally removed in 1635 and the former grazing rights belonging to Sheriff Hutton were converted to land, resulting in the area of 'High Roans' to the south of the River Foss being added to the parish and manor.[22]

The physical and legal divisions between the forest and Sheriff Hutton deer park might also have been blurred, at least in the 13th century, due to the fact that various members of the Neville family were also associated with the forest. For example, Geoffrey Neville was Keeper of the Forest between 1217 and 1223, and this position was continued by his son, John Neville, until 1236. Hugh Neville was also Steward of the Forest in 1227 and Ralph Neville was granted the bailiwick (jurisdiction) of the lawn of Ingolthwayt in 1340.[23]

East Lilling Deserted Medieval Village

The history, development and the surviving earthwork remains of the deserted medieval village of East Lilling have been described in great detail by Swan *et al*,[24] and so only a brief summary is given here.

The overlordship of East Lilling belonged to the manor of Sheriff Hutton, and it passed to the Nevilles in 1331 when the 5th Peter de Mauley released it to Ralph Neville. However, both St Mary's Abbey in York and Marton Priory also held land in the township of East Lilling. The main tenants from the late 12th to the early 14th century were the 'de Lillinge' family, but their interests began to wane after c.1300 and, from the mid 14th century, East Lilling was let out to sub-tenants, perhaps passing to the Neville family in the late 14th or early 15th centuries.

The earliest recognisable phase of the village, a regular single row of houses with rear plots ('A' to 'E' on figure 4/6) laid out along the north side of an east-west aligned street ('J' to 'Q'), probably dates to the early post-Conquest period. The regular appearance of the earthworks suggests that they are a deliberately created settlement, probably by one of the de Bulmer family who were then lords of the manor. As noted in Chapter 1, exactly the same scenario, although on a larger scale, has been proposed for Sheriff Hutton. Subsequent

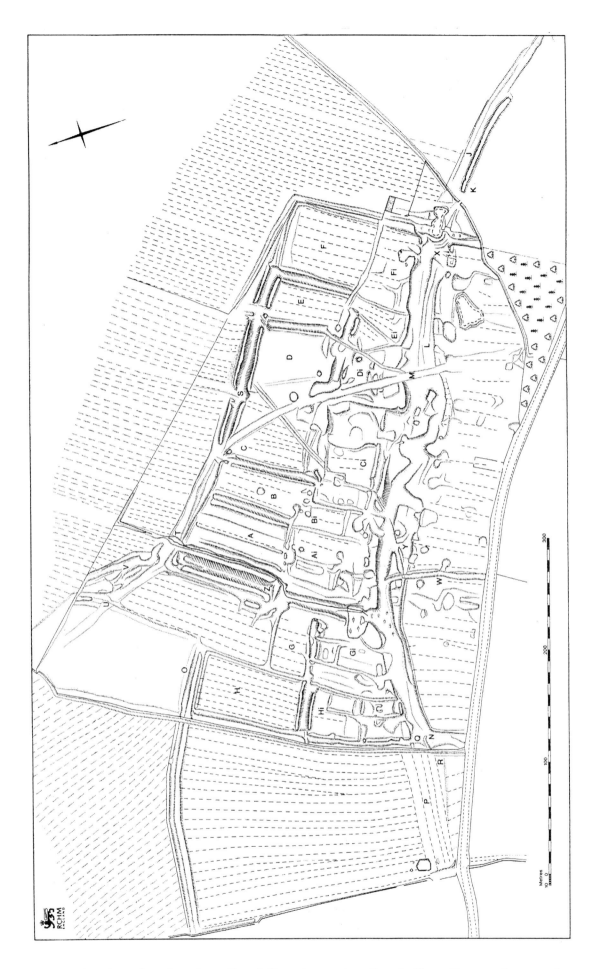

Fig. 4/6: Plan of earthworks at East Lilling deserted medieval village (Source: Swan et al 1990). © Crown Copyright/NMR.

49

expansion resulted in additional plots being added to the east ('F') and to the west ('G' and 'H'), and a sub-division of the original plots. Other earthworks on the site represent a set of fishponds ('Z') and extensive ridge and furrow cultivation. A manor house probably lay slightly further off to the east, in the area of the present Lilling Hall.

The village was probably already in a weakened state by the mid 14th century, due to a declining population, possibly in part caused by the Black Death. In 1377 there were probably five or six families in the village, and some of the agricultural land was taken into the Sheriff Hutton deer park (see below). Bctween 1471 and 1485, when there were probably only two or three households left, the village was deliberately demolished following an agreement between the Lord of Sheriff Hutton, Richard III and the Prior of Marton, and the village site was incorporated into the park (see below). By the early 17th century the site was partly re-occupied by the 'Little Lodge'.

The First Deer Park

It is not known when the first deer park at Sheriff Hutton was established, or even what area it originally covered – more research and investigation is needed before these and related questions can be satisfactorily answered. Nevertheless, some educated guesses can be made, using a combination of the surviving landscape evidence, aerial photographs and the results of previous research.[25]

It is assumed that the first deer park was associated with the first castle located at the east end of the village (or whatever structure was located at this site, see Chapter 6), and it was certainly in existence by 1282-83, when it is mentioned as a 'park with deer' in the *inquisition post mortem* of Robert Neville.[26] However, it is possible that the park had been established slightly earlier, as ten oaks from the 'park at Hoton' are mentioned in an Inquisition of Sales in the Forest of Galtres in 1199-1216.[27] Another inquisition dating to 1257 asks whether the king's Forest of Galtres would suffer any loss if he allowed Robert Neville to enclose the wood at Hoton which covered 60 acres; the jurors said not, because the "wood lies towards Rydale which is outside the forest and the deer are accustomed to stray into that wood, to remain there and go out of the wood towards Rydale which is outside the forest" – the jurors also note that there was almost one and half leagues between the covert of the forest and the wood, which would place the wood on the north side of the village.[28]

Primarily on the basis of aerial photographic evidence, Swan has suggested that the first deer park lay to the east and south of the first castle, in an area characterised by a block of predominantly east-west aligned ridge and furrow (see figures 4/7 and 4/9 below). This ridge and furrow actually post-dates the early park, and it might represent an area of land belonging to Marton Priory which was given back and returned to cultivation in compensation for other land taken into the later deer park by Robert Neville; the ridge and furrow therefore reflects the subsequent ploughing of this area after the 1330s. If this interpretation is correct, the north side of the first deer park is probably represented by a track ('Riddings Lane') shown on the later 1765 plan of the manor[29] and a continuation of this line which runs east from the village as far as the former boundary between the townships of Sheriff Hutton and Stittenham. The east side of the park follows this township boundary south for a short distance, and then continues on a general south-west alignment as far as an area of modern plantation to the north of the Hall. This latter section is also visible as a substantial, but intermittent, bank on aerial photographs dating to 1946 and as ploughed out parallel lines on others taken in 1992 and 1993.[30] The southern, more sinuous, boundary of the park, around the south side of High Park, is now virtually lost, this area having been ploughed and improved, but it was visible for part of its length as a ditch until fairly recently; the boundary is still marked on the Ordnance Survey maps. A bank running through the southern part of High Park is also visible on an aerial photograph taken in December 1966, but it appears ploughed out a few years later.[31] The suggested alignment then passes around a field called 'The Postern' on the 1848 tithe map[32] (field 28 on figure 5/7), and turns north back towards the village, before returning to the east around the first castle site.

Fig. 4/7: Aerial photograph taken in June 1970 showing part of the area of the first park with its later ridge and furrow, with the presumed Roman enclosure in High Park and the 'Postern' field to its left (Copyright reserved Cambridge University Collection of Air Photographs, BBQ75).

Unfortunately, there is little evidence now surviving on the ground for the line of the first park boundary or pale (see figure 4/9). Nothing remains of the track which leaves the north-east corner of the village, and much of the former eastern boundary has been destroyed. The point at which the first pale crosses a later park pale is marked by a mature oak tree. Within the field to the south, the line of the presumed first pale (the section noted above as a bank or parallel lines on aerial photographs) can just be seen from a distance as a very slight depression, and closer up as a change in vegetation approximately 4m in width. The alignment in the south-west corner of the park around 'The Postern' is still followed by a drain or ditch, some 3m wide and 1m deep, whilst the west side may survive as a very spread south-west facing bank.

51

In 1331 Ralph Neville received a grant of free warren over his demesne lands in Sheriff Hutton, as well as in Midelham [Middleham], Thornaldby, Carleton, Crakehall, Snape, Welle, Raskelf and Sutton in Galtres.[33] This gave him the right to hunt the smaller game for the table, such as hare, rabbit, woodcock, pheasant and partridge, as well as fox, wildcat, badger, marten, otter and squirrel which were classed as vermin.[34] As noted in Chapter 2 above, a grant of free warren was often a precursor to emparkment, and this appears to have been the case at Sheriff Hutton.

The Second Deer Park

The original, rather small, deer park may have remained in use until the 1330s, but in February 1334 a licence was issued to Ralph Neville to "enclose his woods of Middleham and Sheriff Hutton and make parks there, with a deer leap in the same park of Sheriff Hutton, not withstanding that it is close to our [i.e. the king's] Forest of Galtres, and that he will be able to hold these enclosed woods and the parks made there together with the aforesaid deer leap to himself and his heirs in perpetuity without interference or impediment from us or our heirs".[35] It is also important to note that, had the park still been in the Forest of Galtres at this time (see above), the construction of the deer-leap would probably not have been permitted, as the king would not have approved of his deer moving from his forest into the park. As mentioned in Chapter 2 above, Ralph Neville did exactly the same thing some 50 years later in 1389 at Raskelf, where he enclosed some woods to make a park with three deer-leaps each 100ft long.[36]

Fig. 4/8: Artist's impression of the park pale with a deer-leap, looking towards the stone castle.

The area of this expanded park is thought to lie to the south and south-west of the original park, between the villages of the Sheriff Hutton and East and West Lilling[37] (see figure 4/9) but once again, the precise alignment of the eastern boundary has not yet been determined. The majority of the new park covered ground previously given over to arable cultivation, as evidenced by the large areas of ridge and furrow seen on aerial photographs; only the area of

High Park and 'The Postern' remained from the earlier park. Most of the newly emparked land lay within the former open fields attached to Sheriff Hutton village, although it also included a small part of East Lilling's fields. As noted in Chapter 1 and above, perhaps some of this land was owned by Marton Priory, and they were then given other land in the area of the original but now disused deer park as compensation, resulting in the east-west aligned ridge and furrow and the field names of 'Kirk Lands' recorded in 1765. The central part of the north edge of the new park was also called 'Kirk Launde' in 1598 (see below).

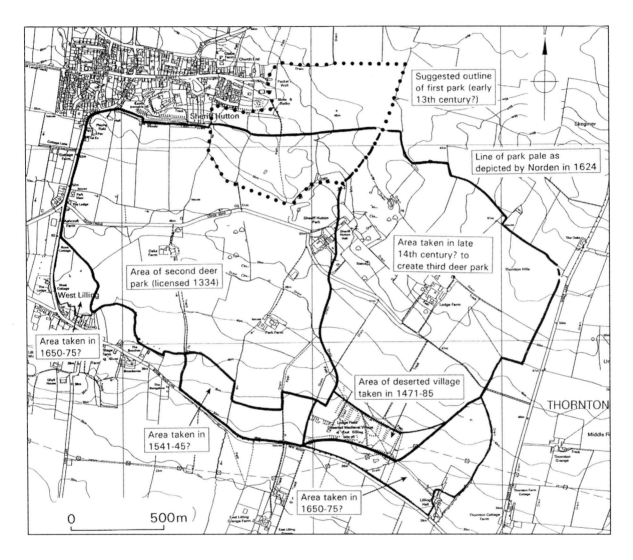

Fig. 4/9: Plan showing the outlines of the medieval deer parks at Sheriff Hutton.

It is possible that the area of former woodland mentioned in the 1334 licence lies in the south-west corner of this park, where the boundary is very irregular and where several of the field names, as recorded on the 1848 tithe map, contain the element 'hagg', a term indicative of land cleared of trees[38] (see figure 5/7); this area of Lilling Hagg still contained trees and coppices in the late 16th century and the area is named as 'Copes' on Norden's plan of 1624-25 (see Chapter 5 below). The presence of this woodland might also explain why several fields in this part of the park do not appear to have been ploughed in the past, as evidenced by the distribution of the ridge and furrow seen on the aerial photographs.

Although the emparking licence is dated to 1334, we cannot, as yet, really be sure when the earlier park was actually extended. It may well have been done in or soon after 1334, as by this date Ralph Neville had gained overlordship of the manor (in 1331) and so had the power and authority to empark a large area of the former open fields belonging to the village or other landowners. Alternatively, it could have happened slightly later, perhaps around the 1380s when the new stone castle was started (in 1382), although the current evidence suggests that this was associated with a later phase of deer park expansion (see below). The *inquisition post mortem* of Ralph Neville, dated to 1367, notes 'a park with game (rather than just deer) worth nothing a year apart from its upkeep'.[39]

As can be seen from figure 4/9, the suggested east side of the second park has a meandering line from north of the Hall, skirting around the east side of Park Farm and then southwards towards the north-west corner of East Lilling village. To the north of the Hall, the line is the same as that taken for part of the suggested east side of the first park described above, visible on aerial photographs and on the ground as a very faint earthwork. The earthwork is aligned on a break in the plantation to the south-west, part of a belt around the Hall. Within the plantation, a slight south-east facing bank can be seen on the same alignment. This has been disturbed by 20th century drainage works, but it becomes more prominent to the south-west; at this point the earthwork is a spread bank, c.4m wide but only 0.5m high, with a shallow 2m-3m wide depression running parallel to the eastern side. The bank then curves around to the south-west before fading out at the edge of the plantation, where it is assumed to have been destroyed by the construction of Arthur Ingram's New Lodge and associated landscaping work in the early 17th century.

Fig. 4/10: Possible re-cut line of the pale forming the east side of the second park in the plantation to the north of the Hall.

The eastern boundary becomes visible again to the south-east of The Rangers House complex next to the Hall. Here, it can be seen as a slight spread bank running along the west side of a field boundary. An oak tree with a circumference of 7.9m survives on this section of the pale line (see Chapter 10 and plate 66). This oak, which is one of the oldest surviving within the park, is estimated to be approximately 600 years old, giving a planting date which broadly coincides with that of the 1334 licence. The line of the pale then continues south beyond a trackway as two parallel spread banks with an overall width of c.8m flanking a shallow linear depression. These run as far as a sinuous hedge line and ditch which then follow the suggested eastern side of the second park to the north-west corner of East Lilling. The hedge line appears to have a spread bank along its western side in some places.

The detailed survey work previously undertaken at East Lilling[40] identified part of the second park pale as a substantial earthwork bank and ditch ('O' on figure 4/6) which crosses over the west part of the now deserted village. To the west of here, the line of the pale has been largely removed by the modern agricultural regime, although a massive bank survived well into the second half of the 20th century;[41] there are now a number of small oak trees along a part of the alignment. This and the other parts of the third park's pale line are discussed in more detail below.

The Third Deer Park

The creation of the third and final phase of the deer park at Sheriff Hutton was a significant event, for it almost doubled the size of the existing park (see figure 4/9). The land newly taken in mostly covered the north part of East Lilling township, as well as small areas of West Lilling and Sheriff Hutton townships.

Once again, we do not know precisely when this expansion took place. To date, only a few documentary references have been found that may relate to this third park. The *inquisition post mortem* of John Neville in 1388 notes 'a certain park with deer worth 10s. per annum apart from its upkeep'.[42] In 1441 Cardinal Beaufort and others leased Sheriff Hutton, including the park,[43] and in 1483 the Abbot of St Mary's in York was to get 'ii bukkes' in summer and 'ii does' in winter from the 'Park of (Myddeham) Sherefhoton'.[44] Robert Wilne, the king's Gentleman Usher of the Chamber, was granted the office of Keeper of the Park, to hold himself or by his deputy,[45] while in 1483, Nicholas Heddlam (or Hedlaw) received the parkership at the same time as becoming Porter of the Gate and Keeper of the Wardrobe at the castle; his wages for the parkership were 2d. per day.[46]

It is possible that this third and final expansion may not have occurred until the 1470s, when the area of the former village of East Lilling was taken into the park (see below). However, it is presently thought much more likely that this third expansion took place at around the same time as the construction of the stone castle, at the end of the 14th century. As noted in Chapter 1, the new castle resulted in the almost complete re-arrangement of the village morphology and was accompanied by a market grant (in 1378), and these actions, together with a massively expanded park, can be seen as deliberate 're-development' package undertaken by the Neville family, reflecting their greatly increased status by this period. The newly extended park, which would have accommodated greater numbers of deer and made more ground available for hunting, would have complemented their newly-built permanent and impressive residence in Sheriff Hutton, as well as maximising their profits from timber and associated park products. In addition, the population of East Lilling had entered a period of gradual decline from the early 14th century onwards, and this decline was probably hastened by the Black Death of 1348.[47] It may be therefore that the village's fields were already largely abandoned by this date and the Nevilles could have taken them into the expanded park without the need to provide replacement land elsewhere. The alignment of the new park pale around the east end of the expanded park is not known in detail, although it is assumed to more or less follow the line as depicted in 1624 by Norden; this is the line which is depicted on figure 4/9 and which is described further below.

Fig. 4/11: Hunting in progress, based on a medieval illustration.

Although the addition of this extra land meant that the deer park now covered a substantial area to the south of the village, it is not the end of the story, and further small-scale extensions were made as time went on (see figure 4/9). For example, the previous work at East Lilling has shown that the remaining village, probably amounting to no more than two or three households by the middle of the 15th century, was deliberately 'demolished and turned into grazing' between 1471 and 1485 following an agreement between the Lord of Sheriff Hutton (i.e. Richard III) and the Prior of Marton.[48] The village site was then added to the deer park, and the displaced villagers were possibly given some land in Bulford Tofts as compensation.[49] Over the following century, the village site was adapted to form an enclosed garth on the southern boundary of the park, and a park keeper's lodge (the 'little lodge') was built over two of the former crofts; this structure is depicted on Norden's plan of 1624 (see Chapter 5 and plate 37). The parish boundary was subsequently altered to coincide with the line of the new park pale.[50]

As with the second park, most physical traces of the east boundary of the third park have been removed by modern agricultural practices. Those that do survive along the general line are described in Chapter 5 below, but a few points are worth noting here. The modern township boundary between Sheriff Hutton and Thornton-le-Clay follows a very angular route, reflecting later field boundaries, and is unlikely to represent the east end of the park as it was in c.1400. This may have been set slightly further to the west, running south-west towards the north end of a triangular block of post-1855 plantation. From here, the line of the pale ran along the west side of the plantation as far as the New Road. However, this probably represents the pale line as it was post-1471, after East Lilling village had been emparked. Prior to this, the c.1400 pale line may be represented by a linear depression, c.4m wide and 0.5m deep, aligned north-east/south-west and with a number of smaller oak trees along its line, which cuts across the well preserved ridge and furrow to the north-east of the village; although relatively slight, the earthwork does not coincide with any field boundaries or drains shown on 19th century maps, and it could represent the former park boundary. The line may then have run along, or be represented by, a very prominent ditch forming the north side of the village earthworks.

Fig. 4/12: Ditch on the north side of East Lilling deserted village, separating the village to the left from the pre-1471 park pale to the right.

Deer Park Buildings and Structures

As yet, there is little clear documentary evidence for any medieval buildings within the park, although it would almost certainly have contained the same range of structures as can be seen in other contemporary late medieval deer parks. These might have included, for example, a lodge or house for the park keeper, possibly a separate lodge for the hunters, and/or agricultural-type buildings to provide deer shelters or fodder stores. Given the status and wealth of the Nevilles by the late 14th century, some of the buildings would be expected to be fairly grand examples of their kind. The possibility of the first castle being a detached lodge to the earliest (or perhaps even the later) park will be discussed in Chapter 6, and it is possible that another early lodge may lie under the existing Hall (see Chapter 5 and below). Another alternative is that the presumed Roman enclosure in the High Park might actually be the site of a medieval hunting lodge, surrounded by a ditch and bank to keep the deer out.

There are several places within the park where earthworks possibly representing early buildings or features survive, but they are generally poorly defined. For example, the field approximately 200m south-west of the first castle ('The Postern') contains a large but poorly defined raised platform in its north-west corner (see figure 4/7). Other, possibly natural, landforms in this field are crossed by spread but regular north-east/south-west aligned ridge and furrow earthworks.[51]

The only place within the park where there is any convincing earthwork evidence for possible medieval buildings is to the north-west of Lodge Farm. The name of the farm may be significant, although by itself it is not convincing; hundreds of Victorian houses and farms were re-christened 'The Grange' or 'The Manor House' during the 19th century without having the slightest connection to either manorial centres or monastic sites. However, some 160m north-west of the farm, there are three slight terraces, sloping slightly downwards from south to north and occupying an area approximately 60m square. There are least three platforms, possibly the sites of buildings, within these terraces, with a well at their centre. The well is covered with a concrete slab and when it is lifted, a sub-circular, almost oval, structure is revealed, 0.98m in diameter. The top few courses of the well are built of 19th century brick but the remainder (where visible) is of worn roughly coursed sandstone rubble. At the time of inspection, the well was filled with water to within 1m of the top, but rough measurements taken with weights and rope suggest that it is c.18m deep. The site is located adjacent to the linear earthwork noted above as a possible Roman road alignment, although a detailed survey is needed to establish the precise relationship between the two. The earthworks may form a small complex associated with the management of the deer or even the 'other animals' implied in John Neville's *inquisition post mortem* of 1388, or it could also be the 'helme' (agricultural building) mentioned in the 1598 documents (see below). It is also interesting to note that this area is marked by several small fields on the 1848 tithe map named as 'Garth', a term synonymous with the sites of former buildings (fields 104, 105 and 106 on figure 5/7).[52]

Ridge and Furrow

Mention has been made above of the ridge and furrow which was once extensive within the area of the park, and which is visible on aerial photographs predating the recent agricultural improvements and ploughing.[53] The ridge and furrow, and the field systems that it defines, will have had a complex development over time. Some parts will pre-date the areas of the park in which they are located, others may sit within areas of the park that were dis-parked and then ploughed at an early date, whilst still others may date from much later period, when areas of the park were converted back to agricultural land.

Within this complex pattern, three broad areas can be identified. We have already mentioned one large block of east-west aligned ridge and furrow to the east of the village, mostly lying outside the park pale as shown in 1624 (see figures 4/7 and 6/5). As noted above, this block seems to define the area of the earliest park, and some of this ridge and furrow probably dates to the period when this land was returned to arable once the second park was created. However, the relationship between this block and other swathes of differently orientated ridge and furrow is as yet unclear, and it may actually continue much further to the east, perhaps forming part of an early field system associated with the early development of the village.

Within the area occupied by the later (third phase) park, the ridge and furrow divides into two broad areas. In the eastern half of the park, the general trend is for the earthworks to run north-east/south-west, while to the west they are generally orientated north-south. This difference appears to reflect the division between East Lilling township to the east and Sheriff Hutton township to the west, which were broadly emparked at different times.

Ploughing and arable farming over the past 50 years has removed much of the ridge and furrow within the park and in the surrounding area, and now only isolated fragments remain. Apart from the area immediately adjacent to East Lilling village (see plate 62), the most extensive and best preserved area lies to the south of the stone castle, within the area of the later-named 'Lawnd' or 'West Launde'. Here, the ridge and furrow covers a block measuring some 440m long by 220m wide, the broad north-south ridges set at approximately 10m centres and standing up to 0.4m high. There is also a raised flattened strip running along the east side of the ridge and furrow, approximately 11m wide and 0.4m high, possibly with two platforms surviving towards its centre; another possible platform can be seen in the north-west corner of the same field.

Fig. 4/13: Surviving ridge and furrow earthworks at East Lilling.

The other surviving areas of ridge and furrow are fragmentary and scattered. There are a few well preserved blocks around Lodge Farm, and a prominent strip south of Sheepclose Farm, just outside the park's northern boundary. Well preserved ridge and furrow can also be seen in the fields immediately to the south of the earthwork castle (see plate 41).

Archaeological Finds

A small number of artefacts dating to the medieval period have been found in and immediately around the park. One of the most impressive, and visually striking, was found during small-scale building work at Stile House which, as noted in Chapter 1, is thought to lie very close to a possible gatehouse leading from the market place into the stone castle complex. The find was a diamond-shaped plaque or mount of plated copper alloy, inlaid with green champlevé enamel and bearing an unidentified heraldic design set within a lozenge[54] (see plate 34). It was thought that the object was either a book fitting, or possibly a brooch or badge, and it was dated to the mid 13th to 15th century.

The other significant find was discovered at the beginning of the 20th century 'between the moats at Sheriff Hutton castle'.[55] This was a late 15th century gold posy ring, engraved with Old French love mottoes or 'posies': *bon. core. de. core.* was inscribed on the outside face and *le. toute. voutre.* on the inside. The ring measured only c.18mm in diameter, and so was thought to have fitted a lady's second finger. The ring was also in very good condition, suggesting that it had not been worn for long before it was lost.

There have also been a number of finds from within the park itself. A cast copper-alloy pouring spout from an ewer or bowl, the design of the head looking rather like a bat and dating to the 15th or 16th century, has been found at Lodge Farm. A coin of Edward I was found in the field to the south of the stone castle, and other coins of Elizabeth I and Queen Mary have been recovered from the High Park (see plates 32 and 33). Finds suggestive of late medieval hunting activity have also included a horse-shoe with a flange at the front and the remains of a spur (see plate 35). Two lead ampullae (a small flask designed to contain holy oil or water, often attached to clothing and work by pilgrims), dating to the medieval period, have also been found, one in Sheriff Hutton village during the development of 'Laurels Garth' in 1997 and one at West Lilling. Other coins dating to Henry III, Edward I and Charles I, and a casket key dating to 1350-1400, have also been discovered by metal detectorists in West Lilling, on the south side of the park.

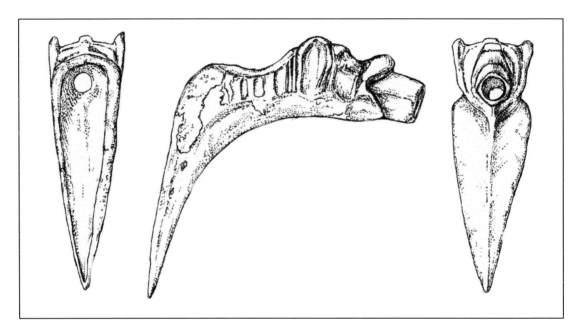

Fig. 4/14: Pouring spout from an ewer or bowl, 15th-16th century date, found at Lodge Farm.

The Park in the 16th Century

The line of the pale

A major alteration to the park pale during the 16th century was centred around the construction of the double canals along the southern side of the castle. As will be discussed in Chapter 8, this was almost certainly undertaken in conjunction with the creation of the 'Lawnd' area to the immediate south of the canals, the castle and 'Lawnd' being linked, in the later 16th century at least, by a wooden bridge ('the Lady Bridge') which spanned the canals. The form of the canals, with their raised central walkway, indicates that they were intended to act both as a viewing platform in their own right but also to function as a giant version of a ha-ha, giving unimpeded views from the castle's gardens, and indeed from the castle itself, into this area of the park. The same was true in reverse, the 'Lawnd' giving impressive views back across the canals to the castle. As will be mentioned below, the 'Lawnd' may have contained a building to which those walking through the gardens and across the bridge could have progressed. It is also possible that deer were let into the same area or tempted in by feeding stations, creating a suitably idyllic scene when viewed from the walkway or the castle.

There were undoubtedly other minor and perhaps also major alterations to the line of the pale during the 16th century, but documentary or archaeological evidence to mark their position is as yet sparse. Swan notes that in the period 1541-45, an area of land formerly belonging to West Lilling may have been taken into the park, perhaps the area immediately to the west of East Lilling, whilst in Sheriff Hutton village a garden called 'Kylngarth' was 'enclosed within the park there'.[56] The former area might be represented by a number of fields on the north side of New Road, between West Lilling and the deserted village. The northern edge of this area is marked by a prominent bank and ditch which runs west from the deserted village for some 250m before being ploughed out, although its alignment can be traced further west on aerial photographs and perhaps beyond as a dry ditch and hedged boundary on a slight bank.[57] This northern alignment represents the course of the park pale prior to c.1540 and the land to the south was taken in by c.1545, a period partly coinciding with the residence of the Duke of Norfolk at the castle. The 'Kylngarth' in Sheriff Hutton village might be represented by the small 'bump' in the pale line shown by Norden in 1624 (see plate 37), immediately adjacent to the south-east corner of the castle garth; a small area of scrub and trees survives in this general area today, at the bottom of one of the plots leading off from the south side of the village green (the former market place).

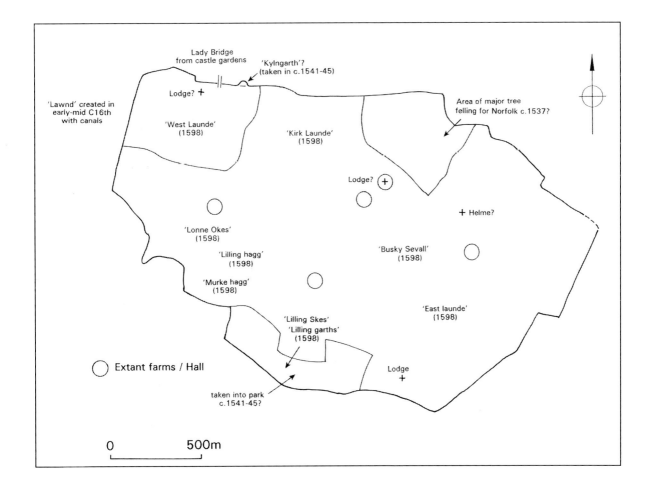

Fig. 4/15: Interpretation of the park in the 16th century.

Internal divisions

It is likely that some alterations were undertaken to the park during the time that Henry Fitzroy, Earl of Richmond, resided at the castle (from c.1525 to 1532) and there is clear evidence that the residence of Thomas Howard, Duke of Norfolk (1537 to 1541-42) affected the park. As will be set out in Chapter 11, some 300 to 400 loads of structural timber were felled in the park, together with the same amount of 'loppes and toppes of trees'.[58] The area from which the trees had been cleared was referred to as a 'spryng' and it was dyked and hedged around by the duke's men. In 1545 wood had to be taken from the Forest of Galtres, rather than the park itself, 'for the repair of Sheriff Hutton Park', which implies that the timber inside the park was severely depleted.[59]

It is important to avoid the pitfall of associating major alterations to the park with the scattered references surviving in the documentary record. Such references represent only the small proportion of the documents which have actually survived into the present day, and these in turn, even in much fuller form, may not have recorded all of the many items of repair, maintenance and alteration associated with the park and its pale. Nevertheless, it is tempting to link one of the enclosures in the park later shown on Norden's survey of 1624[60] with the large amount of timber felled for Norfolk in c.1537. The description suggests that the cleared area was enclosed so that new timber could be grown there – might it be the large sub-rectangular enclosure shown to the north of Ingram's New Lodge in 1624? (see plate 37).

The longest period of occupancy of the castle during the 16th century was that of Henry Hastings, Earl of Huntingdon, between 1572 and 1595, although it is probable that he was resident only very sporadically and then perhaps only for short periods (see Chapter 11). It was during this period, in 1577, that the park was depicted on a map for the first time, although Christopher Saxton showed only a circular wooden pale in approximately the right place.[61]

A series of depositions made in 1598 as part of an inquisition into the custodianship of Richard Pollerd, the then Keeper of the Castle who had been granted the Keepership of the Park as a means of payment, provide valuable evidence regarding the use and organisation of the park towards the end of Huntingdon's residence.[62] This document has been transcribed by Tony Wright, and is discussed further in Chapter 11, although a few points of interest can be given here.

The 'Lawnde' to the south of the stone castle (referred to as the 'West Launde' in the depositions) had been de-pastured due to winter grazing by sheep. During the early 1590s about 140 sheep (all ewes according to one source[63]) belonging to John Broughe had been over-wintered in the West Launde for many years, but by 1597 this had fallen to 60 and by 1598 only about 20 remained. The presence of sheep in the deer park is rather surprising, as they were generally kept out because they eat the same fodder as the deer, although they do start to appear in parks generally from the 16th century onwards.[64] One deposee stated that he leased a parcel of ground within the West Launde, suggesting that it was sub-divided, either temporarily or permanently, by the late 16th century.[65] Pollerd also leased out Kirk Hill or Kirk Launde, which contained a mixture of wood and lawn over approximately 18 acres, to a group of York businessmen for £22 per year, and they were required to put a new pale around the area which they proposed to fell and make a spring.[66]

The grazing by sheep notwithstanding, deer remained an important part of the park's economy at the end of the 16th century. Several of the deposees thought that there had been about 300 deer in the park in the early 1590s, but shortly before 1598 this had been increased to around 400. These numbers were too many for those areas of the park still grazed by deer to sustain, and each year ten loads of hay from land to the north-east of the village were allowed for their nourishment, possibly stored in a building referred to as the 'grese (grass?) house' located on that land.[67] 'Gresegarths' appear quite regularly in the documentary record at this time, and they may be connected with getting the deer 'in grease', i.e. fattened up for the hunt; it is thought that they were areas of pasture set aside for growing fodder for the deer. The deer were still keen to seek out other food sources, and had entered and destroyed some 3 acres of corn contained in a parcel of ground covering some 20 acres called 'sevall' around the lodge.[68]

Fig. 4/16: Sheep grazing in the area of the West Lawn today.

Two areas, called 'Lilling hagg' and 'murke hagg' also occur regularly in the 1598 depositions. The wood and underwood in Lilling hagg, including oak trees, had been felled and sold in 1597, while the timber in 'murke hagg' appears to have been felled and sold slightly earlier, in c.1590. Twenty ashes felled in 'Lilling garthes' during the same period had been used towards paling the east side of the park. The deposition also notes that "Certain Thornes to the number of tenn hundreth lods" (a thousand loads) were taken out of 'the daile Croftes', 'Lilling garthes', 'Busky sevall', the 'Kirke Launde' and the 'east Launde'. One deposee makes an interesting reference to a 'Kilne lately builded' by Richard Pollerd in the castle which had done no harm to the woods;[69] this infers that the kiln might have been for the production of charcoal, although as it was in the castle (at the end of the new stable), it may have been a malting kiln with wood from the park being used as fuel. Other parcels of land mentioned within the park include 'Lonne (long?) Okes' and a meadow known as 'Lilling S(i?)kes'. Pollerd also spent some £50 on repairs to the pale, using both oak and ash from the park.

Locating the various enclosures and areas mentioned in the 1598 deposition can, as yet, only be done generally (see figure 4/15). Some, such as the 'West Launde' are relatively straightforward but others are more difficult. The 'Lonne Okes' was probably in the area later referred to as 'the Oaks' in 1650, namely the central part of the west side. 'Kirk Launde' may well be the same as the 'Kirk Hill' of 1650, located on the highest ground of the park with a view to the church (the present 'High Park'); the name 'Launde' suggests that it was clear of trees and used mostly for grazing during the late 16th century. The references to 'Lilling hagg' and 'Murke hagg' are more problematic as 'Lilling' could still refer to either East or West Lilling at this time. However, as noted above, the 1848 tithe map[70] has a concentration of 'hagg' fieldnames in the area marked as 'Copes' in 1624 and 'Horse Hagg' in 1650, and it is possible that both were located here, in the south-west corner of the park. Similarly, in 1848, several fields known as 'East Lawn' formed a large block of land situated between the present track leading to Lodge Farm and the former northern boundary of East Lilling (see figure 5/7), perhaps providing a clue to their late 16th century 'east Launde' predecessor.

These discrete areas were probably already part of a tripartite division of the whole park which is referred to in 1650 (see Chapter 5). It is tempting to place the origin of this division into the early to mid 16th century, and to associate it with the residences of either Henry Fitzroy or the Duke of Norfolk, but there is as yet no clear evidence to do so.

Buildings and Structures

The deposees of 1598 also provide some clues to possible structures in the park at the end of the 16th century. There are several references to a 'lodge' in the depositions, and they all seem to refer to the same building; the word appears only in the singular, perhaps suggesting that there was only one such structure in the park at this date, although of course the question being answered by the deposition may have been directed to only one building in particular. The use of the term 'lodge' also changed over time,[71] and so the deposees may not necessarily have been referring to a hunting structure by this date, perhaps more of an agricultural complex. However, the Earl of Huntingdon sometimes stayed at the lodge, perhaps due to the removal of fixtures and fittings from the castle's principal apartments during the late 16th century (see Chapter 7). Some items went from the castle to the lodge including 'one lesser pann wch was Carried to the lodge in the said Parke'.[72] Lead was also taken from the castle to the lodge, apparently to be stored rather than re-used there, and was later sold on to local plumbers. From the information given, the lodge sat within a small enclosure, including 3 acres of ground sometimes sown with corn, and paled/ditched around although, as noted above, this did not prevent the deer entering to eat the crop within. The lodge had been repaired, as had 'the helme' (see below), although it not certain from the depositions if the two were associated or on the same site.

'The helme' is mentioned several times in 1598, possibly in association with the lodge or as a separate structure. The meaning of the word 'helm' has also varied over time but, during the early post-medieval period in the north of England, it was most commonly taken to mean a store for hay, corn or other crops, raised off the ground on posts with space for cattle or carts below. Such structures could be associated with farmsteads, or be in isolated positions in the fields.[73] However, during the later Middle Ages, a helm may denote a building within a field system used to house cattle, and there are also occasional references to such buildings within the medieval parks in West Yorkshire.[74] There are also references to helms within the Forest of Galtres, where the term is considered to be a shed for storage.[75] A further building within the park is referred to in 1532-33, when the 'making of the hekes [palisade] new round about the deer house' cost 2s. 3d.,[76] although this could, of course simply be another reference to the helm noted above.

Unfortunately, none of these documents provide much idea as to the specific location of the 'lodge', the 'helme' or any other structure(s). The details of the lodge given in 1598, in particular its location in a small garth and its possible association with other agricultural buildings, are reminiscent of the 1649 description of the 'Little Lodge' (see Chapter 5), although any link remains, at present, unproven. Alternatively, the 1598 lodge may have stood on the site of Ingram's New Lodge but again, there is little firm evidence; only the central location of Ingram's building within the park makes it likely to have replaced an earlier structure, as this position is where an earlier lodge might have been expected to be found.

Conclusions

Originally quite limited in size, the deer park at Sheriff Hutton was massively expanded during the later medieval period, so that by c.1400 it had assumed a size and scale which was commensurate with the Neville's great new castle. The two were intimately connected, and for the following 150 years both park and castle accommodated a succession of titled and royal residents. From Ralph Neville to Henry Fitzroy, the park was doubtless the scene of hunts equally as elaborate and exciting as those portrayed in the medieval manuscripts (see Chapter 3). However, intimate relationships have their disadvantages; whilst the castle and park had once complemented each other so perfectly, by c.1600 the decay of one was hastening the decline of the other. Although the castle staggered on into the 17th century, it did so very much as a shadow of its medieval self. Similarly, the park still retained substantial numbers of deer at this date but its tripartite division, dating back to at least the mid 16th century, shows that agricultural and economic uses had taken precedence over hunting. The castle was unable to find a role during the 17th century and it fell into ruins. In contrast, the park proved to be eminently more adaptable. The story of this adaptation is set out in the next chapter.

Footnotes

1   Beresford 1954, pp.283-284 & 302-303; Beresford 1957, pp.219-225.
2   The details of the various artefacts mentioned in the text have been produced from records and information kindly supplied by Robin Wardell, Tony Wright, Jim Halliday, the North Yorkshire Sites and Monuments Record, English Heritage and Anne Hodgson.
3   Radley 1974, p.21; Rowe 1966, p.240; Watkin 1987.
4   Clinch 1907, p.413.
5   Ottaway 2003, pp.137-139; Horne 2003.
6   e.g. Jones 1988.
7   Swan *et al* 1993, 20-21.
8   Information kindly provided by Nick Pearson of On Site Archaeology.
9   e.g. Cambridge University Collection of Air Photographs (CUCAP) BBQ75 taken 4/6/70; BAT4 taken 6/2/70; CBV15 taken 3/3/77 amongst others.
10   Aerial photograph held by Robin Wardell.
11   Oldfield 1867, pp.325-26; Clark 1935, p.129-130.
12   Margary 1973, p.431 (road 80a); Clark 1935, p.71
13   Margary 1973, pp.426-427 (road 800).
14   Swan *et al* 1993, pp.20-22.

15 Gelling 1984, p.167; Smith 1928, p.31.
16 Cowling 1967, p.153.
17 National Archives C47/11/6 no 27, perambulation 1316.
18 Dormer 2003, p.79; Swan *et al* 1993, pp.13-14.
19 Swan *et al* 1993, p.13.
20 English 1996, p.78; Farrer 1914, p.330; Cowling 1967, p.153 and plan.
21 Cowling 1967, p.153.
22 H.M.S.O. 1967, p.511; National Archives E178/5742.
23 Cowling 1967, pp.161 & 164.
24 Swan *et al* 1993.
25 The authors would like to thank Vivien Swan for discussing her unpublished research on the various deer parks with us, and for allowing us to use this information; thanks are also due to Bridgett Jones for translating some of the relevant documentation in the National Archives.
26 Swan *et al* 1990, p.99 note 50 quoting Cal IPM II, p.294, no. 483, 10th February 1282-83.
27 National Archives C47/11/1/1.
28 National Archives C143/2/41.
29 West Yorkshire Archive Service (WYAS) Leeds WYL/100/SH/B4/2.
30 Winton 1993, Site 4; aerial photograph AJC 322/30-31 taken 13/1/93.
31 CUCAP AQH29 taken 13/12/66; CUCAP BBQ75 taken 4/6/70.
32 Borthwick Institute TA411S.
33 Calendar Charter Rolls vol 4 (1327-1341), p.229; Calthrop 1923, p.178.
34 Bond 1994, p.116.
35 National Archives Patent Roll C66/184; Calthrop 1923, p.173; Cantor 1983, p.88; Beresford 1957, p.222.
36 Calendar Charter Rolls 1341-1471, p.310.
37 Swan *et al* 1990, p.108 ; Vivien Swan, *pers. comm.*
38 Borthwick Institute TA411S; Field 1972, p.94.
39 National Archives C135/195/1: Ralph de Neville IPM 28th August 1367.
40 Swan *et al* 1990.
41 John Armitage, *pers. comm.*
42 National Archives C136/56/1: John de Neville IPM 2nd November 1388.
43 Calthrop 1923, p.177
44 British Library Harleian MSS 433 f.153.
45 Calendar Patent Rolls 1452-1461, p.552.
46 British Library Harleian MSS 433 f.31b; Calendar Patent Rolls 1476-1485, p.434.
47 Swan *et al* 1990, pp.97-98.
48 ibid., pp.98-99.
49 Swan *et al* 1993, p.17.
50 Swan *et al* 1990, p.100.
51 Vivien Swann, *pers comm.*
52 Borthwick Institute TA411S.
53 This ridge and furrow has been mapped by Swan and also Winton (1993); thanks to Vivien Swan for giving us a copy of her research and discussing it with us.
54 Dennison 1999, Appendix 2.
55 Lascelles 1929; Lascelles, no date.
56 Swan *et al* 1990, p.99 note 55, quoting National Archives Ministers' Accounts Henry VIII (1541-42), SC6/Henry VIII/4198.
57 Swan *et al* 1990, p.97; aerial photograph taken by Tony Pacitto in 1981 held by Tony Wright.
58 National Archives E101/484/3 'The Works of Shirefhoton Castell' by Bartholomew Stable (1537), f.4v.
59 Jamison 1966, p.173.
60 British Library Harleian MSS no. 6288; WYAS Leeds WYL100/SH/B4/1.
61 Lawrence & Hoyle 1981; Butlin 2003, p.242.
62 National Archives E178/2792.
63 ibid., testimony of Christopher Richardson.
64 Bond 1994, pp.131-132.
65 National Archives E178/2792, testimony of Christopher Sharr.
66 ibid., testimony of Bryan Pereson.
67 ibid., testimony of Robert Stable.
68 ibid., testimony of John Broughe.
69 ibid., and testimony of John Skarr.
70 Borthwick Institute TA411S.

71   e.g. Moorhouse 2003c, pp.346-347.
72   National Archives E178/2792, testimony of Bartholomew Smith.
73   Brunskill 1999, pp.192-194.
74   Moorhouse 1981, pp.758-759.
75   Cowling 1967, p.180.
76   National Archives E101/484/2.

CHAPTER 5: THE ARCHAEOLOGY OF THE PARK – 2: FROM THE 17TH CENTURY

by Ed Dennison, Tony Wright and Shaun Richardson

The Park in the 17th Century

The number of documents which are of direct relevance to the park, and which help us to understand how it was managed, used and resourced, increase during the 17th century. To date, four surveys are known, dating to 1609-11, 1624, 1650 and 1675-85, and each are discussed in turn.

The 1609-11 Special Commission

This document[1] has not yet been translated in full, and only a summary is currently available. However, it tells us that the number of deer in the park had declined from the time of Richard Pollerd's parkership in the late 1590s. One of the witnesses to the Commission, John Richardson, said that 'diverse men' had taken meadow in the West Lawne and had entreated William Clarke (the present Keeper) to make a hedge to stop 'the raskall deere' from entering their ground. There had also been a severe drought just recently, and so the 'rails betwixt the East Lawne and Oakes [were] laid open'. It was also said that several other men had cut down 61 trees in the park and used them to enclose a parcel of ground adjacent to Bushie Severall 'wherein was planted crabtree stocks which were grafted Plumtrees, Cherry Trees, nut trees, birch trees, arkhornes [acorns], hawes and others'. William Clarke's workmen had also paled Kirk Hill, repaired the pale around the East Lawn and enclosed a piece on the West Lawne as a harbour for the deer. Several witnesses reported that William Clarke had allowed 16 or 17 trees to be cut down, partly for the building of a stable in the park, and that he had sold browse wood in return for straw which he used for making bricks. Some trees had also been cut down for 'burning bricks'. Both John Richardson and George Gibson grazed milk cattle in the park, and had been doing so for several years.

Norden's 1624 Survey of the Manor of Sheriff Hutton

This survey[2] provides the earliest known detailed cartographic depiction of the park (see plate 37). The description of the bounds of the whole manor as given by Norden has previously been reproduced by Franks,[3] while a description of the alignment of the pale is given below, as it survives today. The pale itself has, of course, been much altered in the subsequent 400 years; repairs would have been carried out on a yearly basis and there may well have been some minor re-alignments, either by accident or design. Some of the surviving earthworks on or adjacent to the 1624 line almost certainly belong to earlier or later periods. Nevertheless, given that Norden's depiction is the earliest yet known, it is a reasonable starting point from which to discuss the pale's overall surviving form. The alignment as shown by Norden has been plotted, as far as is possible, on the modern Ordnance Survey maps (see figures 1/3 and 4/9).

The line of the park pale

The route is described below, starting at the stone castle and proceeding around the circuit in a clockwise direction.

To the immediate south of the stone castle, the line of the pale is defined by two parallel canals associated with the castle gardens which are described further in Chapter 8. The depiction of the canals on the 1624 survey is very schematic but the line of the pale does contain a definite dog-leg in this area. One interpretation of this might be that the angled western portion of the southern canal, which runs further west than the northern canal (see figure 8/2), was included within the park at this date, perhaps to provide water for the deer when they were in the 'lawnde' and to attract them closer to the castle. Alternatively, the kink might lie slightly further to the east, where a later plan of 1765[4] shows the boundary going across the ponds, in the approximate position of the late 16th century 'Lady Bridge' (see Chapter 8). To the east of this kink, the line of the pale runs along the south side of the southern canal.

The parallel canals continue east as far as the eastern boundary of the castle's outer court, where they terminate. However, a footpath running between them carries on to the east, through an area which is later called the 'Hop Garth' on the 1765 plan. This area has a very wet boggy area approximately 2m wide on its north side, perhaps a remnant of a ditch defining the pale line, and an area of scrub and plantation possibly defining the site of a kiln mentioned during the 16th century and perhaps represented on Norden's plan as a 'bump' in the pale alignment here. While the footpath then curves around to the north-east to enter 'The Croft', the pale continues to the east along the line of a hawthorn hedge. This hedge sits on a spread bank, approximately 3m wide and 0.4m high, with a shallow ditch of similar dimensions to the north.

Fig. 5/1: Line of the park pale to the south of The Croft, looking south-east.

After the line of the pale crosses the footpath leading from the church into Sheriff Hutton park, the ground begins to slope downwards away from the east end of the village. The pale is aligned almost exactly east-west here, and is defined by a steep-sided ditch, recently improved, between two tall hedges. These features continue east for some distance, the ditch gradually reaching maximum dimensions of 3m wide and 1.5m deep. A number of mature oak trees, up to 1.4m in diameter, are incorporated into the inner hedge-line along this part of the ditch; one of these marks the point at which the suggested line of the east end of the first park crosses that of the 1624 line (see figure 4/9). The pale then returns to the south for some 160m, dog-legging to the east and south again before resuming a more general south-easterly direction. As with the section nearer to the village, the line of the pale survives here as a tall double hedge sat on top of a very slight bank, flanking a steep-sided ditch, and sometimes with a shallow depression on the south side as well; part of this alignment is followed by a footpath shown on the Ordnance Survey 1855 1st edition 6" map[5], but it is now abandoned. The line of the pale continues south-east as far as a small plantation to the south of Sheepclose Farm. The north side of the plantation is defined by a spread south-facing bank, approximately 3.5m wide and 1.2m high, whilst the south side has a similar bank of lesser dimensions. Beyond the plantation, the pale passes through an area of arable land where almost all physical traces have been removed, apart from very slight ditches or banks adjacent to the hedgerow which could represent its former course.

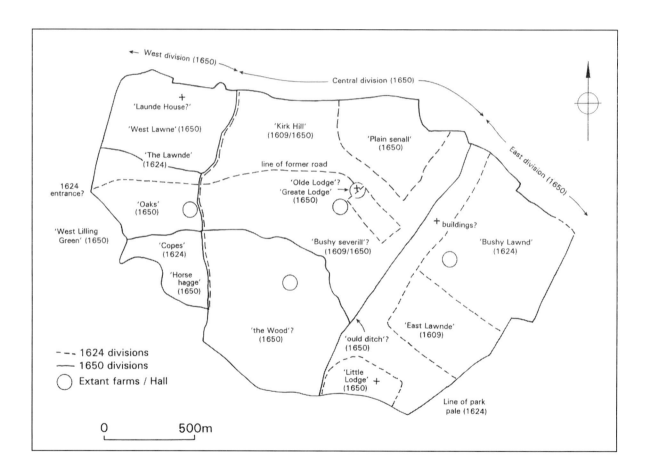

Fig. 5/2: Interpretation of the park in the 17th century.

The north-east corner of the park, as depicted by Norden, is now difficult to define precisely. Slight earthworks indicate that the course of the pale was probably more rounded and sinuous than the present field boundaries to the west of Moor Lane, which are formed by later enclosures on Thornton Hills. The return to the south appears to run virtually parallel to Moor Lane for a short distance, an alignment now represented by the straightened parish boundary separating Sheriff Hutton from Thornton-le-Clay, although it is possible that the edge of the park actually ran along the west side of Moor Lane for a short distance.

70

However, Norden's plan clearly shows the alignment to take several sharp returns before crossing the track leading to the Hall and Lodge Farm. Beyond this track, the line of the pale is preserved by the existing boundary marking the division between the modern civil parishes of Sheriff Hutton and Lillings Ambo. The line continues to curve around to the south-west, along the west side of a triangular-shaped post-1856 wood and to the west of Lilling Hall; much of the alignment here is still hedged (see plate 62), but with few earthworks apart from a shallow 2m wide ditch at the north end of the woodland.

Beyond this woodland, the pale line formerly returned to the west, along the southern boundary of the deserted medieval village of East Lilling; as noted in Chapter 4, it previously ran around the north side of the village but this area was taken into the park in c.1471-85. It seems clear from Norden's plot of East Lilling (see plate 38) that the line of the pale followed the earlier holloway running along the south side of the former village; the Norden drawing of the East Lilling plot depicts the pale here as series of upright stakes, although this may be a diagrammatic representation. The area of the site has been much disturbed but at its west end, a short length of east-west aligned ridge and furrow, running counter to the prevailing north-south ridge and furrow, perhaps marks the westward continuation of the pale as it converged with the New Road.

The line of the pale as shown in 1624 then runs along the north side of New Road for some 700m, where it is marked intermittently by a low bank, and around a further area taken into the park c.1541-45, before returning sharply to the north for a short distance along the line of a substantial ditch which again marks the parish boundary. It then turns west and follows a sinuous course around the back (north) of West Lilling, again along the parish boundary. There are few physical traces of the pale in this area of arable land, apart from the odd shallow linear depression where the alignment crosses a field track. However, there is one section where the pale survives as a low spread bank, 6m-7m wide but only 0.4m high. A bank of similar dimensions runs northwards from West Lilling close to the pale line, curving around to the north-west of the area referred to as 'West Lillin Green' in 1650 but fading where it meets a modern field boundary. The actual green lay slightly further to the west, and the area bounded by the pale comprises a sub-oval enclosure measuring a maximum of 220m across (north-south). The east side is defined by a curvilinear remnant of the pale bank but the north side is bounded by a curving linear depression, approximately 11m wide and 0.6m deep. This curves around to meet a pond, adjacent to which are the sub-rectangular remains of a possible building platform. This depression corresponds to a former route into the park, which is shown on the 1765 plan and named, within the park, as 'Foot Road to Lodge Being an Odd [Old?] House and also to Sheriff Hutton'.[6] The interior of the enclosure is bisected by a narrow north-south linear depression, which is flanked by north-south aligned ridge and furrow, corresponding to a division shown in 1765.

The western boundary of the park ran along the east side of Finkle Street, back towards the village. A denuded bank is visible within the narrow strip of land flanking the east side of Finkle Street to the south of 'The Lodge'; it is possible that this c.10m wide strip represents the former width of the pale, although it is more likely to be an area of waste created as a result of the formalisation of the road at enclosure and on which a few houses have subsequently been built. The bank of the pale becomes more prominent between 'Rose Cottage' and 'The Lodge', where it runs along the east side of the former waste, but it does not comprise a substantial earthwork until it passes 'The Lodge' and enters the garden of 'Park View'. At this point, there is a substantial bank with a gently rounded profile, 4m wide and 1.4m high; although it is likely to have been 'improved' after being enclosed in the garden, it is nevertheless a significant earthwork which probably represents the bank of the pale. The bank has been breached to provide an access road to 'South View' and fades out in the field immediately to the north. The alignment continues to follow the east side of Finkle Street (see plate 39), curving around to the north-east of the cricket ground and village hall, before rejoining the double canals to the south of the castle.

Fig. 5/3: Remains of the park pale in the garden of 'Park View', looking north.

Norden's 1624 plan also appears to show that the main entrance into the park, off the unenclosed West Lilling green, was slightly further to the south than at present, possibly in the area of the present parish boundary junction; nothing can now be seen here in an arable field although there is a gap in the pale at about the right location. The route to the Lodge also appears to have followed a more direct easterly alignment once within the park (see Chapter 15). The later 1765 plan shows a gap in the boundary further to the north, in the area of the present entrance.

Internal sub-divisions

Norden's plan shows that the majority of the area enclosed by the pale was lightly wooded, with isolated trees depicted in a widely dispersed pattern (see plate 37). However, the western third of the park is shown as containing one large tree-less enclosure, named as 'The Lawnde', in the north-west corner, and the still wooded 'Copes' in the south-west, both separated from the central area by a dead-straight, almost north-south aligned boundary. Today, this boundary survives as a significant ditch with a steep-sided V-shaped profile to the south of Oaks Farm, measuring up to 6m wide and up to 4m deep, and a prominent hedge line which runs down to the southern boundary of the park; in its southern section it forms part of the parish boundary and the line of the pale (see above and figure 5/4). However, to the north of the Coach Road it is more difficult to follow and there are no obvious features. The boundary may be marked by a very straight surviving north-south aligned field boundary, or perhaps a sinuous hedge and drain further to the east which run along the west side of 'The Postern' field; this latter line is also marked as a footpath on the Ordnance Survey 1856 1st edition 6" map. Norden has drawn the boundary as running up to the south-east corner of the Castle Garth, in which case the correct alignment would lie between the two – no earthworks are visible in the field, which has been ploughed and improved, and no features can be seen on the historic aerial photographs. On balance, it is currently thought that the boundary is represented by the more sinuous eastern alignment, and this is the course depicted on figure 5/2 above.

Fig. 5/4: Line of the internal division depicted by Norden in 1624, to the south of Oaks Farm.

In 1624, another large wooded but unnamed enclosure is shown to the north of the rectangular walled enclosure containing Sir Arthur Ingram's New Lodge and garden. The eastern third of this enclosure remains as woodland today (named as 'Sawtry Plantation' on the Ordnance Survey 1855 1st edition 6" map), although the trees are of relatively recent date. The eastern side of this wood follows a similar line to that shown in the 1624 enclosure; there are no traces of the earlier boundary surviving within the woodland, although there may be the very slight remains of a spread bank running parallel to the woodland some 4m to the east. The west side of the enclosure is marked by an existing field boundary. At its north end, the boundary is formed by a shallow linear depression approximately 3.5m wide, but after some disturbance, it resumes as a spread bank of a similar width. The south-west part of the enclosure is lost in the present woodland around the Hall.

The eastern end of the park contained two sparsely wooded enclosures in 1624, the northern one marked as the 'Bushy Lawnd' and the other unnamed. Little or no above-ground evidence for these enclosures survives today, the area being predominantly arable land, and it is difficult to relate the surviving field boundaries to those shown on the map. There is a prominent flat-topped linear earthwork to the north-west of Lodge Farm which might represent the west side of the 'Bushy Lawnd' although, as we have seen, it is also possibly the causeway of a Roman road. However, there is another north-east/south-west aligned bank just to the east, while to the west there is a ditched field boundary which runs across the full extent of the park; this was described as an 'ould ditch' in 1650 and it has been assumed to represent one of the major boundaries of the park at that time (see below). The southern enclosure might correspond to the 'East Launde' mentioned in 1609.

The final enclosure shown on Norden's survey surrounds the area of the deserted village of East Lilling, depicted as devoid of trees and containing a building. The schematic depiction appears to show an L-shaped structure, or perhaps a main house with a smaller wing, both parts served by a single chimney stack (see plate 37). This building is almost certainly the 'Little Lodge', which is discussed below.

The 1650 survey

It is assumed that the general line of the pale had changed little in the time between Norden's survey of 1624 and the Parliamentary survey of 1650, and the principal interest in the later survey lies in its description of the internal divisions of the park at that date.

As will be noted in Chapter 12, the 1650 survey states that the 741 acre (300 hectares) park "is commodiously .. divided for the purchaser advantage .. into three pts (parts)".[7] These three main divisions, described as west, central and east, are themselves further sub-divided. The survey suggests that the major divisions were separated by ditches while the minor ones were defined by 'mounds' or banks. Using the evidence provided by the previous Norden survey and the subsequent 19th century tithe and Ordnance Survey maps, and the surviving field remains, it is possible to re-create these sub-divisions (see figure 5/2 above); it should be noted that further research may lead to the revision of some of these boundaries.

The west division covered just over 128 acres (88 hectares) and comprised, from north to south, the 'West Lawne', the 'Oaks' and the 'Horse hagge'. The first two had been created out of the larger 'Lawnde' depicted in 1624; the probable boundary between them survives as a generally east-west aligned drain with a spread bank on the south side, 5m wide and up to 0.4m in height. The present Oaks Farm stands on the east side of the former sub-division of the same name. The 'Horse hagge' was created out of the 'Copes' shown in 1624. The boundary between the west and central divisions probably re-used the boundary shown here in 1624 which, as noted above, is represented by a substantial ditch to the south of Oaks Farm and a more sinuous field boundary to the north of the Coach Road. The 1650 survey notes that the west division of the park retained some woodland, comprising 462 trees in total.

The central division (366 acres or 148 hectares) was divided into four parts, the 'Kirk Hill', the 'plain senall', the 'Bushy severall' and 'the wood'. As previously noted, Kirk Hill probably lay in the northern part of the division, corresponding to the present 'High Park', and it may be so named because it either gave clear views to Sheriff Hutton church or that it was previously part of a monastic landholding. 'Plain senall' and 'Bushy severall' probably lay further to the east and south, occupying most of the central part of the central division - the names 'Plain Severn Hills' and 'Busky Severn Hills' continued to be recorded by the 1848 tithe map[8] (see figure 5/7), but the division between the north and central areas is not immediately obvious. The southern half of the central division was occupied by 'the wood'; the northern boundary of this area may be represented by a sinuous drain located half way between Park Farm and the Hall, and the north-west corner was shown as still being wooded on the tithe and Ordnance Survey 1856 1st edition 6" maps. The central division retained by far the highest number of trees in 1650, comprising 3,229 in total of varying quality.

The 1650 survey notes that the east division of the park covered 219 acres (88 hectares) and was separated from the central part by 'an ould ditch' which crossed the full width of the park. Although the exact location of this ditch is not certain, there is still a significant boundary running north-east/south-west through the park just to the west of Lodge Farm. The drain which follows this boundary has obviously been re-cut and improved many times since 1650, but it is still 2.5m wide and over 2m deep. If the drain does mark the 1650 boundary, then the 'Bushy Lawnd' and associated enclosure shown here in 1624 had been somewhat enlarged. The third division contained only 23 trees in 1650 and must have been virtually completely open land at the time the survey was made.

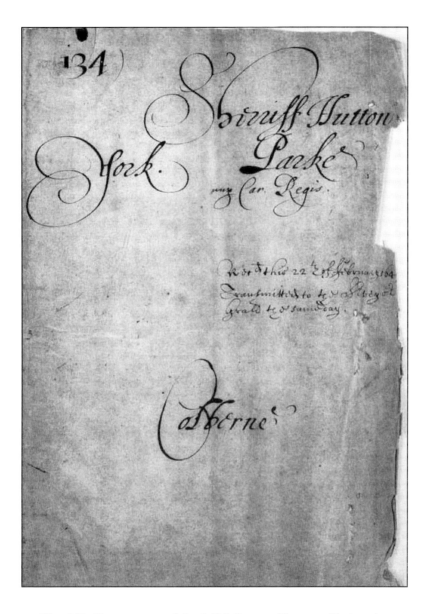

Fig. 5/5: Front cover of the 1650 Survey (Source: National Archives E317/York S/54).

Whilst the 1650 survey description plays up the tripartite division of the park as a ploy to make it more attractive to potential purchasers, it is very likely that this division made use of an arrangement that had been established considerably earlier than the mid 17th century. It can be seen from figure 5/2 that the major boundaries separating the three divisions may have also been those shown, in part, in 1624, and many of the names used in the 17th century surveys were already in use by the late 16th century. This three-part division also had a profound impact on the park that endured into the late 18th and early 19th centuries. Each division was subsequently provided with a single farm or centre; Oaks Farm to the west, the Hall (and later Park Farm) in the central division, and Lodge Farm to the east. Although none of the existing farm buildings pre-date the late 18th century, and there are no clear traces of earlier earthwork settlements immediately around them, their distribution was apparently influenced by a pattern of land use that had been established more than 200 years earlier.

The 1675-85 Particular of Sheriff Hutton Park

Once again, this document[9] only came to light towards the end of the project and will be subject of further study. However, it does show that the park now covered a total of 816 acres (330 hectares), an increase in 84 acres since 1650. It is not clear where the additional acres were situated, but they may have been in the areas of West Lilling Green and around Lilling Hall (see figure 4/9); these areas equate to c.82 acres.[10]

The 'particular' shows that the sub-division of the park had increased apace, and by now some 27 separate closes or enclosures are listed. It is not at present possible to identify all of them, with any degree of accuracy, but some specific areas can be identified from the field names recorded on the 1848 tithe map (see figure 5/7). For example, the 'West Lawn' had four separate occupiers, John Richardson, Clarkeson, Stable and Duckett, the 'Postern' had been lately 'laid to pasture', and the 'Church Hills' (the Kirk Hills above) was let to William Harrison and Tomas Bainsby for £11 2s. 6d. The central division of the west end of the park noted in 1650 as 'The Oaks' appears to have been divided into a number of enclosures, namely 'North Oaks', 'Studies Oaks', 'Pond Oakes', 'Plain Oakes', and also possibly 'Hockings Close' and a 'New Plantation'; the latter had been lately laid to pasture. The 1848 tithe map suggests that 'Studies Oaks' lay in the north-west corner of the earlier plot while 'Plain Oakes and Pond Oakes', which formed one tenancy, lay around the present Oaks Farm. There is no evidence (as yet) for any farmsteads within the area of the park.

Other areas can also be identified from a comparison with the previous survey, and their general locations suggested, such as Lodge Close, Horse Hagg, Horse Close, Plain Several and Bushey Severall. A large part of the 'Bushy Lawnd', which comprised the northern end of the east main division of 1650 was now known as 'Thorneton Hills', while the southern part was 'East Lawne'. It is expected that further study of this document will enable us to locate all of these 1675 enclosures in due course.

Land Use within the Park

It is clear that, by the early 17th century, much of the park was no longer in use as a hunting reserve, and that its value lay primarily as let or leased land. The park underwent increasing sub-division during the 17th century and also increased slightly in size; as has been noted above, in 1650 the pale enclosed 714 acres whereas by 1675-85 this had risen to 816 acres. This increasing sub-division reflects the national trend, which sees a major phase of disafforestation and dis-parkment in the late 16th and early 17th centuries.[11]

Documentary evidence indicates that there were some 400 deer in the park at the end of the 16th century, but that this number had dwindled to about 250 by the beginning of the 17th century. By 1650 the number was around 189, and they may well have been largely confined to the central division, which retained by far the most trees. The other parts of the park were given over wholly or partially to grazing by both cattle and sheep; as early as 1609-11, William Clarke, Keeper of the Park, was accused of having 'overcharged the park with cattle'.[12] These areas were fenced or paled off, to prevent the deer from entering and to stop stock moving between areas under different tenancies, although this was not always successful; the 1609-11 Commission notes that the 'rails betwixt the East Lawne and Oakes

[were] laid open' to compensate for a recent drought.[13]   Other areas were given over to specific use, for example an enclosure beside Bushy Severall had been separately enclosed and planted with plum trees, cherry trees, nut trees, birch trees etc, and William Clarke's men had paled the Kirk Hill and a piece on the West Lawn as a harbour for the deer. In the 1675-85 Particular it was noted that the Postern had been 'lately laid to pasture', implying that it had previously been arable or wooded.[14]

Fig. 5/6: Cattle grazing in the park today.

Buildings and Structures

The 17th century park was dominated by Sir Arthur Ingram's New Lodge, built between 1619-24 towards the centre of the park and approached by the Coach Road from the west; this building is discussed in detail in Chapter 15. As discussed in the same chapter, an earlier 'lodge' was present at an uncertain location within the park in the late 16th century. Further references to a building described only as a 'lodge' continue throughout the early 17th century, although they are not always what they seem. In 1609, Gilbert Shrewsbury, in preparing an estimate for repairs to the 'lodge' wrote that he desired to meet with 'two Verdurers … at ye Lodge in ye Lawnde in Galtres Forrest'.[15] Although the estimate forms part of the Temple Newsam archive relating to Sheriff Hutton, the reference to 'Verdurers' (officials regulating the royal forest) and Galtres Forest suggests that it relates to a lodge elsewhere and not in Sheriff Hutton park.

However, other references can be proved to relate to Sheriff Hutton, and these show that monies were being spent on an earlier house (i.e. pre-New Lodge) somewhere within the park before 1619. In 1617, Rafe Brocke, Arthur Ingram's steward, recorded in his accounts that building work was taking place in the park and in that year, during a visit to York, King James I had a days hunting at Sheriff Hutton park, being entertained to lunch in the 'Laund House' by Sir Arthur, who provided imported almonds and oysters for the occasion.[16] Large quantities of lead and probably also panelling were being removed from the chambers of the castle in 1617 by William Clarke,[17] perhaps in connection with the building work noted by Brocke. Furthermore, in 1618, the German glazier Barnard Dininghof requested 'the some of six pounds of lawfull English money in prte of payment of a greater some of and for glayssnge of Sir Arthur Ingrams house at Sheriff Hutton'[18] (see Chapter 15). A few of the possible locations for this earlier building or buildings are discussed below.

The Little Lodge

One possible candidate for the earlier house is the 'Little Lodge' noted in 1650. It is almost certainly the structure shown by Norden in 1624 standing within its own enclosure on the south side of the park on the former site of East Lilling village (see plate 37); the name 'Little Lodge' was probably acquired once Ingram's New or 'Greate Lodge' was finished in 1624. The Little Lodge might have been constructed around 1609-11, as the Special Commission of that date records that pales were being made to enclose a 'Lodge Garth'.[19] However, this could equally relate to the renewal of an existing feature and, as such, would not rule out the Little Lodge being of a much earlier date. It could, for example, have been built soon after 1471-85 when the former village site was incorporated into the park, to serve the area to the north which is thought to have been emparked in association with the construction of the second castle.

In 1650 the Little Lodge is described as:

> *"situate and beinge at the south side of the said parke consistinge of a hall a parlour, and three other litle rooms below the stayres, and other three rooms above stayres, a litle stable with a hay howse thereunto adjoyninge, one litle barn and a garth or yard round the said tenemt now in occupacon of Anthony Blanch ...".[20]*

The building was still occupied by Anthony Blanch of York in 1651,[21] and in c.1675 'Lodge Close' was occupied by Christopher Wilkinson and others for an annual rent of £25.[22]

The 1609-11 Special Commission also notes that 16 or 17 trees had been cut down to build a stable in the park,[23] and this might be the one mentioned in connection with the Little Lodge in 1650. Swan suggests that the Little Lodge may have been demolished as early as c.1670, whilst a tithe assessment of 1697 makes reference to 'East Lilling and Lodges' paying a small sum.[24] The site of the lodge has been identified as being within the central part of the former village, in the area marked as 'Ci', 'C', 'Di' and 'D' on figure 4/6 where there appears to have been post-village disturbance, while a track running to the north as depicted by Norden might be represented by a break in the outer boundary of the village ('S' on figure 4/6).[25] The area of disturbed earthworks on the south side of the village street, i.e. on the north side of New Road, was also thought to lie within the lodge enclosure as depicted by Norden.

The Laund House

From at least the late 16th century, there were two cleared areas within the park that were described as 'lawnde' or 'launde'. The 'West Lawnde' had probably been created in the early 16th century as part of a comprehensive remodelling of the landscape immediately to the south of the stone castle. An aerial photograph of Sheriff Hutton taken in 1956[26] shows some cropmarks in the field immediately to the south of the castle, apparently forming three conjoined rectangular structures or perhaps a building of three cells; the northernmost cell has a small square projection from the east side. The age of the cropmark is uncertain; it could be the remnants of a 20th century farm building or perhaps even a wartime structure, erected and demolished in quick succession as many such buildings were. The cropmarks could also be associated with the harbour for deer noted as being created in the West Lawnde by the 1609-

11 Special Commission.[27] However, it might equally be something else. As will be shown in Chapter 8, the castle was once linked to the West Lawnde by a substantial wooden bridge crossing the double canals. Where might this bridge have lead to? – perhaps to a 'Laund house' situated on the 'Lawnde', with the castle forming a spectacular backdrop? Unfortunately, the bridge had been largely dismantled by 1598 and any such house had clearly gone by 1624 when the Nordens surveyed the park, making it unlikely to be the site of the kings' entertainment.

Based on the field names given in the 1848 Sheriff Hutton tithe map[28] (see below), the late 16th century 'east Launde' lay in the area immediately to the north of the Little Lodge. Might the Little Lodge therefore be the 'Laund House' of 1617? A case could certainly be made for it. The location of the building, tucked away in one corner of the park, would not have made a very spectacular setting for a royal visit, but by 1617 the decaying castle was no longer the focal point in the park landscape that it once had been and James may have been more concerned with the quality of the hunting than where he took lunch.

A third possibility exists, namely that advanced by Gilbert in 1966, that the 'Laund House' stood on the same site as Ingram's New Lodge.[29] Given its name, it might be considered unlikely that the 'Laund House' was placed within the central area of the park which was still the most heavily wooded in 1624 and 1650, although a clearing could have been created within the woodland. Writing in 1946, Mrs Egerton knew of a theory that the stables (adjacent to the existing Hall and close to the site of Ingram's New Lodge) 'were made out of an existing house there called the Lawnd House, but so far I have not been able to verify this'[30] (see Chapter 15). It is certainly true that the only surviving fragment of the Laund House may be the coat of arms carved in stone, formerly set into the wall of the stable complex (latterly known as 'The Rangers House').[31] The arms cannot be any earlier than James I and could have been carved to commemorate his visit in 1617. Support for Mrs Egerton's theory may be provided by a letter from Richard Pollerd to Thomas Lumsden in June 1620 concerning hunting in Sheriff Hutton Park, which was written at the 'Lawne House'.[32] Pollerd was presumably not living somewhere that had either been demolished or was in the process of being incorporated into the much larger New Lodge, and so it is feasible that the Laund House was close to, but not on exactly the same site as, the later house. Alternatively, we may be thrown back to the possibility that the 'Little Lodge' is the 'Laund House' and that this was where Pollerd was living in 1620. Perhaps some clue is contained in Arthur Ingram's 1623 account with Thomas Lumsden, which includes a comparison of the 'old and new plotts at Sheriff Hutton'.[33]

The Park in the 18th Century

Sheriff Hutton is fortunate in that a series of superbly executed and well preserved maps of the village survive from the late 18th century, depicting the area both prior to, during and after enclosure. Unfortunately, as the park had already been enclosed long before this date, it is excluded from the maps, and so we lack the same detailed information as that which exists for the village and surrounding area. There is a similar lack of evidence concerning the way the park was farmed during the early to mid 18th century. Brief surveys of the existing farms within the park have shown that no surviving buildings are earlier than the late 18th century, and there is nothing to suggest that they were established any earlier, at least as farms. Late 18th century maps, such as Jeffrey's 1771 map of Yorkshire, shed little further light on the subject and so, as for the 17th century, we are forced to presume that the park was farmed 'in hand' from the Hall with other substantial areas leased to tenants who had farm buildings on the edges of the park, presumably in Sheriff Hutton or West Lilling. It was during Leonard Thompson's time at the park (1772 to 1815) that two of the existing three farms were built, namely Oaks Farm and Lodge Farm; the farms in the park are discussed in Chapter 16.

The Park in the 19th and 20th Centuries

The main documentary and cartographic source for the park in the early 19th century is the 1848 tithe map and award;[34] the map provides a key to the award which records the name of each field, its owner and occupier, its size and what it was used for. The award shows that, although Leonard Thompson is the owner of the whole, over two thirds of the area was let, mainly to his steward, William Wright, who farmed the area from Oaks Farm, and to John Flawith of Lodge Farm. A few of the other fields around the north and western edge of the park were let individually, while the area around the Hall was in hand. The majority of the former West Lawn was let to John Foster, while George Fawcett and Mary Morley had smaller areas; John Blenkarn 'and others' had the field in the north-west corner of the lawn, which is shown as being 'Cottage Gardens' in 1856 and so perhaps it was given over to allotments at this time as well.

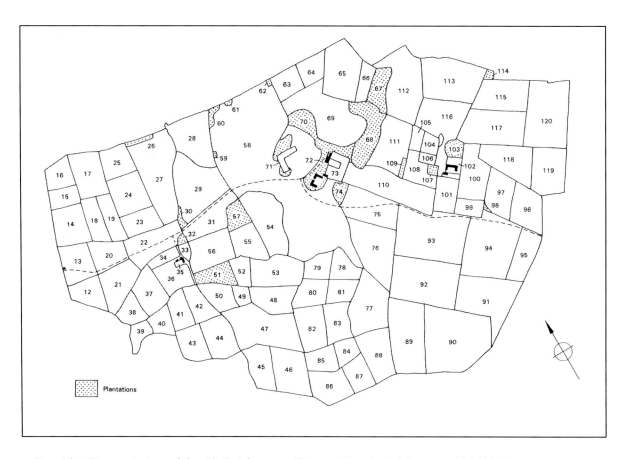

Fig. 5/7: Transcription of the 1848 tithe map (Source: Borthwick Institute TA411S).

Field names as recorded on the 1848 tithe map:

Field no	Field name	Field no	Field name
12	First Sturdy Oak	67	Plantation
13	Sturdy Oak	68	Plantation
14	Part of Redus	69	Little Serverhills & Washhouse Close
15	Part of Redus	70	Plantation
16	Part of Redus	71	Plantation & Fish Pond
17	Upper Lawn	72	Shrubberies, Walks and Gardens
18	Winter Lawn	73	Mansion House & gardens (the Hall)
19	Winter Lawn	74	Orchard
20	Sturdy Oak	75	Near Busky Severn hills
21	Second Sturdy Oak	76	Low Ox Pasture
22	Plain Oaks	77	Snowdale Hagg
23	Low Lawn	78	Upper Meadow Field
24	Lawn	79	Upper Meadow Field
25	Lawn	80	Upper Meadow Field
26	Plantation	81	Upper Meadow Field
27	Lawn	82	Switchen Close
28	Postern	83	Switchen Close
29	Puckerings Close	84	Part of Little Lilling
30	Plantation	85	Part of Little Lilling
31	Great Warwick Oak	86	Great Lilling
32	Plantation	87	Great Lilling
33	Orchard	88	Dale Croft
34	Plain Oaks	89	Lodge Close
35	Homestead Gdn Lane (Oaks Farm)	90	Lodge Close
36	House Close	91	East Lawn
37	Plain Oaks	92	East Lawn
38	Hagg	93	East Lawn
39	Hagg	94	East Lawn
40	First Hagg	95	East Lawn
41	Horse Hagg	96	Third Corn Close
42	Hesp Hills	97	Second Corn Close
43	Far Horse Hagg	98	Plantation
44	Near Horse Hagg	99	Far Corn Close
45	Part of Brecon Hagg	100	First Corn Close
46	Part of Brecon Hagg	101	Front of House Close
47	Winter Hagg	102	Homestead Gdn & Stackyard (Lodge Farm)
48	First Hesp Hills	103	Plantation
49	Hesp Hills	104	Eastmost Garth
50	Hesp Hills	105	Garth
51	Plantation	106	Eastmost Garth
52	Hesp Hills	107	Orchard
53	Hesp Hills	108	Croft
54	New Laid Close	109	Plantation
55	Hesp Hills	110	Avenue
56	Great Warwick Oak	111	Plain Severn Hills
57	Plantation	112	Part of Thornton Hills
58	Park	113	Part of Thornton Hills
59	Plantation	114	Plantation
60	Plantation	115	Part of Thornton Hills
61	Plantation	116	Part of Thornton Hills
62	Plantation	117	Part of Thornton Hills
63	Part of Horse Hagg	118	Part of Thornton Hills
64	Part of Horse Close	119	Part of Thornton Hills
65	Great Sawtry	120	Part of Thornton Hills
66	Little Sawtry		

The majority of the area to the north and south of Lodge Farm was given over to arable, whilst there was more equal distribution of arable and grassland around Oaks Farm. The Hall was sheltered by belts of plantation, some named as 'shrubberies, walks and gardens', with the surrounding fields largely given over to grass. There are also some 17 areas of plantation, the largest being around the Hall but with smaller parcels scattered around the in-hand land. It is assumed that these woods were laid out for shooting, and it is known that the Thompson family were keen shooters (see Chapter 13). Edwin Dalton, born in Sheriff Hutton in 1845, notes in his unpublished memoirs that: "Still further from the Hall stands the large rookery where one of England's commonest fowls gather in great numbers and the youths look forward with pleasure to the shooting day which comes once a year".[35] Percy Wright, a much loved villager of Sheriff Hutton who died at the beginning of the 21st century aged 83, also told of how, as a boy, he used to shoot rooks in the park with a catapult and take them home to his mother who made rook pie.[36]

As has already been noted, many of the 1848 field names refer to parcels of land or sub-divisions of the park which had been in place since at least the end of the 16th century. In the former west division of the park described in 1650,[37] 'Horse Hagg' (where the Earl of Surrey and Elizabeth of York had once grazed their horses) had become 'Hagg', 'First Hagg', 'Near Horse Hagg' and 'Winter Hagg', while 'the Oaks' had become the various 'Sturdy Oaks', 'Plain Oaks' and 'Warwick Oaks' (but nowhere near the tree which had been designated the Warwick Oak). The 'Weste Lawne' had become 'Upper and Lower Lawn', 'Lawn', 'Winter Lawn' and three fields named 'Redus'. In the middle section 'Kirk Hill' had gone to become simply 'Park' (the parkland around the Hall), part of the former 'Bushy Severalls' had become 'Near Busky Severn Hills' and the former 'Plain Severall' had become 'Plain Severn Hills'. In the east, where the Parliamentarians had omitted to name the lands, the area of the 1624 'Bushy Lawnd' is now a number of fields named as 'Thornton Hills', after the adjacent parish of Thornton-le-Clay. As previously described, the area to the south, which might correspond to the unnamed block of land shown in 1624 (see plate 37), is represented by a block of five fields all named as 'East Lawn'. These presumably reflect the position of the former east lawn, which might have been associated with the former Little Lodge which lay on the site of the deserted East Lilling village; this latter area is called 'Lodge Close'.

Some of the field names recorded in 1848 refer to the use of the land, for example 'Corn Close' and 'Meadow Field', while 'Park' distinguished that area retained as parkland around the Hall. Two fields named as 'Part of Brecon Hagg' in the south-east of the park may refer to the bracken plant - it was used as bedding and so may have been allowed to grow for this purpose,[38] but a 'bracken' was also a type of medieval hunting dog and so perhaps this is a reference to an earlier activity. 'Switchen Close', to the south of the present Park Farm, may refer to coppiced land, on which the coppices are kept very young to produce thin, flexible 'switches' for making hurdles. The significance of the field name 'Postern', adjacent to the High Park, has already been noted in connection with the former lands of Marton Priory in the 14th century (see Chapter 1), as has the occurrence of the numerous 'Hagg' names which indicate earlier areas of woodland (see above).

The Ordnance Survey 1st edition 6" maps of the mid 19th century[39] provide a detailed depiction of the park as it appeared at that time. These maps provide the first accurate survey compared to the previous 1848 tithe map, which has a few inaccuracies. The Ordnance Survey, as might be expected, show the field boundaries with their correct orientation, together with other details such as water courses, footpaths and minor outlying agricultural structures. Examples of the latter include many buildings now demolished, such as the 'Dog

Kennel' to the south-west of the Hall complex and a small enclosure and barn in the north-east corner of the High Park. There is basically little difference in the field pattern as shown on the maps of 1848 and 1855-56, although there is some sub-division of larger fields on the latter; there are however, some differences in the depiction of the farmsteads, as noted in Chapter 16. The area named as 'Sheriff Hutton Park' is much smaller than the total park area that existed during the 17th century and before – the area is concentrated around the Hall itself, reflecting the area that was 'in hand' at this time.

Fig. 5/8: Hare coursing, based on a mid 19th century illustration.

Reference was made above to shooting, and the opportunities for shooting and hunting within the park were certainly considered a prime attraction when it was put up for sale in 1880. Lot 1, which comprised just over 203 acres and included the entire park area, was described, amongst other things, as being:

> *"To Lovers of Field Sports this Estate must have many attractions, as it affords excellent Shooting and is in the midst of a capital Hunting District, situate about midway between the Kennels of Lord Middleton's and the York and Ainsty Hounds, and within easy reach of many of the Meets of these noted Packs".*[40]

The plan accompanying the sale catalogue (see plate 40) suggests that little had changed in terms of the overall appearance of the park since the previous tithe and Ordnance Survey maps, the major difference being the construction of Park Farm (then referred to as Home Farm). This was built between 1855 and 1871 to the south of The Rangers House complex, and most of its land was taken from the former Oaks Farm holding (see Chapter 16).

The 1880 sale catalogue shows that the estate was put up for sale in nine lots (see plate 40). The Hall and surrounding parkland comprised 203 acres and was sold for £14,500. Lodge

Farm comprised 283 acres, Home (Park) Farm was 102 acres, and Oaks Farm was 108 acres. The area between the Postern and Finkle Street was sold as four separate lots, and there was a further separate parcel of ground on the south side of the Coach Road. It should be noted that the 900 acre (365 hectares) estate extended slightly beyond the former park pale, into parts of the West Lilling, East Lilling and Thornton-le-Clay townships.

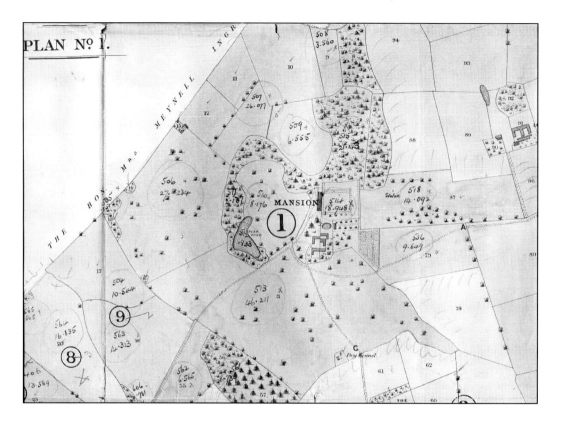

Fig. 5/9: The Hall and surrounding area as depicted in the 1880 sale catalogue.

The story of the park during the 20th century has been one of adaptation to modern agricultural techniques. As land holdings changed and fragmented, the pale line became increasingly irrelevant to the agricultural landscape. The remaining sections were gradually removed or ploughed out, until only a few upstanding fragments were left. However, as this and the proceeding chapter have demonstrated, nothing disappears without a trace, and both pale and park continue to exert a subtle influence on the landscape today.

Footnotes

1   National Archives E178/4839.
2   British Library Harleian MSS no. 6288; West Yorkshire Archive Service (WYAS) Leeds WYL100/SH/B4/1.
3   Franks (no date), pp.23-25.
4   WYAS Leeds WYL100/SH/B4/2.
5   Ordnance Survey 1855 6" map sheet 141, surveyed 1854.
6   WYAS Leeds WYL100/SH/B4/2.
7   National Archives E317/York S/54; this document was transcribed by Tony Wright for this project.
8   Borthwick Institute TA411S.
9   WYAS Leeds WYL100/SH/B3/1.
10 Vivien Swan, *pers. comm.*
11 Bond 1994, p.132.
12 Swan *et al* 1990, p.104.

13   National Archives E178/4838.

14   WYAS Leeds WYL100/SH/B3/1.

15   WYAS Leeds WYL/SH/A4/23.

16   Upton 1961, p.150; Rushton 2003, p.204; Drake 1736, pp.256-7; Gilbert 1966a, p.548.

17   WYAS Leeds WYL/SH/G/4.

18   WYAS Leeds WYL100/SH/A3/2/5.

19   National Archives E178/4839.

20   National Archives E317/York S/54.

21   WYAS Leeds WYL100/SH/A1/32.

22   WYAS Leeds WYL100/SH/B3/1.

23   National Archives E178/4839.

24   Swan *et al* 1990, pp.101-104.

25   ibid., p.105.

26   Reproduced in Beresford & St Joseph 1979, fig. 63.

27   National Archives E178/4839.

28   Borthwick Institute TA411S.

29   Gilbert 1966a, pp.548-551.

30   Egerton 1946, p.13.

31   The arms are shown in Gilbert 1966b, p.628.

32   WYAS Leeds WYL/100/SH/A4/17.

33   WYAS Leeds WYL/100/SH/TN/G/1.

34   Borthwick Institute TA411S; the apportionment was transcribed by Tony Wright.

35   Edwin Dalton unpublished memoirs (privately held).

36   Percy Wright *pers. comm.* to Barbara Walker.

37   National Archives E317/York S/54.

38   Field 1972, p.26.

39   Ordnance Survey 1856 6" map sheet 140, surveyed 1851-52 & 1855 sheet 141 surveyed 1854.

40   Sedgwick, Son & Weall 1880 "The Sheriff Hutton Park Estate". Copies held within the village and at the Borthwick Institute (PR/SH/80).

CHAPTER 6: THE FIRST SHERIFF HUTTON CASTLE
by Ed Dennison

Introduction

A complex of earthworks representing the remains of the first castle at Sheriff Hutton lies at the east end of the present village, just to the south of the church. As has been noted in Chapter 1, this end of the village was probably the area of the original, possibly Saxon, settlement, and the juxtaposition of castle, church and settlement nucleus is a common characteristic of many early villages.

Historical and Documentary Accounts

It is surprising that the first castle site at Sheriff Hutton has not attracted more attention in the past, but the majority of work seems to have been concentrated on the more impressive, later, stone castle located at the west end of the village. Nevertheless, the earthworks have not gone unnoticed, and they were first accurately depicted on the Ordnance Survey 1st edition 1855 6" map where they were named as 'mounds'.[1] A later 25" edition map shows the same series of earthworks, but names them as 'Tumuli',[2] possibly because they were so-called by both Todd and Tempest.[3] The Victoria County History notes that the 'curious' earthworks probably represent "a transitional form from the motte and bailey to the later keep and bailey castle" while Illingworth describes them as a 'mount and bailey'.[4] The plan of the site as published by the Victoria County History shows a sub-rectangular ditched earthwork with a number of raised platforms within the slightly raised interior, with lower banks extending to the west.

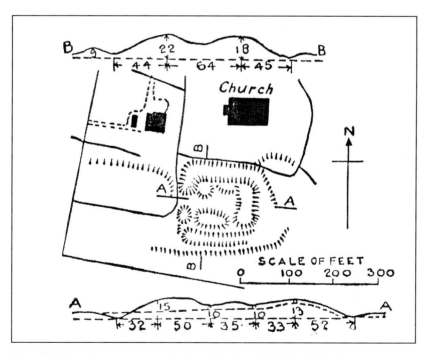

Fig. 6/1: The first castle as depicted by the VCH in 1912 (Source: Armitage & Montgomerie 1912).

At present, there do not appear to be many documentary references for this first castle complex, although research is still continuing. It is not mentioned in the 1086 Domesday Book, but this need not be significant as castles were sources of expenditure rather than taxable assets, and so they are only infrequently recorded in this source.[5] The construction of the castle has always been associated with Bertram de Bulmer in c.1140,[6] although this date actually refers to a siege at the site.[7] It now seems more likely that it was built slightly earlier by his father, Ansketill de Bulmer, either when he was enfeoffed of [Sheriff] Hutton by Nigel Fossard in 1106 or 1115, or when he was made Sheriff of York in 1115.[8] The site is not mentioned as being one of the castles reduced during the 12th century Civil War between Stephen and Matilda.[9]

The *inquisitions post mortem* of various members of the Neville family do, however, give some clues about the site. That for Robert Neville, dated to 1282-83, describes it as a 'capital messuage' held from Peter de Mauley which, together with fruits and herbage, was worth 10s. per annum.[10] The *inquisition* of Ranulph Neville in 1331 notes that the capital messuage with a garden was only worth 2s. per annum,[11] and by the time of Ralph Neville's *inquisition* in 1367 it still had an orchard and garden, but it was worth nothing, 'apart from its repairs', presumably reflecting the fact that the site had been more or less abandoned.[12] It was similarly described and valued in 1388.[13]

As yet, little is known about the Neville's occupation of the site, or indeed whether they actually lived there for any period of time, particularly after they gained the overlordship of the manor in 1331. Apart from the evidence produced from an earthwork and geophysical survey (see below), little is also known about the size and disposition of any structures within or around the site. It is assumed that there would have been a building sufficient to accommodate the sheriff's retinue, but the only known documentary reference to a hall at Sheriff Hutton occurs in 1320 when the burghers of Beverley requested that Ranulph Neville's bailiff release one Stephen Russel of Elstonwick who they believed had been imprisoned there.[14] There are several references to a 'Court' at Sheriff Hutton in the Neville *inquisitions* of 1376 and 1388, which suggests that there was a suitable building either on the site or in the vicinity,[15] and Ranulph Neville claimed several important manorial powers including the right to have a gallows and 'amends of the assize of ale' between 1274 and 1280.[16] The various lay subsidies also note that Mistress Ida Neville was one of the two biggest taxpayers in the village in 1301 and Ranulph also paid a significant sum in 1327[17] (see Chapter 1). It has been suggested that Edward II's wife and Edward III visited the castle on several occasions, although this is disputed by some authors.[18]

It is not known what happened to the complex once the second, and much larger, stone castle was built at the west end of the village. It appears, from the limited range of documentary sources so far consulted, that the complex was simply abandoned and then leased out. In c.1532 the site may have been held by Marton Priory as part of their holdings in the manor, and it was described then as 'a waste called Castlehill'.[19] Some years later, in 1571, it belonged to the Duke of York and was itemised as 'one waste called Castle Hill',[20] while in 1607-08 a close called 'Castle Hill', covering 1 acre and 2 roods, was included in a Survey of Sheriff Hutton manor taken at this time.[21] In 1646 the site had been let out for grazing, as it is recorded as 'herbage of parcel of land called Castle Isle near Sheriff Hutton church'.[22]

The detailed plan which accompanies the 1765 survey of Sheriff Hutton[23] depicts five sharply pointed earthwork mounds, arranged more or less in a square, with a field boundary running east-west between them before it returns to the south. The plot which forms the north half of the castle site is named as 'Hilly Garth' in the accompanying schedule, and there is a square structure positioned towards the east end of the enclosure, presumably representing a house. The plot which forms the south side of the castle site is part of a larger and elongated field which runs off to the west, which is named as 'Croft Garth and Hill Garth'.

The site remained in private hands until 1863, when Hugo Ingram swapped the 4½ acres for other land to the north of the village with the Church Commissioners.[24] It then became glebe land and remained so until 1982, when it was bought by a group of villagers who formed the Sheriff Hutton Glebe Conservation Trust; the site is now managed as a traditional meadow.[25] The site was designated as a Scheduled Monument on 4th January 1937 and is described in the documentation as a 'ringwork and bailey'.[26]

Recent Survey Work

In 2004 a detailed earthwork survey was carried out on the site, and this represents the first accurate plan of the complex. As can be seen from figure 6/3 below, the broad outline of the earthworks is not significantly different from that mapped in 1912, although considerably more information has been gathered for the peripheral areas.

The most prominent earthworks lie in the centre of the site, forming what has been described as a raised 'collar' or 'banquette' (the latter term being used by I'Anson in 1913)[27] measuring c.50m by c.40m overall and open on the west side. The banks of this feature are steep, rising some 2.5m high out of an encircling ditch which is most prominent on the north and south sides where it is up to 10m wide and 1m deep. The ditch has been partly infilled around the west side of the collar, whilst a very slight depression suggests that it also once continued around the east end. The south side of the ditch is set at a much higher level than that to the north, and it is unlikely that it was ever wholly water-filled to create a moat.

Fig. 6/2: The first castle, looking west, showing the central mound and the ditch on the south side.

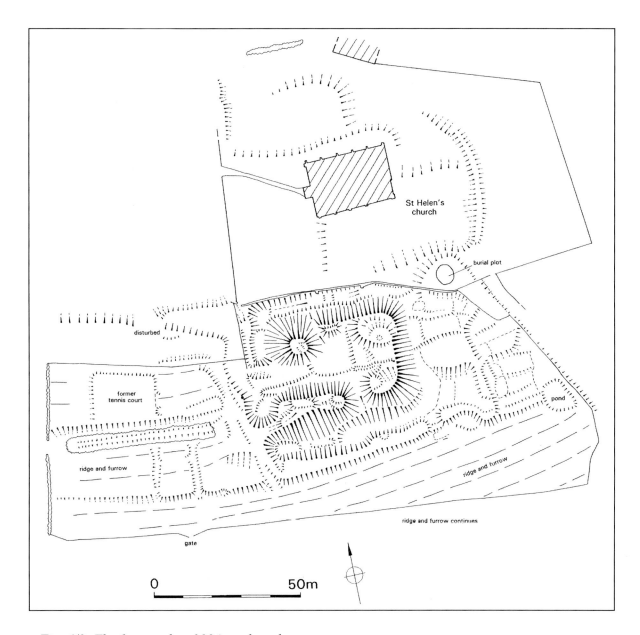

Fig. 6/3: The first castle – 2004 earthwork survey.

The north-west corner of the collar is marked by a prominent flat-topped mound, and a similar but more elongated feature forms most of the south side. The east side also appears to have two mounds at either end, with a central raised section in between, combining to produce an area c.25m long by c.10m wide. The width of these earthworks suggests that they represent the sites of buildings, i.e. large separate ranges forming the east and south sides of the rectangle. It is also possible that there was another building in the centre of the north side, connecting the east range with a mound in the north-west corner. There is a single prominent sycamore tree on the top of this mound, and the tops of two of the other mounds are disturbed; perhaps they all had trees on, planted for ornamental purposes, possibly when the area formed part of the Vicarage Garden; the former Vicarage lies immediately to the west of the church (see figure 6/1).

If the interpretation of the building ranges is correct, they would appear to surround a small rectangular internal courtyard, perhaps c.25m east-west by c.10m north-south. The opening on the west side of the defensive enclosure is c.10m wide and this would represent the main entrance into the site, perhaps with a bridge across the encircling ditch which has since been infilled. There is also perhaps another entrance, located between the south and east ranges. This latter entrance may have been associated with a bridge which crossed the southern ditch to the flat earthwork beyond, although any such bridge might be a later addition to the site. The courtyard is significantly higher than the surrounding ground, and it is crossed by a slight east-west bank which represents the field boundary shown on the 1765 plan; this boundary is still depicted on the Ordnance Survey 1855 1st edition 6" map.

To the west of the central rectangle is an area of ridge and furrow earthworks, representing former arable cultivation. This area is divided by an east-west bank, now a hedge, which marks the south end of the former Vicarage garden, and there are also north-south divisions in the southern half, perhaps drains. The site of an abandoned tennis court, now seen as a square earthwork platform, lies in the centre of the northern block, and there are further disturbed south-facing banks in the present garden just to the north. It is thought that this area to the west of the mound represents a bailey or other enclosure, which has been subsequently ploughed when the castle fell out of use. The bailey would have been about 60m wide (north-south) and at least as long, but the west end has been lost to a modern housing development; a continuation of the ridge and furrow is shown in this western area on aerial photographs that pre-date the development.[28] Any traces of castle structures within the bailey, as might normally be expected, have been destroyed by the later ridge and furrow ploughing.

Fig. 6/4: Entrance to first castle, looking west towards the second castle.

There are further, more complex, earthworks to the east of the main mound, within an area which slopes gently down from north to south. This area seems to contain numerous small platforms placed either side of a disjointed north-south bank. On the west side of the bank, at its north end, there is perhaps one large sub-divided structural platform measuring c.25m by c.15m, which appears to overlie the eastern ditch of the main rectangle and to be terraced into

90

the east side. To the east of the bank, there are a number of slight parallel east-west terraces or platforms running down the gentle slope towards a pond in the south-east corner. At least three of these terraces have smaller platforms at their west ends. It is possible that these earthworks once continued beyond the east boundary of the site, now a footpath but which is marked as 'Road to ye Lodge' in 1765.[29] However, this area is now covered by a dense plantation which has obscured any features here, although no earthworks are visible on aerial photographs (see below).[30]

The whole castle complex is divided from the adjacent ridge and furrow to the south by a well defined bank, up to c.4m wide and flat-topped, although with a slight slope to the south (see plate 41). Towards its east end, the bank is breached or broken by a c.2m wide gap. The ridge and furrow lies very close to the south side of the castle but seems to respect its general alignment, and there is no direct evidence to suggest that the complex was superimposed into a pre-existing agricultural landscape as has been previously implied.[31]

Fig. 6/5: Aerial photograph taken in March 1956 showing the first castle surrounded by ridge and furrow, looking west (Cambridge University Collection of Air Photographs, RU62). © Crown Copyright/MOD.

In an attempt to try and increase our understanding of the complex, a geophysical survey was undertaken in December 2004.[32] This survey covered as much of the castle and associated earthworks as was practicable, using a variety of techniques. The interpreted results are shown below and on plate 43. A probable well was located towards the centre of the east end of the internal courtyard ('4' on figure 6/6), together with a few other possible wall lines; unfortunately it was not possible to survey the large platforms of the rectangular earthworks due to the tree cover. The readings within the area of the western bailey were heavily masked by a scatter of iron and other near-surface material and no underlying features were revealed, although a possible small structure ('A') was identified just beyond the west end of the southern moat.

The main area of interest, as revealed by the geophysical survey, lay to the east of the main enclosure. The north-west part of the area, previously noted above as a possible building platform, did contain anomalies suggestive of a building ('C'), within an area of magnetic disturbance. However, the anomies continue to the south, suggesting a substantial rectangular north-south aligned structure ('D') , with additional wall lines to the east. Further intrusive investigation would be needed to confirm these results, and it is currently impossible to determine whether these anomalies are associated with the medieval castle, or the 18th century house depicted in this area.

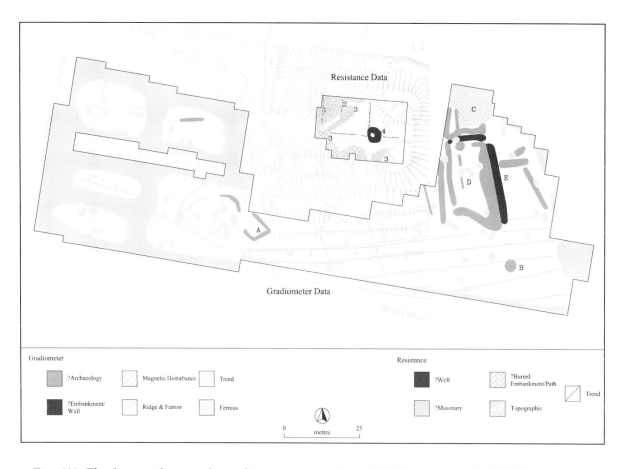

Fig. 6/6: The first castle - geophysical interpretation (from GSB Prospection Ltd 2004).

Interpretation – What does it all Mean?

The core of the castle complex is obviously the central rectangular enclosure, and it would appear that the earthworks represent a number of building ranges and possibly towers or turrets arranged around an internal courtyard. This is not the traditional view of a ringwork, in which a large central single structure is surrounded by a palisade or wall.[33] It more closely resembles a 'courtyard castle', the plan forms of which do tend to appear in the 12th century. The site also has similarities with two other mid 12th century, but temporary, castles in Burwell and Rampton in Cambridgeshire.[34] However, the size of the courtyard at Sheriff Hutton does seem rather small, and it is possible that the castle did originate as an earlier pre-Conquest ringwork which was subsequently modified within a constricted site by later generations of the Bulmer and Neville families. Clark has drawn comparisons between this site and Helmsley castle in North Yorkshire, the latter also traditionally interpreted as a ringwork but which has more characteristics of a courtyard design.[35] It is interesting to note that the adjacent church is also first documented to 1100-15,[36] precisely when the castle is thought to have been first constructed, and it is possible that the two represent the deliberate creation of a 'magnate core' within or adjacent to a pre-existing settlement.[37]

At present, it is not possible to say whether the bailey attached to the west side of the castle is part of the original design, but it would seem more likely that it was a later addition. Perhaps it was added in the mid 12th century when the Bulmers became more closely associated with the manor, and when the adjacent small planned settlement appears to have become established, when the 'Sheriff' prefix was added to the village name, and when there was a substantial rebuilding of the church (see phase 2 in Chapter 1 above). The bailey would normally have contained a number of ancillary structures, such as barns and stables etc, but subsequent arable cultivation has removed all surface and near-surface remains.

The first castle site would have been held by the Bulmers and then, from 1190 to 1382 or slightly beyond, by the Nevilles. None of the Neville documents so far examined suggest any permanent occupation here, although two family members were taxed in the village in 1301 and 1327, and perhaps they simply 'called in' as they progressed around their northern estates. The site is described as a 'capital messuage' and so some degree of importance was attached to it, and it also probably served as the administrative centre for their lordship. However, the complex, in whatever form it took, would also have provided the Nevilles with a base for hunting in their adjacent deer park, and perhaps the site took on an added significance once they gained overlordship of the manor in c.1331 and when the relatively small deer park was expanded a few years later (see Chapter 4).

It is to be expected that the capital messuage would have had some gardens attached to it, particularly in its later phases, and orchards and gardens are mentioned in the Neville *inquisitions post mortem* noted above. It is possible that the shallow earthworks to the east of the main mound represent their remains, and the small parallel platforms or terraces on the east side of the disjointed north-south bank have the appearance of a medieval garden. However, the *inquisition post mortem* of Ralph Neville in 1367 shows that the site was worth nothing, implying that it had been abandoned, although the gardens are still mentioned.

It would be nice to think that the first castle site still performed some function once the new stone complex at the west end of the village was complete, and perhaps the site was re-occupied once the Nevilles had their more permanent base. For example, does the sharply defined east range at the first castle site represent a later structure, possibly a platform or building, even perhaps a detached lodge or 'dower house' complex, from where views could be gained looking west towards the new castle and/or south over the extensive deer park? Similarly, does the flat-topped mound in the north-west corner of the rectangle represent a prospect mound? The flat-topped bank on the south side of the castle may also be associated with this later use, perhaps acting as a walkway with a bridge leading over an altered south ditch into the central courtyard. This southern ditch may have been water-filled with a sluice located in the c.2m wide gap adjacent to the pond. If this is the case, perhaps some of the 'garden' earthworks on the east side of the main mound belong to this ornamental and/or detached lodge phase; the trees on the corner mounds are likely to be remnants of the Vicarage garden, but they could have replaced others. A ramp also leads on to the top of the south-west mound, which might be another viewing point into the courtyard or south to the deer park. These theories are not without precedent, and there are other examples of earlier castles being converted into ornamental garden features, such as at the Percy family's manorial complex at Topcliffe near Thirsk.[38]

It is interesting to note that the first and second castle sites are not only intervisible (see figure 6/4), but are still linked by a footpath. The Nevilles would have been able to look out from their new castle back towards where, both physically and metaphorically, they had come from, and the deliberate retention or re-use of the earlier castle site would have provided not only a pleasant place to visit but also a visual reminder of their origins. There are precisely these same connections between an earlier ringwork and a later massive replacement stone castle at Middleham in North Yorkshire, another important Neville estate.

However, the site appears to have been properly abandoned by c.1532, when it formed part of another landholding, and it is assumed that it was no longer required following the death of Richard Neville in 1471 and the transference of the Sheriff Hutton estates to Richard, Duke of Gloucester.

At least part of the site was re-occupied in the 18th century when a house is depicted to the east of the main mound on the plan of 1765. Perhaps some of the 'garden' earthworks seen in this area are therefore associated with this house. The position of the actual building appears to correspond with the larger, structural, sub-divided platform and magnetic disturbance seen in the north-west part of this area, and the platform seems to have been partly created by infilling the east side of the earlier ditch. The geophysical survey suggests that there are further structural remains to the south, perhaps a small garden enclosure rather than an actual building. It is possible therefore, that this later building and garden were superimposed on the much earlier castle gardens.

Footnotes

1   Ordnance Survey 1855 6" map sheet 141, surveyed 1854.
2   Ordnance Survey 1911 25" map sheet 141/1.
3   Todd 1824, Addendum; Tempest 1875, p.28.
4   Calthrop 1923, p.174; Armitage & Montgomerie 1912, pp.45-46; Illingworth 1938, p.130.
5   Creighton 2002, p.93.
6   e.g. Beresford & St Joseph 1979, p.154; Illingworth 1938, pp.130-31.
7   King 1983, pp.525 & 528.
8   National Archives Lists of Sheriffs; Farrer 1915a, pp.281-85; Rushton 1986, p.22.
9   Rushton 1986, p.24; Tony Wright, *pers. comm.*
10   National Archives C133/35/1: Robert de Neville IPM 10th Februray 1282/3; I am grateful to Bridgett Jones for providing translations of this and subsequent IPMs.
11   National Archives C135/27/19: Ranulph de Neville IPM 22nd April 1331.
12   National Archives C135/195/1: Ralph de Neville IPM 28th August 1367.

13   National Archives C136/56/1: John de Neville IPM 2nd November 1388.

14   Leech 1898, p.384.

15   Cal. IPM 12 no. 160; Cal. IPM 16 no. 736.

16   English 1996, p.265 ; these manorial rights were 'inganenthief' (the right of the Lord of the manor to try and punish a thief caught in the manor), 'outfangenethief' (the right of the Lord to pursue a thief outside the manor boundary and bring him back for trial), and 'toll and team' (either the right to collect tax or hold a market).

17   Brown 1896, p.77; Parker 1929, p.143.

18   e.g. Wheater 1888, p.217.

19   National Archives E315/199, f.98.

20   National Archives E310/27/163.

21   National Archives LR 2/193, Land Revenue Misc. Book.

22   West Yorkshire Archive Service (WYAS) Leeds WYL100/SH/A/27.

23   WYAS Leeds WYL100/SH/B4/2.

24   Borthwick Institute TA P.

25   Robin Wardell, *pers. comm.*

26   Scheduled Monument documentation provided by English Heritage, AM 30114.

27   I'Anson 1913, p.379.

28   e.g. Cambridge University Collection of Air Photographs (CUCAP) AQH 29 taken 3/12/66 and RU62 taken 26/3/56; Beresford & St Joseph 1979, p.155.

29   WYAS Leeds WYL100/SH/B4/2.

30   e.g. CUCAP BBQ 75 taken 4/6/70 and RU62 taken 26/3/56

31   Beresford & St Joseph 1979, p.154; Creighton 2002, p.211.

32   GSB Prospection Ltd 2004.

33   Leech 1988.

34   RCHME 1972, pp.41-42; Brown & Taylor 1977, pp.97-99; I am grateful to Chris Taylor for drawing my attention to these sites.

35   Dr Jonathan Clark, University of York, *pers. comm.*

36   Tony Wright, *pers. comm.*

37   Creighton 2002, p.111.

38   Moorhouse 2003b, p.200.

CHAPTER 7: THE SECOND SHERIFF HUTTON CASTLE
By Tony Wright and Shaun Richardson

Introduction

The reader might be surprised to find such a lengthy chapter on the second of Sheriff Hutton's castles in a book that purports to be the story of the park. However, the two have an almost symbiotic relationship and it is impossible to consider one without the other. The one feature that remains constant in the park landscape is the castle, which is visible from almost everywhere within the park, even the far eastern and southern edges (see plate 27).

The purpose of this chapter is to describe the structure of the castle and how it evolved over time. However, one must be careful not to forget the people amongst the crenellations, buttresses, halls and chambers, as without people the castle is little more than a rather large pile of stone. One of the main purposes of the castle was to provide a certain type of lifestyle for parts of the Neville family, but different members of that family, their households and the villagers of Sheriff Hutton would have experienced the castle in different ways. Therefore, rather than giving a detailed history of the people who lived *at* the castle, this chapter seeks to explore *how* it was lived in.

The Construction of the Castle

Chapter 1 gave a summary of how, during the 14th century, the Neville family greatly increased their status, power and wealth through military service, clever marriages and royal patronage, culminating in the careers of John (d.1388) and Ralph Neville (d.1425). As a result, John and then Ralph were able to undertake a widespread programme of ecclesiastical and artistic patronage, and they embarked upon an extensive scheme of improvements to many of their residences, including Raby, Brancepeth and Middleham.[1]

It is against this background that the construction of the second and greater castle at Sheriff Hutton needs to be considered. By the late 14th century, the existing site at the east end of the village was simply not commensurate with John Neville's status; the second castle and its attendant courts cover an area approximately seven or eight times greater than the earlier complex. The late medieval aristocracy were an intensely competitive group, and John Neville would certainly have been aware of the regional building programmes of his contemporaries, such as the Scropes at Bolton castle in Wensleydale and the Percys at Wressle castle in East Yorkshire.

But why choose to build at Sheriff Hutton? At first glance, it seems an odd decision, given the involvement of John Neville in Anglo-Scottish border governance and the concentration of many of his estates further to the north. However, given that the deer park accompanying the earlier castle was extended in 1334-35, and that John Neville gained a licence to hold a market at Sheriff Hutton in 1378, it is reasonable to propose that John and perhaps also his immediate ancestors had a long-term plan from the mid 14th century to develop the village as the centre of their estates (see Chapter 1). As was also noted in Chapter 1, Sheriff Hutton had several other advantages to recommend it, including being close to York and on an important transport route.[2]

Construction of the new castle started in or about April 1382, when John Neville was granted:

"License for John de Nevill of Raby, Knight, to enclose within a wall of stone and lime and crenellate a plot in his own ground at Shirefhoton, York and make a Castle there".[3]

The castle was built on an entirely new site, on a prominent ridge at the west end of the village, and there is no evidence, either structural, earthwork or documentary, to suggest that it incorporates the remains of any earlier buildings, although the existing layout of the village was much altered to accommodate it (see Chapter 1). There was, however, some landscaping undertaken to provide a level platform upon which to set the new building. Although there are much higher points in the landscape close by, for example, at Stittenham, the castle's end-ridge location greatly enhances its visual impact for miles around – it can clearly been seen from Terrington and Stittenham to the north-east, it stands out against the Vale of York beyond, and in winter it can be seen from just outside Strensall to the south and Flaxton to the south-east (see for example plate 48). The castle is also a prominent landscape feature when viewed from the vicinity of Easingwold and Crayke to the north.

Fig. 7/1: Aerial view of the castle, showing its location at the west end of the ridge, taken June 1991 (Aeroscene Ltd, AJC 260/24).

As has been noted above, the castle ruins still form a constant focal point from within the park and it quite possible that its location was chosen partly with this in mind. When complete, and viewed from within the 'forest setting' of the deer park during a hunt, the castle must have looked not unlike some of the illustrations of the Duc de Berry's castles illustrated in his *Tres Riches Heures*[4] (see plate 47). The view looking outwards from the upper parts of the castle is equally spectacular and on a clear day, three great Yorkshire icons, York Minster, Penhill in Wensleydale and the Drax power station, can all be seen.

The construction of the castle was obviously a major undertaking, requiring the provision, organisation and accommodation of vast amounts of labour and material. The design of the building would have been under the overall control of a master mason but as yet, no such official has been identified. It has been suggested that it might have been John de Hyndeley, or perhaps even John Lewyn who was already engaged at Bolton castle in Wensleydale,[5] but to date no firm documentary evidence has been produced; one possible agreement between Hyndeley and John Neville proved to be erroneous.[6]

Fig. 7/2: Construction work in progress, based on medieval illustrations.

It has been estimated that the remains of the north-east tower alone incorporate about 1,400 tons of stone.[7] As there is approximately only one third of this tower left, one might estimate that the completed structure contained c.3,000 tons of stone. If this amount is multiplied by four, for the main towers plus the other parts of the castle which are known once to have existed (see below), then a very approximate estimate of about 25,000 to 30,000 tons of stone is reached. Geologists who have examined the surviving structure have identified that the majority of the building stone used in the castle is an iron-rich oolitic limestone rubble, whilst the quoins, window and door surrounds are of a grey to brown medium-grained sandstone, frequently iron rich, thus giving it a 'rusty' appearance (see plates 15 and 46).[8] The most likely source for both these types of stone are the quarries at Mowthorpe, near Terrington, some 2 miles to the north-east of Sheriff Hutton; this concurs with the statement made by John Leland in 1534, that "the Stone that the Castel was buildid with was fetchid from a Quarre at Terington a 2. miles of."[9]

The main area of quarrying at Mowthorpe covers an area at least 1km long by 500m wide and over 10m deep, indicating that sufficient rock was removed to build the castle and to supply other structures (such as the Castle Howard estate wall) into the 19th century.[10] It is hoped that ongoing geological and archaeological survey work at Mowthorpe and the surrounding area will identify the remains of any activity associated with the quarrying and construction work, such as workers' accommodation, stone grading and sorting areas, and ancillary buildings such as smithies.

If Leland and the geologists are right, and the stone was quarried at Mowthorpe, then how did it reach the castle? In the 19th century, one story had it that the stone was passed from hand to hand along a human chain.[11] If one stands at Mowthorpe, and looks towards the ridge upon which Sheriff Hutton stands, the majority of the area between the two settlements is formed by an almost featureless flat-bottomed valley, once occupied by a post-glacial lake,[12] and an obvious transport route. Despite extensive drainage works in the 19th century, the valley is still prone to flooding in the winter and has done so at least once since 2000.[13] This flooding may be significant, as there is a long standing local legend that the stone was punted across a flooded lake to the castle using rafts, and like many local legends, it may well contain an element of truth. There are even suggestions, and some circumstantial evidence, for an artificial waterway of some kind running from the quarries towards the castle, which was possibly re-used at a later date as mill race.[14] Yet another local legend, current during the 1920s, says that the stone was dragged on sleds across the low-lying marsh from Terrington during the winter,[15] and sleds were certainly used to move heavy materials from York to Sheriff Hutton during repairs to the castle in 1537.[16] There are also possibilities of an overland route, as a well-graded and constructed trackway crosses the line of the Bulmer Beck opposite the quarries, and then winds its way up towards Stittenham. Although sometimes suggested as part of the line of the Roman road of Braygate, the gradient of this track would make it equally suitable for use by quarry carts. As with the quarries themselves, it is hoped that ongoing archaeological survey work in this area will provide more information in future years.

Once the stone, timber, lead, glass, slates and other materials had been assembled at the castle, construction work would have progressed on a seasonal basis. The recent archaeological survey of the north-east tower undertaken during consolidation and repair work identified a number of clear building breaks on several of the elevations.[17] At a lower level, these breaks are marked by a change in the colour of the sandstone used for the corner quoins, and they also occur at the same height on several of the other towers. Higher up, the building breaks are spaced at vertical intervals of between 2.5m and 3m; they are stepped across the elevation, rather than running level, and in some cases their positions may be marked at the corners by the use of a brown sandstone quoin. In addition, series of regularly spaced 'putlog' (scaffolding) holes have been recorded in some of the elevations, which probably relate to several different episodes of construction and/or repair. On the north elevation, putlog holes rise to 13m above ground level and then appear to stop, but on the west elevation they begin at this height, and have occasional larger blocked recesses set at the same level as the building breaks, perhaps representing former crane positions or beams to support larger scaffold platforms.

One piece of constructional evidence notably lacking at Sheriff Hutton are masons' marks. When any major stone structure such as a castle was being built, numerous masons would be needed to dress and prepare the different types and shapes of stone needed in its construction. It is perhaps best to imagine these masons working either individually or in groups, stockpiling finished stones which then went to the labourers working on the building. A clerk of works would have recorded who had produced which pieces of stonework and how many, and each mason or perhaps group of masons identified his/their stone using a unique mark. These marks vary from the very simple (e.g. crosses) to the more complex (e.g. interlocked triangles) and, as well as performing a practical function, they may also reflect the wish of the mason to leave a record of his presence on the building. In castles where the stones were regularly cut, masons' marks can be very common; for example, at Harewood castle in West Yorkshire, hundreds of examples of about 12 different marks have been recorded, and it is clear that some masons produced walling stone whilst others were responsible for the more complex mouldings around windows.[18] However, Sheriff Hutton is primarily a castle built of rubble, and so surviving masons' marks are very few and far between. To date, only four have been identified, including a complex 'daisy' mark noted on a piece of the machicolations which fell off the south-east tower in December 1982, and much simpler triangular marks which can be seen on some of the corner quoins; the latter are similar to ones noted in the choir of York Minster (c.1400), at Bolton castle (1378-96) and also in the tower of Sheriff Hutton church.

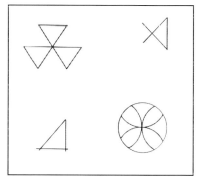

Fig. 7/4: Masons' marks recorded at Sheriff Hutton castle.

Fig. 7/3: Stone masons at work, based on a medieval illustration.

We do not know how long the castle took to build, but a reasonable estimate might be 20 years. Bolton castle, a similar structure in many ways, took 18 years to complete, and the first reference to the stone castle at Sheriff Hutton occurs in 1398.[19] Ralph Neville is often given credit for the construction[20] which is not unreasonable, as John Neville died in 1388 and so Ralph must have overseen more than half of the work. It is possible that the effects of John's death can still be discerned in the castle ruins, in the south-east corner. At first glance, the castle appears to have had a relatively symmetrical and regular layout, but a closer examination of its plan reveals that there are several discrepancies (see figure 7/6). The north-east, north-west and south-west towers, and the ranges that once connected them, all have a reasonably regular plan. However, the south-east tower, and the adjacent gatehouse, are on a slightly different orientation and there is also a marked change in alignment in the centre of the south wall, meaning that entire south range has a shallow-V plan; both Todd and Sharp recorded a similar shallow-V plan to the wall between the porter's lodge and the north-east tower.[21] The walls of the south-east tower are also thinner than the other towers, and this is the only tower to be buttressed (see plate 45). The fabric of the gatehouse shows that it was originally meant to be recessed, but it was then brought forward in a later phase.

It might reasonably be suggested that these changes result from a hiatus in work following the death of John Neville, at which point the construction of the south-east tower and gatehouse were well underway, and the recommencement of work by Ralph Neville, with a different set of demands and expectations of a (possibly different) master mason.[22] Work at other castles is increasingly beginning to recognise that apparently different phases of construction may relate to changes in design during the original or a protracted building programme, rather than widely separated re-buildings or alterations.[23] It is likely that detailed archaeological recording on the other towers as part of future consolidation works will reveal a yet more complex sequence of events. Finally, it should be remembered that when viewed from eye level, as it would have been by those living in and around it during the 15th century, the castle has a relatively symmetrical and regular construction. What we now perceive as irregularities worthy of comment may have been of no consequence whatsoever to the castle's original inhabitants.

The Completed Castle

The surviving ruins at Sheriff Hutton, impressive as they may be, represent only a small fragment of the original structure. In c.1400, the completed castle would have resembled other late 14th century residences in the region such as Bolton castle or Wressle castle. Such buildings are generally described as 'palace-fortresses' – they were built as grand residences for great magnates who wished to have a palatial home, albeit it one with all the latest military trappings, and they are perhaps best thought of as secure rather than overtly defensive places. However, although there are broad similarities between Sheriff Hutton, Bolton, Wressle and other contemporary residences in Yorkshire, each site has its own characteristics, reflecting the differing status, outlook and aspirations of those who lived in them.

Using a combination of the archaeological, structural and documentary evidence, and inevitably some comparison with other sites, a brief description of the castle as it may have appeared during the later Middle Ages can be given. This is inevitably a generalised picture, and based partly on 16th century documents, which make references to elements that may not all have been present in the late medieval building. However, it provides some idea as to the original scope and grandeur of the site, and brings some colour to the existing gaunt ruins.

The Outer Court

It is important to remember that the castle and its immediate surroundings were originally formed by three separate areas, described in the 16th century as wards or courts; an outer or base court, a middle court, and an inner court (see figure 7/6). The outer or base court is the area bounded by double canals to the south, the rear of those properties fronting the south side of Main Street to the north, and to the west by Finkle Street (see figure 8/2). The eastern extent of the outer court is less certain, but it probably coincided with the west side of the long plot which runs south from the south-west corner of the green, more or less along the existing north-south footpath to the east of Castle Farm. This outer court is also known in the documents as the 'castle garth', and it is named as 'Castle Yard' on the 1765 map.[24]

It is as yet uncertain what the outer court wall looked like, or precisely what it was built of, but a possible small section of it was seen during drainage work in 2003 behind Main Street.[25] At this point it was relatively narrow and to the north of the castle it evidently retained the back of the properties forming the south side of Main Street. A spread of heavy rubble and gravel seen in the garden of Stile House in 1999 might also represent the foundations for the now robbed away wall on the east side of the outer court.[26] The outer court wall may have been studded with towers, and a description made in 1839 suggests that the remains of one survived in the north-west corner of the outer court.[27]

Fig. 7/5: Possible location of the entrance into the outer court from the market place, looking east.

The main formal entrance into the outer court appears to have been at the north-east corner, off the west side of the market place, in approximately the same position as an existing footpath, next to Stile House. It is likely that there would have been a second entrance into the outer court, although its location is as yet uncertain. The 1765 plan[28] shows a gap in the houses fronting onto Main Street in approximately the same position as the modern track approaching Castle Farm, although no track is shown here in the 18th century. An approach from this direction could have led to a small passage shown in 1618 at the east end of the middle court's north range, named as 'the incoming to the back court with horse or wain',[29] but it is not clear whether this is an old feature or one forming part of the conversion of this part of the castle proposed at the time (see Chapter 15). An 1824 engraving by Todd appears to depict a small gatehouse with an arched entrance on the extreme left side,[30] but the perspective of the engraving is such that this building, whatever it was, may have lain on either Main Street or Finkle Street.

It is assumed that there was some kind of gatehouse structure marking the main entrance into the outer court from the market place. A public footpath once ran south-west from this point towards Castle Farm, and its line survives as a slight bank ('j' on figure 8/2); the current path deviates slightly from the original line. This bank almost certainly marks the course of a much more substantial paved track or causeway, which survived as late as 1839, when Samuel Sharp noted that "The present occupier pulled up a few years ago a well-formed pavement of cobble stones leading precisely to the centre between where the two extreme towers [of the middle court] stood".[31]

Writing in 1534, Leland stated that the base or outer court contained 'Houses of Office afore the Entering of the Castelle'.[32] A slightly earlier survey of 1525 had been more explicit, referring to a brewhouse and horsemills as well as 'stables, barns, garners and offices'.[33] Some of these structures can be traced right through to the end of the 16th century. Both the horsemill and the brewhouse received extensive overhauls in 1537 in anticipation of the Duke of Norfolk's arrival. Payments were made to 'the sledmen of yorke' William Plomton and William Wells for the carriage of ''one payre great myllestones to grynd whete [wheat]'' by sled from York to Sheriff Hutton; some idea of the weight of the millstones can be gauged from the 24 oxen required for their carriage.[34] A 'gret copp kettyll' [great copper kettle] was installed in the brewhouse and other necessary equipment purchased, such as the 'cooler' and 'a coole Rake'. A new slaughterhouse was also built in the outer court at the same time.[35]

One of the barns noted in 1525 and 1537 in the outer court must have been a substantial stone and timber-framed building, if the evidence of depositions made to an inquisition held in 1598 into the state of the castle and park is correct.[36] It was usually described as the 'greate barne' or 'greate laithe' which had stone walls 14 feet high. The barn was roofed with stone slates and had 'two greate doors and two Little ones'. It had been dismantled before 1595 and the salvaged elements employed for diverse other uses. The slates and three 'great Beames' of timber, perhaps tie-beams from roof trusses, had been carried to the 'brickhouse' at the complex now known as the King's Manor in York and used there. Some of the other timber had been temporarily stored in one of the castle's stables and then "imployed about building of a Chamber in A house where John Broughe now dwelleth"; the same man also apparently burnt 'some shorte spars' as firewood. Similarly, other barn timber was sold to William Roe to make a home whilst yet other parts went into the making of wains or large carts. Some was however of no use, 'by reason of the many mortices' that it contained, and this might also have found its way onto John Broughe's fire.

At around the same time as the barn was being dismantled, the 'great Copper pann' and other equipment installed in the brewhouse was being moved to the King's Manor in York. The stone of one of the porches of the 'greate stable' had also been taken down.[37] This 'greate stable' appears to have been located in the outer court, and to have been in addition to another stable in the middle court (see below). The stone porches suggest a building not unlike the large barns with porches built on West Riding farmsteads in the late 16th and early 17th centuries, although projecting porches had been a feature of larger agricultural buildings since the Middle Ages.

The precise locations of many of these buildings in the outer court are not known, and there are few clues in the surviving earthworks (see figure 8/2). However, perhaps some of the barns and yards lay outside the north-east corner of the middle court, where walls and cobbled surfaces have been revealed by recent drainage work.[38] Other buildings may have been located further to the east, nearer the market place gatehouse, either side of the paved causeway. Still others may have been built against the north wall of the inner court's kitchen range (perhaps the brewhouse and slaughterhouse?) where some slight earthworks might represent building platforms. It is almost certain that there were none of these structures to the south of the castle, as this area seems to have been reserved for the castle gardens (see Chapter 8).

The Middle Court

After passing through the outer court, with its stable, barns, bakehouse and brewhouse etc., one would have arrived at the middle court. The middle court was formerly about 60 metres or 180 feet square, covering an area approximately twice the size of the late Victorian brick farm buildings of Castle Farm which have recently been converted to residential accommodation. The above-ground structures of the middle court have been almost entirely swept away, apart from a low buttressed section of the south wall and a much altered north-west corner, and we are again reliant on earlier documents, historians and writers to gain an idea of its appearance.

When Leland visited in 1534, he stated of the middle court:

> *"I markid yn the fore Front of the first Area of the Castelle self 3. great and high Toures, of the which the Gate House was the Midle".*[39]

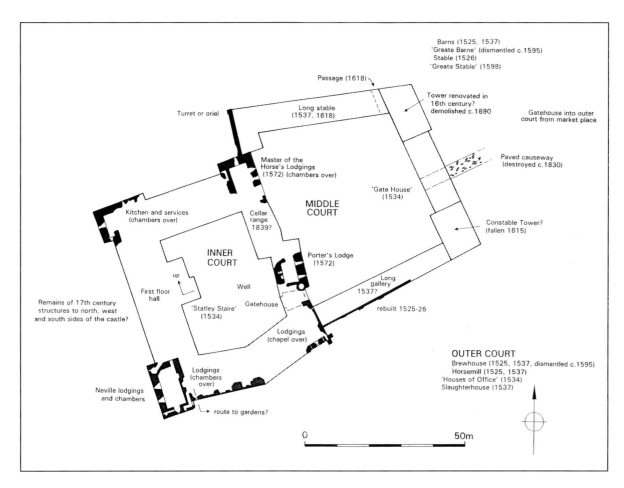

Fig. 7/6: Schematic reconstruction of the inner and middle courts (after Emery 1996, Dennison 1998a, Field Archaeology Specialists 2003).

The gatehouse may have resembled a grander and larger, but perhaps more austere, version of the Neville gatehouse still surviving at Raby castle.[40] The stump of one of the towers flanking the gatehouse survived into the late 19th century. It was drawn by the architect Samuel Sharp, who depicts similar detailing to the windows to those which survive within the inner court today (see below). This suggests that the middle court was contemporary with the inner court, and not a later addition, although Sharp noted that some of the windows in the tower had flat double-centred brick arches of 16th century appearance.[41] The 1765 plan shows Sharp's tower breaking forward slightly from the rest of the east side of the middle court, and this alignment was uncovered during a recent archaeological watching brief.[42] What little that remained of the tower appeared to be faced with more regularly cut stone than that surviving in the four towers of the middle court, suggesting a greater element of display towards the direction from which the castle was approached.

The tower and the surviving part of the north range of the middle court which Sharp drew in 1839 were used as the meeting place for the manorial court for many years, but by the time that they were photographed in c.1889, both had been largely converted to housing. Prior to being used as a courthouse, the north range had consisted of the 'longh stable' and is named as such on a drawing of 1618.[43] This 'long stable' may have been one of two such named structures built as part of the 1537 works. These were apparently timber-framed although the watching brief carried out in 2003 recorded stone walls beneath the brick walls of the existing farm range that could easily have supported a single-storey stone building; a large contemporary gutter or drain was also observed running along the south side of the 'long stable'.[44]

Fig. 7/7: View of the castle farmhouse c.1889 showing the remains of the tower in north-east corner of the middle court (Source: Sheriff Hutton WI 1975).

Fig. 7/8:Remains of south wall of the middle court, rebuilt c.1525.

The Inner Court

From the middle court there was access into the heart of the castle, the inner court, now represented by the four ruined towers which dominate the skyline of the village (see plate 15). Like the middle court, the inner court was approximately 60m or 180 feet square. Once again, using Leland's 1534 description as a guide:

> *"In the secunde Area ther be a 5. or 6. Toures, and the statley Staire up to the Haul is very Magnificent, and so is the Haul it self, and al the residew of the House: in so much that I saw no House in the North so like a Princely Logginges".*[45]

The inner court was entered through a gatehouse located towards the south end of the eastern range (see plate 45). The outer wall of this gatehouse still stands, although the tall entrance arch is now somewhat truncated by the raised ground level beneath it (see figure 7/14 below). In 1824, Todd depicted machicolations (overhanging openings along the top of a wall through which projections can be dropped) on the upper part of the gatehouse and, whilst it is possible that such structures were once present, there is much about the engraving to doubt its accuracy;[46] they were not mentioned by Sharp in 1839.[47] If there ever were any machicolations surmounting the gatehouse, their presence may well have drawn the visitor's eye upwards to the heraldic achievements of Ralph Neville displayed above the arched entrance. There are four escutcheons of carved stone over the gate, mounted in a panel, in a row, with surrounding blocks, which appear to make the panel replaceable (see figure 7/14 and plate 46). It is therefore impossible to date the completion of the castle from these arms.[48] These escutcheons are, from left to right:

- (gules) a saltire (argent) - that is the plain saltire (diagonal cross) of the Neville family – surrounded by a plain garter;
- the same, although there are small dimension changes and there might be the remnants of a bell below the garter;
- a saltire on the dexter (right) side with France and England quarterly on the sinister (left) side ('Neville impaling France and England quarterly'), surrounded by a twisted wreath;
- the saltire with what might be a defaced charge on the dexter lower branch of the saltire, surrounded by a twisted wreath.

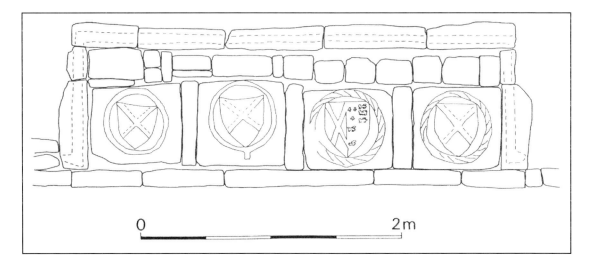

Fig. 7/9: Drawing of heraldic frieze over the inner court gatehouse (Source: Dennison 1998a).

There have been a number of different explanations for these arms, but it is now generally agreed that the garters are no earlier than 1402 when Ralph Neville, Earl of Westmoreland, was granted the Order of the Garter, rather than relating to his father John's elevation to the same order in 1369. Unfortunately, the absence of differences (changes which distinguished different members of a family) leaves the interpretation unclear. The amount of packing stone around the arms suggests that they are either a later insertion, either together or individually, or that the space they fill may have been designed to take a somewhat different frieze.[49] Perhaps it was originally intended to fill the space with the achievements of John Neville, and after his death in 1388 it was adapted to contain those of Ralph.

In 1525, it was noted that 'The gate of the inner ward is worn and needs three tons of iron to mend it'.[50] This has been taken to suggest that the gatehouse was fitted with a portcullis, rising flush with the east side,[51] although the surviving structural evidence is slight. There certainly were the remains of a portcullis stored within the castle in 1598, when someone saw 'three peeces of olde pcullis in the storehowse' along with some 'olde arrows' sat forlornly on a chest.[52] Sixteenth century surveys also make sporadic references to pieces of ordnance stored around the castle, although to what extent they were used in anger is open to debate. In 1525 'six brass falcons with their carts, 10 score iron shots, 6 barrels of powder, a barrel of bowstrings, 6 coffins of bows and arrows, 21 hagbushes, 2 bullet moulds' were noted[53] but by 1598 any surviving ordnance had been removed by locals to the village blacksmith to be either cut up or re-worked into more useful items, such as agricultural tools and fittings for a nearby mill. No one could ever remember have fired any of it, apart from during a 'Lord of Misrule'.[54]

Passing through the gatehouse, one entered the courtyard of the inner court, which was probably cobbled or paved in some way. Here, one could glance up at the four massive corner towers, each approaching 100 feet (30m) in height. The sharp-eyed reader will have noted that Leland described five or six towers here in 1534, and that there are now only four. One of the missing towers can probably be accounted for by the gatehouse, which may well have risen to the same height as the corner towers. The sixth tower may have enclosed Leland's 'stately Staire' rising up to the hall, as suggested by Sharp in 1839 and endorsed by more recent studies.[55] If one remembers that there would have been connecting ranges running between these towers, the substantial nature of the inner court in its completed form becomes apparent. Perhaps the best impression of what the inner court at Sheriff Hutton once looked like can be gained by studying a bird's eye view of Wressle castle made in c.1600, which shows a similar arrangement.[56]

Drawing on a wide variety of sources and comparative evidence, it has most recently been suggested that the different elements of the inner court can be placed as follows[57] (see figure 7/6 above). The lodging chambers and great chamber of Ralph Neville and his family were located in and around the south-west tower. The south range had several different levels of lodgings, with more chambers on the upper floor and perhaps also the castle chapel at the east end of the same floor. The hall was located on the first floor of the west range, accessed via the external staircase tower which had so impressed Leland. The kitchens and service rooms were located in the north range, and perhaps also at the base of the north-west tower. The north-east and south-east tower both contained further lodgings, whilst the gatehouse in the east range had a porter's lodge on the north side. Like any other large and complex building, the spaces would have been adapted over time and changed function; excavation of the first floor of the north-east tower during the recent consolidation works revealed a series of substantial changes to the room here, denoting a change from a high status space to a lower status one.[58]

Fig. 7/10: Interior view of south-west tower, with views over deer park to the south.

Fig. 7/11: Interior view of north-west tower.

Only the north-east and south-west towers now have vaulted basements or cellars beneath them, although there was evidently once also a vaulted cellar range running beneath the north range and Sharp suggests that another was visible beneath the east range;[59] a doorway in the south wall of the north-east tower's cellar may once have lead into this now lost cellar range. Each tower contained four or five different floor levels, of which only the cellar and ground floors were vaulted, with timber floors to the upper levels. Each level within the towers was lit by one or two-light trefoil-headed windows. In terms of the distribution of features such as doorways, windows, fireplaces and garderobes, the towers were all quite different internally, reflecting their differing uses. Although the surviving remains suggest a relatively austere external appearance, it is also quite possible that there were subtle differences in the overall height or form of the towers, which also reflected their uses. For example, the south-west tower has large round-headed rear arches to the windows not seen elsewhere in the castle, probably reflecting its use by the Neville family as part of their lodgings and chambers, whilst the south-east tower has the only surviving machicolations on the castle and is the only tower to be buttressed (see plate 45). These buttresses may be explained by the thinner walls of the south-east tower, when compared to the other towers, but the machicolations might serve a less functional purpose, perhaps supporting a projection or parapet from which views could be obtained southwards over the park. It is probable that all of the towers were crenellated,[60] and perhaps also the connecting ranges too; the last surviving crenellations, on the south-west tower, were blown off by a lightning strike on April 16th 1927.[61] Each of the towers may well have risen to small corner turrets; one of the deposees at the 1598 inquisition, when describing where lead had been taken from, referred to the 'Coverings of seaven Little towers which was taken away', while another mentioned four or five towers or turrets.[62] Indeed, the whole roof line of the castle may have been far more articulated than we now imagine, as evidenced by the great leaded lantern which was removed from the roof of the hall by persons unknown in the 1590s.[63]

Fig. 7/12: Interior view of the south-east tower, with views over the deer park to the south.

Fig. 7/13: Garderobe in the south range of the inner court, showing window and chute.

The connecting ranges between the towers would have been similarly complex, with rooms and spaces spread over several different levels, some connected by spiral staircases and others by stairs rising within the walls. Studies of better preserved castles, such as Bolton or Harewood, have revealed complex patterns of movement or circulation within the structure, with easy access to some parts but much more restricted and convoluted routes to others. The whole three court castle complex at Sheriff Hutton would have unfolded like a series of boxes or spaces in front of the visitor, family member or servant. How far you progressed into these spaces would have depended on who you were, what time of day it was, and/or what position you held within the household. The rooms within the ranges of the inner court may well have been divisible into suites, so that Ralph Neville and his wife could maintain separate households, and these households themselves may have been even further sub-divided, with some areas of the castle perhaps accessible only to those personally attending upon the lord himself.

Fig. 7/15: Interior view of the north-east tower, after consolidation.

Fig. 7/14: Exterior view of the gatehouse leading into the inner court.

As yet we have no idea as to the exact size of the Neville household at Sheriff Hutton, but documents dating from a century later relating to Henry Fitzroy's residence provide an idea of just how many people made up the 'castle community' living and working in and around the building. In the 16th century the staff of the castle numbered about 100[64] and in 1526 Henry Fitzroy's retinue was 140 people, creating a total population of about 240 when he was in residence.[65] These numbers of people, accompanied by their horses and equipment, coupled with the normal business of an administrative centre carried out at the castle, illustrate just what an impact the complex would have had on Sheriff Hutton. Clearly the facilities needed to cope with such numbers were vast. Consider just one part, the kitchens. The main kitchen alone must have been on a par with the magnificent two-storey kitchen surviving at Raby castle; in 1598, it was described as the 'greate kitching' and 'one Copper pann standing in a ffurnace with Leade about' was taken from it to the lodge in the park.[66] The kitchen would have been provided with numerous related departments, some of which are named in Henry Fitzroy's household accounts; these include the pantry, buttery, scullery, napery, spicery, wafery, saucery, poultry, boiling house and wine cellars, together with numerous staff such as carvers and cup bearers who fulfilled important ceremonial functions at mealtimes.[67] Catering on such a scale probably meant that the kitchen was almost always active when the lord was in residence, and the kitchen fires, coupled with the chimneys from the many other fireplaces distributed throughout the building, must have produced enough smoke to give the castle the appearance of a small factory during the winter.

Perhaps the most difficult aspect of the castle's appearance to re-create is the internal decoration. Many of the rooms would undoubtedly have been richly decorated, using wall paintings, tapestries, wall panelling and other fitted furniture. For example, one item in Ralph Neville's (d.1425) will notes "Item I give … to my son, Richard Nevill, 2 chargers, 12 plates and a shield with an ewer, (all of) silver and an arras bed with tapestries divided into colours of red, green and white which (..) hanging in the great room inside the Castle of Sherifhoton …".[68] A wall painting of unknown date apparently survived in one of the towers as late as the early 18th century, but it had gone by the time that Todd went to look for it in 1823, all apart from "a trifling scroll in the arch of one of the widows".[69] There was also much panelling surviving in the upper rooms of the castle in the late 16th and early 17th centuries, some of which was removed to Arthur Ingram's new lodge in the park (see Chapter 15). Decoration may not have been restricted to the interior of the castle, and it has been proposed that the entire exterior of the building was rendered and whitewashed.[70] Whilst there is currently no structural, documentary or archaeological evidence to support this theory, it is an exciting suggestion; imagine the effect of sunlight striking a building the size of Sheriff Hutton castle that was painted almost entirely white.

The Castle during the 15th and 16th Centuries

As has been mentioned in Chapter 1, following Ralph Neville's death in 1425, the castle appears to have been occupied by his second wife Joan Beaufort until her death in 1440. It then remained with the younger branch of the Neville family until Richard Neville, Earl of Warwick, was killed at the Battle of Barnet in 1471. Thereafter, his estates were divided by Edward IV and Sheriff Hutton passed to Richard, Duke of Gloucester (the future Richard III). After acceding to the throne, in the second year of his reign (1484), Richard III created a Council to run the north of England and a household in which its members could live, and during his reign they were present at least once at Sheriff Hutton.

Following Richard III's death at the Battle of Bosworth in 1485, Sheriff Hutton seems to have become the administrative centre for much of the amalgamated Neville and York estates in central and east Yorkshire, and it remained an important venue for the Council of the North.[71] Monies continued to be spent on its upkeep and repair, and in 1502 and 1504 the Earl of Surrey received £46 from the exchequer towards the cost of repairing the castle.[72]

However, despite evidence such as the above, the maintenance of the castle was a huge undertaking and, unless a lord and large household were present all the time, parts evidently started to decay. A survey undertaken in 1525 prior to the arrival of Henry Fitzroy, Duke of Richmond revealed significant defects:

> "*View of the Castle at Sheriff Hutton taken by Tho. Magnus, Sir George Lawson and John Uvedaile.*
>
> *The lead on the roofs is so worn that three of the old webs will scarcely make one; at least 16 fowder will be required to repair it. It is thought the timber is sufficient if any faults are found. There is enough to repair them. The corbels, water tables, stone*

spouts and other necessaries of masonry, esp. the crests and loops must be newly set up and mended with lime and sand. Most of the chimneys and draughts require mending for they are very noisome when occupied. There are three wards: the inner one contains the hall, kitchen, lodgings for the Lord, chapel, se ... r, buttery, pantry, and offices. The walls and towers are strong and high but must be mended with lime and sand. Great part of the mantlewall of the middleward towards the park is broken down, 21 yards long, 6 yards high and 7 qrs in breadth. The north wall also requires mending for 14 yds in length and to be increased 2½ yds in height. Another part is also defective, 36 yrds long by 6 qrs high. There is a well of fair water in the inner ward, and ponds for baking and brewing, near the walls outside. The bakehouse, very good, is within the inner ward. The brewhouse and horsemills both good, are in the outer ward or base court with stables, barns, garners and offices. The base court is all open, the walls decayed and the gates gone. The gate of the inner ward is worn and needs three tons of iron to mend it. Of ordnance there is 6 brass falcons with their carts, 10 score iron shots, 6 barrels of powder, a barrel of bowstrings, 6 coffins of bows and arrows, 21 hagbushes, 2 bullet moulds".[73]

In the Duke's household accounts, covering the period from 12th June 1525 to 31st March 1526, there is an entry of £321 19s. 10¾d. for 'repairs at Sherefhooton'.[74] Some evidence of these repairs can be seen in the surviving castle structure. The south wall of the middle court, described as 'broken down' in 1525, was rebuilt using coursed squared stone unlike that seen elsewhere in the castle (see figure 7/8) and the new construction clearly butts the south-east tower. It is probable that those fireplaces with tile or brick backs visible in the north-west tower were also inserted during the same period.

In 1537, prior to the arrival of Thomas Howard, Duke of Norfolk, the castle needed another extensive overhaul. Henry VIII had written to Sir George Lawson, then Receiver of the Lordship, to put the castle in order.[75] However, Lawson had only limited money at his disposal and he wrote to Cromwell on the 18th of April that the "reparations of Shirefhoton Castle ... will amount to a goodly sum".[76] He had £180 surplus from his accounts for the Lordship of Sheriff Hutton[77] - still devoted to the upkeep of the Citadel of Berwick[78] - and during the first six months of 1537 he spent £196 2s. 8d. on a general overhaul.[79] The roofs were repaired, numerous windows mended and '54 cartloads of elder bushes and earth were removed from the inner court'.[80] Sir Bartholomew Stable, a priest and Chaplain who was probably of a local family, was the Clerk of Works.[81] Timber was brought from the park to rebuild many of the service buildings, such as barns, stables and bakehouse, and a new slaughterhouse was built (see Chapter 11). It is also possible that a long gallery was built in the castle at this time, perhaps at an upper level in the south range or along the south side of the middle court.[82] Towards the end of the repairs to the castle, preparations were made for the arrival of Henry VIII himself. Extra timber was brought from Marton woods[83] and extra cupboards and storage were built for his wardrobe,[84] but in the end the king did not come.

As part of his role in overseeing the dissolution of the monasteries in the north, Norfolk was involved in the transfer of former monastic goods - directly to London if convenient, to Sheriff Hutton if not.[85] At Bridlington Priory he admired the enormous lead roof of the barn and proposed that it should be sent to London by coaster.[86] His successor, Bishop Tunstall and his council requested that sufficient lead be left in the north to repair the roofs of Pontefract and Sheriff Hutton castles and their other houses.[87] But by then it was approaching the end of the season and the roads were impassable, so Richard Bellycys, the man responsible for dismantling Bridlington Priory, asked for permission to delay their movement until the following spring.[88] His request was granted and now only legend says that Sheriff Hutton castle was roofed with the lead from Bridlington Priory.[89]

Following Norfolk's departure in 1547, the castle seems to have been occupied only sporadically by the Council of the North, as they preferred to use the King's Manor in York which had been at their disposal since 1538.[90] The castle continued in use mainly as a prison, a role it had fulfilled since at least the 1530s. During the 'Wakefield Plot' of 1541,[91] although the terms of imprisonment do not appear to have been long, condition were most definitely severe, with 'jeyrons' (irons) being made to hold the prisoners; these included the 'traitors' William Lee and Sir William Grene, Sir Robert Holdynq and Sir Robert Barton, who were held from 20th April to 9th May and 16th April to 9th May respectively.[92]

The Decline and Fall of the Castle

What turned out to be the last major overhaul of the castle began in the 1570s, following the appointment of Henry Hastings, 3rd Earl of Huntingdon, to the post of President of the Council of the North in 1572 (see figure 11/5). A full survey of the castle was undertaken in 1572.[93] A further survey, made in December of the same year by carpenter John Jameson and plumber Richard Peckitt, noted that the porter's lodge and its two adjacent towers "one at the north end called the Master of the Horses lodging and thother at the southe end" needed major repair. The towers needed their roofs repaired and the porter's lodge needed almost complete rebuilding of its floors, roof and battlements, at an estimated cost of £69 10s. The rest of the castle was "in some decay everywheare namely of the leade, which is sore worne with long continuance and so thynne that it must neded be all new casten, or the moste part thereof", which would seem to be further evidence that Bridlington Priory barn roof went elsewhere. However, an 'expert survey' would have required "a great tyme and like consideration by the advice of skillful workmen" (when doesn't it?) and the commissioners (William Fairfax, Sheriff of Yorkshire, and others) "deferred to travell about the views of the same" without further instructions.[94]

Despite this, more than £700 was apparently spent on repairs between 1573 and 1575 according to the later testimony of Richard Hebborne, the then Clerk of Works, when he requested payment for his three summer's work.[95] He also testified that no more was spent in the following 20 years.[96] Others testified that lead was removed from the roof but no-one could say whether it was for sale or for the repair of the King's Manor.[97] Possibly a roof was not thought necessary as the castle was being used mainly as a gaol for the wives of recusant (Catholic) gentlemen,[98] Mrs Babthorpe of Osgodby, Hemingbrough, among them; in 1592 she later wrote a description of her time there.[99]

It is not clear to what extent Huntingdon had ever been resident at Sheriff Hutton, although a substantial amount of his goods remained at the castle at the time of his death in 1595,[100] and his wife went to some expense to build a bridge over the double canals to the south of the castle (see Chapter 8). There is circumstantial evidence to suggest that the earl was staying at a lodge in the park rather than the castle itself in his later years, whilst the 1598 depositions indicate that the stripping out of the fixtures and fittings of the castle's high status chambers was well underway by his death,[101] although one was still known as 'my Lo: of Huntingdon's chamber' in 1617.[102] What might have been one of Huntingdon's final sights of Sheriff Hutton was described by John Flood in 1598;

"And he saith that the said Erle Comyng to the said castle in a Rainy Day And seeing the said house at Sheriff hutton to be in decay in dives places Comanded the said Richard Pollerd to repayre it. And the said Erle did then appoint the said Richard Pollerd to take c-taine pcells of Leade of the said house in c-taine places thereof and commanded The same to be brought to yorke to be solde And the mony be distributed towardes the chardge of Repayringe of the said house ..".[103]

Although the grammar may now sound peculiar, the image conjured up of the earl standing in the pouring rain before the decaying hulk of the castle, watching water stream in through holes in the roof, is still a memorable one. By the end of the 16th century, the castle was clearly going to need more than patching to the roof to remain in use as a grand residence.

However, it is probably wrong to think of the preceding century as being one of alternating neglect and repair of the castle. The documents that survive refer only to the major overhauls and there are few records for the small-scale yearly or even monthly maintenance works that were required to keep the building in good order. It is probably these expenses, rather than the major outlays, which were the deciding factor in the decline of the castle. Sheriff Hutton was a long way from the royal court in London, with much more convenient residences available throughout the south-east and the midlands, and people's ideas of what constituted fashionable accommodation had changed. The point was reached in about 1600 when no-one was interested in spending money on the castle anymore.

The demolition of the structure proper, as opposed to the removal of fixtures and fittings, does not appear to have commenced until the early 17th century. In 1613 Thomas Lumsden, Gentleman of the Privy Chamber, was granted a range of offices at Sheriff Hutton, including Constable of the Castle.[104] In that office in 1615 he received letters from one William Clarke, who tenanted rooms in the castle, complaining of people stealing the lead and mentioning that the 'Constable Tower' had fallen.[105] The castle was henceforth treated as irreparable and in 1618 it was granted to Lumsden in terms which make it clear that it was to be treated as a source of materials:

June 1618
"Grant to Thomas Lumsden, ..., of the ruinous castle of Sheriff Hutton and the castle garth and three or four acres of ground adjoining with benefit of waste and spoils, since 30 Elizabeth."[106]

August 1618, Letters Patent James I to Thomas Lumsden
"grant of the Castle of Sheriffe Hutton alias Sherrie Hutton (in ruins) with stone, iron, timber, lead &c., the castle garth, orchards, fishponds and all other appurtenances by fealty only with all profits of all wastes since 30 Elizabeth I."[107]

The following year, Lumsden received proposals for altering the gatehouse and flanking towers of the middle court into a house 'with such addission as is needfull and convenient for a gentleman to dwell in' from Barnard Dinninghof, a noted glass painter and architect[108] (see Chapter 15). Whether it was to pay for this work or because he was already in debt, seven days later Lumsden mortgaged his ownership of the castle to William Ferrers of London.[109] It is unlikely that Lumsden ever had the alterations carried out as he was frequently in debt and progressively sold or mortgaged each of his offices at Sheriff Hutton.[110] William Ferrers was Sir Arthur Ingram's father-in-law and it is possible that Ingram intended all along to obtain the castle[111] and use it as a source of building materials for his new lodge in the park[112]

114

(see Chapter 15). The account book of John Mattison, Ingram's steward at York, who supervised the building of the lodge, records the transportation of many loads of stone, timber, lead and fittings from the castle[113] and on one occasion Ingram sent the instruction to "Take Ventris and a mason to the castle and see what mantle trees be there …".[114] The massive fireplace arch in the lodge's basement kitchen (now Sheriff Hutton Hall) may be one from the castle and much of the panelling has been trimmed from a size intended for other rooms leading to suggestions that it may originate there as well.[115]

In 1622, Lumsden objected to the 'ruination' of a tower which he had been preserving as a prison; it had been stripped of "lead, timber, casements, iron bars, doors, bolts, hinges and hooks".[116] He succeeded in obtaining £53 compensation for the theft of "383 yards of wainscot, 10 doors and 44 cwt of lead" but that same year he had to concede his offices to Ingram.[117] There were subsequent complaints of the ruinous state of the castle from its tenants[118] and the description accompanying Nordens' 1624 survey noted:

> "*It appeareth that there was and yet is the case of a stately Castle, the inward materials transported and the walls ruined, situate as it seemeth upon a natural but not much advanced grounde … The bowels of this worthy pyle and defensive house are rent and torn and the naked carcase … aliened in fee … to … Mr Lumsden*".[119]

However, some parts of the castle clearly survived, as it had tenants throughout the 17th century,[120] and it was described as an armoury for 'foot arms' for the Wapentake of Bulmer in 1633.[121] In 1639 when Sir Thomas Ingram and his wife of two years,[122] Frances Belasyse, had a new stable block and brewhouse built adjacent to the lodge in the park, some 940 loads of 'squared rubble' were taken from the castle[123] (see Chapter 15). As well as materials being taken from the castle to the lodge, even a cursory examination of Sheriff Hutton village shows that many of the older houses are also built from castle stone.[124] It is also possible that some of the earthworks and stone footings attached to or immediately adjacent to the north, west and south walls of the castle represent the remains of 17th century re-use. Although some foundations just to the west of the west range have been thought to be the remains of a projecting bay possibly supporting a 16th century addition to the hall,[125] their insubstantial nature suggests that they were in fact lean-to structures and minor agricultural buildings, perhaps dating to the 17th century or later.

In 1662, Marmaduke Rawdon and his companions, who were lodging in the village, recorded that the castle was roofless and 'mined' (presumably undermined with the best stone having been purloined), and placed the blame on one 'Lumbsdell'.[126] In 1690, Alderman Thompson of York gathered his tenants and broke open the castle gate for no recorded reason, but to the consternation of the steward, John Roades.[127] Given all that had been taken from the castle in the preceding 100 years, it seems amazing that there was enough left to break into.

The Later History of the Castle

From the early 18th century, the castle began to attract antiquaries, artists and much later photographers, and its importance passed from being a grand residence to a picturesque ruin. The earliest surviving, authenticated, picture of Sheriff Hutton castle was drawn in 1715 by Francis Place, who was then touring Yorkshire.[128] His picture shows an interior view of the south-east tower and the gatehouse, with large barrel vaults which are now gone. Samuel Buck visited in 1719 or 1721 in the company of John Warburton and, although his sketchbook shows a faint, distant view,[129] much as the castle appears today, the engraving which he later published shows the castle nearly intact.[130] It is clearly a fake, and could be a view of Bolton castle superimposed on another engraving 'A Distant View of York'. However, it could be a copy of a 17th century engraving, possibly by William Lodge,[131] of which the Tate Gallery has a copy.[132] Although the windows are shown in both Buck's and Tate's engraving as being square, rather than with pointed arches, this might be consistent with the tenants fitting shuttering after the carved window quoins had been removed.

Fig. 7/16: Buck's 1721 engraving of Sheriff Hutton castle.

In 1824, George Todd of York wrote and published his *Castellum Huttonicum, Some Account of Sheriff Hutton Castle*. In it he reports that a Mr Plows of York had recently spent three months repointing and refastening stones on the castle at the cost of £80-90 to the 'noble proprietor'.[133] Between the publication of *Magna Britannia* in 1738 and that time, two of the outer towers (in the middle court?) had been dismantled, one which had "quite overhung its base and was forcibly pulled down with the aid of 20-30 horses yoked to it, within the recollection of the present tenant of the court-house".[134] Henry Cave also drew two pencil sketches[135] of the castle and Todd engraved and published them, for those prepared to pay an extra 1/6d.

In 1839, Samuel Sharp gained the Soane Medal of the Royal Institute of British Architects for his reconstruction drawings of Sheriff Hutton castle. These reconstructions are highly imaginative and incorporate parts of many other medieval structures in northern England, including Raby castle and Micklegate Bar in York. However, Sharpe also produced a valuable drawn record and written description of the castle ruins as they then appeared, including one of the few known drawings of the last remnants of the middle court.[136] Luckily, these survived long enough to appear on some of the earliest known photographs of the castle, which date from the early 1880s onwards.

As well as amateur photographers, there were evidently also some very keen pigeon fanciers in Sheriff Hutton during the 19th century, as before 1855 a crude pigeon cote was built on the first floor of the north-east tower after over 1.5m of stone had already fallen in from the decaying rooms above.[137] The pigeons did not have long to enjoy their elevated roost, as in March 1875 Samuel Tempest recorded that 'the top of the first floor room' in the tower fell down.[138] This collapse may have occasioned the 1880s repairs carried out by Noah Banks of Lilling, who placed an iron-tie through the uppermost garderobe passage in the tower and carved his initials on the doorway as a record.[139]

Fig. 7/17: Sheriff Hutton castle drawn by the Revd. Allen in 1840 (Source: York City Art Gallery).

Numerous pictures of the castle appeared during the 19th century, many based on Todd's engravings but containing more errors. However, scattered amongst these there are a few gems, such as the sketches of the castle made by the Rev. Allen in 1840. In the later 19th century, as well as providing an inspiration for artists, the masonry of the castle itself became a canvas for numerous generations of locals. The south-west tower was a particularly favoured spot, and some of the immaculately carved graffiti here commemorates Queen Victoria.

The last human occupant of the castle, apart from occasional campers, was a joiner who planned to live there towards the end of the 19th century.[140] Like the Duke of Norfolk in 1537, he found it too cold and lived elsewhere, using the buildings as a workshop. Castle Farm was built in the middle court around the turn of the 20th century, and the castle remained in the hands of the Ingram family until 1919 when it was sold to Benjamin Jagger. In the early 20th century it was used on at least one occasion by a travelling circus to house its elephants![141] In 1940 the site passed to the Wagstaff family, and to the present owner, Dr Richard Howarth, in 1952. The farm ceased to function as an agricultural unit in 1981, and Dr Howarth has since cleared away most of the more temporary agricultural buildings from the site.[142] This improving work has also included the recent conversion of the late 19th century farm outbuildings into residential accommodation.

Finally, the life of the castle has almost come full circle, for in 2002 a programme of consolidation and repair work was started on the north-east tower which was in danger of imminent collapse. Through limited rebuilding, the replacement and re-positioning of fallen stone, the judicious use of hidden reinforcements and stainless steel pins, and wholesale repointing, this work has ensured the structural stability of the remains for future generations (see plate 44). The work was funded by English Heritage, with additional contributions by Dr Howarth, and the accompanying archaeological recording has provided a considerable amount of new information on the construction and layout of the tower, and the castle as a whole.

Fig. 7/18: Aerial view of castle taken in July 1949 showing agricultural buildings inside the inner court (Cambridge University Collection of Air Photographs, DQ35).

Footnotes

1   Emery 1996, p.133.
2   Ormrod 2000, pp.75-98; Harrison 1984, pp.3-8.
3   Calendar Patent Rolls 1381-1417, p.243; see also Cal. IPM 12 (1376) no. 160; Cal. IPM 16 (1388), p.280, no. 736; notably, the Inquisitions make no reference to a castle at Sheriff Hutton whereas the 1367 one does at Middleham. "Feudal Aids" first mentions a castle at Sheriff Hutton in 1402 (p.262).
4   Musee Conde 1969, p.13.
5   Dr Jonathan Clark, York University, *pers comm.*; Dr E. A. Gee, *pers. comm.*; Harvey 1972, pp.128 on; Harvey 1983, pp.181 on; Hislop 1998, pp.171-2.
6   Field Archaeology Specialists 2003, p.14; National Archives E326/6674 – kindly translated by Bridgett Jones.
7   Tony Wood, *pers. comm.*
8   Myerscough 2005; Myerscough 2003.
9   Brayshaw 1889, p.325.
10   Myerscough 2005.
11   Miss Ursula Lascelles reporting (in a notebook, 1949) the then forester of Castle Howard, Mr Nash, who was reporting the estate workers when he first worked at Castle Howard, who were quoting their grandfathers! The Castle Howard estate included part of Stittenham Hill in the 19th century and still includes Mowthorpe Dale.
12   Myerscough 2005.
13   Stephen Gibson, *pers. comm.*

14   From SE658667 to SE666672. It is very faintly visible on aerial photos (e.g. York Archaeological Trust 1977, 4/6, 36 & 37). It follows the track of a footpath which was moved in the 1970's by Mr Easterby, the farmer. On both the 1624 and 1765 plans of the manor, this is shown as the remains of a tail race for a mill sited at the base of Carr Hill (SE658667). The mill-race is shown extending for about 3 miles towards Dalby. On the 1765 plan the 'tail-race' (called Angram Beck) is paralleled at about 100 feet by another stream, Carr Beck.

15   Tony Wright's father, Donovan Wright, reporting his grandfather, Joseph Lascelles, who was born in Sheriff Hutton in 1855.

16   National Archives E101/484/3.

17   Richardson & Dennison forthcoming (a).

18   Richardson & Dennison forthcoming (b).

19   Jackson 1973, p3; List and Index Society vol 124 'Exchequer Augmentation Office Calendar of Ancient Deeds Series B', no. 4517.

20   e.g. Brayshaw 1889, p.325.

21   Todd 1824, p.6; British Architectural Library at the Royal Institute of British Architects (RIBA) X(079)So 728.81 (42.74 SH) (Samuel Sharp's survey).

22   Dr Jonathan Clark, University of York, *pers comm*.

23   see for example, Richardson & Dennison forthcoming (a).

24   West Yorkshire Archive Service (WYAS) Leeds WYL/100/SH/B4/2.

25   Richardson & Dennison forthcoming (c).

26   Dennison 1999.

27   RIBA X(079)So 728.81 (42.74 SH).

28   WYAS Leeds WYL/100/SH/B4/2.

29   WYAS Leeds WYL/100/SH/A3/2/1.

30   Todd 1824, frontispiece.

31   RIBA X(079)So 728.81 (42.74 SH).

32   Brayshaw 1889, p.325.

33   Camden Society 1855, p.xxvi; Letters & Papers, Henry VIII vol 4(2), no.2436.

34   National Archives E101/484/3.

35   ibid.

36   National Archives E178/2792.

37   ibid.

38   Richardson & Dennison forthcoming (c).

39   Brayshaw 1889, p.325.

40   Heritage House Group Ltd 2001, p.12.

41   RIBA X(079)So 728.81 (42.74 SH).

42   WYAS Leeds WLY100/SH/B4/2; Richardson & Dennison forthcoming (c).

43   WYAS Leeds WYL/100/SH/A3/2/1.

44   National Archives E101/484/3; Richardson & Dennison forthcoming (c).

45   Brayshaw 1889, p.325.

46   Todd 1824, p.6.

47   RIBA X(079)So 728.81 (42.74 SH).

48   e.g. Calthrop 1923, p.175 who says "Nevill impaling Beaufort" but there is no border on the France and England and no space for one. Gill ("Vallis Eboracensis" 1852, p.425) describes the arms correctly but again attributes the impalement to Joan Beaufort (wife of Ralph Neville and the daughter of Edward III). We know of no other male Neville betrothal to any lady entitled to a variant of France and England; Todd 1824, pp.3-30.

49   Dennison 1998a, pp.35-36.

50   Letters & Papers, Henry VIII, vol 4(2), no. 2436.

51   Field Archaeology Specialists 2003, p.43.

52   National Archives E178/2792, testimony of John Broughe.

53   Letters & Papers, Henry VIII, vol 4(2), no. 2436.

54   National Archives E178/2792, testimony of John Humfreyson.

55   RIBA X(079)So 728.81 (42.74 SH); Field Archaeology Specialists 2003, pp.17-20.

56   Emery 1996, p.418; Pevsner & Neave 1995, p.767.

57   Emery 1996, pp.390-392; Field Archaeology Specialists 2003, pp.14-21.

58   Richardson & Dennison forthcoming (a).

59   RIBA X(079)So 728.81 (42.74 SH).

60   There are castellations visible in several pictures, e.g. that of Place drawn in 1715. The height of the corner in the photographs of the 1880's suggests that there were turrets.

61   *Yorkshire Gazette* w/c 18th April 1927.

62   National Archives E178/2792, testimony of John Broughe and Richard Heburne.

63   ibid., testimony of John Fisher.

64   Camden Society 1855, pp.xxiv-xxvi.

65   ibid., pp.xxii-xxiv.

66   National Archives E178/2792, testimony of John Broughe.

67   British Library Harleian MSS, 589, f.192 quoted in Camden Miscellany III.

68   Borthwick Institute Register of Wills II, ff.495-495v.

69   Todd 1824, pp.8-9.

70   Dr Jonathan Clark, University of York*, pers. comm.*

71   Brookes 1954, passim; Reid 1975.

72   Colvin *et al* 1975, p.293 quoting National Archives E404/80/610; E404/81 – writs dated 26/4/1492 & 5/2/1493-4.

73   Letters & Papers, Foreign & Domestic, Henry VIII vol 4(3-2), no. 2436.

74   Letters & Papers, Foreign & Domestic, Henry VIII vol 4(2), no. 2063.

75   National Archives E101/484/3, f.4v; Letters & Papers, Foreign & Domestic, Henry VIII vol 11, p.562, no. 4; Colvin *et al* 1975, p.294.

76   Letters & Papers, Foreign & Domestic, Henry VIII, vol 12(1), p.438, no. 968.

77   ibid.

78   ibid.; special arrangements were made for the payment of Norfolk's garrison: Letters & Papers, Foreign & Domestic, Henry VIII, vol 11, no.1410(3).

79   Colvin *et al* 1975, p.294.

80   ibid., quoting National Archives E101/484/3.

81   Borthwick Institute PRSH13, f.2r. His father was probably Robert Stable (d.1512: Will R.T., 8/85), his mother Agnes (named in Robert's will) and a brother was William (also in Robert's will). Colvin *et al* 1975, p.294 note.

82   Field Archaeology Specialists 2003, p.23.

83   National Archives E101/484/4 f.25v.

84   ibid., f.30r & f.30v.

85   Woodward 1966, p.105.

86   Letters & Papers, Foreign & Domestic, Henry VIII, vol 12(1), p.592, no. 1307.

87   Letters & Papers, Foreign & Domestic, Henry VIII, vol 12(2), no. 1076.

88   Burton 1758, p.266.

89   Dugdale 1846, vol VI, pp.284 onwards: dismantling seems to have started in March 1538; Sheriff Hutton WI 1975, p.2.

90   Reid 1975, p.156.

91   Dickens 1955, p.13.

92   Letters & Papers, Foreign & Domestic, Henry VIII, vol 16, p.413, no. 875; Lee (or Leigh) and probably others as well, was later executed (see Dickens 1955, p.12).

93   Field Archaeology Specialists 2003, p.24.

94   Colvin *et al* 1975, p.294, quoting SP 12/90, f.51.

95   ibid., also the accounts of the Receiver for Yorkshire: SC 6 Elizabeth I / 2750, m.27, 2751, m.27 & 2753, m.23; Calendar Patent Rolls 1575-78, no. 5, 159 & 1366 (he received payment of £74 3s 8d).

96   Colvin *et al* 1975, pp.294-95, quoting National Archives E178/2792.

97   ibid., p.295.

98   Burton 1888, p.317.

99   Morris 1872 vol 1, pp.229 on & Appendix 10.

100   Harley 1928, p.335.

101   National Archives E178/2792.

102   WYAS Leeds WLY/100/SH/G/4.

103   National Archives E178/2792, testimony of John fflood.

104   WYAS Leeds WYL/100/SH/A1/4.

105   WYAS Leeds WYL/100/SH/A4/3.

106   Calendar State Papers Domestic, James I, vol 9, p.549.

107   WYAS Leeds WYL/100/SH/A1/8A.

108   WYAS Leeds WYL/100/SH/A3/2/1; Upton 1961, p.150; Kitson 1929, pp.55-58; Brighton 1978, pp.7-10.

109   WYAS Leeds WYL/100/SH/A1.

110   WYAS Leeds WYL/100/SH/A1/10.

111   As in WYAS Leeds WYL/100/SH/A1/11.

112   Gilbert 1966a & 1966b.

113 Gilbert 1966a.
114 ibid., p.549: Thomas Ventris, a local Mason; ibid., p.550.
115 Egerton 1946, pp.9-10; some may also now form the backdrop to the sanctuary in Sheriff Hutton parish church.
116 Gilbert 1996a, p.550; WYAS Leeds WYL/100/SH/A4/13 & Appendix 9.
117 WYAS Leeds WYL/100/SH/A1/12.
118 WYAS Leeds WYL/100/SH/A4/2.
119 British Library Harleian MSS, 6288, f.2; WYAS Leeds WYL/100/SH/B4/1, p.2.
120 WYAS Leeds WYL/100//SH/A4/Passim.
121 Wheater 1888, p.231.
122 Gilbert 1966a, p.551.
123 Gilbert 1966b, p.628.
124 Dennison 1998a, pp.69-70.
125 Dr Jonathan Clark, University of York, *pers. comm.*
126 Davies 1863, pp.153-4.
127 WYAS Leeds WYL/100/SH/A4/7.
128 York Art Gallery, D5: Place is known to have visited in 1715 although the picture bears the date 1718. Perhaps derived from a sketch. Francis Place, William Lodge, Martin Lister, John Lambert and Thomas Kirke travelled together, making sketches of antiquities and calling themselves the 'Club of Virtuosi'. As Lodge died in 1689, the sketch could have been much earlier.
129 British Museum Lansdowne MSS, no. 914, published by Wakefield Historical Publications 1979.
130 It was published in two versions, one with the tree to the right bare, the other with it in leaf. York Art Gallery has a copy of the former. The view of York is correct (even now!) but the middle ground is stylised.
131 Lodge published an engraving (mentioned in "Walpole's catalogue of Engravers...", Various editions and dates, p.98 in 1786) and he lived from 1640 to 1689.
132 *www.tate.org.uk* T11607. This engraving is un-attributed and undated. The background to the castle seems authentic.
133 Todd 1824, p.30.
134 ibid, p.6.
135 York Art Gallery, PD 424 a & b.
136 The notes are RIBA reference X(079)So 728.81 (42.74 SH) and the drawings are PA22/16-22. John Armitage supplied the original reference.
137 Richardson & Dennison forthcoming (a); Grainge 1855, p.242.
138 Tempest 1875, p.41.
139 Robin Wardell, *pers comm.*
140 Miss Lascelles Green Book (unpublished scrapbook held in Sheriff Hutton Village Hall).
141 Story from Tony Wright's great-grandfather, Joseph Lascelles.
142 Dr Richard Howarth, *pers. comm.*

CHAPTER 8: PARK AND GARDENS AT SHERIFF HUTTON CASTLE

By Sylvia Roberts and Shaun Richardson

Castles and their Gardens

It is becoming increasingly acknowledged that many castles or important houses are surrounded by a designed landscape, incorporating gardens, water features, elaborate drives and planting schemes, all designed to impress visitors, friends, and enemies alike.[1] Probably the most famous example is that of Bodiam in West Sussex, where a convoluted entrance drive through formal ponds and water gardens was created at the same time as the castle in the 14th century.[2] However, many other equally complex examples have been identified throughout the country, including North Yorkshire.

The gardens at such sites would have comprised a mixture of private and more open spaces, some perhaps placed so as to be visible from specific parts of the castle, while others were covered or shaded so as to be concealed from prying eyes. There were places such as the kitchen garden which had practical functions, and others which were designed just as pleasant places to be, and no doubt yet others which combined the two. Different parts may have appealed to different senses, stimulating sight, smell or touch, whilst other parts conveyed subtle emotional or religious messages which are now difficult for us to understand. Nevertheless, medieval illustrations show that there were equally many features and indeed plants with which the modern gardener would be familiar, including fountains, raised beds, trellis-work, lawns, galleries, seating, orchards, herbs, flowers and fruit.[3] The medieval gardeners depicted in such illustrations no doubt suffered from exactly the same aches and pains after a hard day's work as their modern counterparts, and cursed just as loudly when they saw the damage that slugs and snails had caused to their plants!

The Gardens at Sheriff Hutton Castle

The earthworks which surround the castle have previously been surveyed and described elsewhere,[4] but they were re-visited as part of the current project in April 2005.

The gardens are concentrated to the south of the castle, in the area between it and the double canals or moats. They may once have been reached using the small external doorway at the west end of the south range of the inner court. This doorway led out onto a broad flattened area or terrace. In a curious contrast, the garderobes from the south range also discharge in this area, and so there must either have been pits with wooden covers here or regular cleaning by members of the household to save those wishing to visit the gardens from a nasty surprise! From the terrace, a castle guest or visitor may have progressed down a ramp or inclined path into the garden area proper. There are the remains of several such pathways to the south of the castle, although their original form has been much disturbed by the extensive cattle churning which is shown in this area on cine film taken during the 1940s and 1950s.[5]

The flat area of ground to the south-east of the castle contains a number of different garden features. Most prominent amongst these are two ponds. The smaller pond ('f' on figure 8/2) may have had a platform or building running along its south-east side. It is set slightly higher than the larger pond ('g') to the east and it is likely that water flowed from one into the other, although there is now no remaining visible connection. The eastern pond is over 45m long, with a short northern return at its west end, which is overlooked by a flattened mound at the north-west corner; there may also be a long narrow building positioned adjacent to one side. A probable sluice at the south-east corner allowed water out into a wide shallow channel, which once again appears to have been overlooked by another building or structure. This channel may once have been linked to the northern of the two prominent canals which form the southern boundary of the garden area (see below).

Fig. 8/1: View towards the area of formal gardens with pond ('g'), looking south-east.

A gap between the two ponds leads down to the formal gardens ('o'). The earthworks here are very slight, but they suggest that there was an angled entrance into a rectangular space, surrounded by a wall or fence, and sub-divided into a number of smaller compartments or areas. In the centre of the western half, there is a narrow, slightly sunken feature, noticeably boggy in wet weather, perhaps a pond, with level terraces to either side. Similar features are visible in the eastern half of the gardens. A gap in the eastern boundary may once have been another entrance or exit, although it does appear to open out into the shallow channel draining the large ponds.

After viewing these gardens, the castle guest or visitor could have left the entrance at the south-west corner and walked over the 'Lady Bridge' (see below), which crossed the parallel double canals to the south of the castle. The surviving earthworks suggest that this bridge might have been positioned towards the east end of the canals (at 'p'). Even in their current overgrown state, the canals remain very impressive features. The northern canal is 265m long and the southern 355m long, they are both c.11m wide, and both kink slightly to the north-west at their western ends. They have U-shaped profiles and are separated by a wide flat-topped bank ('k'). This bank, part of which is now used a footpath, is between 7m and 5m wide, and a shallow slope at either end gives the impression of a raised walkway running between the ponds.

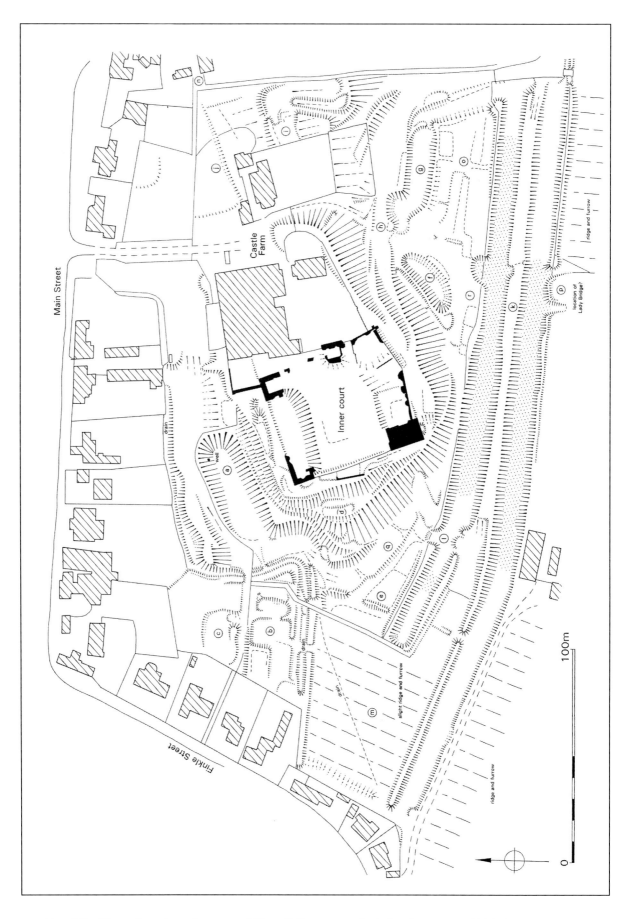

Fig. 8/2: Plan of earthworks around Sheriff Hutton castle (after Dennison 1998a).

124

Fig. 8/3: View along the walkway between the canals, looking west.

When on the Lady Bridge, perhaps the visitor had a choice of two routes. They could either cross both canals and go into the park to the south of the castle, or they could walk west along the central walkway. They could have continued further along this bank to overlook an almost flat area of ground ('m' – perhaps an orchard), or they could perhaps have crossed back over the northern canal via another smaller bridge ('l'); a footbridge survived in this position as late as 1979.[6] On the north side of this canal there are a number of other poorly defined sub-rectangular terraces ('q') that might represent another formal garden. From here, the visitor might have returned east past several possible buildings on the north side of the north canal ('r') and then back up the sloping walkways to the castle, or they could perhaps have continued around the north side of the castle, following a circuit which is now lost to us.

Although all of the different elements of the garden landscape described above once existed, it is important to appreciate that they evolved over time, and the circuit outlined above may only have been possible in the latter years of the castle's life, if at all (see below). The surviving earthworks probably represent activity spanning a period of nearly 200 years. For example, one of the ponds to the south-east of the castle ('f') may be a remnant of an original part-encircling moat, only a small section of which ('a') now survives; it was then converted into a pond as part of a later scheme. Comparison with other late 14th century castles in Yorkshire[7] indicates that Sheriff Hutton would undoubtedly have been provided with gardens when it was first finished in c.1400, although extensive later remodelling has helped to obscure exactly where these were. It is possible that the enclosed space to the south-east of the ruins ('o') marks their position, even if the existing earthworks might be later; some early gardens may also have been destroyed by the construction of the double canals at a later date (see below).

The documentary evidence shows that the castle gardens persisted throughout the medieval period into the early 16th century. For example, Thomas Wilson was appointed as Gardener to the Castle in 1485 but he had been succeeded by William Wyly in 1497. Wyly was also

Keeper of the Castle Orchard, but by 1512 both posts had passed to William Hogeson. Robert Hogen, the 'Chief Master of the King's Kitchen' became Keeper of the Orchard in 1534.[8] The extent to which any of the men holding these titles actually carried out gardening or landscape activities is debatable, as they would have been supported by numerous staff. However, the continued references to gardeners into the early 16th century at Sheriff Hutton forms an interesting contrast with one of Richard III's other castles, Middleham, where it is suggested that the absence of gardeners recorded after 1485 indicates that these gardens were abandoned following Richard's death at the Battle of Bosworth.[9]

Herbs and Healing

The study of the plants shown in medieval illustrations, together with detailed investigation of seeds and plant remains preserved elsewhere in, for example, waterlogged cess pits,[10] provides a good idea of the range of species that might have appeared in the medieval gardens at Sheriff Hutton castle and the surrounding village. Amongst these it is likely that a range of herbs would have been present, grown for both culinary and medicinal purposes. Such use had been made of herbs for centuries, if not millennia, before they appeared in medieval gardens, and knowledge of their properties would have been handed down from generation to generation by word of mouth long before written records existed.[11] In 400 BC Hippocrates wrote about the curative and healing properties of herbs, and when the Romans invaded Britain they brought with them new species to add to those already used by the native Britons. Although monastic institutions are often cited as being the centres of knowledge for medicinal and culinary herbal usage during the medieval period, ordinary people all over the medieval countryside and in each village or hamlet would have made use of a range of plants which would have been both cultivated domestically and picked wild.

Fig. 8/4: Andrew Baird tending herbs in the garden at the Ryedale Folk Museum. (Courtesy of Ryedale Folk Museum).

Fig. 8/5: Gathering the herbs, based on an early 15th century illustration.

During the medieval period, whilst the posts of physician, surgeon and apothecary were usually occupied by men, the vast majority of the day-to-day care of the sick from the lord to the lowliest worker was carried out by women. Whatever their station in society, women were expected to fulfil the role of healer and carer. In 1390, an elderly husband in Paris wrote a manual of instruction for his young bride as a guide, and one of hcr duties was to assume responsibility for the health of both himself and his staff. As part of this, she was to maintain a fully stocked herb garden, filled with all the necessary plants used for everyday medicines.[12]

In smaller communities, such duties would have fallen to a local 'wise woman' practised in the art of herbal healing but also utilising prayer and other beliefs such as astrology. Although detailed documentary evidence for the practices of such women in the medieval period is rare, they must have played an especially important role in attending childbirth; indeed, it is interesting to note that when the pregnant wife of one of the authors was taken ill on holiday in France, the hospital midwife who attended her wore a badge still giving her title as 'femme sage' – wise woman.[13] Many of these 'wise women' trod a dangerous path, as their mixture of herbs, potions, prayers and charms were viewed rather dimly by the church authorities and many were accused of witchcraft and sorcery.[14]

In cooking, herbs would be used by the lower classes to flavour dishes that might otherwise have been bland, and many medieval households would have had a pan of pottage boiling on the fire. Pottage was most commonly made using a collection of herbs and vegetables, although meat and cereals or pulses could also be added.[15] Herbs were also strewn on the floor to keep the house smelling sweet and sometimes they were mixed with straw or rushes to make it easier to change them regularly. In the towns, ladies would often carry a 'tussie mussie' - a small bouquet of sweetly smelling herbs and flowers to counteract the many noxious smells.[16]

The following account lists just a few of the plants that were in such common usage, and it is very probable that they were grown and used in the village and at the castle. An account is also given of the folklore and other beliefs surrounding each plant.

Elder (Sambucus nigra)

Traditionally the best place for the elder (see plate 50) was at the back door where it was thought to keep evil spirits away.[17] The basis of this piece of folklore may have been common sense in that the leaves were known to repel flies, which could indeed have brought disease into the house. Every part of the elder can be used.[18] The bark can be used as an infusion for its diuretic and mild laxative properties, and for making whistles and pipes after the pithy centre has been removed from the stem. The leaves were used as an infusion for purifying the blood and also, when crushed with olive oil, butter or lard and applied to haemorrhoids, the poultice will relieve the pain. The flowers were used as an infusion for treating bronchial catarrh, fevers, gout and rheumatism. The berries can be made into wine or used in jam. The Romans also used them for dyeing their hair.[19] And of course, if you want to meet a fairy the best place to lie is under an elder or boretree on Midsummer's Eve.

Rosemary (Rosmarinus officinalis)

It is well known that rosemary has long been used as a seasoning for meat, but the Romans also thought it was a sacred herb which brought happiness to the living and peace to the dead.[20] They plaited it into crowns which were worn on special occasions, weddings in particular. Rosemary was used in ointments for curing wounds and it was a regular remedy for jaundice, debility, vertigo and memory loss; if you preserved its flowers in sugar, it was also considered an excellent guard against the plague or at the very least would make the heart merry.[21] Today it is used to make essential oils which are anti-bacterial and anti-fungal, or added to the bath to ease the pain of rheumatism, gout and circulatory disorders.

Meadowsweet (Spirea ulmaria)
also known as Queen of the Meadows, Lady or Maid of the Meadow, and Bridewort

This is a herb which looks good (see plate 49), is sweet scented and very versatile.[22] It is alleged that it was regarded as sacred by Iron Age druids and in medieval homes the floors would often have been covered with this herb;[23] it was deemed particularly efficacious, in conjunction with verbena, marjoram, thyme and valerian, all sacred to Venus, when used on the floor of the bridal chamber.[24] John Gerard, the famous herbalist of the 16th century, says "The leaves and floures of Meadowsweet farre exelle all other strowing herbs for to decke up houses, to straw in chambers, halls and banqueting houses in the summer-time, for the smell thereof makes the heart merrie and joyful and delighteth the senses".[25] Since the 19th century, when it was discovered that the natural occurring methyl salicylate in Meadowsweet could be converted into salicylic acid, it has been used extensively in modern medicine, but before this it was being used as a diuretic, aromatic, astringent, and for the relief of diarrhoea and as a remedy for dropsy. It also made a pleasant beverage that would often be drunk in the harvest field.

Hops (Humulus lupus)

The Romans referred to this plant as *lupus salictarius* which translates into 'good wolf' because it grows among the osiers (young willow trees) and strangled them by its light, climbing action as the wolf does a sheep.[26] They brought the plant here and ate it as a vegetable long before it was used in beer making. Hops were used in breweries in the Netherlands at the beginning of 14th century, but they were not used in England for the concoction of beer until nearly two centuries afterwards.

Henry VII forbade brewers to put hops or sulphur into ale, Parliament having been petitioned against the hop as 'a wicked weed that would spoil the taste of the drink and endanger the people'. In 1551-52 however, privileges were granted to the hop growers, though in the reign of James I the plant was still not sufficiently cultivated to meet the demand, as we find a statute of 1608 against the importation of spoiled hops. Sheriff Hutton castle probably had its own hop garden, and an area of ground is so named on the 1765 plan of the manor of Sheriff Hutton;[27] the hops cultivated here were presumably used to make beer in the castle brewhouse (see Chapter 7).

Fig. 8/6: Site of the Sheriff Hutton hop garden, looking west.

Culpeper's Herbal recommends that half a dram of the seed in powder, taken in drink, kills worms in the body.[28] A pillow filled with hops was also known as a cure for insomnia. Hops have tonic, nervine, diuretic and anodyne properties, their volatile oil produces sedative and soporific effects, and the lupamaric acid or bitter principle is stomachic and tonic. For this reason, hops improve the appetite and promote sleep.

Parsley (Petroselinum crispum)

In the medieval period, it was believed that if you said your enemy's name while pulling a root of parsley he would die a sudden death.[29] Similarly, one should never take a house with an established garden that did not include parsley, as you would not see the year out if you did. Parsley was perceived to be difficult to germinate, most probably because it took an honest man to grow it, or perhaps because the seed had to go back to the devil nine times before it would grow; however, sow it on a Good Friday and all these problems could be avoided. All parts of the parsley plant are used; the roots would go into soups, the leaves into salads, and the seeds would supply the nurserymen for the following year. Parsley was also used to relieve urinary infections, kidney stones and rheumatism, and finally, where it grows well, it is the man of the house who wears the trousers.[30]

Tansy (Tanacetum vulgare)

This was used as a strewing herb and was especially good if used with elder as it keeps the flies away.[31] It was also used in tansy cakes which were used to purify the humours of the body after the limited fare of Lent. In time, this custom became symbolic as a remembrance of the bitter herbs eaten by Jews at the Passover, and the cakes were then called 'Tansies'. They were also used for expelling worms in children. Tansy was found to be beneficial in small doses but in large amounts was a violent irritant. Modern day herbalists advise against eating it.[32]

* * * * *

In general, the plants listed above could be used in four main ways. They would have been administered internally as infusions, made by pouring water over the herb in order to extract its active qualities, or as decoctions, extracts obtained by boiling. Externally, the herb might be administered as either a compress, a cloth moistened with an infusion and put on the skin, or as a poultice, formed by soft cooked herbs wrapped in a piece of muslin and applied to the affected area.

In order to maximise the effectiveness of the treatment, one needed to know exactly when and in what way to pick the plant. The time, place and manner of picking were extremely important, as was the person undertaking this activity. For example, in order to preserve the medicinal property of betony, it was specified that it should be picked in August by a small child. Similarly, those picking sage leaves should recite certain prayers to enhance the plant's powers.[33]

Pity then the poor herbalist sent in search of a mandrake plant. The mandrake (*Mandragora officinalis L.*) is a relatively innocuous plant but, due to the size and shape of its root, which often resemble bodies complete with 'limbs', it attracted a whole host of folkloric beliefs. When mandrakes were pulled out of the ground, they screamed deafeningly, instantly killing the person trying to extract the plant; Hildegard von Bingen, the great 12th century German abbess, believed that the devil's influence was more apparent in the mandrake than any other plant. Of course, there were various ways of countering its dangerous properties. Before it was picked, one should draw a circle on the ground around it and then soak the ground at intervals for three months using a solution of one part honey to 18 parts boiled water. The actual picking should take place at sunset and no iron tools should be used. Finally, it was advisable to tie a dog to the upper part of the mandrake as it was lifted, as the plant's scream would then kill the dog and not the herbalist. But why would anyone have gone to all of this trouble? The mandrake, when hung at the bedhead, was deemed to imbue a powerful aphrodisiac effect and, given the problems of obtaining a root, it commanded a high price. However, lovers were warned against unscrupulous herbalists who obtained the roots of bryony and then carved them to resemble the real thing, and they should certainly not have infused powdered mandrake root, as its lethally narcotic properties would have had the opposite effect to that intended on the honeymoon night.[34]

Lest the reader is tempted to laugh at some of the more outlandish beliefs outlined above, they should remember that the medicinal use and application of plants was based on hundreds of years of acquired experience, and that this persisted far beyond the medieval period into a supposedly more rational age. Indeed, plants still form the basis of many modern medicines, and the search for new treatments based on plants obtained in remote habitats around the world continues today.

We are fortunate to have a few records of how illnesses were treated using plants and other ingredients in Sheriff Hutton during these later periods. For example, the churchwardens' accounts between 1707 and 1783[35] advise the following in the case of receiving the bite of a mad dog:

> "*Dr Troutsbecks cure for the Bite of a mad Dog*
> *Take 6 ounces of kue shred small, 4 ounces of Garlik*
> *Rill's & stamped, 4 ounces of Mithridate, or Treacle 4*
> *Spoonfull of scraped tiring. Boyle these in 2 Quarts*

Of stale Ale in a pot well cover'd for the space of
An hour, then strain it and give of this Decoction in
Ye morning, 3 mornings together 8 or 9 spoonsfull
Warme to a man & cold to a beast, bind to yen
Some of ye dregs yt were strained out 8 of
Will sent either man or beast 3 to a sh
Dogg provided it be given within 9 days of
Biteing of any Creature

An other of Mr Thompsons
R Carduus, Kue and wormwood, of each a handful
Them in 4 Qrts of Ale till half be consur
Strain ye Herbs & put into the liquor 2 ounces
The fillings of pewder, & ounce of Methre
Then give to a man or a dog yt is bit, 3 spoons
3 mornings together, & again ye same Quant
3 or 4 days before ye change of ye moon give
Threec as much to a horse, and oxe, or a cow".

Fig. 8/7: Picking a mandrake, based on an early 16th century illustration.

The meanings of some of the words or phrases reproduced above have been lost and some are different to those which we would now use. It is thought that 'kue' refers to the herb rue (*Ruta graveolens*), whilst to 'rill' is an old word for chopping or shredding. 'Mithridate' would have been used as a precaution against poison and 'Carduus' is probably the cardoon (*Cyanara cardunculus*).

It would appear that local people were well accustomed to treating themselves, as demonstrated by a list of potions recorded by Thomas Plumer in his memoranda book, and which were used to treat his son (unfortunately he left no record of his son's ailment).[36] Plumer lists both apothecaries' weights and avoirdupois weights, and he apparently 'shopped around' a number of suppliers, because he compares prices to get the best value. The following were the ones that he finally chose:

Spirits of Lavender	6/-
Powdered Peruvian Bark	1/6d
Unpowdered Peruvian Bark	6d
Tincture of Alfafatida	4d
Salts of Wormwood	4d
Saffron	6d
Hartshorn Spirits	1/6d

The Castle Gardens in the Post-medieval Period

The castle gardens, and their relationship with the park, underwent several radical changes in the period between c.1400 and c.1600, and this is reflected in the surviving earthworks. At some point, the part-encircling moat, now represented only by a few surviving parts ('a' and 'f' on figure 8/2), was largely infilled. To the south-west of the castle, the moat was replaced by a series of terraces and enclosures ('q'), perhaps a formal garden, whilst to the south, the cutting of the double canals ('l') destroyed much of its former course. The orientation and form of both the enclosed garden area 'o' and pond 'g' to the north suggests that both may be contemporary with the double canals, as is the enclosure 'm' at their east end. But when were all these alterations made?

Of course, they may not all have been carried out at the same time, although the creation of such intrusive features as the double moats must surely have had a great effect on the area between them and the castle. It seems logical to assume that such a substantial alteration could have been made as part of one of two general scenarios. In the first, someone who was resident at the castle for a substantial period of time and therefore had a reason to make long-term investments had the canals created. In the second, they were created by or for someone who was resident only for a short period, but that person was sufficiently important to merit such a creation.

The first scenario might be applied to Thomas Howard, Earl of Surrey, who was resident at Sheriff Hutton from c.1489 until c.1500 (and perhaps as late as 1504) and who married for the second time in the castle chapel in 1497.[37] Whilst such a date might be considered slightly early for the canals, work at Whorlton castle in North Yorkshire, led Everson to advise caution in immediately assigning a similarly large water feature to the 16th century, rather than being an original part of the 14th century castle landscape.[38] In the second

132

scenario, the canals could well have been created either for the residence of Henry Fitzroy, Earl of Richmond (c.1525 to 1532) or Thomas Howard, Duke of Norfolk (1537 to 1541/42), both of whom were important enough to have merited such treatment. On balance, it is currently thought most likely that the canals were excavated as part of the changes undertaken in preparation for Henry Fitzroy's arrival.

As has been noted in Chapter 7, the scale of the investment that Henry VIII made in his bastard son was very substantial and indicates his importance to the king. It is quite probable that the castle grounds received the same overhaul as the structure itself, repairing and modernising them as a suitable venue for the education and pleasure of a possible future monarch. Unfortunately, published documentary sources of this period are of little use in dating the features. The 1525 survey made prior to Fitzroy's arrival notes only 'ponds for baking and brewing, near the walls outside';[39] this might refer to the two ponds still surviving to the south-east of the castle. Similarly, in 1534, the visiting antiquary Leland stated briefly that "The Castelle self in the Front [i.e. to the east] is not dichid but it stondith in loco utcunque edito [in an elevated position]",[40] a comment which could be equally applied to either the early part-encircling moat or the later double canals.

The excavation of the double canals along the south side of the castle garth created more of a formal link between the gardens and the park than had existed up to then. It is almost certain that, at the same time as the canals were created, a substantial area of the park immediately to the south was cleared of trees and put down to grass. This change of use is recorded as a place name in the late 16th century, when the area was still known as the 'West Launde' (see Chapter 4). Although the canals are currently overgrown, they would originally also have been cleared of all vegetation, and would have acted very much like a giant version of an 18th century ha-ha.

Fig. 8/8: pre-1887 photograph showing an uninterrupted view from the park to the castle across the double canals.

From the raised central walkway between the canals, people had unimpeded views towards the cleared area of the park, and back to the castle, especially the looming south-west tower, but with the water stopping the deer and other animals from entering the castle garth. The cleared area would have been equally visible across the canals from the south side of the castle, whilst the castle itself formed a spectacular backdrop to the cleared area from within the park (see plate 47). It is also possible that deer were kept within the grassland to create a suitably idyllic scene, or less peacefully, that they were driven into this area to be hunted here in full view of the walkway and castle. Allied with this more 'open' landscape however, there may still have been a desire to have some more private enclosed spaces within the castle grounds. Both ends of the north side of the north canal are formed by slight banks in front of the terraces ('q') and enclosed gardens ('o'), suggesting that walls or fences were used here to shield these areas from the eyes of those on the raised walkway.

The Countess of Huntingdon and the Lady Bridge

Although the castle, its gardens and the park were linked both by views and in the imagination of the viewer from at least the early 16th century onwards, there is no evidence for a physical link between all three until later on in the century. The depositions made as part of the 1598 inquisition into the Keeper of the Castle, Richard Pollerd, contain several fascinating snippets of information regarding the 'Lady Bridge'.[41] There is no doubt as to where the bridge was, as John Skarr stated that "he Knewe one Bridge called the Lady Bridge that did stand betwene the Castle and the West Launde", whilst another deposee said it was "leading over two motes [moats] from the castle to Sherif huton parke". The deposees suggest that the bridge was made at the appointment of the Countess of Huntingdon and that she had given £10 for its construction in addition to the cost of the timber. It was clearly a substantial structure, one deposee estimating that it was about "ffower skore yerdes [80 yards or c.73m] long". It had a base of planks and was also fitted with rails. However, it was already ruinous by 1595 and had diverse pieces 'purloyned' since, including parts seen at the door of Mr Raif or Ralph Mansfield's house in the village. The wooden parts of the bridge appear to have largely gone by 1597.

As stated above, the probable site of the bridge survives as a series of earthworks crossing the line of the canals towards their eastern end ('p' on figure 8/2). It is likely that the bridge consisted of two spans or arches, linked by the central walkway, and that it was provided with stone abutments, although the earthworks still fall well short of the estimated 80 yards length. If the bridge was built on the order of the Countess of Huntingdon, then it can be no earlier than 1572 when the Earl of Huntingdon took over the presidency of the Council of the North, but it had clearly fallen into disrepair by 1595, if not some time before, a period of only c.20 years. Neither the Earl of Huntingdon nor the Countess, Catherine Dudley, are thought to have been resident at the castle for anything other than short periods and so it is puzzling as to why such a substantial structure would have been erected.

One clue may lie with the Countess herself. Catherine Dudley was a favourite of Elizabeth I and spent much of her time at court with the queen. It is just possible that the bridge could have been built in anticipation of a royal visit to Sheriff Hutton as part of a royal progress around the north which subsequently never took place.[42] The late 16th century nobility sometimes went to extraordinary lengths in creating festivities and spectacle when receiving the queen at their residences, like, for example, those undertaken by Robert Dudley, Earl of Leicester at Kenilworth in 1575.[43] If this were also to have been the case at Sheriff Hutton, it is interesting to speculate just how much else of the garden and park area might have been altered at the same time; perhaps some of what we assume to have evolved over hundreds of years was actually laid out in a very short time for a very specific purpose.

The End of the Gardens

It is probable that the construction of the Lady Bridge marked the last major addition or re-modelling of the castle's designed landscape. By the early 17th century, the focus of the park and any garden activity had shifted south-east towards Ingram's New Lodge (see Chapter 15). The former garden area surrounding the castle was gradually given over to agricultural use, whilst the canals slowly silted up and the castle itself decayed away. However, where ordered flower beds, artificial terraces and controlled walkways had once reigned, nature returned, bringing flora and fauna of an entirely different kind.

Footnotes

1   Taylor 2000.
2   Everson 1996.
3   see, for example, Harvey 1981.
4   Dennison 1997; Dennison 1998a & 1998b.
5   Cine film of the castle taken during the 1940s and 1950s by the owner Dr R. Howarth.
6   Ordnance Survey 1979 1:2500 map (sheet SE6566).
7   e.g. Everson 2003, pp.24-33.
8   Calendar Patent Rolls 1485-1494, p.55; Letters & Papers, Henry VIII vol 1(1), p.684; these references kindly provided by Tony Wright.
9   Moorhouse 2003c, p.330.
10 Murphy & Scaife 1991.
11 Boxer & Black 1980.
12 Rawcliffe 1997, pp.180-183.
13 Shaun Richardson, *pers comm.*
14 Rawcliffe 1997, pp.199-202.
15 Black 1985, pp.13-14.
16 Examples can be seen at the Ryedale Folk Museum in Hutton-le-Hole, North Yorkshire.
17 "Mythology and Folklore of the Elder" (*www.treesforlife.org.uk/tflmythe.html*).
18 Palaiseul 1976, pp.107-109.
19 "Mythology and Folklore of the Elder" (*www.treesforlife.org.uk/tflmythe.html*).
20 Palaiseul 1976, p.275.
21 Podlech 1996; Boland 1977, p.50.
22 Podlech 1996, p.142.
23 Grieve 1931.
24 Boland 1977, p.12.
25 Palaiseul 1976, p.208.
26 Grieve 1931, p.411.
27 West Yorkshire Archive Service (WYAS) Leeds WYL100//SH/B4/2.
28 Culpepers Herbal.
29 Palaiseul 1976, p.236.
30 Boland 1977, p.32.
31 Grieve 1931, p.790.
32 Podlech 1996, p.74.
33 Rawcliffe 1997, pp.98-99.
34 Boland 1977, pp.13 & 35-38; Telesko 2001, pp.44-45.
35 Borthwick Institute PRSH3 (Sheriff Hutton churchwardens accounts 1707-83), f.8r.
36 North Yorkshire County Record Office (NYCRO) *Thomas Plumer's Memoranda Book* (Z1001); see also Chapter 17.
37 Tucker 1962, pp.71 & 74; *Testamenta Eboracensia: A Selection of Wills from the Registry of York vol III* Surtees Society 1865 vol 45, p.360.

38   Everson 1998, pp.34-35.
39   Camden Society 1855, p.xxvi; Letters & Papers, Foreign & Domestic, Henry VIII, 4(2), no. 2402; ibid., no. 2063; ibid., no. 2436.
40   Brayshaw 1889, p.325.
41   National Archives E178/2792.
42   Professor Claire Cross, York University, *pers. comm.*
43   Johnson 2002, pp.156-158.

CHAPTER 9: THE ECOLOGY OF THE PARK
by Ovie Wallis and Don Smith

Introduction

The ecological survey of the park was divided into two separate elements. One dealt with the trees and hedges, and this is reported separately elsewhere (see Chapter 10). The other covered the three farms, some rented land and the moats belonging to the castle. The latter survey was undertaken by members of the Sheriff Hutton Field Naturalists between January and May 2005.[1] The work would normally have been done over a 12 month period, to record details of all species over the four seasons, but the truncated timescale available to us meant that we had to rely heavily on information provided by the farmers.

The Ecology of the Farms

The three farms visited by the survey teams were Oaks Farm, Park or Home Farm, and Lodge Farm, and these are reported individually. The total acreage of the farms and rented land covered by the survey was some 617 acres (249 hectares). The farms are mainly mixed arable and pasture with some woodland and a reservoir. The acreage of arable land was 366 acres (142 hectares), while pasture amounted to 248 acres (100 hectares). Woodland covered 1¼ acres and the reservoir 2 acres.

All the farmers reported a decrease in House Sparrows and Starlings and an increase in Kestrels, Sparrow Hawks and game birds. An increase in roe deer was also indicated as well as large stocks of Finches, Tits and Wrens in the winter. It is hoped that a survey of small mammals will take place at a later date. The total number of birds species so far recorded is 75, together with 69 species of flowers and six species of mammals - bats, roe deer, foxes, rabbits, hares and moles were present on all the farms as well as field mice and bank vole.

Oaks Farm

This farm is presently in the tenancy of Mr Robin Barker who also owns land outside the park. The farm is approximately 110 acres (44 hectares) growing spring and winter sown cereals, oilseed rape and field beans. Potatoes have been grown in the past, and there is also a reservoir of approximately 2 acres. Mr. Barker tenanted the farm in 1987 and made the reservoir in 1991 for irrigation reasons which have now lapsed, and so the reservoir is now used for wildlife and perhaps eventually for fishing. The presence of the reservoir has, of course, meant birds being recorded which the other farms do not have, for example Grey Lag Geese, Wigeon, Teal, Tufted Duck, Black-backed Gull and Cormorant. The field sizes within the landholding have been increased to cater for modern farming practices which require larger machinery. This has, of course, meant that some hedges have been removed - Mr Barker has removed three hedges, but others had been removed before he tenanted the farm. There is a small stream running through the landholding, now diverted to the boundary of a field.

Mr Barker takes a pH reading of the soil every two years. A friend of Mr Barker is collecting acorns from some of the veteran oaks around the farm, and has grown them on and planted them back on the farm. It is intended to continue this and form a wood. Mr Barker and another friend supplied the survey team with a list of birds and flowers which appear in the schedules below.

Altogether on this farm, 67 species of birds were recorded, including three species of owls and also Golden Plover. These were also 54 species of flowers (see the schedule below) and six species of mammals.

Park Farm

This farm, which is currently farmed by Michael and David Armitage, has been in the family since 1886. The present family, that of Mr David Armitage, has lived in the farm since 1954. The holding covers approximately 100 acres (40 hectares), comprising 80 acres of arable and 20 acres as permanent pasture. The farm was managed as a dairy farm until last year. It is now partly arable with the remainder of the land being used for breeding good quality dairy cows. Once again, some hedges have been removed and field sizes increased. There are also more winter sown cereals, namely wheat and barley, and 6½ acres are currently set aside land. Some pH values are taken at intervals of between 4 and 6½ years. The Armitages apply lime and use chemicals sparingly, mainly as a fertilizer, and the crops are rotated. All three species of owls are reported, and also bats in good numbers. A total of 53 species of birds were recorded on this farm, as well as four species of butterflies (see the schedule below).

Lodge Farm

The Rickatson family moved to this farm, which is rented, in 1961 and the son Michael Rickatson who now manages the farm was born there. He took over full control in 1992 when his father died. The farm covers 250 acres (101 hectares) and is managed mainly as a dairy farm with short term grass leys and some areas of permanent grassland. There are 120 acres of wheat and barley, 30 acres of maize and 100 acres of permanent pasture. Michael also runs a shoot and has grown some cover crops for this purpose. In addition, he also rents a further 50 acres of pasture and approximately 1 acre of woodland. Lodge Farm still retains many of its hedges, some of which are old historic boundaries. All three species of owls were recorded as were Golden Plover, Redwing and Fieldfare, and a good number of bats. He has a small pond and believes that one pair of shell duck has nested in the past. PH values are taken irregularly, the last more than two years ago. He uses chemicals, but also some lime. A total of 58 species of birds were recorded on this farm (see the schedule below).

Other land

Mr Peter McPherson has a farm in Lilling (Village Farm), outside the park, but farms 104 acres (42 hectares) within the park which he rents. He has farmed for 50 years. The land within the park comprises 26 acres of arable, wheat and barley, as well as 78 acres of permanent pasture for sheep. None of the hedges have been removed. Again, all three species of owls were recorded as well as 36 species of birds (see the schedule below).

The Schedule

Key to columns: OF – Oaks Farm; PF – Park Farm; LF – Lodge Farm; McP – Mr Peter McPherson; Hall Pond / Mrs P – Mrs Palmer at The Hall; RH – Mr Richard Howarth; JW – Mrs J Wood; BL – Brian Liddle

Birds

	Species	*Oaks Farm*	*Park Farm*	*Lodge Farm*	*McP*	*Hall Pond*
1	Little Grebe					Y
2	Cormorant	Y				
3	Grey Heron	Y	Y	Y		
4	Grey Lag Goose	Y				Y
5	Canada Goose	Y	Y	Y		Y
6	Wigeon	Y				
7	Teal	Y				
8	Mallard	Y	Y	Y		Y
9	Tufted Duck	Y	Y			Y
10	Hen Harrier		Y			
11	Sparrow Hawk	Y	Y	Y	Y	
12	Kestrel	Y	Y	Y	Y	
13	Red Leg Partridge	Y	Y	Y	Y	
14	Grey Partridge	Y	Y	Y	Y	
15	Pheasant	Y	Y	Y	Y	Y
16	Coot	Y	Y	Y		Y
17	Moorhen	Y	Y	Y		Y
18	Oystercatcher	Flew from park				
19	Snipe	Y	Y	Y		
20	Woodcock	Y	Y	Y		
21	Curlew	Y	Y	Y		
22	Black Headed Gull	Y	Y	Y	Y	
23	Lesser Black Backed Gull	Y	Y			
24	Herring Gull	Y	Y			
25	Stock Dove	Y	Y	Y		
26	Wood Pigeon	Y	Y	Y		
27	Collared Dove	Y	Y	Y		
28	Turtle Dove	Y	Y	Y		
29	Cuckoo	Y	Y	Y	Y	
30	Barn Owl	Y	Y	Y	Y	
31	Tawny Owl	Y	Y	Y	Y	
32	Little Owl	Y	Y	Y		
33	Swift	Y	Y	Y	Y	
34	Green Woodpecker	Y		Y		
35	Great Spotted Woodpecker	Y	Y	Y		
36	Lesser Spotted Woodpecker		?	Y		
37	Skylark	Y	Y	Y	Y	
38	Swallow	Y	Y	Y	Y	Y
39	House Martin	Y	Y	Y	Y	
40	Meadow Pipit	Y	Y	Y		
41	Pied Wagtail	Y	Y	Y	Y	
42	Wren	Y	Y	Y	Y	
43	Dunnock	Y	Y	Y	Y	
44	Robin	Y	Y	Y	Y	Y

45	Blackbird	Y	Y	Y	Y	Y
46	Fieldfare	Y	Y	Y	Y	
47	Redwing	Y	Y	Y		
48	Song Thrush	Y	Y	Y	Y	
49	Mistle Thrush	Y	Y	Y	Y	
50	Sedge Warbler	Y				
51	Blackcap	Y	Y			
52	Chiffchaff	Y	Y	Y		
53	Willow Warbler	Y	Y	Y		
54	Long Tailed Tit	Y				
55	Blue Tit	Y	Y	Y	Y	
56	Great Tit	Y	Y	Y	Y	
57	Magpie	Y	Y	Y	Y	
58	Jackdaw	Y	Y	Y	Y	Y
59	Rook	Y	Y	Y	Y	Y
60	Crow	Y	Y	Y	Y	
61	Starling	Y	Y	Y	Y	
62	House Sparrow	Y	Y	Y	Y	
63	Tree Sparrow					Y
64	Chaffinch	Y	Y	Y	Y	Y
65	Goldfinch	Y	Y	Y		
66	Yellowhammer	Y	Y	Y	Y	
67	Greenfinch	Y	Y	Y	Y	
68	Corn Bunting		Not for some years			
69	Golden Plover	Y	Y	Y		
70	Lapwing	Y	Y	Y	Y	
71	Siskin	Y	Y		Y	
72	Bullfinch				Y	
73	Treecreeper	Y				
74	Jay	Y		Y		
75	Shellduck					Y

Flowers

	Species	OF	PF	LF	McP	Mrs P	RH	JW	BL
1	Common Field Speedwell	Y	Y	Y					
2	Creeping Buttercup	Y	Y	Y				Y	
3	Meadow Buttercup	Y	Y	Y				Y	
4	Dandelion	Y	Y	Y					
5	Corn Marigold	Y	Y	Y					
6	Pink Campion	Y							
7	Primrose	Y	Y	Y		Y			Y
8	Snowdrop	Y	Y	Y					
9	Lords & Ladies (Arum)	Y	Y	Y	Y		Y	Y	
10	Scarlet Pimpernel	Y	Y	Y					
11	Field Violet (Pansy)	Y			Y				
12	Common Dog Violet	Y							
13	Queen Anne's Lace (Cow Parsley)	Y	Y	Y			Y		
14	Ragwort	Y		Y					
15	Bluebell	Y	Y	Y		Y	Y		
16	Daisy	Y	Y	Y					
17	Lesser Celandine	Y	Y	Y	Y		Y	Y	
18	Groundsel	Y	Y	Y					
19	Redshank	Y	Y	Y					

#	Species								
20	Scentless Mayweed	Y	Y	Y					
21	Shepherds Purse	Y	Y	Y					
22	Hemp Nettle	Y	Y	Y					
23	White Dead Nettle	Y	Y	Y					
24	Red Dead Nettle	Y	Y	Y					
25	White Clover	Y	Y	Y					
26	Red Clover	Y	Y	Y					
27	Spurge Laurel	Y				Y	Y		
28	Dogs Mercury	Y	Y	Y	Y	Y	Y		
29	Brook Lime	Y				Y	Y	Y	
30	Ivy	Y			Y		Y		
31	Dog Rose	Y					Y		
32	Bramble	Y					Y		
33	Ground Ivy	Y					Y		Y
34	Forget Me Not	Y					Y		
35	Lesser Stitchwort						Y		
36	Spear Thistle	Y		Y		Y	Y	Y	
37	Water Starwort			Y		Y	Y	Y	
38	Water Crowfoot			Y			Y		
39	Floating Sweet Grass						Y		
40	Watercress			Y			Y		
41	Hard Rush			Y			Y		
42	Soft Rush			Y			Y		
43	Rose Bay Willow Herb			Y			Y		
44	Pignut	Y		Y				Y	Y
45	Common Chickweed			Y					
46	Nettles	Y		Y	Y	Y		Y	
47	Common Duckweed			Y		Y			
48	Marsh Thistle			Y			Y		
49	Wood Avens					Y	Y		Y
50	Hogweed	Y		Y		Y	Y		
51	Hemlock			Y					
52	Goosegrass	Y			Y	Y			
53	Honeysuckle	Y							Y
54	Ramsons	Y							Y
55	Creeping Thistle	Y		Y			Y	Y	
56	Broad Leaf Dock	Y				Y			
57	Garlic Mustard					Y	Y		
58	Hedge Woundwort					Y	Y		
59	Barren Strawberry	Y							
60	Herb Robert	Y							
61	Yarrow	Y							
62	Mugwort	Y							
63	Mullein	Y							
64	Dove's Foot Cranesbill	Y							
65	Thyme Leaf Speedwell	Y							
66	Hairy Bittercress	Y							
67	Greater Plantain	Y							
68	Nipplewort	Y							
69	Burdock	Y							

Butterflies

	Species	Oaks Farm	Park Farm	BL
1	Large White	Y	Y	
2	Small White	Y	Y	

3	Red Admiral	Y	Y	
4	Tortishell	Y	Y	
5	Peacock	Y	Y	Y
6	Holly Blue	Y		
7	Wall	Y		

The Moats

There are two linear moats or canals to the south of the stone castle, now heavily overgrown, with a public right of way running between them. These moats belong to the castle, which is owned by Dr Richard Howarth, who inherited from his late father Mr John Howarth. The following results were obtained from this area.

Birds
1. Mallard (one pair swimming)
2. Kestrel (high in the air - very near)
3. Pheasant
4. Moorhen (once only)
5. Wood Pigeon
6. Collared Dove
7. Swallow (overhead)
8. Wren
9. Dunnock
10. Robin
11. Blackbird
12. Song Thrush
13. Blackcap
14. Willow Warbler
15. Chiffchaff (usually two, one at each end)
16. Marsh Tit
17. Blue Tit
18. Great Tit
19. Treecreeper
20. Jackdaw (nests on Castle)
21. Rooks (Rookery)
22. Chaffinch
23. Greenfinch
24. Goldfinch

Butterflies
1. Orange Tip
2. Holly Blue
3. Brimstone
4. Lesser Tortoiseshell
5. Peacock
6. Wall
7. Ringlet
8. Small White

Mammals
1. Squirrel
2. Tadpoles

Trees
1. Blackthorn
2. Ash
3. Oak
4. Hawthorn
5. Field Maple
6. Willow
7. Hazel
8. Crab Apple
9. Holly
10. Beech

Flowers
1. Lesser Celandine
2. Violets
3. Primrose
4. Red Dead Nettle
5. Dandelion
6. Dogs Mercury
7. Jack by the Hedge
8. Bluebell
9. Greater Stitchwort
10. Milkmaids
11. Queen Anne's Lace
12. Purple Milk Vetch
13. Herb Robert
14. Daisy
15. Creeping Buttercup
16. Tufted Vetch
21. Ribbed Plantain
22. Narrow Leaved Dock
23. Nettle
24. Cleavers
25. Barren Strawberry
26. Broad Leaved Dock
27. Sow Thistle
28. Red Clover
29. White Clover
30. Flag
31. Nipplewort
32. Meadowsweet
33. Loose Strife
34. Ragwort
35. Leafy Hawkweed
36. Spear Thistle

17. Marsh Marigold
18. Germander Speedwell
19. Herb Bennet
20. Sorrel

37. Chickweed
38. Lesser Stitchwort
39. Lesser Pignut
40. Forget me Not

Fungus, Lichen and Insect Survey

The following species were recorded in the park:

Lichens

On Blackthorn:	Xanthoria parietina
	X. polycarpa
	Physcia tenella
On tree bark:	Lepraria incana
On rotting plywood:	X. parietina
	X. polycarpa
	Candelariella vitellina
	Phaeophyscia orbicularis
	Physcia caesia
	P. tenella
	P. adscendens
	Lecanora dispersa
On iron-work:	Caloplaca citrina
On brickwork:	Psilolechia lucida

Fungi

In hedge line:	Conocybe appendiculata (toadstool)
On fallen branches:	Coriolus versicolor (bracket fungi)

Galls

Quercus petraea	Neuroterus numismalis (silk-button galls) – gall wasp
ditto	Neuroterus quercusbaccarum (common spangle galls) – gall wasp
Fraxinus excelsior	Phyllopsis fraxini – leaf hopper nymph
Acer campestre	Aceria macrochelus (=Eriophyes) – Acaria (mite)
ditto	Aceria aceriscampestris (=Eriophyes) – Acaria (mite)

Plant bugs

Hemiptera Heteroptera
    Capsus ater (black form)
    Leptopterna dolobrata
    L. ferrugata
    Notostira elongata
    Scolopostethus grandis
    Anthocoris nemorum
    Lygocoris lucorum

Hemiptera Homoptera (froghoppers)
    Aphrophora alni

Lacewings

Neuroptera
    Chrysopa carnea f.carnea

Caddisflies

Trichoptera
    Glyphotaelius pellucidus

Moths

Lepidoptera
    Lomaspilis marginata (Clouded Border)
    Eudonia truncicolella
    Dichrorampha petiverella
    Udea olivalis

Beetles

Cantharis nigra (Soldier beetle)
Microcara testacea
Tachinus signatus (Rove beetle)

Flies
Diptera
    Cheilosia albitarsis
    Chloromyia formosa
    Chrysopilus cristatus
    Chrysotus cilipes
    Dolichopus trivialis
    D. nubilus
    Geomyza balachowskyi
    Lyciella platycephala
    Nephrotoma quadrifaria
    Opomyza germinationis
    Phaonia variegata
    Poecilobothrus nobilitatus
    Sciapus platypterus
    Sicus ferrugineus
    Syritta pipiens
    Syrphus vitripennis

Sawflies
Hymenoptera Symphyta
    Athalia lineolata

Discussion

It is difficult to draw many conclusions from the results of what can only be described as a partial survey, undertaken over part of the park and only for a limited period of time. Furthermore, we are not aware of any previous survey work having been done in the park, or any previous records or other documentation with which to compare our efforts.

We were, however, very pleased to find that the three farmers were all very interested in wildlife. They were doing what they could to conserve wildlife without interfering with their normal farming activities. The creation of the reservoir and the planting of acorns on Oaks Farm is very commendable, although the general reduction of trees and hedges will have affected numbers of insects, hedge nesting birds and flowers. The most interesting birds were the winter birds on the reservoir at Oaks Farm, and the finding of Spurge Laurel (see plates 56 and 57) and Brook Lime, neither of which are common, is also significant. Otherwise the range of bird and plant species is such as might be expected for similar habitats in this area.

Footnotes

1   The following individuals are gratefully acknowledged for having helped with, or provided information for the survey: Mr Robin Barker, Messrs Michael and David Armitage, Mr Michael Rickatson, Mrs P. Palmer, Mr P. McPherson, Dr R. Howarth, Mrs J. Wood and Mr Brian Liddle.

CHAPTER 10: THE WOODS, TREES AND HEDGES OF THE PARK

by Barbara Hickman

Medieval Woodland Management

In the medieval period trees were carefully managed in order to supply the population with a huge number of essential products. A distinction was made between timber and wood; timber was taken from trunks and main branches and provided beams and planks for any large construction, while wood from smaller limbs was used for fuel, and made into implements and palings. Tree bark provided tannin for leather, and wood ash was used for dyeing and soap-making. Domestic fuel was in constant demand, and some wood was converted into charcoal which gave more heat and no smoke; it was also needed for iron and glass making.

There were three sources of wood and timber, from woodland, from wood pasture, and from individual and hedgerow trees. It is not clear how much planting actually took place - it is probable that natural regeneration was managed to ensure that the age of trees in a specific locality ranged from sapling to mature to meet the constant demand. Areas of new trees would need protecting from grazing animals by thorny plants and/or banks or fences.

Almost all medieval woodmanship was based around the principle of cutting wood in such a way that natural regrowth was ensured and encouraged. Those who managed the trees were especially skilled in coppicing and pollarding. Coppicing is the process by which a tree is cut at ground level, to produce a stool from which many new stems grow. These thin straight stems were usually used for poles and hurdle making. The new growth was cut again in rotations of between seven to 15 years depending on the size of wood required. Ash, lime, hazel and sweet chestnut are particularly suited to coppicing and whole woods managed in this way are called 'coppices'; in Yorkshire they are recorded in the Domesday Book as *silva minuta*.[1] Sometimes one stem would be allowed to grow into a mature tree to supply a particular timber – such trees were called standards. When an oak was felled, a standard was usually left to mature in its place. In most medieval woods there was a mixture of coppice wood (also known as underwood) and larger mature standards. Normally oaks were allowed to mature, for perhaps 70 years or longer, before being cut, sawn or split into the major timbers needed for building works.

Wood pasture, recorded in Domesday as *silva pastoralis*, is a less intensive system of land management. Mature trees such as oak, ash and beech were dotted around grazing and pasture land, to provide animals with shade and food, whether as fallen nuts or from the leaves. Other trees, such as holly, were planted specifically to provide fodder, although the wood would also be utilised.[2] The trees were either left to mature as standards, or were pollarded. This was another way of getting smaller wood from a tree. The trees were cut at a height of between 2m or 3m above ground level, above the animals reach to prevent them eating off the new growth. Only a small number of stems would be allowed to grow on to provide timber.

Coppice stools can survive indefinitely as long as they are regularly cut, and they can be hundreds and even thousands of years old. Pollarding can make a tree more susceptible to wind damage and it is very difficult to date pollarded trees accurately. Growth is stimulated by cutting; the tree 'springs' into growth, hence the names of some ancient (pre-1600) woods include the word 'spring' indicating that the woodland would have been managed by coppicing and pollarding in the medieval period.

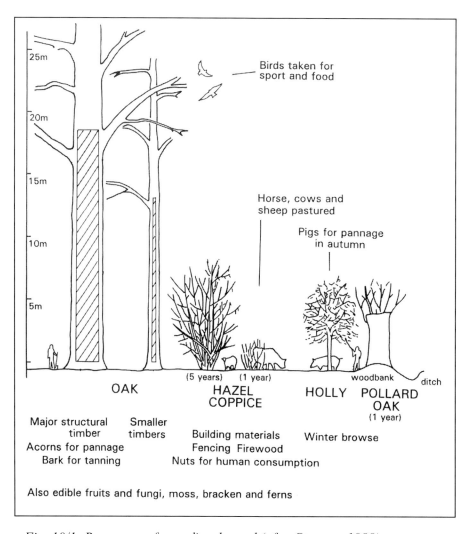

Fig. 10/1: Resources of a medieval wood (after Stamper 1988).

A Brief History of Woodland Management in England

Until the 12th century, the extraction of wood and timber did not exceed supply. The natural vegetation of these islands is woodland, although this had been considerably reduced even before the Roman era. However, in the medieval period, there were a large number of huge construction projects, cathedrals, monasteries, castles and mills to name but a few, which led to a massive programme of felling and a reduction in woodland cover. The supply of suitably large timbers for these projects was often problematic, and they often had to be transported for considerable distances across the countryside. There are also numerous records of timber being given to institutions by owners of woods to help with their building projects; for example, in 1343 the Crown gave 500 oaks from the Forest of Galtres to repair the staithes at Ravenser Odd on the Spurn peninsula, while in 1227 Hugh de Neville gave four oaks from Galtres to repair Topcliffe Bridge and ten oaks for the fabric of Marton Priory church.[3]

Fig. 10/2: An ancient pollard.

Fig. 10/3: A coppiced hazel.

In the Tudor period, the expanding iron and ship building industries began to consume vast amounts of timber. Oak is ideal for ships as it does not rot in water and the huge upper branches grow with a natural curve making 'ship-shape' timbers. Woodland management had become less rigorous by this time, but the huge demand for timber meant there were occasional shortages and some wood had to be imported. The Elizabethan period saw some tree planting to replenish the stocks, marking the beginning of plantation forestry.

The Restoration of Charles II in 1660 saw another move to plant trees. The king had seen great forests and estates in France during his exile, and explorers were bringing back exotic trees from their travels beyond Europe. The 1660s also saw the publication of John Evelyn's book *Silva* (the Latin for trees and woodland), which was the first study of trees to include commercial as well as aesthetic values. As a result, the later Stuart period saw much ornamental tree planting, and plantations on country estates. Some landowners were inspired by Evelyn, and this led to the tree collections and landscape gardening of the 18th century.

Samuel Pepys, the founder of the modern navy, foresaw the need for good timber for future ship building and encouraged the establishment of oak plantations. However, the overall lack of planning and woodland management continued, although there was another burst of oak planting during the Napoleonic period; as a result, many of the oaks in our landscape are approximately 200 years old. Little woodland management took place after 1850, and it was only after World War I, when most lowland woods were clear felled, that national woodland management became necessary and so the Forestry Commission was formed in 1919. The 20th century saw mass plantation forestry, much of it coniferous and in upland areas.

The Management of Sheriff Hutton Park for Timber and Wood

The Domesday entry for Sheriff Hutton notes the presence of 'woodland pasture' covering an area one league long by two furlongs wide.[4] It is not known where this woodland was located, but it may well have been in the area of the present park, to the south of the village. It was also noted in Chapter 4 above that a 'park at Hoton' was recorded in 1199-1216, and this may have lain on the north side of the village.

The original deer park at Sheriff Hutton would have provided the necessary timber for the buildings and defensive structures of the first castle site. In 1334 the Nevilles were given permission from the Crown to enclose their woods in Sheriff Hutton to create a new deer park (see Chapter 4)[5] and, although it would have been laid out principally for the pleasure of the hunt and the recreation of the castle guests, it would also have provided the timber used for the construction of the later castle and all its associated buildings. The park would have also supplied the fuel and wood needed by all those who lived in and worked for the castle, while the villagers would have exercised their common grazing and pasture rights ('pannage', 'berbiage' and 'herbage') in the wood, as well as their rights to take wood for fuel ('firebote'), building materials ('housebote'), fencing ('fencebote') and for making agricultural equipment ('ploughbote'). The pale or fence surrounding the deer park would almost certainly have been predominately made of oak.

Fig. 10/4: Cutting trees and clearing ground, based on a medieval illustration.

Under Henry VIII major repairs were made to the castle using oaks from the park – an account of 1537 shows that three or four hundred loads of wood were felled in the park to repair or rebuild various structures, and payments were made for the 'dyking and hedging of the spryng' which had been previously been felled.[6] However, in 1545 wood had to be brought in from the Forest of Galtres for repairs in the park.[7] Was this an example of the

Tudor deterioration in woodland management, or had so much timber been extracted that insufficient of the necessary size was available?

As mentioned in the preceding chapters, there was an inquisition into the state of the park and castle in 1598, and this provides much interesting detail on the way the wood within the park was managed (see also Chapter 11). For example, many oak and ash trees and coppices had been sold from 'Murke Hagg' and 'Lilling Hagg' by Richard Pollerd,[8] who had been granted the Keepership of the Park, and the general impression is that much of the wood had been or was in the process of being sold off. One Christopher Richardson complained that he had been sold three oak trees from Lilling Hagg, but that two of them were rotten.[9] There are also records of selling ten hundred loads of 'certaine Thornes', as well as firewood, and some of the wood appears to have been used to fire a new kiln built at the castle.[10] Oak and ash from the park was also used to repair the pale at the same time.

A Special Commission of 1609-11 noted that several men had cut down 61 trees in the park and used the timber to enclose an area of ground within which were then planted young oaks and birch, as well as cherry and plum trees.[11] A further 16 or 17 trees had been cut down to build a stable in the park.

Following Arthur Ingram's purchase of the estate in the early 17th century, John Norden, in his survey of the park in 1624, recorded around '4000 decayde and decayinge okes, the most of them headed' i.e. pollarded.[12] It is assumed Ingram had used his own oak to furnish the interior of his new lodge. This was well before the Restoration enthusiasm for tree planting – we know he established a fine garden (see Chapter 15) but was there any planting for timber?

A Parliamentary survey of 1650[13] stated that there were 512 trees 'of the better sort' in the park, that is able to provide timber, although none were allocated for the Navy. There were also 3,222 other trees, referred to 'ould decayed trees fitte for little other than the fire'. If these 3,000-4,000 trees were already decayed and decaying in the 17th century, they may well have been over 300 and possibly over 500 years old, although poor management over the previous two centuries may have hastened their demise.

Major changes then occurred between 1651 and 1675-85 when the park was sub-divided and became 27 separate closes.[14] The Hall and its immediate environs remained as they had been, and the rest become farm land. In c.1675 the park covered some 816 acres, and there was £300 worth of timber about the house.[15] Many of the trees remained, but only if they did not interfere with the farming regimes.

The Oak

The Pendunculate or English oak, *Quercus robur*, is the oak of lowland Britain. It has become synonymous with the English character, strong and unyielding in conflict, and with a somewhat eccentric form. According to Richard Mabey,[16] we can be justifiably proud of our ancient oaks, nowhere else are they of such good quality or so numerous. Over the centuries they have provided for the needs of the population and their domestic animals. They were also planted in commemoration of events and people, and to mark boundaries; for example, the Anglo-Saxon boundary of Old Drax contains 'Sighere's Oak' while a 13th century boundary at Ripley had 'Godwin's Oak'.[17]

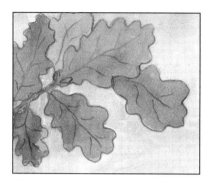

Fig. 10/5: The Oak.

Oaks are said to be 300 years growing, 300 years maturing and 300 years dying. Solitary trees can reach girths (circumference) of 25-40 feet; grown in plantation they are tall, straight and more slender. In their maturity they begin to develop 'stag heads', that is some dead limbs protruding from the crown of foliage (see plate 65). Sometimes great bulbous burrs expand the trunk (see plate 63), and the heartwood can rot leaving hollows big enough to hold a number of people. There are some outstanding examples around the country.[18]

Oak trees support more wildlife than any other living organism, including birds, mammals, lichens, fungi and some 200 insect species (see plate 58). They are one of the last trees to come into leaf and produce a second flush of leaves in August, sometimes replacing the earlier damage of caterpillars. Like the beech, they retain some of their leaves throughout the winter.

The oak is slow to regenerate as it needs light to germinate so it relies on birds and animals to take acorns away from the dense shade of the parent tree. They do well in hedgerows as the thorns protect the young saplings. Unlike many trees which are shallow rooted, oaks put down strong tap roots which help support the huge weight of branches above.

The Sheriff Hutton Oaks Today

The woods, trees and hedges of Sheriff Hutton park were surveyed and assessed in April 2005, as part of the wider ecological survey mentioned in Chapter 9 above.

Time has taken its toll on the 4,000 oaks recorded by Norden in 1624. They were clearly well into maturity at that time so not many would have survived to the present day. There are some good trees surviving in the hedgerows and along the line of the pale with trunk girths of between 12ft and 20ft (3.5m and 6.0m). One particular example, which might well lie on the eastern boundary of the second (1334) deer park, to the south of the farm buildings at the Hall, is a splendid example with a girth of approximately 7.9m, estimated at over 600 years old (see plate 66). There are also some very large trees close to both Park and Lodge Farms, and a few also remain in the middle of fields; some of these were damaged in the gales of January 2005. A prominent line of six trees at Park Farm represents the line of a field boundary shown on the Ordnance Survey 1855 1st edition 6" map,[19] but now removed. The farming policies of the 1980s led to the destruction of many of the very old trees in parts of the park. Nevertheless, the line of the park pale to the west of East Lilling deserted village is marked by a number of smaller oak trees.

Around the park there are trees which have the appearance of being pollarded and many which would fall into the category of ancient trees. These are trees which are of interest biologically, aesthetically or culturally because of their age – the trees have character, dead and damaged limbs, perhaps evidence of woodland management and yet continue growing (see plates 64 and 65). A tree with a girth of more than 4.5m has conservation value; if it is more than 6.25m it is considered ancient.

Fig. 10/6: Oak c.3m girth, showing evidence of former pollarding, east of Park Farm.

Fig. 10/7: Ancient oak adjacent to the Hall.

Trying to determine the ages of trees is notoriously difficult, although there is a relationship between the size of a tree, expressed in girth or diameter measured at chest height and avoiding any distorting bulges, and its age.[20] It has also been suggested that a tree growing in an open situation gains 1" (26mm) of girth every year, while one in a wood gains only ½" a year.[21] If a tree has been pollarded, its girth can be up to 30% smaller as the removal of branches slows growth.

Today, the largest specimens are seen along the Coach Road and to the north-west of the Hall where there are over 20 ancient trees; it was not possible to examine the area to the south-east of the Hall. Most of these have girths of over 20ft (6m), and there are two distinct separate clusters, to the north-east of the Hall and south of the lake. The number of ancient trees in this area suggest that they were deliberately left in place when Ingram was constructing his New Lodge in the 1620s, but the central area was cleared to provide an uninterrupted vista along the north-west/south-east axis (see Chapter 15). The deliberate retention of pre-existing trees from an earlier landscape, often a medieval deer park, and their incorporation into a new designed 'garden landscape' has been noted elsewhere,[22] and many of the trees in front of the Hall are surrounded by 19th century cast-iron railings. The oaks, together with the occasional lime, copper beech and horse chestnut, now form part of a landscape which both pleases the eye and allows sheltered grazing. In 2004 a hollowed tree stump in woodland adjacent to the Hall produced the very rare fungus, the oak polypore (*Piptoporus quercinus*). Ancient tree specialists who have visited the site state that the oak polypore is rarely seen (only 18 sightings in the last 30 years), and they always occur at a site which has seen little change for centuries. They have rated the central area of the park as one of the top 300 ecological sites in Europe,[23] although some of the trees are reputed to be filled with concrete to prevent them falling over.[24]

Old oak trees cannot live for ever, but their genetic make-up is very special and its continuation needs to be encouraged. The aesthetic value of the landscape cannot be easily quantified, but it must be cherished for future generations.

Fig. 10/8: Hollowed tree stump in the wood adjacent to the Hall.

Fig. 10/9: Ancient oak surrounded by cast-iron railings, adjacent to the Hall.

The Hedges and Woods of the Park

In early April 2005, some of the hedgerows, which included sections of the pale, were also surveyed. They included:

(1)   the internal division of the park which appears at the west end of Norden's 1624 survey (see plate 37), i.e. the hedge running north-south from the village to Oaks Farm and on to the Lilling wood;

(2)   the hedges in the fields immediately to the south of the second castle;

(3)   the hedge running east along the pale from the first castle;

(4)   East Lilling deserted village.

The hedges are mixed, generally with a dominance of hawthorn, blackthorn, field maple, holly, hazel and elder, with rose, bramble and ivy. In some places there are mature trees in the hedges, mostly oak with some ash and occasional field maple, crab apple and elm. Most of the hedges are not laid. Some have been allowed to grow comparatively tall, and even into full sized trees. There are some strangely shaped trees where laid hedges have been left to grow.

Hedgerows are an extension of woodland and often have a very similar habitat. The surveyed hedges are all thick with dog's mercury, wild garlic, celandine, bluebells, wild arum and primrose. All the usual rapid colonisers are also present, such as cow parsley, dead nettles, thistles, dandelions, docks, nettle, hogweed, cleavers and burdock.

Along the ditch which follows much of the hedge on Norden's survey, there are many clumps of the comparatively rare Spurge Laurel (*Daphne laureola*) (see plates 56 and 57). It is a small evergreen woodland shrub, generally liking some lime in the soil. It flowers in January and February and is scented. All the ditches contain Brook Lime with its graphic Latin name V*eronica beccabunga*.

The most interesting hedge is that to the south of Oaks Farm, namely the one forming the boundary between the 'Copes' and the area to the east in 1624 (see figure 5/2). The ditch here is very deep and has plants of much older woodland species including barren strawberry and pignut, as well as speedwells and those mentioned above. The trees are more varied with willow, holly, and an English elm present.

The woodland to the north of the Hall is well carpeted with bluebells although the current levels of sheep stocking mean that few will flower. On a visit in March one plant stood out with its pale green feathery leaves, Monkshood (*Aconitum dephinifolium*) (see plate 68). It had not been grazed as it is *extremely* poisonous. It is a native wildflower, but could also be a garden escapee. It was used to add poison to arrow heads in medieval times, and used with care it was also a pain killer but not always successfully! Even touching it can cause a severe reaction.

The hedges at the deserted village site are mixed, generally hawthorn, blackthorn, hazel and elder, with rose, bramble and ivy. There are some hedgerow trees, mostly oak with some ash. This area also has many wet areas so the flora reflects this with water crowfoot, starwort, rushes and reed grass. Generally the flora within the park as a whole is what would be expected from an area which, like most of lowland Britain, shows much evidence of modern farming methods. Wildflowers are restricted to field margins, tracks and ditches.

Footnotes

1 Gledhill 1998, p.111.
2 Spray 1981.
3 Kaner 1998, p.125; Calendar Close Rolls 1227-1231, p.8 (14th December 1227).
4 Faull & Stinson 1986, 5N54.
5 Calthrop 1923, p.173; Beresford 1957, p.222.
6 National Archives E101/484/3; these and other documents are discussed further in Chapters 11 and 12.
7 Jamison 1966, p.173.
8 National Archives E178/2792, testimony of John Boughe: ".. the two yeres last past did sell all the underwood in Lilling hagg and Cropte and lopte the Oke wood there growing w[ch] wood so cutt downe, lopte and cropte, The defend[t] solde after the Raite of viij[s] a hundreth of Kidds And the other ffier woode after two shilling six pence a Lode ..".

9   ibid., testimony of Christopher Richardson "..he saith that he did in winter last buy thre Oke trees in Lillinh hagg of m^r Pollerd One of theme soaund And the other two Rotten And he paid for the same to the said pollerd xl^s And at the same tyme he bought more of the said Pollerd Two heapes of ffier wood ffor wch he paid v^s..".

10   ibid., testimony of Bartholomew Smith: "..he saiythe that he thinketh The Kilne Latelie builded by the def^t [defendant – Richard Pollerd] hath done no harm to her matie [majesty] or her woodes ..".

11   National Archives E178/4839.

12   British Library Harleian MSS no. 6288; see Chapters 4 and 12 which discuss the survey in more detail.

13   National Archives E317/York S/54.

14   Beresford 1957, p.224.

15   West Yorkshire Archive Service (WYAS) Leeds WYL/100/SH/B3/1.

16   Mabey 1996.

17   Alexander 1993, p.48.

18   see, for example, Pakenham 1996.

19   Ordnance Survey 1855 1st edition 6" map (sheet 141), surveyed 1854.

20   Muir 2000, p.101.

21   Mitchell 1966.

22   Rackham 2004.

23   Ted Green, Luke Steer and David Clayden (English Nature), *pers. comm.*

24   Robin Barker, Oaks Farm, *pers. comm.*

25   Information kindly provided by Don Smith.

Other references:

Hadfield, J (ed) 1979 *The Shell Guide to England.* Book Club Associates, Rainbird Reference Books Ltd and Michael Joseph.

Readers Digest 1988 *The Ever-changing Woodlands.* Readers Digest, New York (originally partwork The Living Countryside, Eaglemoss Publications Ltd and Orbis Publications Ltd).

Plate 1: The Pale Project Committee (L-R): Jean Farnaby, Barbara Foreman, Sylvia Roberts, Nancy Megginson, Janet Towse and Ruth Wood.

Plate 2: Planning the work – village meeting in progress.

Plate 3: Public field trip around the castle.

Plate 4: The start of the fieldwork – surveying the scene.

Plate 5: Fieldwork in action – mapping the park pale.

Plate 6: Fieldwork in action – measuring the park pale.

Plate 7: Fieldwork in action – discussions.

Plate 8: Fieldwork in action – measuring the trees.

Plate 9: Fieldwork in action – geophysical survey on the first castle mounds.

Plate 10: Fieldwork in action – ecological survey in woods.

Plate 11: Fieldwork in action – discovery of the underground game larder at Lodge Farm.

Plate 12: Explaining the project – BBC Look North interviews.

Plate 13: View to Sheriff Hutton castle from the park.

Plate 14: View to Sheriff Hutton Hall, north elevation.

Plate 15: Sheriff Hutton castle, looking south-east.

Plate 16: Sheriff Hutton church.

Plate 17: Aerial view of Sheriff Hutton village, taken June 1991 (Aeroscene Ltd, AJC 260/22).

Plate 18: Effigy of Ralph Neville and one of his wives in Staindrop church, County Durham.

Plate 19: View of first village green, looking east towards the church.

Plate 20: View of the market place, looking south-east.

Plate 21: Hunting 'par force de chiens' – the quest. Huntsman with a lymer hunts out the quarry (Source: BnF FR616, fol.63).

Plate 22: Hunting 'par force de chiens' – the assembly. The Master of the Game assesses the reports of the trackers and the fumes are examined (Source: BnF FR616, fol.67).

Plate 23: Hunting 'par force de chiens' – the lymer leads the coupled running hounds to the selected hart (Source: BnF FR616, fol.55).

Plate 24: Hunting 'par force de chiens' – the unharbouring and the chase is on (Source: BnF FR616, fol.85v).

Plate 25: Hunting 'par force de chiens' – after the death, the unmaking begins (Source: BnF FR616, fol.70).

Plate 26: Hunting 'par force de chiens' – the final act, the curée when the hounds are rewarded (Source: BnF FR616, fol.72).

Plate 27: View towards Sheriff Hutton castle, looking north across the park.

Plate 28: Typical flint arrowhead and wheel scraper, Neolithic-Bronze Age in date.

Plate 29: Selection of Roman Crambeck ware pottery found in the High Park.

Plate 30: Convex keel scraper of mid Bronze Age date, found in the parish.

Plate 31: Typical Roman trumpet brooch, similar to one found recently near the church.

Plate 32: Edward I 'long cross' silver penny, found in the park (20mm diameter).

Plate 33: Elizabeth I silver penny found in the High Park.

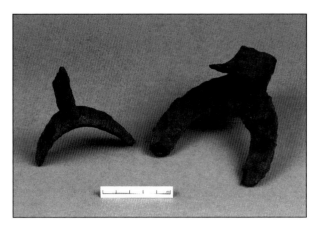

*Plate 35: Fragment of iron spur and horseshoe
with front flange found in the park,
post-medieval in date.*

*Plate 34: Inscribed medieval plaque, found at
Stile House in 1999.*

*Plate 36: View across the High Park (Kirk Hill) and site of the presumed Roman enclosure, looking
north towards the church.*

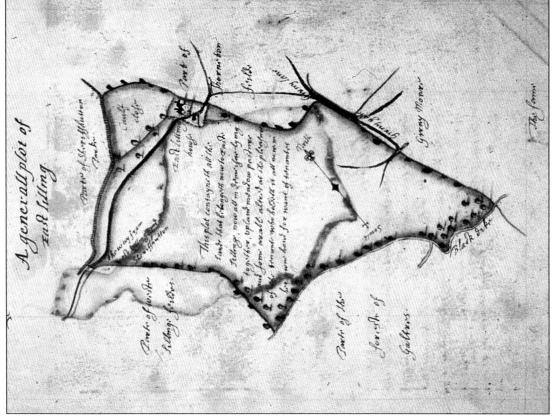

Plate 38: John Norden's 1624 plan of East Lilling (reproduced by permission of the British Library).

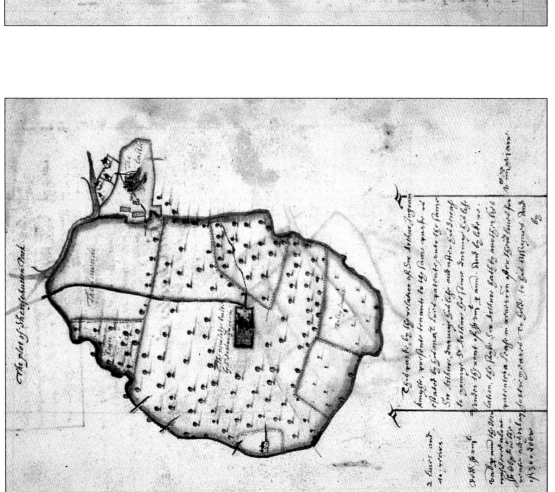

Plate 37: John Norden's 1624 plan of Sheriff Hutton Park (reproduced by permission of the British Library). (North to right).

Plate 39: Line of the park pale along Finkle Street to the south of the village.

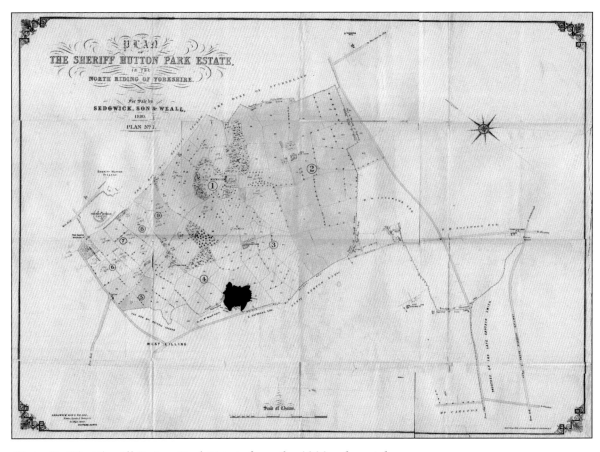

Plate 40: The Sheriff Hutton Park Estate from the 1880 sale catalogue.

Plate 41: First castle with ridge and furrow in foreground, looking north-west.

Plate 42: First castle, looking west.

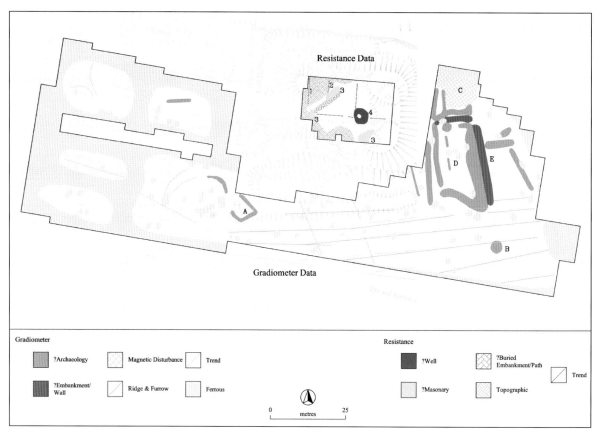

Plate 43: Interpretation of geophysical survey of first castle site (from GSB Prospection Ltd 2004).

Plate 44: Sheriff Hutton castle, north-east tower after repair and consolidation.

Plate 45: View of Sheriff Hutton castle from the gardens, looking north-west, showing the inner court buildings.

Plate 46: View of heraldic frieze on the inner gatehouse.

Plate 47: View of Sheriff Hutton castle from the west lawn, looking north.

Plate 48: Distant view of Sheriff Hutton castle, looking west.

Plate 49: Meadowsweet.

Plate 50: Elder.

Plate 51: View towards the area of formal gardens at Sheriff Hutton castle.

Plate 52: Thistle.

Plate 53: Rose bay willow herb.

Plate 55: Primroses.

Plate 54: Cow parsley.

Plate 56: Spurge Laurel in hedge to the south of the stone castle.

Plate 57: Spurge Laurel – detail.

Plate 58: Woodpecker hole in an oak tree at East Lilling deserted village.

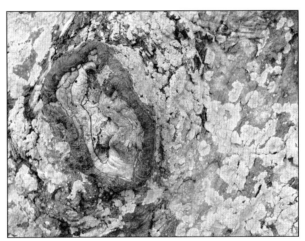

Plate 59: Lichen (Diploicia canescens) on an oak tree in the park.

Plate 60: Common spotted orchid.

Plate 61: Bank vole.

Plate 62: Line of the park pale north-east of East Lilling deserted village, showing ancient oak trees and ridge and furrow.

Plate 63: Old oak tree stump in East Lilling deserted village.

Plate 64: Ancient oak trees to the north-east of the Hall.

Plate 65: Ancient oak tree to the north of the Hall.

Plate 66: Ancient oak tree on the line of the 1334 park pale to the south of the Hall.

Plate 67: Ancient oak tree adjacent to the Hall.

Plate 68: Monkshood in woodland adjacent to the Hall.

Plate 69: Bluebells in woodland on the east side of the park.

Plate 70: 1963 Christmas card showing Colonel Percy Ledgard, his wife and daughters in the grounds of The Park; Percy has his pet macaw 'Sinbad' on his right arm.

Plate 71: 1963 Christmas card showing Sarah, Annabelle and Lavinia Ledgard out with the hunt in front of The Park.

Plate 72: Sheriff Hutton Hall, north elevation.

Plate 73: Sheriff Hutton Hall, south elevation.

Plate 74: General view of Oaks Farm, looking north-west.

Plate 75: View of farmhouse at Lodge Farm, looking north.

Plate 76: View of farmhouse at Park Farm, looking north.

Plate 77: View of The Rangers House, looking east.

Plate 78: View of Sheriff Hutton castle from the park.

Plate 79: Snow at Sheriff Hutton castle.

Plate 80: Dawn at Sheriff Hutton castle.

Plate 81: Sunset over Sheriff Hutton castle and park.

CHAPTER 11: THE PEOPLE AND THE PARK - 1: 1485 TO 1596
By Tony Wright

Sheriff Hutton Castle, the day after the battle of Bosworth

Soon after dawn on 23rd August 1485, three figures could be seen standing below the south wall of the immense inner court of Sheriff Hutton castle. One, a grown man in worn and stained travelling clothes was talking urgently to the other two, both of whom were teenagers and both were richly dressed. The boy was considerably younger than the girl, who had a clear view of the gardens and ponds at the bottom of the slope in front of them. Behind them, keeping a discrete distance were two bodyguards, carrying spears, swords and each with a bow strapped across his back, a quiver of arrows at his belt. The boy's view of the gardens, lakes and the immense lawn of the deer park beyond was blocked by the body of the man. A herd of deer, which had been eating the food put out for them by the ponds, had been disturbed by the stridency of the man's speech and were standing, watchful, a hundred paces beyond the far side of the far pond. It had been stormy the previous day so they didn't lack for water and they had been agitated by the unaccustomed comings and goings of the night.

'The Duke of Hereford's men will be here soon! If you do not leave within the hour, you will never be able' the man urged the boy. 'Leave now, my Lord. Go to Kingston and take ship for France.'

The girl interrupted: 'France is refuge for neither the Earl of Warwick nor myself' she said.

'Nor is Scotland'

'Spain then'

'I doubt that we would reach Spain alive and I do not wish to leave. Where are you going, Sir Geoffrey?'

'I am going to the hills near my estate, ma'am' replied the man and paused respectfully, as the boy was stammering something.

'C c c c can we go and see the horses Lizzie?' he asked. The man had moved in his agitation and the boy was now pointing to the shapes of grazing animals, just visible in the rising mist in a paddock about half a mile to the south.

'Later Eddie' she answered, then spoke to the man.

'I am as safe here as anywhere and the Earl of Warwick..' she inclined her head to the boy, whose concentration had wandered to the deer '.. Surely they cannot believe that he is a threat to anyone. He scarcely knows the season of the year'

'Your brothers ma'am..' he started but he had angered the girl.

'King Edward may yet live, as may Prince Richard' she retorted fiercely. 'My eldest brother is compos mentis and the Duke will, no doubt, release him from the Tower to take his place as King. Then, Sir Geoffrey, you may return from your refuge in the hills and resume your duties here.'

She took the boy by the hand. 'Come Eddie.' and, as they descended through the garden terraces, her voice faded in the distance: 'Which one's your favourite, Eddie?'

'Lady Elizabeth' replied the Earl of Warwick and she laughed.

Sir Geoffrey Frank turned to the two bodyguards and said 'Follow them and guard their Royal Highnesses with your lives. The new king, whoever he is, will reward you.' He turned back and raised his voice

'Your Highness!'

The children stopped but only the boy turned, enquiringly so he called again.

'My Lady, the Princess Elizabeth!'

She also turned and smiled broadly. Frank bowed deeply and backed respectfully until she could no longer see him, then he turned and leaped up the steps and into the castle by the nearby postern, where the darkness swallowed him.

Whilst the conversation above is invented, the circumstances surrounding the end of the House of York are well known. The messenger bearing the news of the death of Richard III arrived in the City of York late in the evening of the Battle of Bosworth.[1] There is no record of the immediate transmission of the news to Sheriff Hutton castle but it is likely that the Corporation of York sent someone. Geoffrey Frank, Receiver of the Lordship of Sheriff Hutton, did flee to his estate,[2] Elizabeth of York (who could have anticipated being restored to her title of Princess) was fetched within a few days to the Tower of London, to be reunited with her mother and ultimately to become queen to Henry VII (known to us as Henry Tudor but, until 1485, his major title was Duke of Hereford) and Edward, Earl of Warwick, reputedly lacking some of his wits, was imprisoned and then executed in the Tower some 17 years later.

Local legend has it that Edward was permitted to walk in Sheriff Hutton park as far as an old oak tree, which acquired the sobriquet of 'The Warwick Oak'. It had blown down by 1824[3] but was propped up and fenced, surviving, after a fashion, until the construction of a piggery in 1970;[4] it stood (or leaned) to the south of The Rangers House. Elizabeth also had rights to graze her horses 'below the park'[5] and the location of the paddock seems to have been in the area later called 'Horse Hagg', about half a mile directly south of the castle (see figure 5/2).

Fig. 11/1: The remains of the Warwick Oak in the late 1960s.

For Sheriff Hutton park, as with the rest of the manor and the lordship, the end of the House of York marked the end of the era of ownership by a great northern lord and it became a royal manor. The Tudor kings and queens used the revenues of the manor and all its 'appurtenances' to pay for the rule of the north and the castle became one of the seats of the President of the Council of the North (or his Lieutenant).[6] The incumbent of this title would live at the castle unless he possessed his own estates nearby.

Henry VII immediately revoked all of Richard III's appointments and the next Keeper of the Park was a John Dawnay, who was appointed on the 6th October 1485.[7] Such an appointment was, almost certainly, purely to reward Dawnay for services to Henry or to pay him for something he was about to do. Someone else will have actually carried out the functions involved in caring for the deer, maintaining the pale, preventing poaching and organising the hunts.

The first Leader of the Council (or alternatively President, Lieutenant and/or Lieutenant-General - the title is not certain) was Henry Percy, Earl of Northumberland but, when he was killed on his manor of Topcliffe in 1489, he was replaced by Thomas Howard, Earl of Surrey. Thomas's father, John, Duke of Norfolk, had been killed at Bosworth, fighting for Richard III, and Thomas, who had also been wounded there, was still under the family attainder which was not lifted until his famous victory over the Scots at Flodden Field in 1513. Thomas had been appointed Lieutenant-General of the North under the nominal presidency of Prince Arthur, who was then just a baby, and he retained this position until 1499. His predecessor, Henry Percy had family estates and other castles nearby, so he probably hardly used Sheriff Hutton, but the castle became Howard's main residence in the north.

Fig. 11/2: Thomas Howard, 3rd Duke of Norfolk (Source: National Portrait Gallery, London).

Fig. 11/3: John Skelton (Source: National Portrait Gallery, London).

The Garland of Laurel

In May 1495, Howard had a group of people staying at the castle and, amongst the family and northern officials, was the poet, John Skelton. The poem he composed in this year gives us a list of the ladies present at the castle, and therefore, by inference, their men folk.[8] It also provides a tantalising glimpse of the park and of a hunt:

> *A Right Delectable Treatise upon a Goodly*
> *GARLAND OR CHAPLET OF LAUREL*
>
> *By Master Skelton, Poet Laureate, studiously Devised at*
> *Sheriff-Hutton Castle, in the Forest of Galtres, wherein*
> *are comprised many and divers solacious and right pregnant*
> *electuaries of singular pleasure, as more at large it doth*
> *appear in the process following.*

Skelton imagines a review of his life to date and anticipates a debate between the Queen of Fame and Dame Pallas as to whether he should be admitted to the Court of Fame. This occurs after he has wandered into the park and becomes drowsy…

> *….me to rest, I leant me to a stumpe*
> *Of an oak, that sometime grew full straight,*
> *A mighty tree and of a noble height,*
> *Whose beauty blasted was with the boystors wind,*
> *His leaves lost, the sap was from the rind.*
>
> *Thus stood I in the frithy forest of Galtress,*
> *Ensoaked with silt of the miry moss,*
> *Where hartes bellowing, embosed with distress,*
> *Ran on the range so long, that I suppose*
> *Few men can tell now where the hind-calf goes;*
> *Fair fall that forster that so well can bate his hound*
> *But of my purpose now turn we to the ground.*

In practice, Sheriff Hutton had not been within the Forest of Galtres since 1228-29 (see Chapter 4) but it lay within a peripheral area called the 'purlieus', where the forest laws were less restrictive.[9] In this passage, Skelton regrets the passing of the medieval huntsman's skills, then imagines the pavilion in which his fate is to be debated.

After the debate, in which it is decided that he will be admitted to the Court of Fame, he returns to the castle, where the Countess of Surrey, her family and retinue are weaving and embroidering his Crown of Laurel.

> *Thus talking we went in at a postern gate;*
> *Turning on the right hande, by a winding stair,*
> *She brought me to a goodly chamber of estate,*
> *Where the noble Countess of Surrey in a chair*
> *Sat honourably, to whome did repair*
> *Of ladies a bevy with all due reverence.*
> *Sit downe, fair ladies, and do your diligence!*

Come forth, gentlewomen, I pray you, she said,
I have contrived for you a goodly work,
And who can work beste now shall be assayed.
A coronal of laurel with verdures light and dark
I have devised for Skelton, my clerk;
For to his service I have suche regard
That of our bounty we will him reward.

Skelton then composes a short poem to each of the ladies present in forms and length which accurately reflect their age and status. The most important of this company was the countess's daughter, Lady Elizabeth Howard, mother of Anne Boleyn and grandmother of Elizabeth I, and Margery Wentworth, who may have married John Seymour and became mother of Jane Seymour and therefore grandmother to Edward VI.[10] The other ladies were Mistress Margaret Tilney (the countess's sister-in-law), Lady Anne Dacre of the South (wife of Thomas, Lord Dacre), Mistress Margery Wentworth (daughter of Sir Richard Wentworth), Mistress Jane Blennerhasset (daughter of Sir Thomas Blennerhasset), Mistress Gertrude Statham, Mistress Isabel Knight, Mistress Margaret Hussey, Lady Minel Howard and Mistress Isabell Pennell.

First Neglect

Thomas Howard, the Earl of Surrey, had the same privilege of pasturing his animals 'below the Park' as had Queen Elizabeth during her stay at the castle in Richard III's reign. This was reckoned part of his payment for being Lieutenant-General of the North, worth £6 13s. 4d. per year, as was his holding of the park, which was worth 60s. per year.[11] He also had the right of 'herbage' (the pasturing of any animal on the demesne except swine) and 'pannage' (the right to pasture pigs in the park).[12] He may also have been the Keeper of the Park, although this office (or more probably Howard's gift of it) had been successively held by John Dawnay in 1485, Ralph Bigod in 1486 and Thomas Hargyll in 1487; the latter's wages were not to exceed 2d. per day but he also had the right to pasture 12 animals within the park.[13] These appointments were recorded in government rolls but Howard's commission as lieutenant had been 'by word of mouth'[14] from the king, so his other remunerative posts may have been as well. Howard stayed as Lieutenant-General until about 1500 and was then replaced by Abbot Sever of St Mary's Abbey in York. Prince Arthur died in 1502, still a child and never having visited his northern fiefdom, and his successor as President was Thomas Savage, Archbishop of York.[15] Each of these presidents had their own estates and residences nearby, and so had no need for the castle.

Howard's departure opened up some opportunities for enhancement, and Sir Thomas Darcy (who, for some reason, had been given control of the Marches and was made Constable and Steward of Sheriff Hutton castle but was not made Lieutenant of the North[16]) gained the rights of herbage and pannage in the park and was paid 40 shillings more than his predecessors.[17] According to his priest, John Baxter: "...we went to Schyryff Howton and there we kept a court ...where [Darcy's] patyn was read and everyman was glad; for they said that they had had heard much good spoken of him".[18] Whilst they were there, they had a survey done and "Master Evers took a few (view) of the deer and I trow he fewed them to ten score deer".[19]

If Master Evers counted 200 deer, he found about the right number. Any more and the park would not have been able to sustain them. Any fewer and they would not have been a viable herd. Evers also made an inventory of goods within the castle and 'be ye assured it is of little valour'.[20] Perhaps his inventory was useless but it is more likely that, with no resident lord, the castle was devoid of the necessities of life and being allowed to decay.

A little over a year later, a reshuffle of offices saw Richard Cholmley become Master of the Game as well as Constable of the Castle, and he received the rent of the herbage at the same rate as Darcy.[21] He seems to have held this post for some years, being re-appointed in 1509 after Henry VIII's succession.[22] The Keepership of the Park, however, changed hands much more frequently after Thomas Hargyll handed the post over to Thomas Berkeley in September 1506, shortly before he died;[23] Berkeley also became pallister (the person responsible for maintaining the pale) at the same time. However, Henry VIII did not renew Berkeley's appointment but gave it to William Cheyney, who was then replaced by Lawrence Ecclesfield in April 1513.[24]

Later in that year, Thomas Howard, Earl of Surrey, returned to the area, mustering troops on his way to a famous victory at Flodden. We do not know if he called in at his old stamping ground of Sheriff Hutton park but the men of the village still remembered the battle 40 years afterwards, in the same way that 20th century folk talk of the time before and after the Second World War.[25]

Henry VIII's son at Sheriff Hutton

The Earl of Shrewsbury became Lieutenant of the North in 1523 but he had the choice of Sheriff Hutton, Barnard Castle and Pontefract castles as a residence;[26] there is no sign that he chose Sheriff Hutton which seems to have continued to decay. As a result, when Henry VIII, lacking a legitimate heir, decided to send his illegitimate son, Henry 'Fitzroy', Duke of Richmond, to be educated at Sheriff Hutton as a possible future king, the whole place was in serious need of repair (see Chapter 7).

John Palsgrave, Richmond's schoolmaster, tried to make his young charge's studies as pleasant as possible, so that "his officers wot not whether I learn him or play with him".[27] His education was not confined solely to the schoolroom. Richmond was to be a true renaissance prince – he was taught archery and "He also developed a love of hunting, keeping hawks, greyhounds and bloodhounds in order to do so".[28] Indeed, Palsgrave soon started to complain that his own teachings were being ignored in favour of hunting, hawking and riding. He was replaced but the new schoolmaster, Richard Croke, made the same complaints, namely that his pupil was being taken out of classes to learn archery and other sports.[29] It is possible that at least some of the £321 19s. 10¾d. spent between June 1525 and the following March in 'Reparations on the Manor of Sheriff Hutton'[30] was spent on the park, although the lack of any specific mention may simply reflect that the park was self supporting.

There are no records in Richmond's accounts for expenditure on hunting, except for £4 10s. 0d. for 'Greyhounds and other hounds'. In the stables there was the Master of the Horse with four servants, a 'Clerk of the Avery' with two servants, a yeoman and two grooms 'of the stirrope', a yeoman and two grooms as farriers, a yeoman and two grooms as cartiers, a similar threesome as 'somptermen' and again as 'lyttermen', and ten 'horsekeepers'. But these do not seem excessive for a household which numbered 245[31] and which depended on horses for travel and carriage.

The Pilgrimage brings Another Duke

Henry Fitzroy, Duke of Richmond, had left Sheriff Hutton by 1532, when William Reskymer, 'one of the Pages of the King's Chamber', was made bailiff of the Lordship of Sheriff Hutton and was granted the offices of Keeper of the Park and 'paler' in place of Lawrence Ecclesfield, who had died.[32] Two years later, Henry VII's historian, Leland passed by and, whilst fulsome in his praise for the castle, noted merely that "There is a Park by the Castel" and that there was little wood in the nearby areas of the Forest of Galtres.[33] Clearly the castle was allowed to deteriorate again for, when Richmond's father-in-law, Thomas Howard, the Duke of Norfolk, was sent here to complete the suppression of the Pilgrimage of Grace in 1537, a massive programme of repair was required.

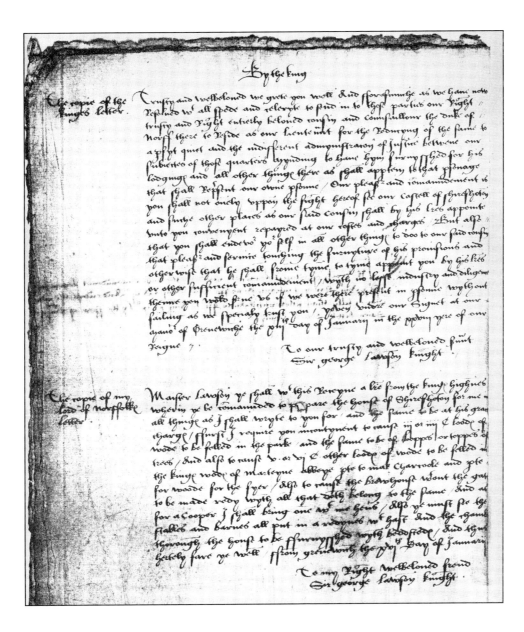

Fig. 11/4: Copies of Henry VIII's and the Duke of Norfolk's letters to George Lawson (Source: National Archives).

161

Before he left Greenwich, Norfolk wrote to Sir George Lawson instructing him to arrange for three or four hundred loads of wood to be felled in the park 'and the same to be loppes and toppes of trees'. This appears to be intended as structural timber, as the five or six hundred other loads he requested from Marton Woods were to be for charcoal and firewood.[34] Nine carpenters worked in the park and castle from the middle of January until the middle of July, felling, hewing and squaring the timber, which was used to rebuild the barns, stables, bakehouse, brewhouse, horsemill and other buildings, and for building a new slaughterhouse. It was also used for new beds, tables, trestles, 'forms', stools and cupboards, and fitting out the kitchen, pastry and larderhouses, and those buildings which had been repaired.[35] However, the fresh timber was not suitable for making watertight vats, tubs and barrels and for these, 'full shronken' planks and boards had to be brought from Crayke and York.[36] Nor, apparently, was the wood suitable to make the table for the duke to eat off. The timber for this had to be bought from Hull, shipped to York and then carried from there.[37] The costs of transporting all this timber was significant: several Sheriff Hutton men were paid 2d. a load to bring seven score and eighteen loads of timber from the park to the castle, but this was cheap compared with ferrying the loads from Marton and Crayke which cost 12d. each.[38]

The timber taken from the park needed to be replaced, and an area where new trees were to be allowed to grow (here called a spring) was set aside for the duke: "Item paid to John Cobbe and his fellows of Shirefhoton for dyking and hedging of the spryng within the park of Shirefhoton which was felled for my lord of Norfolks household spent within the castell of Shirfhoton" ... at a cost of £2 12s. 9d.[39] The length of this new boundary amounted to 210 rods, which equates to approximately 1060m.

There are other incidental references to the park at this time, for example, the duke took Robert Southwell for a walk in the park for private discussions after the latter had delivered a letter from Thomas Cromwell.[40] Detailed preparations were also made in 1537 for the arrival of Henry VIII[41] but he didn't travel north until 1541 and the duke left Sheriff Hutton before the end of the year. In the following year (1538), the offices of the park were granted to Sir Thomas Curwen, who had been loyal throughout the Pilgrimage of Grace, and the reversion was granted to Sir George Lawson, another loyalist who had overseen the works at the castle.[42] The grant records that Sir George received the herbage and pannage, which cost him a rent but he received fees for Keeping the Park and the game in return.

After the Howards

In 1538-39, a comparison can be made between the number of deer kept in various northern royal forests, chases and parks:[43]

Park	No of Deer	Type
Galtres Forest	800	Fallow
Sheriff Hutton	400	Fallow
Sherwood Forest	1000	Red
Hatfield Chase	700	Red
Topcliffe Great Park	435	Fallow
Topcliffe Little Park	247	Fallow

A park of about 600 acres, of which about a third was wood, could not have supported a population of 400 fallow deer without additional water and feed. There are several wells and ponds scattered over the area of the park, and it will be shown later how the trees were managed to provide feed, but it is probable that this number was an overestimate or that it was a temporary overstocking. It seems that 300, for which later tenants covenanted, was a more usual number of deer.

The Duke of Norfolk returned in 1542 and a letter from him suggests that Henry VIII might have hunted at Sheriff Hutton in the previous year as he had left harnesses both here and at Pontefract.[44] Henry's love of hunting was legendary, and his progress to York had taken weeks, in which he had dispensed benevolent royal justice "bringing desolation only to the hundreds of stags, deer and swans who fell to the lavish royal hunts which punctuated the progress and which must have swept clean of much of its wildlife a wide track from London to Yorkshire".[45] Rejuvenated by his relationship with Catharine Howard, the duke's second niece and later to become one of his queens, Henry had resumed the regular routine of rising at five or six and hunting until ten.[46]

However, the duke does not appear to have been staying at Sheriff Hutton at this time, for in 1539 Archbishop Holgate had been appointed as President of the North and was given the King's Manor in York as a residence and headquarters.[47] Never again was Sheriff Hutton to be the main residence of a major lord, although they continued to hunt in the park. For example, the duke entertained the Scottish ambassador to a hunt on the 23rd of September in 1542, but was expected back to York in the evening, in time to dine.[48] Sir Thomas Curwen died in 1543-44 and his park offices reverted to Sir George Lawson, but they were re-granted to Charles Brandon in the following year.[49]

An idea of the state of the park in 1545 may be inferred from a memorandum from George Talbot, 6th Earl of Shrewsbury, who noted that "the Lord Treasurer is to grant a warrant for wood from the Forest of Galtres for the repair of Sheriff Hutton Park".[50] This implies that there was no longer enough good or substantial wood to maintain either the pale or the building(s) within it – was it the taking of sufficient good trees for the repairs to the castle in 1537 or that grazing 400 fallow deer in 600 acres was too much and the woodland had to be sacrificed to feed the deer?

The Puritan Earl

Probably the longest serving President of the North arrived at Sheriff Hutton in 1572 in the person of Henry Hastings, 3rd Earl of Huntingdon.[51] Like his queen's father, he was in the habit of rising early but, in his case, it was to hear a good sermon. Known to us as 'The Puritan Earl', he devoted his life to Protestantism and good government, and refused to allow anyone to put forward his (very strong) case as heir to the throne.[52] The earl used the castle mainly as a prison, inevitably for Scots and Border 'pledges' (hostages for good behaviour) but later for the Catholic wives of gentlemen. Notably, their imprisonment was unsympathetic but not harsh, and their descriptions mention successfully importing priests. These accounts suggest that the side of the castle facing over the park was less well guarded, and in 1593 Mrs Babthorpe was not only able to give letters to a priest at a 'grate window of a low room which looked out into a Park' but also to take communion with him there.[53]

The Puritan Earl died in December 1595, leaving debts so great that his family refused to collect his body (which would have instantly acknowledged them) until instructed to do so by the queen. His inability to handle money was exacerbated by her unwillingness to recompense him adequately for his service in the north. He had been partially paid by being allowed to buy land in Sheriff Hutton, notably in Lillings Ambo along the southern border of the park, and it was his desperate need for cash which led him to sell some of this to the Hall family, who had had an interest in Lilling Hall since at least 1556 but were now able to expand their holdings there.[54]   An inventory taken in June 1596[55] shows that he left 75 'ancient and poor' servants bereft of a master as well as a number of named horses:

> *"The names of such as ar at Sherifhutton - Bay Haistinges with a fillie fole, xxxiijs iiijd; Gray Haistinges, a mare, xxxviijs; Dune Ockingham, xvjs; Gray Thorpe, xls; Gray Teyll, xls; Sourell Dyeves, xxiiijs; Blacke thorpe, xxiiijs; Gray Abney, xxvjs viijd; Gray Dawbye xvjs; one calde Ockingham, xxiiijs; Boyneton, xvjs; White Alforde, xxxijs; an iron gray nagg, xxvjs viijd; Gray Hausbye, a colte, xxs; Bay Ockingham, xxvjs viijd; a browne bay nagg with a snipp, xxvjs viijd"* Total 21l 11s. 4d.

Does this impressive list indicate that he came to Sheriff Hutton to go hunting? If so, he surrounded himself with richness:

> *"At Sherifhutton - one cannopie of purple cloth with blewe silke fringe and lace with five curtians agreable and a coveringe, xliijs iiijd;...."*

but slept on a camp bed, perhaps to reinforce his Puritan ideals:

> *'... one feilde bedsteade with girthes, iijs' etc Total 5l 12s. 6d.*

Fig. 11/5: Henry Hastings, 3rd Earl of Huntingdon (Source: National Portrait Gallery, London).

Richard Pollerd's Inquisition

Two years later, in 1598, an inquisition was held into the state of the park and the castle and the custodianship of one Richard Pollerd, who was Keeper of the Castle and had been granted the Keepership of the Park as a means of payment.[56] Someone had accused him of employing the park for his own 'Benyfitt', 'Comoditie and use' to the 'preiudice' of 'Her Maiestie',[57] and so six commissioners questioned 44 local men, a yeoman from Escrick and the late earl's brewer as to what had happened over the last few years. This important document, which has been transcribed as part the Pale Project, gives us a first clear picture of how the park was managed under the Tudor monarchs.

At this time, the park was owned by Queen Elizabeth, who had granted it to the Earl of Huntingdon as part of his payment for being President of the Council of the North. From this payment, Huntingdon had to pay all his costs (except for certain specific ones, mainly military campaigns), and so he had re-granted the park to pay the man he had appointed as gaoler at Sheriff Hutton castle, Richard Pollerd.[58] Pollerd in turn had let out the various enclosures in the park to local men[59] and he also employed local men to maintain the park. There were two local 'surveyors', Sir William Fairfax and John Briggs, who could authorise the felling of trees on behalf of the queen.[60]

Pollerd had his grant renewed in the interregnum between Huntingdon's death and the appointment of the new council president in 1598 directly by the Lord Treasurer.[61] He was able to rent out Kirk Hill (now known as High Park) for £22 per year and the whole of the West End (previously and later called The West Lawn) for £20.[62] Pollerd was probably obliged to leave the park as he received it, and so the sale of trees and coppices from Lilling Hagg was being investigated.[63] He was also accused of removing planks from the 'ruinous' Lady Bridge which connected the castle and the West Lawn[64] (see Chapter 8). However, the evidence was that much of the damage had been done before Pollerd's time and some of it at the command of the earl, who was refurbishing the council's headquarters in York, namely the 'King's Manor'.[65]

Pollerd had sold not only timber trees, such as oaks (usually individually but sometimes selling the 'loppes' and the 'toppes' separately) and ashes (in much larger quantities) but also the underwood, thorne trees, 'dotrells' and brushwood. Firewood was sold in 'kidds', by the hundred.[66]

Pollerd had also incurred substantial expense. The park pale had been in disrepair when he took over and he employed a gang of men to repair it at a cost of £30. The Earl of Huntingdon had not been satisfied with the repairs and extra work had to be done, especially where the park was 'verie waterie', so that new bridges had to be built. Overall, most witnesses agreed that Pollerd had spent about £50 on repairs within his first few years. The park provided all the wood for the pale, both oak and ash being used, but he had had to pay for Lilling Hagg to be 'impayled' with a ditch, bank and fence after felling, to protect the new spring from browsing deer.[67] He had let an enclosure called Kirk Hill, which seemed to have both wood and lawn, to a group of York business men, including Alderman Henry Hall of East Lilling, and the lessees were required to put a new pale around the area which they proposed to fell and make a spring. Another enclosure, Murke Hagg, was being felled. Henry Hall and his associates had bought hundreds of loads of thorn trees and taken them to York.[68] The locations of some of these areas are shown on figure 5/2.

The witnesses disagreed about the animals which had been grazed in the park, although many mentioned that one winter, several hundred sheep had been pastured in the West Laund, which had caused damage. Since then far fewer had been allowed and nearly all agreed that the park was in a better condition than when Pollerd took control, with more and better game. This in spite of reports that an area around the lodge had been cleared, ploughed and planted with oats for two years (which interfered with one of the deer 'walks' - one witness said that the deer had got into the corn in the first year and destroyed it).[69] No one believed that any of the deer walks had been disturbed, and the number of deer had been increased to 400, all well looked after, even though their regular yearly food supply of ten loads of hay had been interrupted. This fodder had previously come from Horse Close (an old enclosure on the edge of the Carrs to the north-east of Sheriff Hutton) but this had been let to one Raif Mansfeld, who had stopped it.[70] The keeper had the right to graze his horses and there were reports of cattle being grazed in the park, although no one said that this was to the prejudice of the queen's interests.

It is clear that full grown oak was regarded as very valuable; the inquisition was also trying to trace all the timber from the buildings around the castle which had been demolished and which had been reused in the queen's manor house at York (now the 'King's Manor'), in a newly built mill near to Sheriff Hutton, and by local people to make wains [carts] and build rooms.[71] Even rotten oaks had a value. Witnesses disagreed as to the effect of Richard Pollerd's newly built kiln in the castle (possibly a charcoal kiln but more probably a malting kiln), although one believed that the wood would be diminished.[72]

One witness said that the Earl of Huntingdon had allowed his relations to hunt freely in the park at one time and another, and that the earl often used to stay at the lodge in the park rather than in the castle.[73] There is also mention of a helm (a barn) in the park[74] (see Chapter 4).

The overall picture from the inquisition is of an area which is being cropped, grazed and used for recreation. There is great pressure on it from men wishing to make money from it and a set of rules, not always clear, intended to preserve it, being implemented by men who also made money from it. Under firm management, this is a good incentive but, if government were to become lax, it looks like a recipe for failure.

Footnotes

1   York Corporation Minute Book, 22nd August 1485 quoted by Davies 1843, p.218; Ross 1981, p.223 states that this was two days after the battle.
2   British Library Harleian MSS no. 433, f.59, f.32b & f.113b.
3   Todd 1824, p.20.
4   *Yorkshire Evening Press*, 30th June 1977 "History in the Re-Making"; Gilbert 1965, p.22; *Yorkshire Post* n.d. 1929 "Yorkshire Archaeological Society Outing".
5   Ministers Accounts for the Lordship of Sheriff Hutton, National Archives, DL/650/10510-10514, quoted by Tucker 1962, p.70
6   There is a degree of continuity as Richard III had created such a council with its seat at Sandal Castle but with the use of Sheriff Hutton amongst others, and there are records of Richard's council at Sheriff Hutton. The revenues of the lordship of Sheriff Hutton were devoted to the upkeep of the garrison of Berwick (see Chapter 1).
7   Calendar of Patent Rolls, Henry VII vol 1, p.54.
8   The poem was composed in 1495 but not published until 1523, when Skelton added further lines. For the dating, a full copy and a definitive description of the poem, see Brownlow 1999. My thanks are due to Professor Melvin B Tucker for pointing me in the right directions. The quotes here are taken from Henderson 1948.
9   Swan *et al* 1993, p13; Cowling 1967, p.153.

10   Brownlow 1999, pp.187-189.
11   Tucker 1962, p.70.
12   Calendar of Patent Rolls, Henry VII vol 2, p.203.
13   Calendar of Patent Rolls, Henry VII vol 1, pp.54, 90 & 192: 'Materials for a History of Henry VII', Rolls Series, vol 60, p.188.
14   Tucker 1962, p.67.
15   Reid 1975, p.83.
16   ibid., p.84.
17   Calendar of Patent Rolls, Henry VII vol 2, p.203.
18   Letters & Papers, Henry VIII vol 12(2), p.61, no.186. This letter, dated 1500, is in a sequence from 1537.
19   ibid.
20   ibid.
21   Calendar of Patent Rolls, Henry VII vol 2, p.269; Letters & Papers, Henry VIII vol 1(1), p.55.
22   Letters & Papers, Henry VIII vol 1(2), no. 2055(44).
23   Catalogue of Ancient Deeds, vol 3, D1214; Calendar of Patent Rolls, Henry VII vol 2, p.496. Also Letters & Papers, Henry VIII vol 1(2), no. 2055(44). Also Duckett 1877, p.94.
24   Letters & Papers, Henry VIII vol 1(1), p.31; Letters & Papers, Henry VIII vol 1(2), no. 2055(44).
25   Purvis 1949, p.88.
26   Reid 1975, p.94 quoting Letters & Papers, Henry VIII vol 4, nos. 2412 & 2439.
27   Murphy 2003, p.71.
28   ibid.
29   ibid., p.72.
30   Nichols 1855, p.xxvii.
31   Murphy 2003, p.67.
32   Letters & Papers, Henry VIII vol 4, p.668 no. 1598.
33   Brayshaw 1889, p.325.
34   National Archives E101/484/3 'The Works of Shirefhoton Castell' by Bartholomew Stable (1537), f.4v; this document was fully translated by me in 1985-86.
35   ibid., f.5r through to f.7v. Sawyers were paid separately (f.9v).
36   ibid., f.20r.
37   ibid., f.24v; f.29v.
38   ibid., f.25r.
39   ibid., f.29r.
40   Letters & Papers, Henry VIII vol 12(2), p.206.
41   National Archives E101/484/3, f .30r & v.
42   Letters & Papers, Henry VIII vol 5, no.1598; ibid., vol 7, p.398, no.1026.
43   Cowling 1967, p.161.
44   Bain 1890, p.184.
45   Scarisbrick 1983, p.428.
46   ibid., p.430. He was to take solace in hunting when Catharine's adultery was proved to him, after a meeting, whilst hunting, with the Duke (ibid., p.432).
47   Rushton 2003, p.190.
48   Bain 1890, p.223, no.176.
49   Letters & Papers, Henry VIII, vol 19(1), 141(22).
50   Jamison 1966, p.173.
51   Rushton 2003, p.190.
52   For his story, see Cross 1987.
53   Morris 1872, vol 1, pp.229-231.
54   Cross 1987, p.338 ; Calthrop 1923, p183; see Chapter 17.
55   Harley 1928, pp.355-361: 'An Inventorie of all the goodes and chattells of the Righte Honourable Henry late Erle of Huntingdon deceased ....' June 1596.
56   National Archives E178/2792 Sheriff Hutton, Inquisition as to the Castle and Park 41 Eliz. I (1598). My thanks to Alice Jowitt of the National Archives for her help in sorting this, at times, confusing document.
57   ibid., testimony of John Skarr.
58   ibid., testimony of Thomas Wetton and John ffloode.
59   ibid., testimony of Richard Chapman.
60   ibid., testimony of Xpofer Share; testimony of Roger Barthrope.
61   ibid., testimony of Roger Barthrope.
62   ibid., testimony of Bryan Pereson.
63   ibid., testimony of Bartholomew Smithe.

64 ibid., testimony of John Broughe.
65 ibid., testimony of Richard Heburne; Heburne had been Keeper of the Park and castle before Pollerd and was aged 70 at the time of the Inquisition.
66 ibid., testimony of Christopher Sharr.
67 ibid., testimony of Xpofer Watles.
68 ibid., testimony of John Broughe.
69 ibid., testimony of John Broughe.
70 ibid., testimony of Christopher Dee.
71 ibid., testimony of Thomas Wetton.
72 ibid., testimony of John Broughe.
73 ibid., testimony of Xpofer Watles.
74 ibid., testimony of John Broughe.

CHAPTER 12: THE PEOPLE AND THE PARK – 2: 1596 TO 1674
By Tony Wright

The Arrival of the Ingrams

Queen Elizabeth lived on until 1603 but, for Sheriff Hutton, the death which defined the end of an era was that of Henry Hastings, 3rd Earl of Huntingdon, in December 1595.[1] He had been President of the Council of the North for 24 years and, whilst his energy had remained undiminished until he took to his deathbed, he had spent this time in religious and moral improvement and in bringing law and order to the Scottish borders. He had lived mainly at the King's Manor in York which had by now become the established headquarters for the Council of the North. However, Sheriff Hutton castle was still used as a gaol, notably for Catholic gentry, it was still the head of the royal lordship of Sheriff Hutton, and the park was always there for the hunting. As noted in Chapter 11 above, Hastings had kept 17 of his own horses there, as well as some harness, a camp bed and a carriage.[2]

For three years there was no President of the Council of the North and then Thomas Cecil, Lord Burghley, was appointed.[3] He had two main objectives: the re-establishment of Protestantism in the north (it seems that the humanity of Hastings had prevented him from crushing Catholicism), and preparing for the death of Elizabeth and the smooth transfer of power to James VI of Scotland. He didn't live at Sheriff Hutton as he had his own castle at Snape but, as he had been granted the use of the castle and the park, he had the profits of the sale of the wood.[4] However, he was replaced in 1602 by Edmund Sheffield, Earl of Mulgrave, who also had his own property nearby.[5]

Elizabeth I died in 1603 and King James was unable to repeat his success in governing Scotland south of the border (he was fond of hunting and spent significant amounts of time at his parks close to London).[6] This opened up possibilities for all sorts of courtiers and business men who could take on the running of royal property and profit from its improvement and subletting. Whilst this had also been happening during the reign of Elizabeth, for example the Earl of Huntingdon had received permission to buy lands in Sheriff Hutton as part of his payment and then sold them on,[7] 'farming' now became the classic method of managing the royal manors.

John Eldred and William Whitmore were granted a lease of some lands in Sheriff Hutton in 1610, in return for a loan of £2,000.[8] Eldred and Whitmore were consistently part of farming syndicates and the man who often put together their syndicates was Arthur Ingram, the son of a London merchant of Yorkshire descent.[9] Ingram had worked for his father, travelling to Italy as a young man[10] and collecting debts, but he first rose to prominence in the customs service. As an able organiser, he improved the revenues but became rich by assembling syndicates to take long leases of customs duties, taking his payment as a fraction of the syndicate, which would, in turn, make its profit by receiving dues greater than the lease. Ingram also took on the debts of peers, taking their property as security. Sometimes he promised staged payments, and paid the first then no more, and retained a number of lawyers to fend off the claimants.[11] It was as a part of one such deal that he acquired his third wife, Mary Greville, only falling in love afterwards.

In 1605, the Keeper and Pallister of the Park had been one Thomas Weldon,[12] but he was replaced in 1606 when James I granted the position to an ambitious courtier, Thomas

Lumsden.[13] He appointed William Clarke who was Keeper in 1609, as by 1611 he was being blamed for overgrazing.[14] This is probably a reflection of the structure of these royal grants, in which a farmer or courtier would be granted the park for a rent (or as part repayment for a loan) but then would re-grant it to local men for the grazing, wood or other profitable enterprise.[15]

A Special Commission was held in 1609-11 to determine the state of the park[16] and, like the detailed 1598 commission described in Chapter 11, this provides some information about how the park was managed at this time. Christopher Dawson reported to the commissioners that Richard Pollerd (the Keeper of the Park in 1598) had left the deer in a good condition, but that their numbers had declined during the subsequent keepership by Sir Charles Kelde. As has been noted in Chapter 5, another witness, John Richardson, said that 'diverse men' had taken meadow in the West Lawne and had entreated William Clarke to make a hedge to stop 'the raskall deere' from entering their ground. The 'rails betwixt the East Lawne and Oakes [were] laid open' because of a recent drought, and Clarke had scoured the ponds at his own expense. Other details relating to this commission are listed in Chapter 5 above.

In 1611, the Earl of Shrewsbury was being instructed to 'send persons who had killed deer in the Park to London'[17] and in 1613 Sir Edmund Sheffield was appointed Keeper and Pallister of the Park.[18] The impression is that potential profiteers were gathering, yet ultimately there would be only one winner and that would be the ruthless Ingram.[19] In 1615, James I granted him the offices of Keeper and Palliciator (presumably a new spelling of pallister or an attempt to create a rank above pallister) and later that year a 'View of game' reported 'eleven score and some odde deare of all sortes' in the park (i.e. more than 242). However, one of the panel making this assessment was Rafe Brocke, Arthur Ingram's steward,[20] and so it is difficult to be sure how accurate this number actually was.

Thomas Lumsden seems to have been granted the stewardship of the manor of Sheriff Hutton in 1606 and then several other offices at Sheriff Hutton in 1613, including Steward of the Castle. In 1615, William Clarke, who was tenanting rooms in the castle, wrote to Lumsden complaining that lead was being stolen around him.[21] Two years later, in 1617, Brocke's stewardship accounts record building activity in the park and in that year, during a visit to York, King James had a days hunting in the park and was entertained to lunch in the 'Laund House' by Sir Arthur, who provided imported almonds and oysters.[22]

Ingram was later to claim that the park had been granted to him for 40 years from 1618 at a rent of £8 per year (and a covenant to keep 300 deer), but this is grossly below a reasonable rent, and he was never able to produce the evidence in the form of a patent. George Kirke of London, the Groom of the King's Bedchamber, did have a patent and a more likely rent.[23] Nevertheless, Ingram had decided to extend his businesses into the north, especially Yorkshire, and he started to build a magnificent house and garden in York and a no less magnificent hunting lodge at Sheriff Hutton.[24] A detailed discussion of Ingram's new lodge, and any other structures that it might have replaced, is contained in Chapter 15.

During this time, Thomas Lumsden retained an interest in the park and in 1620, a Richard Pollard (possibly the same Richard Pollerd who had been keeper in the 1590s) wrote to him about the state of the hunting and the game. However, Lumsden's influence was declining, as Ingram had bought his debts.[25] In the following year Lumsden granted the offices of Steward of the Forest of Galtres and the Mastership of the Game (either in the forest or in Sheriff Hutton park) to William Ferrers, Ingram's father-in-law, and in the year after that,

James I gave another grant of the park, possibly genuine this time, to Ingram.[26] In 1623, with Ingram pressurising his steward and workmen to complete the new lodge, they broke into the castle (which Lumsden was still hoping to convert into a habitable house), stealing lead, good stonework, casements and demolishing one tower.[27] Lumsden sued for, and received, compensation, but Ingram had only to foreclose on the debts and Lumsden had to concede his interests to Ingram.[28]

Ingram also had his problems with the local inhabitants, having to tell his steward, Richard Mattison, to put a lock on the castle and also to "get the names of one or two of the best that hath killed my deer and I will bring them into the Star Chamber". Mattison sent him a list of five names, of which three were marked as 'sufficient' indicating that they were worth prosecuting, the rest being penniless and thus unable to pay a fine.[29]

The Survey in 1624 - First Plan of the Park

Ingram's new lodge in the park, on the site of the present Hall, was completed in 1624 and in August of that year, John Norden, who was well known for his surveys of royal manors, made one of Sheriff Hutton, with his son, also called John.[30] Within the survey is the first, complete plan of the park (see plate 37) and a brief description, with the rent and value as follows:

> *"Sherife hutton parke Trees*
>
> *To this Castle garth adioyneth Sherife hutton parke well stored with fallow deere, And sett with neere 4000 Decayde and decayinge okes, the most of them headed ...*

[next to this castle garth is Sheriff Hutton park, well stocked with fallow deer and set with nearly 4,000 decayed and decaying oaks, most of them pollarded]

> *... 2 lives and 40 years vall viii^li ...*

[leased for the lives of two people plus forty years and of annual value £8]

> *... This parke, by the relation of Sir Arthur Ingram knyghte, present tenante to the same parke is estated by his mats Lres patente unto the same Sir Arthur; during his life and after his decease to younge Sr Arthur his sonne during his life under the rent of 0- viii^li p ann. And by like relation the Sayd Sir Arthur hath by another lre patente a lease in revercion after their lives for fortie yeares to hold to his assignes. And by value p ann the deer considered about 0-Clx^li with the rent and herbage of 300 deer ...*

[This park, according to Sir Arthur Ingram, Knight, who tenants the park, is granted to Sir Arthur during his life and, after his death, to his son, also called Sir Arthur, during his life at a rent of £8 per year. Similarly, Sir Arthur has a lease in reversion for 40 years after their lives for whoever they assign it to. The annual value of the deer is £160 allowing for the cost and feed of 300 deer]

> *... the said last letters patent when it shall happen to commence there is to be yielded and paid to his highness p.a. 50 pounds with covenant to maintain in the same park 300 deer. Sir Arthur Ingram hath raised a very fayre new lodge with brick and with a fayre garden enclosed with a brick wall, and with mount walkes and fayre ornaments".*

[the last Letters Patent says that the rent of the park shall be £50 and a covenant to keep 300 deer. Sir Arthur has built a beautiful new lodge of brick, with a beautiful garden enclosed with a brick wall, with raised walks and statuary].

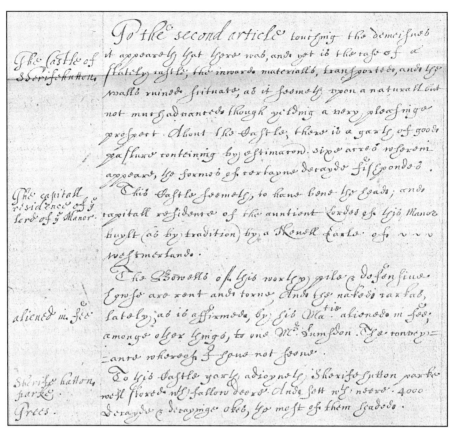

Fig. 12/1: Section of Norden's 1624 survey text (Source: WYAS Leeds WYL100/SH/B4/1).

Clearly the park had been allowed to deteriorate, as a park, and its main value was now as grazing land. Ingram acquired the manor of Sheriff Hutton in 1627 (but not including the park) from the City of London financiers who had bought a first option from James I[31] - he had probably brokered their deal in the first place in return for a percentage - and in the following year he leased the park to two local men, Anthony Blanch of York and George Gibson of Sheriff Hutton.[32] Blanch came to live at the Little Lodge and was still there 20 years later.[33] Ingram (who couldn't produce the patent for his lease) was still engaged in manoeuvrings with George Kirke of London (who could), and in 1630 Ingram believed that Kirke had relinquished his interest.[34] Even the new lodge was now closed up and two years later, when Ingram wanted some Irish lords to be entertained, although there was hunting to be demonstrated, he had to supply 'a pasty of a side of very fat venison' from York and have the rooms opened and aired and the paths weeded.[35] The lords lamented that the house was not used.

But by now, Sir Arthur had already bought the Temple Newsam estate[36] (now within Leeds), and was in the process of converting his large house there (see Chapter 15). The lodge at Sheriff Hutton seems to have been left to languish, with painted glass and the organ from the chapel being transferred.[37] Ingram used his York house for his business in the area, especially that of the Council of the North and for entertaining influential aristocracy, and he

172

had also acquired another park, New Park at Huby, a little to the north-west of Sheriff Hutton.[38] He then raised the value of his estates by having the royal Forest of Galtres disforested. After maybe 500 years of existence, the forest laws were finally removed in 1635. The villagers from Sheriff Hutton, who had grazing rights within the forest, had those rights converted to land and an oddly shaped area, centred on High Roans to the south of the River Foss, was added to the parish (and Ingram's manor).[39] The park was probably little affected by this activity, but it was indicative of the changes to hunting - no longer did royal hunts range across vast areas for deer and boar.

Fig. 12/2: Sir Arthur Ingram (courtesy of Temple Newsam House, Leeds).

Fig. 12/3: Sir Thomas Ingram (courtesy of Temple Newsam House, Leeds).

Sir Arthur, however, was soon to show that he had plans for the lodge, and he gave it to his youngest son, Sir Thomas, who married Frances Belasyse, daughter of Lord Fauconberg of Newburgh in 1638.[40] Young Sir Thomas had followed his father into the Irish customs service but became entangled in an unfortunate love affair, from which he was extracted only by being locked up until he could be returned to England.[41] His marriage into the family of the 1st Viscount Fauconberg must have set the seal on his father's attempts to achieve high status. The newly married couple started alterations at the park within a year, building a new terrace and, in 1639, a new stable block incorporating a brew house and coach house a few yards to the south-west of the main lodge (see Chapter 15); some 940 loads of stone are reputed to have been carried from the castle to build it.[42] The lodge was being transformed into a family home and it was probably intended to become the head of a new estate.

However, the Ingrams still did not own the park, and Lord Sheffield was made keeper in or around 1641.[43] This was more than a symbolic post, or sinecure, to pay the Lord President of the North, as the keeper was supposed to ensure that the park, its buildings and pale were kept in order by the tenants. Nevertheless, before the Ingrams could settle, the Civil War intervened, providing new excitement for the both the park and its tenants.

The Civil War

The divisions of the Civil War are well exemplified by the Ingram family. Old Sir Arthur, who was to die on the day that Charles I raised his banner at Nottingham so starting the war, had been a devout, if ruthless man, maintaining a personal chaplain, setting up an almshouse in York (still extant, in Clifton) and contributing to a prisoners charity. His eldest son, Arthur, was a Puritan but his other son, Sir Thomas, was a royalist who fought for the king. Although Sir Thomas was not noted for his military actions and was mainly a financial contributor, he was probably one of the founding members of the Sealed Knot. By marrying into the Belasyse family, he became brother-in-law to Sir Henry Slingsby, one of the fiercest royalists but, later, when Oliver Cromwell was looking for a husband for his daughter, it was to the Belasyses that he turned and Sir Thomas became her uncle by marriage.[44]

The Belasyse family had fled the threatening Scottish army in 1640 and Sir Henry Slingsby chose to put the River Humber between the family and the threat. After a horrible crossing, they were met on the Lincolnshire side by Frances, Ingram's wife, with a coach.[45] Sir Thomas actually fought at Naseby and the siege of Newark, where he was among those chosen to negotiate with the besiegers. For this, for 'deserting his dwelling' whilst a Commissioner for Array and for being a Member of Parliament, he was forced to 'compound', that is pay a fine to the victorious parliamentary government. He was able to get the fine reduced by half, claiming, amongst other things, that his woods had been damaged to the value of £2,000 but, as he owned estates elsewhere, this may not have been entirely within Sheriff Hutton park.[46] This was a particularly nasty time for Sir Thomas and Lady Frances, as their only child, a daughter, Mary, died in 1651.

The park, meanwhile, had been visited by armies and even seen fighting. Sir Henry Slingsby recorded in his diary that he and his militia camped in the park in January 1643:

> *"We re-marched ye first night to Sheriff-Hutton & lay there two nights. Lieutenant King being sent to view ye place yn after we had our army drawn up together in ye park & so march'd forward to Stamford Bridge".*[47]

Sir Henry had received his Royal Commission on the 12th of December 1642, raised 200 volunteers and was then commanded to join a muster with the Earl of Newcastle's army which they did in Sheriff Hutton park. The earl was on his way to clear the East Riding of scattered parliamentarian forces and to meet the queen, who was due to land at Bridlington.[48] They must have encountered a parliamentarian force at Sheriff Hutton as two officers of Queen Henrietta Maria's Regiment of Foot had been killed in a skirmish in the park; these men were Cornet of Horse William Leyburn, who was buried in York Minster on the 9th of January 1643[49] and Captain Matthew Anderton. Local legend puts the site of the skirmish in 'Duggleby Field', which is located between Park Farm and the site of East Lilling deserted village, and musket balls have also been found there.[50]

The Survey of 1650

In the aftermath of the parliamentarian victory and the beheading of King Charles, the government wanted to dispose of his lands and created 'The Committee of Parliament for Removing Obstructions in the Sale of the Honours, Manors and lands of the late King, Queen and Prince' (frequently shortened to the ominous 'Committee for the Removal of Obstructions'). This body carried out detailed surveys which describe the former royal properties and their legal status.

The survey of Sheriff Hutton park, undertaken in 1650,[51] tells us that it was 714 acres 3 roods and 9 perches in extent, that it was worth £308 00s. 10d. per year, and that it was occupied by Sir Thomas Ingram. After a detailed description of the Great Lodge and the Little Lodge (see Chapters 5 and 15), it values the 189 deer ('of several sorts') at £120 and says that there were just 512 'timber trees' (i.e. suitable for large construction work) left valued at £345 4s. 0d., but that none of them were marked up for use by the Navy. There were also 3,222 "ould decayed trees fitte for litle other than the fire" but still worth £725 1s. 0d. The next section of the survey sounds like true estate agent speak: "The .. Parke is comodiously .. divided for the purchasers advantage.. into three pts [parts]" and, like an estate agent's brochure, it then went on to contradict this statement as each of the three parts (west, central and east) was actually further sub-divided into smaller blocks. The descriptions and locations of the various sub-divisions, as currently known, have been discussed further in Chapter 5.

Of the trees, 20 good ones and 442 of those 'fitte for the fire' were in the west division, there were 492 good and 2,737 firewood in the centre, and 43 firewood in the east. Sir Thomas had the offices of Ranger and Keeper for which he wanted to be paid £4 7s. 6d. per year (payable from the receipts of the Lordship of Sheriff Hutton, which belonged to his half brother, Arthur) and he also claimed the rights to the herbage (grazing) at a rent of £8 3s. 4d. but from which he could expect to earn £160. The Commissioners found letters patent granting the park to Sir Arthur, as well as Sir Thomas (with a covenant to maintain 300 deer in the park but they were allowed to "chase kill take and carry such and soe many Bucks and does as he and they please"), and they were aware of George Kirke's claim to lease the park although they hadn't seen his patent. The lessees were obliged to maintain the pale and the houses, fences, walls, ponds and 'baucks' (banks) during the lease, but the Commission found that the trees would not be sufficient to do this during the 40 unexpired years.

The survey also details various rights within the park which have a medieval ring to them. The lessees were to have 'houseboote' (the right to take wood for the building and repair of buildings), 'paleboote' (the right to wood for the pale), 'fireboote' and 'hedgeboote' (here the right to the hedges, which meant not only using cuttings for animal feed, making hurdles and burning on the fire but, as there were thorn trees growing wild, the right to use these to make hedges).

In their judgements, the Commissioners allowed George Kirke his rights in the manor and park but, separately, also allowed Sir Thomas his; the wording suggests that Sir Thomas had to pay Kirke the rent for the park (£8 13s. 4d.) and Kirke then paid the government £24. Kirke's arrangement was to last for his life and that of a lady called Elizabeth Killigrew (up to a maximum of 80 years) and the Ingrams' was for the life of Sir Arthur (the younger) plus 40 years. As young Sir Arthur died in 1655, this lease, unmodified, would have run out in 1695. However, it is probable that the terms were changed in the following year when the park was sold to a consortium of London businessmen.[52] Curiously, having established his right to the park back in 1650, Sir Thomas had granted a pension from the park to be paid to a John Lambert of Craven, payment to be made at 'Haxbie Tombe' in York Minster.[53]

It is difficult to see how the needs of 300 deer could be met from a park which was so divided and which had been used for grazing cattle for so long. Perhaps the covenant was never enforced and the surviving herd was allowed to dwindle down to the 189 recorded in the survey. It seems unlikely that, under the increasing joylessness of the Protectorate, the Ingrams took part in any big hunts, and the general economic deterioration of the period probably resulted in a need for easier sources of food.

When Charles II was welcomed to the throne in May 1660, Sir Thomas gained his reward for his loyalty. Charles promptly made him a Privy Councillor and Chancellor of the Duchy of Lancaster and, as his duties were mainly in London, Sir Thomas moved there. He subsequently died in 1671, and was buried in Westminster Abbey with his wife and daughter.[54]

But the next occupier of Sheriff Hutton park was already in residence.

The Time of Sir Roger Langley Bart.

We know little of Sir Roger's time at Sheriff Hutton. We don't know if he bought the park and sold it a few years later to move to London or if he merely rented it during his time in the North Riding. If the latter, we don't know whether he rented it from the Crown, the Ingram family or from his successors at Sheriff Hutton park, the Thompsons or, indeed, whether there was another owner in the meantime. These matters are the subject of on-going research and study.

Sir Roger first appears in the Sheriff Hutton parish registers in 1659, when his daughter, Elizabeth, was buried here.[55] Several children were baptised or buried over the next ten years, along with those of his brother, William. His first wife, Mary, was also buried here in 1670. Sir Roger was High Sheriff of Yorkshire in 1663-64 (succeeding his near neighbour, Sir Thomas Gower of Stittenham)[56] and on the 30th May of 1663, he wrote to George Ingram, Lord Irwin and lord of the manor of Sheriff Hutton, recommending his servant, Robert Mulford for the post of gardener at Temple Newsham.[57] In March 1665, the Herald, Dugdale, recorded the arms of 'Langley of Sheriff Hutton Parke',[58] for which Sir Roger had to attend him in York. A banner bearing the arms was still on display in the nave of the church in 1690.[59]

As for the park, a 'Particular' taken in 1675-85 found that it was now covered 816 acres, which means that 102 acres had been added since 1650 (see Chapter 5). It was divided first into 'severall closes' and subdivided into 27 separate closes or enclosures. In law it was still a park, which suggests that it may still have belonged (if only nominally) to the Crown and 'there [was] noe high way through it'.[60] At this time, the park was described as 'well watered' and there was £300 worth of timber trees around the house.

In 1672, Sir Roger was remarried, to Barbara Chapman of Foxton in Leicestershire[61] and in 1673 he paid Hearth Tax on 31 hearths at East and West Lilling.[62] Even allowing for hearths in the stables and brewhouse and in the Little Lodge, this makes Sheriff Hutton park lodge by far the largest house for some distance around. However, the family was not to remain at

Sheriff Hutton for long as Sir Roger's royal duties meant that he had to move to London, and in 1676 the park was bought by Edward Thompson.[63]

Sir Roger may have had other intriguing royal duties, as on the 4th April 1666 he had been allocated £733 out of the Hearth Tax revenue 'for the King's immediate and secret service'.[64] King James II certainly believed that Sir Roger was one of his men, for he was chosen to be the foreman of the packed jury for the Trial of the Seven Bishops, in which James had planned to punish the clerics for refusing to permit his Declaration of Indulgence to be read out in their churches.[65] However, the plan backfired. Sir Roger announced 'Not guilty' and ...

"The shouting and cheers in court lasted a good half hour. The news spread through the city. Soldiers at the camp on Hounslow Heath gave a great shout when they heard it. That night there were bonfires throughout London, ... church bells rang, there were candles in every window and a crowd burned an effigy of the Pope outside St. James's Palace, while the guards looked on.
In Somerset they went one better and burned an effigy of the Prince of Wales as well. Meanwhile, seven men met to draft an invitation to William [of Orange] to invade England, and assured him that the invasion would succeed. 'Nineteen parts of twenty of the people ... are desirous of a change.'. The army officers were 'discontented', the soldiers 'do daily show such an aversion to the Popish religion' that neither they nor the seamen would resist their liberators. Finally, the seven men added, 'we do much doubt whether this present state of things will not yet be much changed to the worse before another year.'. William needed no further encouragement"[66]

... so, in 1688, the two words uttered by Sir Roger Langley, formerly of Sheriff Hutton park, initiated the Glorious Revolution.

Footnotes

1   Henry Hastings died on Sunday 15th December 1596: Cross 1987, p.319.
2   Rushton 2003, p.181; Harley 1928, pp.335-361: 'An Inventorie of all the goodes and chattells of the Righte Honourable Henry late Erle of Huntingdon deceased ....' June 1596.
3   Barnet 1980, p.17.
4   ibid.
5   Rushton 2003, p.190.
6   See the article about James I and hunting in *Chambers Book of Days*, R Chambers 1869, Edinburgh, 'November 20th' quoted on "Hillmans Hyperlinked and Searchable Chambers Book of Days", 2005 (*www.thebookofdays.com/months/nov/20.htm*) by the Greater Emmitsburg Area Historical Society.
7   Cross 1987, pp.312, 319, 326, 338 & 341.
8   Calendar of State Papers Domestic, vol 8 (1603-10), p.595.
9   Upton 1961, passim.
10   Matthew & Harrison 2004 vol 29, p280.
11   Upton 1961, p.194.
12   Calendar of State Papers Domestic, vol 8 (1603-10), p.223.
13   ibid., p.327.
14   National Archives E178/4839, also quoted in Miss Lascelles' Green Book, p.52 (unpublished scrap book held in Sheriff Hutton Village Hall); Swann *et al* 1990, p.101 note 70. Clarke is referred to as a 'past keeper' of the park in a lease of 1628 (West Yorkshire Archive Service (WYAS) Leeds WYL100/SH/A1/16).
15   e.g. see WYAS Leeds WYL100/SH/A1/10 in which Lumsden demises two of his offices to Clarke and a William Tenant.
16   National Archives E178/4839.
17   Wheater 1888, p.222; Calendar of State Papers Domestic, vol 9 (1611-18), p.78.
18   Calendar of State Papers Domestic, vol 8 (1603-10), p.210.

19   Upton, Beresford and Gilbert have all come to different conclusions about the manner and timing of the Ingrams' acquisition of Sheriff Hutton. Many of the documents seem contradictory and other people had interests in the area in the first half of the 17th century. It is not always clear whether documents are outright grants or leases, what the terms are, whether the people referred to are part of a syndicate, individuals or in separate syndicates, and whether they refer to all or part of the manor or park. Royal Parks were subject to different laws and could not be sold, so, for example, the Parliamentary Survey of 1650 disregarded an apparent outright grant of the park to Sir Thomas Ingram.

20   WYAS Leeds WYL100/SH/B8/1.

21   WYAS Leeds WYL100/SH/A4/3.

22   Upton 1961, p.150; Rushton 2003, p.204; Drake 1736, pp.256-7; Gilbert 1966a, p.548.

23   WYAS Leeds WYL100/SH/B4/1 f2r.

24   Butler 1988, p.29.

25   WYAS Leeds WYL100/SH/A1/60.

26   WYAS Leeds WYL100/SH/A1/12; WYL100/SH/F4/4/1, 21st Jan 1622.

27   WYAS Leeds WYL100/SH/A4/13.

28   Upton 1961, p.197.

29   ibid., p.194.

30   There are several copies of this survey, which covered much of the Lordship of Sheriff Hutton. A complete version is in the British Library, Harleian manuscripts No 6288 (including the 'plots'). An abbreviated version, with just Sheriff Hutton, East and West Lilling and Elvington but without the 'plots', is WYAS Leeds WYL100/SH/B4/1.

31   Beresford 1957, pp.220 & 224.

32   WYAS Leeds WYL100/SH/A1/16.

33   'the said tenement now in the occupation of Anthony Blanch': National Archives E317/York S/54 (1650), p.2.

34   e.g. WYAS Leeds WYL100/SH/F4/4/3.

35   Upton 1961, p.150; Gilbert 1966a, p.551.

36   Gilbert 1966, p.551.

37   ibid.

38   Butler 1988, pp.29-31; Gilbert 1973.

39   H.M.S.O. 1967, p.511; National Archives E178/5742.

40   Gilbert 1966a, p.551.

41   Ridsdill Smith 1978, p.27.

42   Gilbert 1966b, p.628.

43   Wheater 1888, 231.

44   Ridsdill Smith 1978, p.27.

45   ibid., p.28.

46   Clay 1895, pp.124-125.

47   Parsons 1836, p.88.

48   Rogers 1992, p.27.

49   For Leyburn's burial see Skaife 1870, p.231 (no. 15). Aveling 1966, pp.302 & 308 puts the two deaths in 1644 during the siege of York in a skirmish between the Scots Army and The Army of the Eastern Association, which was holding the northern sector.

50   Miss Muriel Armitage, *pers. comm.* in 1982. Her nephew David and his son, John confirmed the identification of Duggleby Field and showed us the musket balls, which had been found by metal detectorists.

51   National Archives E317/York S/54 (1650).

52   To John Lambert, Alexander Halsall and Marmaduke Reath. Northumberland Record Office, Papers of the Middleton Family of Belsay, ZMI/B7/1/10.

53   WYAS Leeds WYL100/SH/A1/32.

54   Leeds City Council, Temple Newsam website, 2005
    (*www.leeds.gov.uk/templenewsam/house/port_03.html*)

55   Borthwick Institute PRSH 1, Parish Register, Mixed, 1637-1706.

56   University of York 2000, p.143.

57   WYAS Leeds WYL100/SH/A4/11.

58   Clay 1899, p.300.

59   York Minster Library, Torres MSS, between pp.478 & 479.

60   Beresford 1957, p.224; WYAS Leeds WYL100/SH/B3/1.

61   University of York 2000, p.143.

62 Ripon Historical Society 1991; Purdy 1991, pp.182, 183 & 178; National Archives E179/216/481. Compare the Howards' Castle at Hinderskelfe - now Castle Howard - with 16 hearths and Sir Thomas Gower's Manor House at Stittenham with 19.

63 Gilbert 1966b, p.628.

64 University of York 2000, p.143.

65 Miller 2000, pp.166 & 182. Several people have identified Sir Roger Langley of Sheriff Hutton with the Roger Langley who was Foreman of this Jury (e.g. Gilbert 1966b, p.628; Clay in "Dugdale's Visitation", p.300n.; University of York History Dept., above. note 65) but the City of London Archives have an entry for the 'will of Sir Roger Langley of St. Margaret 1642-1727'
(*www.hmc.gov.uk/accessions/2002/02digests/ london.htm* [December 2004], Accession 2281). The Sheriff Hutton Sir Roger was born in 1627 and was buried, at St Margaret's, Westminster in 1699 ("The Lord Lieutenants ..", above), so it may have been a relative who spoke the fateful words.

66 Miller 2000, p.187.

CHAPTER 13: THE PEOPLE IN THE PARK – 3: THE THOMPSON FAMILY, 1676 TO 1880
By Tony Wright

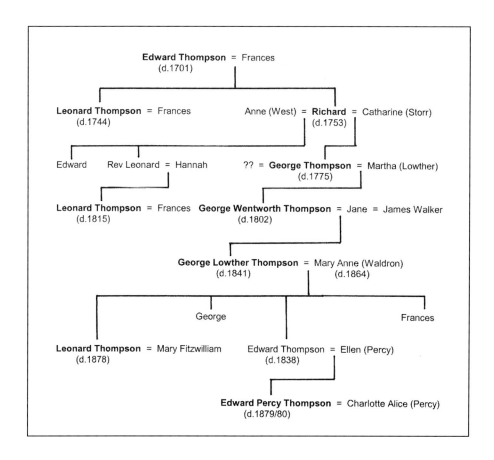

Fig. 13/1: Simplified Thompson family tree.

Edward Thompson MP (from 1676 to 1701)

After Roger Langley moved to the south-east of England, the park and the Lodge were acquired by Edward Thompson in about 1676. The Thompson's were to have the longest tenure of the park since the Nevilles. They were already landed gentry, with substantial estates in the East Riding and they were also established traders, bankers and silversmiths in York and Hull.[1] Edward, along with two of his five brothers, had been apprenticed during the 1650s to his uncle Henry in York. Henry imported wine and was probably keen to bring family members into the business, who could then be placed in trusted positions in the producing countries and in the financial centres, such as London and Amsterdam.

Edward was a friend and business associate of the poet and MP for Hull, Andrew Marvell and at least one letter, dated December 1674, survives from Marvell.[2] Edward had been called into William III's first Parliament (1688) as an MP for York, and he represented the city in the following year, was defeated in 1695, and served again from 1700 until his death in 1701.[3]

He took up the responsibilities of the landed class, attending a quarter sessions at Malton in January 1690 as a Justice of the Peace[4] and sought advice from his neighbour, friend, political ally and business colleague, Thomas Worsley of Hovingham.[5] One of his first duties as a JP was to deal with a complaint against the Constable of Sheriff Hutton for not taking action over a woman with a bastard child and in 1692, whilst sitting at New Malton, being able to 'give liberty to a Sheriff Hutton woman who had her goods destroyed by fire to receive the benevolence of all charitable and well disposed persons' and to 'desire all preachers .. to stir up their auditors to a charitable contribution to her'.[6] In 1696, he was accused of receiving Treasury money for the poor of the city and appropriating it for his own use, but was exonerated by the commissioners.[7]

Edward had married a cousin, Frances Thompson of Escrick. They had six children, of which three sons survived childhood, and from this generation on, the pattern of one son inheriting the land, another going into the business, and another (if there were enough sons) joining the army or the church seems to have been set.

Leonard Thompson (1701-1744)

Edward's eldest son, Leonard, inherited Sheriff Hutton park, although he lived both at the Lodge and at Mint Yard in York, where his daughter was baptised in 1702.[8] Unfortunately, neither his wife nor his daughter were to survive long. He also had married a cousin called Frances and, in keeping with another family tradition, had been to Trinity College in Cambridge. He too became a JP, appearing first in the records at Thirsk in 1708[9] and notably having a 'vagrant from Ganthorpe', Elizabeth Wista, 'publickly whipt' at Sheriff Hutton before sending her back.[10] That record appears in 1712 in the Sheriff Hutton churchwardens' accounts, and he seems to have taken a significant interest in parish affairs, being the first signatory to an agreement to limit the expense of 'ringing' in the parish in 1709 and adding his own 'cure for the bite of a mad dog' to that of Dr Troutsbeck in the same accounts (see also Chapter 8).[11] The family politics were usually Whig and in 1715, Leonard was active in seeking out papists (Catholics), especially in the days after the death of Queen Anne, when a Scottish invasion threatened.[12]

In the meantime, hunting had started to change. The park had been divided into at least 27 enclosures before the Thompson family bought it and it was unlikely to have been suitable for a full scale deer hunt any more (see Chapter 5). Locally, there are records of hunting carted deer (that is, deer taken from their home park and hunted over any chosen terrain) in the early 18th century,[13] and by 1733 the first pack of hounds intended solely for fox hunting had been introduced five miles away by Mr Darley at Aldby Park (ironically now a deer park again) and they hunted all over the area.[14] Hunting with hounds was no longer something done within the confines of a park.

Leonard Thompson, with no use for such a huge house, had the Lodge reduced in size and created a 'Queen Anne' style mansion (see Chapter 15).[15] In keeping with the fashion of the times, the forecourt to the north-west of the house was done away with, and the parterre to the south-east was removed.[16] Leonard also had other property interests. He owned several houses in Ogleforth in York (one backed onto King William's College) and he exchanged part of one with Tobias Jenkins, his father's rival for the parliamentary seat of York, in 1695[17] and had Sir William Lowther MP as a tenant. He had the rectories of Terrington and Brandsby in his gift and gave them to his nephew, also called Leonard, who became unpopular at the latter for underpaying his curate and letting the parsonage house to a Roman Catholic.[18]

Leonard senior died in 1744, after attempting to prolong his life with a visit to Bath. He left legacies to several of his servants and tenants, calling some of them 'godson' and 'god-daughter', and initially left most of his estate (including Sheriff Hutton park) to his eldest nephew, Edward.[19]

Several letters survive from and about the Thompson family in the Worsley family papers, one of which sounds like an excerpt from a Jane Austen novel. It is dated the 4th of September but with no year, and seems to be from the time when Edward was expected to succeed to the Sheriff Hutton estate:

> *"I wrote to Mrs Thompson a little time ago, why wont you make advances to my Cousen Ned Thompson, he has a charming character and the addition of Len's fortune makes him a good match. If you have any objections to Sheriff Hutton for yourself let me know if you approve of my being placed there, 'tis what some of my friends wish extremely, but as I have no acquaintance with him, if you place your affections on him I won't forbid your banns, and promise it shan't break the friendship between us ... distribute my love where you think proper, believe that you have not a sincerer friend than .... Toppy"*[20]

Who was Toppy? She has previously been identified as Fanny Thompson[21] (there were several cousins called Frances!) but in other letters she talks approvingly about Fanny Thompson, so the most likely candidate will be a member of the nearby Topham family, related by marriage.

Edward has also been described as 'of Lisbon' and he probably looked after the Portuguese end of the family wine business, which was becoming ever more important after the Methuen Treaty of 1703 opened up the market for Portuguese wines. Perhaps he stayed in Portugal, or died there but for some reason, Leonard changed his mind about his inheritance and, in a late codicil to his will, left the most part to his younger brother, Richard. He did, however, leave significant sums to several nieces, describing two of them, along with one god-daughter, as those 'who lives with me'. Perhaps he subscribed to the latest fad, that the breath of young women would prolong his life.[22]

Richard Thompson (1744-1753)

Richard was the brother who had run the family business. Active for much of his life in local politics, he was an Alderman (from the age of 29), Lord Mayor (twice) and Freeman of York from the age of 25, a member of the Company of Merchant Adventurers and Governor for three years; his portrait hangs in the Company's Hall, showing an amiable man. As Senior Alderman, he was reported to have attended all the council meetings during the 'anxious days of the '45' and it was he who donated the ebony 'porters staff' to the Mansion House which is still there.[23] He was almost certainly a Whig and anti-Jacobite, but it is unlikely that he was as hostile to Jacobites as his son George, who fought them in the field, at the dinner table and in the street, all before Richard died in 1753 and left him the estate.

Fig. 13/3: Thompson family crest, on the Lodge at the entrance to the park.

Fig. 13/2: Painting of Richard Thompson (by permission of the Company of Merchant Adventurers of York).

George Thompson (1753-1775)

George, born in 1717 to his father's second wife, Catharine, probably didn't expect to inherit the family estate. As the son to a second wife with elder half brothers who had sons, there must have been some powerful reason why he did.

He probably spent some time in Spain as a young man, as he was later to publish *A Description of the Escurial (Palace in Madrid) ... Translated from the Spanish.*[24] He first came to public notice when his father made him a Freeman of York in 1741 at the age of 24.[25] He appears in the records as a Chamberlain in 1744-5[26] and it was during the '45 invasion that he achieved his first fame as one of the 'young bucks' who joined Major General James Ogleforth's 'Yorkshire Hunters'.

This group was formed in the anti-Jacobite cause and the London newspapers said that the General was staying at George's house in York whilst he recruited. Each Hunter had to provide his own horses and be accompanied by two servants. Employed initially as the vanguard of the Duke of Newcastle's army, it soon became clear that the Hunters were best used in free-ranging actions, rounding up stragglers and on one occasion, lifting the siege of Lowther Hall in Cumbria.[27] This could have led to a truly romantic story, as George was later to marry Martha Lowther, but there is no evidence to link the two events. Indeed,

George was already married but his wife died, tragically, in undelivered childbirth early the following year, a few days after he had been elected a councillor for the Micklegate ward.[28] A Whig hero in a generally Whig city, George was elected a Sheriff in September 1746 and his inauguration was the occasion for the 'greatest respect shown to any Sheriffs these 30 years past'.[29] After the ceremony, he entertained the whole company to a bash 'in the politest manner' in the Merchants Hall.[30]

George continued the life of a successful wine merchant and in 1750, the *York Courant* announced:

> "*York Nov 27th*
> *On Thursday last, Mr George Thompson, an eminent Wine Merchant of this City, and son to Mr Alderman Thompson, was married at the Cathedral to Miss Lowther of Seacroft, an agreeable Lady of a considerable fortune*".[31]

He inherited Sheriff Hutton park in 1753, and his father, Richard, proposed him successfully for membership of the Merchant Adventurers Company of York before he died.[32] In 1754, George was the collector of the subscriptions for the new horse racing grandstand on the Knavesmire and may have been instrumental in the choice of architect. The city council had started the project until the councillors of Micklegate objected, as this was their turf (literally), and they selected John Carr's design instead of the city's choice of James Paine. George's accounts have been described as the 'neatest' ever.[33]

But George was in trouble. In 1754 one of the sheriffs was Henry Jubb, an apothecary, and at his inauguration dinner held in his house in Coney Street, a Dr John Burton had taken exception to one of the toasts. Burton was a famous antiquary and physician, but had been accused of Jacobitism during the '45 and was incarcerated for 18 months through the efforts of Jacques Sterne, Precentor of the Minster and ally of the Whig Thompsons. In fact, although he denied it, he was probably a Jacobite and certainly an active Tory, enough, in those times of violent politics, to make him a hated enemy. The toast he had refused to support was 'To the immortal memory of King William III', which had been proposed by the Lord Mayor. George Thompson, 'warmed with a convivial glass' called him an 'impertinent fellow' and flipped a cork at him in derision. Burton, thus goaded, said that he would honour any health proposed and George responded. Later they would dispute the exact words of the toast, George claiming that he had said 'everlasting disappointment to the pretender and all his adherents', Burton saying that George had used the word 'damnation'. As Burton had spent some time in 'the pretender's' company in 1745, he refused to drink and George and his great friend (and possibly fellow 'buck') Matthew St Quintin, tormented the doctor until he struck out at a fellow guest, was attacked, had his professional cane wrested from him, his shirt torn and was ejected into the street. He subsequently brought an action for assault against George Thompson, which came to court in the York Guildhall in March 1756. The jury "without going out of court, brought in the defendant guilty of the said assault". George had to stand on the floor of the Court at Westminster to receive his punishment: he was fined £10, to be paid to the king, and was imprisoned until the fine was paid. It is unlikely that it took very long, as George was by then the owner of large estates. Dr Burton was less fortunate and he was rarely out of debt after his imprisonment. Lawrence Sterne caricatured him in *Tristram Shandy* as 'Dr Slop'. George published a defence of his actions in August and sold it for a shilling a time.[34]

George and Martha's only child, a son, was born in 1759 and they named him George after his father and Wentworth after the Thompson's political guru, the Marquis of Rockingham. George's worship of the peer was perhaps over the top and he once boasted that 'the nobleman would buy over to his interest the whole Corporation of York at the next general election'. This provoked for the following verse from a Tory opponent:

> *"Most noble marquis! Favour'd lord!*
> *Great potent peer! Can you afford*
> *To purchase our whole body?*
> *George Thompson swears, the next election*
> *You'll buy us all without exception*
> *Thus much affirmed that noddy,*
> *Yet know, O most illustrious Sir,*
> *We can't believe this blundering cur,*
> *Though ken him for your tool;*
> *But rather thus conclude o' th' case*
> *Whilst York can show a Thompson's face*
> *'Twill never lack a fool".*[35]

George had taken on one of the posts as collector of Stamp Duties in York in 1760 'where Gentlemen of the Law, and others, may depend on being supplied with stamps of all sorts',[36] so perhaps the wine business was suffering. He died at Bridlington Quay in 1775, close to the old family estates at Hilston and Humbleton, and Martha survived him by five years.

Meanwhile, hunting was by now a very different activity. Hugo Meynell had bred hounds for endurance, rather than speed, so foxhunting as we know it now, with long runs and hunting over great distances became possible (Hugo's son, Hugo Charles had married a descendant of Sir Arthur Ingram and was to inherit the manor and most of the land of Sheriff Hutton). A single park was no longer big enough for a day's hunt. In 1764, Sir Thomas Gascoigne had founded the Middleton Hunt,[37] which was to share the area in southern Ryedale with the York and Ainsty North under a gentleman's agreement. The parliamentary enclosures (Sheriff Hutton was enclosed between 1765 and 1776 – see below[38]) created the ideal landscape for riding to hounds (as the new thorn hedges around the new fields grew, so did the macho image of the young men who dared to jump them). The game laws of 1754, however, were reversing Henry II's dictum that 'no man should die for deer' and by the 1770s imprisoning or whipping for poaching was becoming common.[39]

George Wentworth Thompson (1775-1802)

George and Martha's son was only 18 years old when George died, and so he probably didn't inherit Sheriff Hutton park immediately and it seems that his cousin, Leonard, had previously come to live there[40] and may have been his guardian; in legal documents, he is described as 'tenant for life'.[41]

George, emulating his father's brief service, became an officer in the 4th Queens Irish Dragoons and perhaps it was whilst he was serving with them at Canterbury that he met Jane Sarah Dell of Dover.[42] Possibly, she did not fit into the family aspirations of progressing upwards in the social hierarchy as she was the daughter of a Dover solicitor (although her brother, John, was later to become Mayor of Dover). Equally possibly, they did not intend to marry but circumstances forced their hands, and they were married in Edinburgh (the 4th

Dragoons alternated their service between Scotland and England between 1749 and 1809) on the 30th March 1786,[43] slightly less than nine months before their first child, George Lowther Thompson, was baptised in Manchester on the 15th December 1786. At this ceremony, George Wentworth signed his name with a slight change, to 'Wentworth James Thompson'.[44]

For whatever reason, the marriage was not a success and, although a daughter, Frances, was born in 1797, George and Jane soon formalised their separation.[45] George died of a 'long and painful illness' in 1802 at a rented house in York,[46] and just over a year later Jane remarried, to a near neighbour, James Walker. George had inherited the manor of Hilston from a cousin[47] and created a trust to own the family property and ensured that it was to descend through the male line in future.[48] He left a generous legacy to his daughter, a substantial pension to his wife, and other bequests to two unrelated ladies; one of them, Martha Soulsby of York, may have been his housekeeper in his last years, and the other was Elizabeth Gratwick of Dover.

Leonard Thompson (1772-1815)

For another generation, the heir to the estate was not of age, George Lowther Thompson being just 16½ years old. In the meantime, his father's cousin, Leonard, was still living at Sheriff Hutton Park, as the Lodge was now called.

Leonard has left no great record, yet he presided at Sheriff Hutton Park during significant changes. The parliamentary enclosure of the Manor of Sheriff Hutton and West Lilling was completed between 1765 and 1776 and, although this did not include the park (already an enclosure), there were other cottages and rights within the manor which belonged to the Thompson's and for which they were granted new enclosures. It was during Leonard's time that two of the existing three farms were built within the park, Oaks Farm and Lodge Farm (see Chapter 16).

Leonard made one curious addition to the family estates, when he financed the construction of a lighthouse at Spurn Point, at the mouth of the River Humber, in 1772.[49] This may have been because the family had interests in shipping - either in the goods being shipped or in the ships themselves. They could charge fees for the use of the lighthouses and, in the marriage contract of the last Leonard and Lady Mary, they were valued at over £20,000 but were not included in the settlement as 'the value could fluctuate'.[50]

In the Male Servant Tax of 1780, Leonard was taxed on three servants[51] and co-incidentally, he left generous legacies to three male servants when he died 25 years later in 1815: Thomas Chichester, who seems to have been his personal servant (probably something part way between a valet and a modern butler, to whom he left not only £200 but also all his clothes), his gardener, Richard Chisom, and another servant, Richard Robinson.[52] Leonard's wife had died previously and they were childless, and so he seems to have determined to take care of an unmarried cousin, Grace Thompson (his wife, Frances, had also been a cousin) and the unmarried daughter of the longest serving vicar of Sheriff Hutton, Grace Hawxwell. Leonard asked to be buried in Acomb, next to his mother and wife, where the family had property.

George Lowther Thompson (1815-1841)

George Lowther was an intelligent young man, had been educated at Harrow, was admitted into the family college, Trinity at Cambridge University at 17½ (in 1803), was married when

18 (in 1805) and fathered his first son (Leonard, in 1806) when only 19 years of age.[53] He graduated from Cambridge in 1808, had a second son (another George) in 1809, and went on to gain his Masters degree in 1811. He seems to have contemplated an academic career,[54] living at Chesterton and involving himself in the Classics department, and then he seems to have returned to Sheriff Hutton Park, where his third son, Edward, was born in June.

When his father died in 1802, George took up the mantel of a country squire, becoming a magistrate and Deputy Lieutenant for the North Riding by 1822 and being elected to Parliament in 1823, representing Haslemere until 1830 and then Yarmouth (Isle of Wight) until 1831.[55] According to George Todd, whose *Castellum Huttonicum* was published in 1824, the Thompson's had a copy of Nordens' 1624 Survey of Sheriff Hutton and 'several pictures (paintings) of note'.[56]

George's eldest son, Leonard, then made the most advantageous marriage of this branch of the Thompson family. His bride, Mary Wentworth-Fitzwilliam, was the daughter of Viscount Milton (soon to be Earl Fitzwilliam) and straight away, she was writing to her father from Sheriff Hutton; in the letters, Leonard is described as being 'of Sheriff Hutton.[57] The couple had obviously moved in.

In January 1833, Leonard's brother, George, died and in May, so did his sister, Frances. Young George, aged only 24, had been in the army. Frances was a little younger.[58]

George Lowther Thompson lived long enough to see a grandson Edward Percy born, in 1837, son of his youngest son, Edward. George's wife, Mary Anne, had travelled to Aspatria in Cumbria, where Edward was vicar, for the birth, taking with her Mary Bartle, her maid, who stayed with her for nearly 30 years.[59] Then they saw a further tragedy when Edward died only a year later at the age of only 27. Curiously, he has two monuments placed one on top of the other in Sheriff Hutton churchyard, where he is buried in the family vault.

George survived his son by three years and is also buried in the churchyard. Mary Anne lived out her life until 1864 and, although George had left her the use of nearby Lilling Hall, she based herself at Leamington Spa, where in 1862, Mary Bartle was able to get married.

George's steward for the Sheriff Hutton Park Estate was William Wright, who lived at Oaks Farm and George left him a significant sum in his will.[60] He also named his butler, John Rogers, but no other servants, although he did grant them all 'a half years wages'. The estate was held in trust for the eldest son and, in turn, his eldest son and so on, so Leonard would have use of the house and the rest of George's estate. However, the largest cash bequest was to Edward Percy Thompson, his grandson, then only four years old. As is discussed below, it would prove pitifully inadequate.

Leonard Thompson (1841-1878)

Mary Wentworth-Fitzwilliam brought a substantial estate to her marriage with Leonard and this, combined with the lands which he inherited and bought in the next few years, enabled him to declare in the 1871 census that he was the owner of 7,460 acres, scattered across Yorkshire, Norfolk and Huntingdonshire.[61] He was also lord of the manor of Strensall, a director of the Yorkshire Insurance Company (later Chairman of the Board), Secretary of the Scarborough Railway, founder of the York Association for the Prosecution of Felons (1840), a Deputy Lieutenant and Justice of the Peace in Yorkshire, and 'on the list' for Huntingdon.[62]

He was soon able to pay for the restoration of the chancel of Strensall church (he also owned the right to present the vicar there and was to acquire the same right at Sheriff Hutton[63]) and he and his wife built a new church and vicarage at Flaxton. They also extended The Park, adding a wing in 1848,[64] and buying cast iron railings and gates from the fashionable firm of Walkers of York.[65] They also became leading lights of the new game of croquet, Leonard himself writing a set of rules which were published and went through four editions.[66]

Leonard had graduated from Cambridge in 1829 (passing the time at Trinity College, of course) and gained his M.A. in 1833.[67] Mary was the daughter of the Earl Fitzwilliam of Wentworth Woodhouse and her letters show that she was knowledgeable about their business, her father's business and his politics in which they took an active part, holding election meetings at The Park in 1846.[68] They enjoyed a full social life and were popular with their tenants and the villagers. They hunted and shot, and Leonard was a founder of The Yorkshire Gentlemen Cricket Club.[69] In other words, they were wealthy, solid, well respected members of the landed gentry.

At the end of the century, Edwin Dalton, the noted Methodist Preacher, said in his memoirs:

> *"I must not pass over what is called Sheriff Hutton Park, the seat of Leonard Thompson Esq. and Lady Mary Thompson. The park is a beautiful plot of ground lying between Flaxton Station on the North Eastern Railway, and the village, and must be crossed when going to and from the station. The park is noted for the beautiful oaks it grows, and Mr Thompson took great interest in preserving them. If a branch should be blown off by the force of the wind, he had the exposed place covered with zinc so that it might be guarded against the weather. The Hall stands at the north cast side of the park and is shielded by a very considerable growth of trees.*
>
> *It is one of the ancient family seats and built in a very ancient style. The main front faces the south and opens onto a beautiful pleasure ground and a little in the distance and to the right, an extensive orchard and kitchen garden. Still further from the hall stands the large rookery where one of England's commonest fowls gather in great numbers and the youths look forward with pleasure to the shooting day which comes once a year.*
>
> *All around the hall are beautiful plantations and woods where sly reynard makes his home and roams at will. Here also the coney plays on the little hills and pheasant and woodcock make their nests.*
>
> *One of the notable days of history in the village was the day when the Squire, accompanied by a number of friends went shooting, and it was hard to say whether the bush beaters or the shooters enjoyed the day most.*
>
> *In the hall many happy days have been spent, and many a hungry man and woman been fed. These days however have unfortunately passed away. The old Squire has gone to his Home, and we trust that he has found his way to the Saints Eternal rest. Her Ladyship still remains in the wilderness, awaiting the call of her Master, and has taken up her residence in the Queen of Watering places, Scarborough."[70]*

In 1847, the tithes were commuted for the park, but not for the rest of Sheriff Hutton, which still belonged to the descendants of Sir Arthur Ingram. The tithe map[71] provides the first reasonably detailed and accurately measured plan of the park (see figure 5/7). This shows that, although Leonard Thompson is the owner of all, over two thirds of the park was let, mainly to his steward, William Wright, who farmed the area around Oaks Farm, and to John Flawith, doing the same around Lodge Farm. Some of the other fields around the north and western edge of the park were let individually, and the fields around The Park were kept in hand, although even here Leonard had some down to arable (see Chapter 5).

The plantations shown on the tithe map, not including the ornamental ones immediately around The Park, suggest that the park was laid out for shooting[72] and one visitor around the middle of the century came specifically for that purpose. Harry Dennison was an army officer, who was a great friend of Frederick 'Fred' Thompson, Leonard's cousin, who was living at The Park in 1849. For Thursday 28th November 1850 he wrote:

> *"Went back to Sheriff Hutton for luncheon - found Sir James and Lady Anne Mackenzie staying there and Mr Keene (Bays). He, I and Mr Thompson hunting at Pill Moor - Fred and Sir James shooting - went out after luncheon to join them but did not find them - went to the old castle and shot rats in the moat - played a species of tiddle-I-wink in the evening".*

and for following day:

> *"A hard frost - had a very good days shooting, bagging 104 head - self, 13 har., 6 rab, 4 ph, 2 part. - Ecarte in the evening".[73]*

Harry also enjoyed hunting, although he doesn't mention hunting at Sheriff Hutton but does at nearby at places such as Marton and Lobster House. Ecarte seemed to be the card game of choice and they all, the Thompsons and other landed gentry from north of York and the East Riding, seemed to enjoy parties far and wide as well as balls at the Assembly Rooms.

By the late 1850s a third farm had been built in the park and land attached to it was taken from the other two (see Chapter 16). This was Home Farm (now Park Farm) which was built as a dairy - certainly to supply The Park (Lady Mary used to travel down daily to select milk, cream and cheeses personally[74]) and perhaps to sell, making use of the newly built Scarborough Railway. Flaxton Station was only a mile away and this made getting milk to customers in York very quick indeed. Prior to this, the Bailiff for the estate had lived at Oaks Farm (William Wright was there in 1841) but by 1871, he was here at Park Farm (George Wright, shown on the census that year, William having died in 1855).

The 1871 census[75] gives us an idea of the number and type of staff required to run the estate. In addition to George, his wife and two 'farm servants' (i.e. farm workers) at Park Farm, they had the joiner, William Brough, lodging with them. For a farmhouse of this size, Mary Wright would have expected to be assisted by at least one maid but she had a married daughter staying. For The Park, Leonard Thompson had a butler (there are two butlers recorded in the park, John Hutchinson and Jonathan Smith, the other probably working for Frederick; both were married and neither living in), a gardener (Henry Crament) a coachman (Francis Josland) and stable boy (Alfred Whitwell) and five 'live-in' maids (Emma Shone, Patience Leak, Annie Gilbert, Sarah Fenwick and Annie Archer). This does not include the estate workers who lived in the village and, as there were kennels, someone must have kept the hounds.

In 1849, amongst the company would be 'Mr and Mrs Hudson', yet a year later, Harry Dennison's father was on a commission to investigate George Hudson's affairs.[76]

While Leonard Thompson was seen as the epitome of the landed Victorian gentry, dark clouds were looming on the horizon, starting with the railways. Lady Mary's father had been in negotiation with George Hudson over the cost of transporting coal from the family's mines in the south of Yorkshire to the lucrative London market, where it was in competition with coal from the much closer Kent coalfields. The new rail networks promised cheaper delivery than the coastal colliers via Hull which had been used until then. Hudson was attempting to put together continuous railway routes between major centres and he needed coal not only as freight traffic but also a supply of the right grade of coal for fuel. When he became interested in developing a line to Scarborough, it would pass over Fitzwilliams' land at Malton. Closer to York, it could pass over Leonard Thompson's land at Strensall and East Lilling, and so there were mutual interests.[77]

Leonard certainly became involved in Hudson's enterprises (although how far is unclear) and, when Hudson fell from grace (ironically brought down partly through the efforts of a Thompson cousin, Sir Harry Stephen Meysey Thompson of Newby Hall) almost everyone involved suffered some financial loss. Perhaps it would have been financial disaster but for the involvement of influential aristocratic families in addition to the Fitzwilliams. Leonard's brother Edward had married a first cousin of the Duke of Northumberland, and his nephew and heir to the estate, Edward Percy Thompson, was to marry a Percy cousin as well. In deals for related railways, Frederick Thompson was involved with the Dawnay family of Beningborough, including Viscount Downe. Another partner was the Rev. Frederick Bagot (possibly the nephew of the Bishop of Bath and Wells?).[78]

Fig. 13/4: Leonard Thompson's grave (d.1878) and his wife, Lady Mary (d.1893), in Sheriff Hutton churchyard.

However, it was to be the activities of Leonard's heir which would deliver the *coup de grâce* to the Thompson tenure of Sheriff Hutton Park.

Edward Percy Thompson (1878-1879)

The family of George Lowther Thompson followed the English tradition noted above. The eldest son inherited the use of the land. The second son, George, went into the army and the

190

third son, Edward, went into the church. Edward made an excellent marriage, his wife, Ellen, being the first cousin of the Duke of Northumberland, and they were married at Alnwick, the seat of the Percys. He gained benefices in Cumberland, being Vicar of Aspatria and Rector of Moresby, although they seem to have lived further south in the Lake District at Duddon Hall, a magnificently sited but remote place beside the tumbling River Duddon. Their only child, Edward Percy, was born near Aspatria at Moresby on the 29th of January 1837 and Edward senior died 15 months later.

We know nothing of Edward Percy Thompson's childhood but by 17 years of age he was serving with the Heavy Brigade in the Crimea.[79] Two years later he was admitted into Trinity College Cambridge but there is no record of his graduation.[80] Instead, he continued in the Army and was a lieutenant when he donated a window to Aspatria church in memory of the father he had never known.[81] In 1858, he came of age (21 years), received the bequest of £13,000 from his grandfather and got married to a cousin, Charlotte Alice Percy. They were rapidly blessed and their eldest son, Edward Leonard, was born in August 1860 at Aspatria. As a serving soldier with the 7th Queens Own Hussars, Edward Percy must have been with the regiment (not the active battalion, which was in India at the time),[82] and his wife returned to her mother's for her first lying-in. They had ten more children, one of who lived until 1960.[83]

It was expensive to be an officer in a fashionable regiment and a cavalry regiment like the Hussars especially so. Not only did promotions have to be purchased, mess bills paid and a high social life maintained, but gambling for high stakes was regarded as a sign of strength of character. By 1868, Edward had to borrow £6,000 (could this have been to purchase his promotion to Captain?) and he offered the Sheriff Hutton Park Estate as security.[84] As the estate was held in trust for the use of the eldest son, he had to convince the lenders that he could change the terms of his inheritance, which he did by 'selling' his interest to a lawyer for his (Edward's) own use. If he did not pay back the loan, the lenders would own the estate. Two years later he borrowed a further £6,200, again offering the estate as security and in the following year he hit the big time, taking out a loan of £20,000 and offering to pay back £38,555 six months after the death of his uncle Leonard.

Four years later, Edward breathed a metaphorical sigh of relief. He paid off the urgent £6,200 debt, with interest, and sliced the indenture into little pieces with his pocket knife, throwing the pieces out of the train window whilst travelling home from Waterloo to Portsmouth. Unfortunately, although they may have seemed distant liabilities, he still had his other debts - he certainly forgot that he would have to produce the dismembered indenture later to prove that he had paid it off - and in 1872 he had to transfer a loan of £3,500 to his latest creditors, who also inherited the outstanding £6,000 after the deaths of its lenders. Edward borrowed a further £10,000 to tide him over, on the promise to pay back £21,000 six months 'after the decease of the said Leonard Thompson', a phrase which would literally come back to haunt him. Over the next few months Edward paid off some loans and manipulated others, and eventually they were all consolidated into one loan of £68,000 on his agreement to pay back £126,554 six months after the death of Leonard. All these loans are large but the latter is huge - the repayment would be the equivalent of about £5 million today. The normal rate of interest at that time was 5% per annum and, if Leonard had survived another 13 years, the repayment would have equated to approximately the same amount.

In January 1878, three years later, Leonard was fit enough to sit as a magistrate at York (on the bench with Sir James Meek, an opponent of George Hudson) and he fined and gave six months imprisonment to Joseph Robinson of Sheriff Hutton, who had assaulted PC Holmes at the Pack Horse Inn after he was refused beer there. By now Leonard was in failing health but it wasn't until August that it became serious, and he died on the 27th of the same month.[85]

Six months later, Edward defaulted on the loan. The mortgagees, who included Robert Porcher Broughton, an England cricketer, foreclosed and in July of 1879 they put the Park Estate up for auction. Not only did it fail to realise enough money, but only two small lots were sold (the alternate right of presentation to Sheriff Hutton Vicarage and the brewery). Either the agricultural depression of the time made the estate of little worth or the entangled legal position, in which Lady Mary had the right to a pension and others had rights outstanding and in which Edward Percy's right to dispose of the land was not clear, frightened off any potential purchasers. The mortgagees started the process of obtaining a comprehensive Abstract of Title in which all the Thompsons' affairs were examined, including Edward's own legitimacy and the deaths of his father and his uncle George.

On 10th October 1879, Edward hung himself, at home (Uxbridge House) in Anglesey, Alverstoke, Hampshire, the village to which he had returned five years earlier, relieved because he believed that he had paid off his debts.[86] The last, Thompson, owner of Sheriff Hutton park had kept it for only six months. His eldest son, Edward Leonard, died in April 1880.[87] Three generations had died in 20 months. The mortgagees were able to put the Park Estate up for sale again, this time in smaller lots, on June 11th 1880, but had to accept prices which seem unlikely to have covered the loan, never mind the repayment.[88] They had had to buy an annuity to replace Lady Mary's pension and she retired to Scarborough, dying in May 1893 and was brought back to Sheriff Hutton church to lie beside her beloved husband. She was remembered with great affection in the village, perhaps because of the kindnesses she showed - as, for example in donating all of Leonard's clothes to a village charity, Lady Mary's Clothing Club[89] - or perhaps because of her gay (in the traditional sense), even impish personality; she had once dressed the vicar in woman's clothes, for a fancy dress party.[90]

The purchaser of Lot 1, comprising The Park and 203 acres, 2 roods and 27 perches in the centre of the park was John Coates, Gentleman, of Addingham in Wharfedale. He was able to negotiate terms even on the deposit, payable at the auction. The villagers of Sheriff Hutton lamented the end of an era.

The

SHERIFF HUTTON PARK

Estate,

THE PRINCIPAL ENTRANCE.

NORTH RIDING
YORKSHIRE,
1880

SEDGWICK, SON & WEALL,
Surveyors,
WATFORD.

Fig. 13/5: Front sheet from 1880 sale catalogue.

Footnotes

1 I must record a big thank you to J. P. G. 'Sam' Taylor for pointing me towards many of the sources for the Thompson family. His talk to York Georgian Society in 2003, summarised in the Society's Report of that year (York Georgian Society Annual report 2003, pp39-49) gives the background to the landed side of the family prior to 1676 and tells the story of the cousins at Escrick of who, he wrote more in *Escrick: a village history*. Otley, Oblong Creative Ltd, 1999.

2 "Papers of Henry Thompson, Merchant", Administrative History, Hull University Brynmor Jones Library, 2005 (*www.archiveshub.ac.uk/news/03011503.html*); Capern 2004.

3 Skaife no date, vol 3, no. 2916; Gilbert 1966b, p.629.

4 Atkinson 1889, pp.112, 136 & 144: his first appearance is on 13th January.

5 North Yorkshire County Record Office (NYCRO) ZON/13/1/43, letter dated 17th January. He continued to write to Thomas over the following years about European business, socialising and politics (NYCRO ZON/13/1/62, /74, /113, /67, /70, /97, /194, /196 & /197, 1690 to 1696).

6 Atkinson 1889, p.112.

7 NYCRO ZON/13/1/67.

8 Skaife 1881, p.387.

9 Atkinson 1889, p.217.

10 Borthwick Institute PRSH3, f.8r.

11 ibid., f.7v; ibid., f.8r.

12 Atkinson 1889, p.241.

13 Rushton 2003, p.277.

14 ibid.

15 Gilbert 1966b, pp.629-630.

16 ibid., p.630. Gilbert dates these changes to 1732, citing the date on the Insurance plaque but this could easily have been transferred from or to a converted house. A candidate for the architect is William Etty and there is circumstantial evidence to link him with Leonard Thompson; see Chapter 15.

17 Harrison 1998, pp.53-55; WYAS Leeds TA3/2: Leonard may have lived there in 1703 and leased it (them?) in 1733 to others.

18 "A Short History of Terrington", Gerry Bradshaw; Dymock, M 1964 *Terrington, a History of the Parish*, Appendix A and p.23.

19 His will can be seen at National Archives, Prob. 11/735.

20 NYCRO ZON/13/4/194.

21 Egerton 1946, p.7.

22 White 1963, p.32.

23 Pressley 1946, pp.14-15; Skaife no date, vol 3 "Thompson, Richard" (unnumbered) n.2.

24 Dated 1760. Copy in York Reference Library.

25 Skaife no date, vol 3, no. 2930 ("Free by patrimony").

26 Surtees Society 1899 *Register of the Freemen of the City of York from the City Records Vol 2:* 1559-1759 vol 102, p.259; Skaife no date, vol 3, no. 2930.

27 Oates 2001, pp.123-124; Cash 1975, p.290n.

28 *York Gazetteer*, 19th February 1745-6; *York Courant*, 21st January 1745-6.

29 *York Courant*, 23rd September 1746.

30 *York Courant*, 25th November 1746.

31 *York Courant*, 27th November 1750; Skaife 1873, p.129.

32 My thanks to Jill Redford, Assistant Archivist to the Company for looking up the Membership list for this.

33 Sheffield Archives, Wentworth Woodhouse Muniments, WWM/A/1395 quoted in Wragg 2000, p.71; Wilkinson 2003, p.49. The stand was opened on 25th August 1755. The controversy continued as in 1768, the Council let the grandstand to Rockingham but the 'Gentlemen of Micklegate' maintained that this was their right (Sheffield Archives WWM/R/1/1048).

34 Pressley 1946 p.16; Cross 1909, p.79; *York Courant*, 30th March 1756; *York Courant* 10th August 1756; Davies 1873, pp.408-9 & 421-429.

35 Pressley 1946, pp.17-18.

36 *York Courant*, 22nd July 1760.

37 Master of Foxhounds Association website (2004), 'Middleton Hunt' (*www.mfha.co.uk/hunts/middleton_hunt.html*)

38 West Yorkshire Archive Service (WYAS) Leeds Farrer Add. 313 and 318; Borthwick Institute PRSH 32.

39 Rushton 2003, p.277.

40 In later deeds referring to the building of the lighthouse at Spurn Point in 1772, he is described as 'of Sheriff Hutton' (*www.bopcris.ac.uk/bop1688/ref1381.html*).

41 'Sheriff Hutton Park Abstract of Title' by Roopers and Waleby (1880), Lincolns Inn Fields. I am very grateful to Mrs Phyllis Hull for lending me her copy of this document. Each buyer of a lot from the 1880 sale of the Park was entitled to a copy of this Abstract. This is the only one I know which survives.

42 Foster (no date) 'Thompson'.

43 International Genealogical Index from the website of the Church of Jesus Christ of the Latter Day Saints, June 2005 (*www.familysearch.org*).

44 ibid.

45 His will is at Hull University Brynmor Jones Archives, DDCV/166/27: 'Whereas by certain articles of separation executed between me and my wife, Jane Sarah...'.

46 *York Courant*, 31st May 1802, p.4; *York Courant*, 9th August 1802, p.4 is the advert to re-let the property.

47 Kent 2002, p.52.

48 'Sheriff Hutton Abstract of Title', f.18r.

49 see note 40 above.

50 'Sheriff Hutton Abstract of Title'.

51 Rushton 2003, p.302.

52 His will (National Archives Prob 11/735).

53 Venn 1954b, vol VI.

54 'Papers of the Monk and Sanford families' (*www.janus.lib.cam.ac.uk* 2004), in which he interests himself in the Regius Chair of Greek.

55 'A Topographical Dictionary of Yorkshire for the year 1822' by Thomas Langdale, quoted on Genuki (*www.genuki.org.uk/big/eng/YKS/yrksdict/north/peplnrth.txt*); "House of Commons Register, Thompson"; Venn 1954b, vol VI.

56 Todd 1824, p.34.

57 Sheffield Archives, Wentworth Woodhouse Muniments, WWM/g/83 & WWM/G/16/3.

58 Clifton Parish Registers, 31st Jan 1833; 'Sheriff Hutton Abstract of Title': evidence by Mary Bartle. George was buried at Clifton, Bristol.

59 ibid.

60 National Archives Prob. 11/1957.

61 1871 Census, North Riding Landowners quoted on Genuki (2005) (*www.genuki.org.uk/YKS/Misc/Transcriptions/NRYland/1871T.html*)

62 Bulmers 1890 Directory, Strensall, quoted on Genuki (2005) (*www.genuki.org.uk/big/eng/YKS/NRY/Strensall/Strensall90.html*); Epitaph in the *Malton Gazette*, 31st August 1878.

63 For Strensall, Genuki, above; for Sheriff Hutton, 'The Sheriff Hutton Park Estate' (sale catalogue), 1879 by Sedgwick, Son & Weall, Surveyors, Watford.

64 Gilbert 1966b, p.630.

65 Malden 1976, p.49: The invoice was to 'G. Coates'. A George Coates was involved in developments in York with George Townsend Andrews, architect. Andrews was also architect to George Hudson's railway companies, he designed the Yorkshire Insurance Building and some of his designs for farmhouses are similar to Park Farm. He is therefore a prime candidate as architect for the extension to the hall.

66 York Reference Library: Thompson, L 1864 "The Rules of the Game of Croquet as played at Sheriff Hutton" (and subsequent editions of 1867 & 1874).

67 Venn 1954b, vol VI.

68 Sheffield Archives, Wentworth Woodhouse Muniments, letters quoted above and WWM/G/83/550 & WWM/G/83/552-554; Rushton 2003, p.326.

69 He was responsible for the pavilion on Wiggington Road (now York District Hospital): *Malton Gazette*, 31st August 1878 - the announcement of his death.

70 Edwin Dalton's unpublished memoirs.

71 Borthwick Institute TA411S.

72 *Pers. comm.* with Mr Robin Barker of Oaks Farm, who shoots.

73 East Riding Archives DDSA/1119-21.

74 *Pers. comm.* with David Armitage of Park Farm, quoting family tradition.

75 1871 Census, as above.

76 East Riding Archives DDSA/1119-21.

77 There has been a suggestion that Hudson, Thompson and the surveyor, William Wood, were involved in buying land for the railway and its planned branches (*pers. comm.* with a descendant of Mr Wood, 2004). The rules required that they valued the land so that the company, financed by the shareholders, could buy it but the suggestion is that they bought the land for themselves and then sold it on to the company at an increased price. I have seen no evidence for this.

78 East Riding Archives DDCL/986; DDCL/943/5; DDCL/931/4; DDCL/956; DDCL/534.

79   Venn 1954b, vol VI.

80   ibid.

81   Aspatria church website, 2004 (*www.stevebulman.f9.co.uk/cumbria/1901/ aspatria1901.html*).

82   Regimental History, 2005 (*www.qrh.org.uk/history2a.htm*).

83   Foster no date; International Genealogical Index from the website of the Church of Jesus Christ of the Latter Day Saints, 2005 (*www.familysearch.org*).

84   For Edward's debts, see 'Sheriff Hutton Abstract of Title', passim

85   *Malton Gazette*, 31st August 1878; ibid., 7th September 1878.

86   His death certificate. Paul Theroff's Royal Genealogy Site (*http://pages.prodigy.net/ptheroff/gotha/ northumberland.html*) gives the date of October 1979 for Edward Percy's suicide. The International Genealogical Index gives the date of October 1880 - the former is quoting an early edition of Burke's Peerage, the latter gives no source. Edwin Dalton's unpublished memoirs said "The Hall went to the next heir, but he having led a profligate life; had the estate largely mortgaged, and being unable to meet his liabilities and unable to endure the strain, Judas like, 'He went out and hanged himself'". He was being metaphorical, quoting the King James version of The Bible, Matthew, Chapter 27 Verse 5; Miss Muriel Armitage (*pers. comm.* 1982), relating her family's tradition, told me that he shot himself, a story which David and John Armitage have confirmed (*pers. comms.* 2004); Miss Lascelles, in some notes she made for the visit of the Yorkshire Archaeological Society to the park in 1929 says: "Squire Thompson's nephew unfortunately squandered his inheritance before he came into it & then shot himself, leaving a wife and children" (in the Sheriff Hutton Vicar's file, 1982).

87   International Genealogical Index, 2004 (*www.familysearch.org*): 'Edward Leonard Thompson'.

88   Sedgwick, Son & Weall 1880 "The Sheriff Hutton Park Estate". Copies held within the village and at the Borthwick Institute (PR/SH/80). Lot 1 (the Hall and 203 acres) sold for £14,500. There were 900 acres in total and four farms.

89   *Malton Gazette*, 27th November 1880.

90   Miss Lascelles Green Book, p.76 (unpublished scrapbook held in Sheriff Hutton village hall).

CHAPTER 14: SHERIFF HUTTON PARK AND ITS FAMILIES 1880 TO 2005

By Nancy Megginson

Introduction

The following text has been produced as a result of talking to many local residents of Sheriff Hutton, who have kindly provided me with their anecdotes and reminisces relating to the more recent history of the park and the families who occupied the Hall. Their contributions and time are much appreciated.[1]

It should be noted that the Hall was previously known as 'Sheriff Hutton Park' or 'The Park', and that it was only re-named as 'Sheriff Hutton Hall' in the late 1960s.

The Coates Family 1880-1936

The Coates family came to Sheriff Hutton Park in 1880 having purchased the property from the Thompson family who had lived there for almost 200 years. Mr John Coates was a man of independent means, though it is possible that some of his wealth enabling him to buy the estate may have come from his grandfather who had married Mary Cunliffe, a member of the Bradford mill-owning family the Cunliffe Listers. John Coates was born in Addingham, Wharfedale, and his wife Mary was a Lancashire lass. At the time of their move to Sheriff Hutton there were three children, John, Maude and Eliza, aged three, two and six months respectively, all of whom were born in Lancashire. By 1891 John and Mary had had seven more children, Robert, Mabel, Edith, Samuel, Mildred, Winifred and William.[2]

Fig. 14/1: The Drawing Room in The Park in the Coates' era.

Fig. 14/2: The Park, c.1918.

Reading through Sedgwick Sale Catalogue of 1879,[3] The Park must have been a splendid place when the Coates family arrived there in 1880. It is described as a "Comfortable and Spacious Family Mansion" with "Pleasure Grounds, Gardens and Lawns" overlooking well timbered parkland. The present house with its Queen Anne façade dates back to about c.1730 and contains handsome reception rooms with many fine architectural features (see Chapter 15). The description of the domestic offices also makes very interesting reading. They occupied the basement of The Park, i.e. the old Jacobean kitchens, and comprised

"Housekeeper's Room, Servants' Hall, Butler's Pantry, Large Kitchen with open range and hot plate, Scullery, two larders, Wine, Ale and Beer Cellars, Wine Closet, Store Rooms, Still Room, Lamp Room, Box Room and three bedrooms for the male servants". The female servants were accommodated in eight bedrooms on the attic floor of The Park. The census records of 1891[4] note that there were at least ten living-in servants employed by John Coates.

The 1879 Sale Catalogue goes on to describe the outbuildings in the kitchen yard: "Knife, Wood and Coal Houses, W.C.s, and at a convenient place, is the Ice House, also a Drying Ground and Laundry, with Ironing and Mangling Rooms, Wash-house, Coal and Store House", all provided with "an excellent supply of hard and soft water". Several laundry maids were employed.

The stabling in the Coates' time was well screened from the house by a plantation of trees, and the complex consisted of a stone and slated building with six stalls, a washroom, a saddle and harness room, a Coach House with four bedrooms over for the coachman and grooms, a bacon room and brew house, and attached cart shed. It appears to have remained this way until the Ledgards converted this block in the early 1960s into a dwelling which was to become known as 'The Rangers House' (see below).

In the back yard there was a further range of stone and tiled buildings including more stables, three loose boxes, a gun room, a store room, a curing house, a wood house, a cart shed and a carpenter's shop with a granary over. Nearby there was a three bedroomed cottage occupied by the farm bailiff.

The gardens were also extensive, with lawns, tennis courts, statuary, "sloping banks and terraces". The kitchen garden was well stocked with fruit trees and a range of vineries, as well as having a stove house, and cucumber and melon pits, all heated with hot water pipes. There was also a gardener's room with a fruit room over, a potting shed and a mushroom house. The parkland around the house, which extended to nearly 90 acres, was "studded with some fine old forest oak trees and plantations" and it commanded some "charming views over the surrounding country including the castle ruins". The Coates family obviously lived in some style.

The gardener at that time was a Mr Sykes. He lived in the Lodge Cottage at the end of the Coach Road. He is delightfully described by Miss Lascelles in her 'green book':[5]

> *"He was Head Gardener at The Park in Mr Coates' time. He came from the West Riding, a small man, cheerful, industrious and pleasant. He wore a bowler hat in winter and a straw sailor in summer and a gardener's dark blue apron. He had rather bowed legs. He and Mr Coates used to go round the garden together and examine the wall fruit trees. He sang in the Church Choir and was great help in getting up village concerts. He was a public spirited man and his wife was always neat and trim.".*

Sykes the gardener was eventually succeeded by Harland who also lived in the Lodge Cottage. Harland had another string to his bow and sold sweets from the Lodge.

There are still people living in the village today who remember the Coates family of Sheriff Hutton Park and there are descendants of folk who actually worked there. They all have a story to tell. For example, John Coates Esquire walked to the village each day across the park, through the church yard and up the village street, always arriving around 12 noon and always wearing a long trailing black coat and a bowler hat. Later on, his son Sam followed the same route at exactly the same time, but substituted the long coat for a tweed suit and a trilby.

Ice skating on the fish pond just to the north of the house seemed to play an important part in the life of the village. In the autumn John Coates would engage the services of unemployed village men to clear the pond of leaves and other debris ready for the winter skating. The young Miss Coates' would loan their skates to the servant girls and teach them to skate.

The Coates daughters, Edith, Maude, Mabel and Mildred, all appear to have taken an active part in village life, for example teaching at the Sunday School and showing the other village girls how to mend and patch. They always gave a wonderful party for the Sunday School children in the Jacobean kitchens, and the children enjoyed sandwiches, homemade biscuits and gingerbread men. Miss Maude was also a talented artist. She painted in oils and several examples of her work still survive in the lovely portraits of village girls. However, the daughters always wore very drab clothes, browns, blacks and greys, with straw hats in summer and felt in winter, always in the same style with an upturned brim.

The Coates' era was very much one of the rich man in his castle and the poor man at the gate. After weekend parties at The Park, soup kitchens were set up and the villagers went with cans and jugs for free soup made from the leftovers of the dinner party. This was considered a great treat and the soup was delicious.

What of the people who worked at The Park?

A Miss Walker was governess to the children. The upstairs schoolroom in the house was always full of children of differing ages. Miss Walker prepared the boys for public school, and they went to Uppingham, Radley and Malvern. The youngest of the three girls (Mildred, Edith and Winifred) were the only ones to go to boarding school, in Scarborough. Miss Walker eventually left The Park to marry a local farmer from Stittenham, and the children often visited her there. Their nurse was a Miss Pritchard who looked after the children when they were young and had originally been a nurse at The Vicarage. She stayed with the Coates family for many years. In later years Miss Mabel Coates became the housekeeper.

The maids wore black dresses, white aprons and caps. They were responsible for finding fuel for their own fires, and had to go into the woods and shrubberies to gather wood and sticks. The maids' candles were tallow, but it is not known whether tallow candles were used throughout the house. Story has it that one of the cooks was so fat she had to get a kitchen maid to button her boots! One lifetime Women's Institute member, Nellie Hill, worked at The Park and there is a portrait of her by Miss Maude.

Two of the laundry maids, Emily and Lillian Wrighton, came from Strensall. Their great niece tells how Mrs Coates arrived to interview them. The Brougham stopped outside the girls' home, a very smart equipage with brass headlamps and uniformed coach and footman. Its arrival caused quite a stir and villagers came out to view the proceedings.

In around 1912 Mr Coates bought a Rolls Royce and employed Fred Carter as a chauffeur from about 1918 until the late 1930s. Carter served his mechanics apprenticeship at Robsons of Norton, a firm still in existence today, and he was sent down to the Rolls Royce factory to learn about maintenance and the working of a Rolls. It is probable that Carter lived 'on the job' until his marriage to a local girl, Annie Southam, when they moved to a small roadside cottage on the outskirts of Lilling. Although much altered, the house still stands today.

At a later date, a younger sister of the Wrighton girls, Louisa, came to work at The Park as a nursemaid. She tells how she often had to stay behind with the elderly Mrs Coates (John's mother) whilst the rest of the household were at church. Apparently there was said to be a ghost of a member of the Thompson family who hanged himself and was thought to haunt the servants' staircase.[6] The maids were always very nervous of being in this part of the house alone at night.

Fig. 14/3: Fred and Annie Carter in the 1920s.

Fig. 14/4: William Hill in later years.

Charles Stead was the coachman and he lived with his wife and two daughters in a cottage close to the church. He walked home for dinner every day. A bell was always rung over the west side of the park to call the men to dinner. His wife was a laundry maid. It is thought that another local man, William Hill, was a footman at The Park before 1900.

Bell was the butler in the 1920s. He was a delicate looking man who apparently made a poor job of keeping the drawing room lamps alight. There was always a fuss about the smell and the poor light!

It is known that John Coates dined at the home of William B. Everett of the Castle Brewery, Sheriff Hutton (now Middleton House). Everett and John Coates were the only people in the area with motor cars – in addition to their Rolls, the Coates' had several other cars including a Bentley, an Armstrong Siddley and a Vauxhall 25, and Everett had an Armstrong Siddley.

In 1891, Forrester was the farm bailiff and he lived in a cottage in the grounds of the big house with his wife Annie and their three children, Sarah, Joseph and George. On his retirement he was given a pension by Mr Coates and went to live in Lilling. He was succeeded by a man named Cleasby.

Fig. 14/5: Robert and Annie Forrester in the yard at the back of The Rangers House.

As the years progressed the number of servants decreased. John Coates died in 1935 at the age of 81 leaving three daughters and two sons. His eldest son, Jack, Vicar of Wighill near Tadcaster, pre-deceased him. In 1936 the estate was sold to the Egertons and the remaining members of the Coates family moved to Poppleton just outside York. In later years two of the sisters went to live in the Heworth area of York and were often seen about clad in the same drab garb. The Coates family had lived at Sheriff Hutton Park for over half a century.

The Egerton Family 1936-1950

The Egertons bought Sheriff Hutton Park in 1936, moving up from Sussex. Mrs Jack Egerton was a Yorkshire woman and, prior to her marriage to Rear Admiral Egerton, was the Lady Marion Beckett of Nawton Towers near Helmsley. Jack and Marion had two sons, Edward Gervase and Christopher.

The Egertons did not take up occupancy of The Park immediately, as the Admiral was unexpectedly called to a term of service in Singapore and Marion went with him. As a result, The Park was leased to a Colonel Wyndham who served in the regular army and travelled each day to Fulford Barracks near York. Colonel Wyndham had a butler by the name of Hawkins and Booth was his chauffeur. During the Wyndhams stay the Coach Road was resurfaced so that it could be used by the Army for manoeuvres.

Perhaps the highlight of the Wyndham tenancy was the visit of Queen Mary in 1937. She had come to the village to view the alleged tomb of Prince Edward, son of Richard III and

Anne Neville, and had lunched at The Park before moving on to the church. As the car moved slowly along the York Road, Colonel Wyndham caught a glimpse of his old nurse Miss Plumtree standing in the doorway of a village house. He immediately had the car stopped and Queen Mary chatted to her for a short while. The car then made its way to the church where cheering crowds greeted her along the way.

Fig. 14/6: The Royal Car arrives at Miss Plumtree's home in the village.

Fig. 14/7: Miss Plumtree on the occasion of the Royal visit.

It is said that a Major Howie took a short lease of The Park before the Egertons returned in 1939-40 to take over their property. They brought a number of servants with them from the south of England, including Ernest Rummery their chauffeur. Rummery had two daughters, Madge and Vi, and Madge married the Admiral's butler Frank Amies. Tom Jones was the footman, and he married a local girl, Joan Howard. After war was declared Amies and Jones left The Park to serve in the forces - Frank Amies became Admiral Egerton's batman and Tom Jones joined the Army.

Nancy Wright was a parlour maid at The Park during the Egerton's time and she still lives in Sheriff Hutton. Nancy took over many of the duties that would have been carried out by the butler and footman. She 'lived in' and had a bedroom on the top floor of the house along with the other maids. There was also a bathroom on that floor for their use. Nancy's duties were to clean the silver in the dining room, answer the door, lay the table for afternoon tea to which the family helped themselves, and lay a further table for dinner at which Nancy waited on.

Nancy has also described the Jacobean kitchen which was still in use during the Egerton era. It included a paper and log room, a room for jam and jelly making, and a servants hall and wine cellar at the far end. On the left at the bottom of the staircase was the water distillery. There was a lock up dairy, a large milk dairy, a dairy for poultry and salted vegetables, a shoe cleaning room and a butlers pantry with a bell system. The laundry by this time was located on the top floor of the house. The flower room immediately behind the dining room became a day nursery and latterly, when the Jacobean kitchens fell into disuse, it became the kitchen. The oak panelled room to the right of the staircase was the Admiral's study. Mrs Egerton used the room facing south and to the left of the stairs as a library and sitting room. There would have been about half a dozen servants in the 1940s.

Fig. 14/8: Vice Admiral Jack Egerton and his wife Marion at Cornbrough Villa in October 1958 (Source: Bernard-Wood 1959).

Nancy recalled the wartime visits of Sir Anthony Eden who at that time was Foreign Secretary. Sir Anthony's wife Beatrice was Mrs Egerton's sister and was always referred to as 'my Eden sister'. Eden came to The Park for quiet and relaxation. He would arrive with a police escort and outriders, and was always accompanied by his 7ft tall detective/body guard. She remembers taking telephone calls from the Government which she had to relay to Sir Anthony.

A goodly number of evacuees were billeted at The Park, somewhere around 15 to 20. They were of course hand picked - the crème de la crème. Their washing was sent out and done by two village women, Mrs Haines and Mrs Cordukes, and the ironing was done by Mrs Hull. Mrs Cordukes and Mrs Haines scrubbed the black and white tiled floors and passages in The Park for less than a £1 per week. Mrs Cordukes' husband, Sep, was the gardener. The billiard room/ballroom became the evacuees' dormitory and the water distillery became their dining room. During the wartime years a canning machine was installed in the Jacobean kitchens. It was put to very good use and very often operated by the ladies of the Women's Institute. Margaret Hodgson was billeted at The Park as a Land Army girl and eventually married local farmer Percy Dobson.

Mrs Egerton was in bed with influenza when Nancy Wright had the difficult task of taking to her the telegram informing her of the death in action of her eldest son Edward Gervase Egerton. Nancy told how after this Mrs Egerton would wear jackets, shirts etc belonging to her son - perhaps they brought her comfort.

Mrs Egerton was interested in the history of The Park, and invited over 100 members of the York Georgian Society to tour the house on 22nd June 1946. Her address was subsequently published by the Society,[7] and the resulting text and pictures provide a valuable description of the house at that time. This account for example, describes many of the rooms in the house, and mentions how several old stone mullioned windows and the panelling in the Oak Panelled room were uncovered by the restoration works then underway (see Chapter 15).

Mrs Egerton was for many years President of the local Women's Institute and was very keen on amateur dramatics. She led the Sheriff Hutton Drama Group to victory when they performed a play entitled 'Our Sovereign Lady' on the stage of the York Theatre Royal to celebrate the Coronation. There are a number of villagers still around today who took part in that production. What fun was had rehearsing in the great dining room at The Park and using the cloakroom across the hall as a dressing room!

Audrey Howard, who occupied rooms on the top floor of the house, was needlewoman to Mrs Egerton and she helped a great deal with the making of costumes for the drama productions. Mrs Egerton favoured costume drama. Audrey Howard's husband, Charles, was a joiner and carpenter, and a relative told how he stripped and polished the staircase in the main hall.

The Egertons had built on land adjacent to the Lodge Cottage a pair of agricultural workers cottages to be occupied by men who worked in the park. The cottages were sold off in 1953 as private dwellings. The Egertons sold The Park to Mr and Mrs Dudley Jackson in 1950, "otherwise", Mrs Egerton was heard to say "there will be nothing left for our son Christopher". They stayed in Sheriff Hutton parish, moving to Cornborough Villa where they lived for some years before subsequently moving on to Coxwold.

After the death of Mrs Egerton in February 1972, a memorial service was held in Sheriff Hutton church. At the request of Kit Egerton, the Drama girls sat together in the choir stalls. A plaque to the memory of Admiral and Mrs Egerton can be seen in the church today.

The Jackson Family 1950-1960

Dudley and Nina Jackson and their two sons, Piers and Sandy, moved into The Park in 1950. They were the first occupants to open the house to the paying public, opening each Saturday and Sunday afternoon from 2pm until 5pm, from April until October, using young people from the village as guides.

The tour began in the entrance hall, turning left into the dining room, once the great hall of Jacobean times, then across into the oak parlour, a room which had remained virtually unchanged since Sir Arthur Ingram's time in the 1620s. Visitors then continued up the staircase which dated back to c.1730 and onto the first floor where two bedrooms were on view, the Bird and Baby Room and the Heraldic Room. At this point, the guides would explain that this was a house within a house, a Queen Anne façade encasing a Jacobean building. They were then shown the space between the two walls exposing the iron tie joining the outer to the inner wall. In earlier times this space would have been used as powder closets but in more modem times they became bathrooms. Across the landing, visitors entered the early Georgian drawing room, originally the great chamber of the Jacobean house. It was a beautiful room, elegant and well proportioned. The tour ended, and the visitors left the main rooms by way of the green sitting room and thus into the Victorian wing where afternoon tea was served. The exit was through the conservatory and into the grounds.

SHERIFF HUTTON PARK, YORK

A PORTION OF THE
CONTENTS OF THE MANSION

including

A beautifully-proportioned Regency Mahogany Sofa Table

A Charming Queen Anne pattern Walnutwood Chest

An Important Chippendale Mahogany Pedestal Writing Desk

Small Mahogany Tables in the Chippendale Manner

A Superb Chippendale Mahogany Wing Bookcase

An elegant Chinese teak Side Table. A fine pair of Italian Renaissance Throne Chairs with gilt finials. Chinese Black Lacquer and Leather Screens.

A beautiful Chinese Chippendale Mahogany Serving Table

An oak Firescreen with Old English "Petit-Point" needlework banner.

A fine Chippendale Mahogany Four-poster Bedstead with Tester of pierced rococo outline. An Italian giltwood Dressing Stool. **A very elegant carved and gilt-wood Chandelier** with six scrolled branches for electric candles.

A Magnificent 17th century Italian Canopy Bedstead covered in pale blue damask appliqué with braidwork and rosettes.

An attractive small Bow-front Miniature Mahogany Tallboy

A Handsome Mahogany Breakfront Bureau-Cabinet

A Persian Runner Carpet. 2 charming Wrought Iron Lamp Standards with electric candles An interesting Old Arabian Cassoni.

A Gracefully-proportioned Hepplewhite Settee.
An Important 18th century Dutch Walnutwood Wardrobe

A fine Charles II Oak Dower Chest

A long Run of Wilton Blue Pile Stair Carpeting, *3ft. wide*

Curtains

An Excellent Iron Safe by *Chatwoods, Bolton*

Several Items of Early Chinese Porcelain

Important Oil Paintings of "San Sebastian" by Abraham Storck and "The Daughter's Departure" by F. Wheatley, R.A.

Georgian and Modern English Silver *including* a beautiful pair of George II gadrooned Sauceboats *by William Robertson*, a George II Coffee Pot *by William Shaw and William Priest*, a George II Circular Waiter *by Henry Brind*.

Fig. 14/9: Front page from the Egerton's sale catalogue, held on Friday 28th July 1950 in a marquee in the grounds, conducted by Henry Spencer.

Both Dudley and Nina Jackson were involved in village life. Dudley took part in the drama productions and Nina was President of, and was very active within, the local Women's Institute.

OPEN TO THE PUBLIC EVERY SATURDAY AND
SUNDAY FROM APRIL 10TH—OCTOBER 2ND INCLUSIVE
from 2-0 p.m.—5 p.m.

and at Bank Holidays

MONDAY AND TUESDAY   -   -   -   April 11th and 12th

May 30th and 31st

August 1st and 2nd

between 11-30 a.m. and 5-30 p.m.

Other times by prior arrangement

Routes to the Park:—
York via Malton Road, turn left through Flaxton and Lilling.
Easingwold via Stillington and Farlington.

Fig. 14/10: Details of house opening in the Jackson era, early 1950s.

After Dudley's death in May 1960, The Park was sold and the family moved to a spacious house between Kirbymoorside and Hutton-le-Hole. Mrs Jackson continued her links with Sheriff Hutton and W.I. members were regular visitors during the summer months, maybe for afternoon tea or a buffet supper.

The Ledgard Family 1960-1966

Colonel Percy Ledgard, his wife and three daughters, Sarah, Annabelle and Lavinia, came to The Park in 1960, having purchased the property from the Jacksons. The girls were keen horsewomen and skilled at riding side-saddle, and were often seen around the village and surrounding district on horse back. Percy Ledgard was a former Olympic Pentathlon star, a jazz enthusiast and talented jazz drummer.

Stories are told of the wonderful dances held in the Jacobean kitchens with Colonel Percy on the drums and invariably close by, his pet macaw 'Sinbad', whom we understand lived in a tea chest. It was Colonel Percy who was instrumental in converting the Brewhouse, Coach House and stable block into a dwelling which was to become known as 'The Rangers House'. This building, with its stone mullion windows, is arguably the earliest on the site dating back to 1639 (see Chapter 15). The first floor was for many years living accommodation for grooms and their families. The conversion was done on a very grand scale, and the ornate fireplace, overmantel, panelling and staircase came from nearby Stillington Hall when it was demolished. These items were acquired for the Ledgards by George and Arthur Pearson who were village joiners and they, together with local builders Alan and Jim Coverdale, installed the fireplace, staircase and panelling in The Rangers House.

Fig. 14/11: Christmas card showing Colonel Percy Ledgard, his wife and daughters in the grounds of The Park; Percy has his pet macaw 'Sinbad' on his right arm.

Colonel Percy also produced a short historical guide book to Sheriff Hutton Park. It was compiled by Christopher Gilbert and published in 1965; Gilbert subsequently produced two other articles for *County Life*.[8]

In 1966 The Park was sold to Mr and Mrs Blenkinsopp. However, the Ledgards did not leave the area, but moved into the old laundry block which they had had converted into a dwelling and naming it 'Warwick House'. In the meantime The Rangers House came into its own - the Ledgards were able to use it for parties and weekend guests. Eventually it was sold to John and Pauline Boullier and they, together with their sons, became its first full time occupants. After the Boulliers left it became a country house hotel. It was featured on the BBC 'Holiday Programme' and was run and owned by Syd and Dorianne Butler. They subsequently sold out to the present owner of The Park and The Rangers House has not been occupied since that time.

Warwick House was sold to Mr Robert Brumby, one time potter, sculptor, Head of the Art Faculty at York Technical College and today an artist with London exhibitions. However, he still retains his base at the house, which has been renamed as 'Hall Cottage'.

The Benkinsopp Family 1966-1980

Mr John Leslie Blenkinsopp arrived at The Park with his wife and four children, three boys and a girl, in 1966 having purchased the house from Colonel Percy Ledgard. Mr Blenkinsopp was wounded in the Second World War whilst serving in India and Burma. He was Chairman of Owen and Robinson, a firm of jewellers and silversmiths. It was the Blenkinsopps who changed the name of the house from Sheriff Hutton Park to Sheriff Hutton Hall.

In the late 1970s plans were mooted for a new village hall at Sheriff Hutton. Money needed to be raised and the Blenkinsopps kindly offered the use of their grounds, garden and kitchen facilities for a fund raiser which took the form of a mammoth garden party. This was held on 23rd June 1979. The day was warm and sunny and many of the stallholders were in costume. The walled garden made a perfect backdrop for the stalls which were set up either side of the main lawns. A total of £1,256.72 was raised, a tremendous boost to the coffers, thanks to the generous hospitality of the Blenkinsopps.

Fig. 14/12: Garden party held in the gardens of the Hall in June 1979 to raise funds for the new village hall.

The Hall (as The Park was now known) was put up for sale in 1980-81. Sadly there appeared to be little interest. The villagers thought that it would be converted into apartments. Were its days as a private house numbered? However, this was not to be, and rescue came in the form of a Drama School who decided to make the Hall their northern base.

East 15 Drama School 1981-1997

The East 15 Drama School was a company with a well-established school at Hatfield in Hertfordshire. A northern school was proposed at Sheriff Hutton, taking over the Hall and the grounds, and it was to be run by Wilf and Margaret (Maggie) Bury Walker. The new ownership meant that the Hall took on a new lease of life. The students moved in and the village became involved, helping on the domestic and costume side, even Sheriff Hutton Jumblies lending a hand looking for garments that could be turned into costumes and old jewellery that could be recycled.

Fig. 14/13: Advertisement card for one of East 15's presentations.

The plays, when rehearsals were complete, were open to the village and surrounding district. Sheriff Hutton had its own theatre on its doorstep. There was no set stage or scenery changes, the actors were simply followed from room to room by the audience. The Jacobean kitchens made a wonderful setting for the sleazy 'Street Car Named Desire', and to see the cast in costume strolling in the grounds during the interval on summer evenings was magic.

Maggie Walker kept the house ticking over and in a good state of repair. To this end she employed two old village tradesmen, Alan and Claud Coverdale, both in their 80s, to repoint the walls inside and out where necessary. They carried out restoration work in the Jacobean kitchens including the fitting of an old range which from then on was in constant use both by the students and as settings for some of their productions. The Coverdale brothers then turned their attention to the ice house, clearing out all the old bottles and debris and repointing the walls. The two old men had known the Hall since the Coates' time, and so for them it was a labour of love and they considered it a privilege to work there.

Margaret Bury Walker was a wonderful hostess, injecting new life into the house and making it a part of village life once more. The Christmas Singers were always welcomed into the great hall and plied with mince pies and mulled wine. Sadly all this came to an end in 1997. Once more the Hall and surrounding parkland was up for sale, and it was purchased by Mrs

Pamela Palmer. She has bought back some of the surrounding parkland and is in the process of restoring the house to its former glory.

Footnotes

1 Information on the Coates family kindly provided by Claud Coverdale, Barbara Helliwell, Myrtle and George Hull, Jean Farnaby, Yvonne Jack, Tessa Mitchell, Viv Nelson, Margaret Nicholson, Barbara Foreman, Tony Wright, Alan Coverdale (deceased), Nora Ward (deceased) and Edwin Cooke.

The Egerton family: Nancy Wright, Margaret Nicholson, Yvonne Jack, Jean Farnaby, Barbara Helliwell Myrtle Hull, Phyllis Hull, Barbara Grinham and Yvonne Jack.

The Jackson family: Jean Farnaby.

The Ledgard family: Alan Coverdale (deceased), Pauline Boullier, Robert Brumby, Sheila Clark, Jean Farnaby and Sarah Sherwin (nee Legard).

The Benkinsopp family: Sheila Clark, Wendy Haste and Tony Wright.

East 15 Drama School: Wendy Haste, Robert Brumby, Claud Coverdale and Alan Coverdale (deceased).

Pauline Boullier, Edwin Cooke, Jean Farnaby and Tessa Mitchell also kindly provided photographs, some of which are included in the text above.

2 Information from the 1891 census (*www.ancestry.co.uk*).

3 Sedgwick, Son & Weall 1879 "The Sheriff Hutton Park Estate". Copies held within the village and at the Borthwick Institute (PR/SH/80).

4 Information from the 1891 census (*www.ancestry.co.uk*).

5 Miss Lascelles Green Book (unpublished scrap book held in Sheriff Hutton Village Hall).

6 This is almost certainly a reference to Edward Percy Thompson who hung himself in October 1879; see Chapter 13.

7 Egerton 1946.

8 Gilbert 1965; Gilbert 1966a & 1966b.

CHAPTER 15: THE ARCHITECTURAL HISTORY OF SHERIFF HUTTON HALL

By Shaun Richardson
With contributions by Tony Wright and Mrs Egerton (d.1972)

Introduction

It may seem curious to acknowledge a contribution by a person (Mrs Egerton) who is no longer living, but it is thoroughly deserved. On the 22nd June 1946, the York Georgian Society visited Sheriff Hutton Park (as the Hall was then known) and were received by Mrs Egerton, who lived at the house with her husband, Rear Admiral Egerton (see Chapter 14). Although at the time of the visit, Mrs Egerton had still not been able to remove the Lincrusta from the staircase, she had been exposing 17th century interiors hidden beneath canvas, revealing Jacobean brickwork behind the house's 18th century shell, buying back fittings sold by previous owners and, most importantly, she made a note of it all. Assisted by the Leeds City Archivist, the address that Mrs Egerton gave that day was the first attempt by anyone to understand the history of the house, and she made some interesting observations. It would have been quite understandable if she had thrown up her hands in despair, as Sheriff Hutton Hall has a complex history and, in order to begin to understand this history, it is necessary to discuss not only the earlier house that the existing Hall partly incorporates, namely Sir Arthur Ingram's New or Great Lodge of c.1619-24, but also several other buildings that have long since disappeared, and one or two structures that may never have existed at all.

A decision was made at the beginning of the Pale Project, due to constraints of time and space, not to attempt a full architectural survey of the Hall and adjacent The Rangers House complex. It is hoped that such a survey, combined with a more detailed archaeological survey around the Hall, will take place at a future date, and the information thus gained will go some way to answering some of the questions posed below. Finally, for ease of description, the house is referred to as the Hall throughout the following chapter.

Lodges, Laund Houses and Helms

In 1966, Christopher Gilbert asserted that the Ingram's New Lodge had been built on the site of an old royal hunting lodge known as the 'Laund House' and that parts of its structure were incorporated into Ingram's new house, a view supported by more recent studies.[1] However, the case is not quite as straightforward as Gilbert suggests. As has been set out in Chapter 5, there are several possible predecessors to Ingram's New Lodge, namely lodges, laund houses, little lodges and helms, and not all of them were necessarily located on its site. The evidence is often confusing and contradictory, with some buildings assuming the guise of others, or seemingly different buildings actually being one and the same. The usage of words also changes over time,[2] and so a local wheelwright referring to a 'lodge' in 1598 may have had in mind a very different building to the 'lodge' envisaged by Ingram in 1619.

It would be possible to speculate endlessly, and with no great insight, on the relationship of the various buildings known from the documentary sources, both to one another and to Ingram's New Lodge, and this is before the body of 17th century plans surviving in the West Yorkshire Archives record office in Leeds are even considered (see below). However, a few general themes emerge.

In the late 16th century, there was clearly a building within the park known as the lodge where the Earl of Huntingdon sometimes chose to stay, probably to escape the increasingly decayed state of the castle and perhaps in order to gain some privacy; fixtures and fittings went from the castle to the lodge, perhaps to make it more comfortable. This lodge sat within a cleared enclosure but its exact location is uncertain. Building work was taking place in the park in 1617, James I was entertained at the 'Laund house' there in the same year, and in 1618 Barnard Dinninghof billed Arthur Ingram for glazing his house at Sheriff Hutton, all before construction of the New Lodge started in 1619. As noted in Chapter 5, a case could be made for the 'Little Lodge' in the south-east corner of the park being both the lodge of 1598 and the Laund House of 1617, with the 'helme' located to the north-west of Lodge Farm. However, the position of the former counts against it being the main hunting lodge within the park, which is more likely to have been centrally located. Perhaps, as had been suggested to Mrs Egerton, the Laund House was not on precisely the same site as the New Lodge, but that it stood slightly to the west, and it survived for some years after the larger house was built, eventually being recycled into the stable block along with a good portion of the castle. Thus we have travelled part way, in a rather erratic circle, back towards Gilbert's original assertion that Ingram's New Lodge was built on the site of an earlier building.

The New Lodge

Having put the speculation about what Ingram's New Lodge might have replaced behind us, we must briefly look at the other options for a new house at Sheriff Hutton which were considered before Ingram settled on the site in the park.

Alternative 1: the Castle Gatehouse

In 1618, Barnard Dinninghof produced three plans for Thomas Lumdsen showing how the gatehouse and flanking towers of the middle court of the stone castle in the village could be converted into a residence.[3] Dinninghof, an accomplished German glass-painter and glazier, was probably a foreign refugee who had come to England in the late 16th century. He seems to have been based in York, and his earliest known work is the painted glass at Gilling castle in North Yorkshire, which is signed and dated 1585. He almost certainly produced the surviving painted glass in Fountains Hall in North Yorkshire, and at The Red House at Moor Monckton for Sir William Slingsby. Other glass that may be attributable to him survives at Bishopthorpe Palace in York and Temple Newsam in Leeds; some of the latter was originally placed in the chapel of the New Lodge.[4]

In addition to glass-painting and glazing, Dinninghof produced architectural designs, and interestingly, all the surviving drawings which are signed by him or probably attributable to him appear to relate to Sheriff Hutton. However, others have speculated as to whether he was also involved in the design of The Red House chapel, the Banqueting House at Weston-in-Wharfedale, Gilling castle and Fountains Hall.[5] Girouard noted the similarities between the plans for Fountains Hall and Sheriff Hutton gatehouse, but felt it was more likely that Dinninghof had been influenced by Fountains Hall, and by its probable architect Robert Smythson, rather than vice versa.[6] Dinninghof's eventual fate is unknown for, after signing the Sheriff Hutton gatehouse drawings in 1618, he appears to disappear from history.[7]

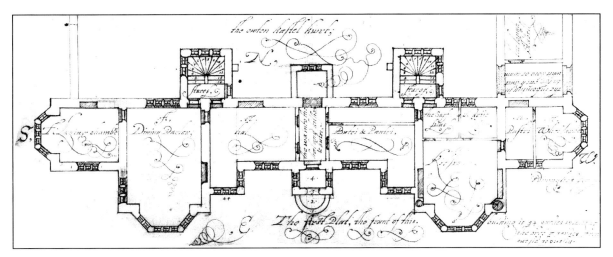

Fig. 15/1: Dinninghof's 1618 plan for the conversion of the castle gatehouse (ground floor) (Source: WYAS Leeds WYL100/SH/A3/2/1).

Dinninghof's plans are designed to be laid one on top of the other, with the staircase spaces cut out on the upper floors so as to illustrate how they rose from the ground floor. According to the ground floor plan, the house was to be "54 yardes in lenght the bret [breadth] 7 yardes from outsid to outsid". It is not clear on the plan exactly which door and window openings were existing, and which were proposed, but it is likely that the canted bays and rear staircase towers were planned additions. The house was to have had a "Galleri or Great Chamber 21 yards in length in bread 25 foot" on the first floor. In his accompanying letter, Dinninghof stated that the whole would cost £440 but that if "you [i.e. Lumdsen] are mynded to take downe the castell theirin will be found much timbre for that purpose all so iron for window barres and bandes for domes and ouremantel ... and also lead for the gutters and wankes and cant windowes".[8]

It is clear from Dinninghof's letter that the inner court of the castle was considered beyond renovation as a house by 1618, and that any conversion of the gatehouse would probably have made use of a re-structured middle court. Maybe Dinninghof settled on the middle court gatehouse because it had already been substantially updated for either Henry Fitzroy or the Duke of Norfolk; Samuel Sharp noted 16th century brickwork here in 1829 (see Chapter 7). For whatever reasons, probably financial ones on Lumsden's part, the gatehouse was never converted. Sheriff Hutton village therefore lost a significant addition to its architecture and architectural historians the chance to see just how competent an architect Dinninghof was. Whether an early 17th century house would have been able to resist the demands of late 19th century farming any more successfully than the Neville's 14th century gatehouse tower is of course debatable.

Alternative 2: 'the first plot agreed upon for the buildinge of my house'

Amongst the Temple Newsam collection in the record office in Leeds is a folder of ten plans and elevations.[9] These were first noted by Mrs Egerton who stated that the plans "bear no relation to the house as it is now, or could have been, and were evidently alternative plans", adding "it would take me too long to explain why the existing ones are obviously not the approved plans".[10] The drawings then seem to have been forgotten about or ignored until 1978 when a PhD student at York University discussed them as part of his work on Barnard Dinninghof.[11]

213

For the purposes of this chapter, Dinninghof's drawings can be divided into three groups. The first group, comprising two plans and an elevation,[12] are in Dinninghof's own hand (see below). The second group[13] are two rather curious elevations of a small house, one of which bears a scrolled 'S' (for south elevation?) suggestive of Dinninghof's handwriting. The third group[14] all comprise plans of a very similar building, distinguished from one another only by their internal arrangements. One of the latter[15] bears Dinninghof's florid script and, although it is unsigned, it is almost certainly his work. It shows a house, described as being 55 feet (c.18m) long by 21 feet (c.7m) wide, with a central cross-passage entered via a small porch (see figure 15/2). The house contained various rooms, including a small rear room named the 'Surveyinge place', equipped with an external doorway; might it have been intended as a room from which to survey the park or the deer? The other plans are in a different hand but show a house of an almost identical overall form with differing internal arrangements, and on the back of one is written 'The first plot agreed upon for the buildinge of my house with Richard Wilson'.[16] The date following this writing is given as 1619 in the accompanying catalogue entry, but it could be 1609.

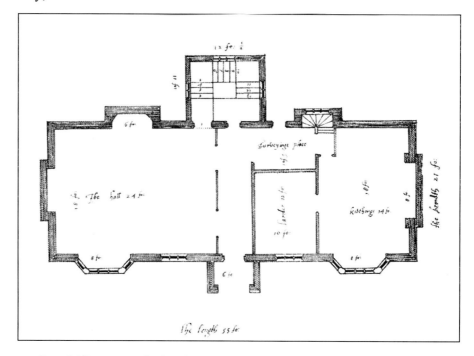

Fig. 15/2: Dinninghof's plan of an unnamed building (WYAS Leeds WYL100/SH/A3/1/6).

Brighton, echoing Mrs Egerton, commented in 1978 that the third group of drawings might be alternative designs for the New Lodge which were never used.[17] Perhaps Ingram did agree to this design in 1619, but then changed his mind and embarked on a far grander project. The identity of Richard Wilson remains uncertain. He does not appear in any standard works of architects/designers of the period,[18] nor is he known in any other capacity at Sheriff Hutton either before or afterwards, although a Richard Wilson, carpenter, did work at Ingram's York Palace after 1618.[19] It has also been proposed that these drawings are of the house that existed on the New Lodge site, which was subsequently demolished to make way for the New Lodge.[20] The fact that plans by two different hands show very similar buildings does suggest that the authors were either working to a set of specific instructions or that they were adapting an existing house. On most of the plans, the rough tripartite (three-part) division of the interior might be a remnant of a late medieval plan form, although the porch, bay windows and stair tower are all suggestive of a late 16th or early 17th century date.[21]

As noted above, the first group of drawings, two plans and an elevation, are undated and unsigned but are in Dinninghof's hand.[22] In some ways these plans are similar to the third group discussed above, but the internal elements are more formalised into distinct cross wings. The plans show a squat H-plan house, with a central ground floor entrance leading through two vestibules into the hall, which occupied the centre of the house (see figure 15/3). The hall was flanked to one side by a service wing with kitchen and brewhouse, and to the other side by a 'Laging' [lodging] and dining parlour with closet. The staircase between the latter rose to a lodging chamber and great chamber on the first floor, with a withdrawing chamber and lodging chamber in the centre of the house, both fitted with closets. The elevation appears to show a design for a similar building from the rear side, but the wings have become more elongated and the house has assumed a half-H or U plan.

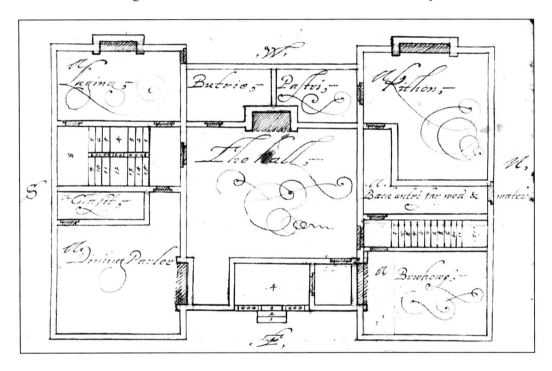

Fig. 15/3: Dinninghof's plan of an unnamed building (WYAS Leeds WYL100/SH/A3/1/2).

Fig. 15/4: Dinninghof's elevation drawing (WYAS Leeds WYL100/SH/A3/1/1).

Like the latter drawing, the finished New Lodge had a half-H plan, but this is where the resemblance ends. It is otherwise an unsophisticated, rather primitive, design and the extruded chimney stacks on the gable ends show no concern for architectural display. Like all the drawings discussed above, it is so far removed in scale and conception from the finished house that it is difficult to see any of them as alternative designs as proposed by Mrs Egerton and others, and extremely doubtful that they had any influence on its design. Is it possible that some do show an existing building (the Laund House?) on or close to the New Lodge site? However, the majority are most convincing as proposals to re-furbish an existing building, rather than make a record of it, but as we have seen above, which one – the Laund House, the Little Lodge, the lodge or the helm?

The building of the New Lodge 1619-24

Whilst the exact relationship of these drawings to the New Lodge is unclear, what is certain is that they were greatly exceeded by the finished house. Only the plans produced by Dinninghof for the castle gatehouse come close in terms of scale and form. It is quite possible that Ingram might have employed Dinninghof to produce designs for the New Lodge; perhaps he produced a new set of plans which are now lost or perhaps he adapted the gatehouse plans to suit a new site. This would go some way to explaining a number of structural features of the New Lodge, particularly the entrance passage which ran the full width of the central block (see below).

The construction of the New Lodge has previously been described in some detail by Gilbert.[23] Building was well underway by October 1619, when John Mattison, Ingram's steward, noted that the "house side down into the garden, also the two parlours next to the garden, likewise one side of the stairs as high as the terrace" were finished and that "the room over the parlour is wainscoted". Later, in 1622, work had started on the gallery, with the stairs, floors and screen at the lower end of the hall finished, and by October 1623 payments were being made for glazing, suggesting that the house was nearing completion. It was certainly finished in 1624, when Norden noted in his survey of the park that "Sir Arthur Ingram has raised a very fair new Lodge with brick of this form, with a fair garden enclosed with a brick wall with mount walks and fair ornaments".[24]

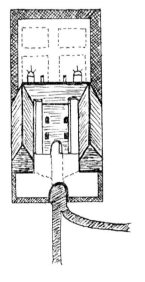

Fig. 15/5: Gilbert's interpretation of Norden's depiction of the New Lodge (Source: Gilbert 1965).

216

The plan accompanying Norden's survey (see plate 37) has a small but relatively detailed depiction of the New Lodge, which was interpreted by Gilbert (see above).[25] However, any interpretation of this drawing from the original is not easy, as even with modern scanning methods, lines merge and blur when it is enlarged. Nevertheless, it seems fairly clear that Norden shows a half-H or U-plan house, approached by a road from the west through an arched entrance into a walled forecourt, and with enclosed gardens containing parterres to the rear (south). The house itself comprised an eastern central block and flanking north and south wings of approximately equal length, all apparently of three storeys, with gabled roofs to the wings and domed towers or turrets to the north-east and south-east corners of the central block. The main entrance was through an archway in the central block, at the base of a slightly projecting storeyed porch with crenellations and perhaps with a heraldic device over.[26]

As described in Chapter 12, by c.1637 Arthur Ingram had passed the Lodge to his son, Sir Thomas Ingram, to use as a home following his marriage to Frances Belasyse. A detailed description of the Lodge (by then called the 'Greate Lodge') is given as part of the 1650 survey of the park, and it provides a good idea of the disposition of the rooms during Thomas and Frances' residence. As they are not known to have undertaken any major alterations to the Lodge, limiting new works to the gardens and stables (see below), the 1650 form of the house was probably still very close to what Arthur Ingram had finished in 1624:

> "*that Messuage dwelling house or Lodge fairly builte with brick with the aputenutes situate and linige, somewhat, Northeast of the Midst of the said Parke consistinge of Large and hansome Roomes on the firste ffloore, one Entry or passage leading out of this Court on the Northweste side of the said howse, into the Garden, on the Southeaste side thereof; one the lefte side of the said entry, one faire hall, with Large windows, jetinge out upon the said Court one parlour, with a Closett or Studdy adioyninge, and a very faire Chappell at the upper end of the said hall, on the right side of the said entry, the Pantrey, one dyneinge roome for servants, with two other necessary rooms over against the parlour doore one faire lodginge Chamber, a nursery and a withdrawinge roome; seaven Stepps descending from the entry, there is one Large and spatious Kitchin with two sellers and other necessary offices: Onto the second floore ascendinge by very faire and large stayres out of the entry into a half space, on the right hand side, a faire and lofty dininge Roome, one large lodgeinge Chamber, a large and hansome Gallery with a balcony towards the North, on the left hande, are five hansome lodginge Chambers, with four Closetts; on the Thirde floore ascendinge by other large staires are two great Lodginge Chambers, and seaven other roomes fitt for lodginge or other uses; on the left side of the Court are several out offices, the said Court is encompassed with a strong and high brick wall, with a faire gate or entrance thereinto*".[27]

What then, did the New Lodge look like in c.1650 and how did it compare to other contemporary houses in the region? Taking all the evidence outlined above, the following can be suggested. The 1624 plan, although schematic, indicates that the width of the Lodge's central block, including the wings at either end, was approximately the same as the walled garden to the south, which was formed by a four-plot parterre surrounded by the 'walks' or 'mounts' noted in contemporary descriptions (see below). Comparison of the surviving garden walls to the south of the house with earthworks depicted in 1911 and the 1624 plan suggests that the total width of the Lodge was something in the order of 45m, with each wing being slightly shorter.[28] Such dimensions are impressive; they fall 13m short of the principal front of Arthur Ingram's vast residence at Temple Newsam in West Yorkshire (see below) but actually exceed other examples of late 16th and early 17th century 'prodigy houses' in the same county.[29] A further indication as to the scale of the Lodge comes during the residence of Sir Roger Langley, who in 1673 paid Hearth Tax on 31 hearths at East and West Lilling.[30] Even allowing for a number of hearths in the surrounding outbuildings, this still suggests that the Lodge was a very substantial dwelling, given that on average only 22% of houses in the northern Vale of York were listed as having more than one hearth in 1673.[31] It also bears comparison with some of the West Yorkshire prodigy houses noted above, exceeding the number of hearths at Ledston Hall (remodelled c.1629-41) but falling short of Temple Newsam (remodelled after 1622), which had 45 (including outbuildings and later additions).[32]

It is quite possible that Arthur Ingram had some of the earlier West Yorkshire 'prodigy houses' in mind when he settled on the final designs for the Lodge, as he would doubtless have been familiar with them through his Yorkshire estates. Contemporary houses around London and the south-east that he had encountered when at Court prior to 1616, such as Hatfield in Hertfordshire and the Smythson houses of the north Midlands, probably also had an influence. Like some of the southern houses, Ingram chose to build in brick rather than stone, but it is likely that the quoins and the storeyed entrance porch were emphasised by the use of good quality stone taken from the castle.[33] The exterior of the wings and central block would have been of largely symmetrical appearance, but given some variety by the use of projecting bays provided with tall mullioned and transomed windows; the remains of such bays and windows were uncovered during restoration works in 1937.[34] One of these projecting bays (sexagonal, according to Mrs Egerton in 1946) probably formed part of the storeyed porch and housed the windows lighting the hall to the north of the entrance. Mrs Egerton also makes reference to the remains of 'sexagonal bays at each corner' exposed externally in 1937, later interpreted by Pevsner as polygonal angle turrets.[35] The drawing of the Lodge made in 1624 certainly appears to show domed towers or turrets to the angles of the garden front of the central block, and such features commonly occur in late 16th and early 17th century houses of this scale. The gabled west ends to the wings shown in 1624 are also likely to have been enriched or articulated in some way, reflecting the importance of the skyline to such houses.[36]

The interior layout of the Lodge resembled that of other large contemporary houses, reflecting the needs of their builders to provide suites of rooms capable of accommodating itinerant monarchs or peers; it also incorporated some of the most recent developments such as compact planning and a service basement.[37]

At Sheriff Hutton, the principal entrance was centrally positioned on the ground floor of the east side of the central block. The entrance also appears to have functioned as a screens passage, running through the width of the central block and flanked to the north by the screen leading into the hall. The oak screen with Tuscan columns, made by Henry Duckett in 1622, still survives but it was originally higher, reflecting the former open height of the hall internally. The hall would have functioned as the principal public room within the Lodge, and served a variety of purposes, from a reception area to an extra dining room if required; as such, it may have been relatively sparsely furnished. The hall led through into the Oak Parlour (described as a parlour with closet adjoining in 1649-50), the chimneypiece, ceiling and panelling of which survive virtually unchanged since 1624; like the other surviving examples within the Hall, the chimney piece was by Thomas Ventris and the plasterwork by John Burridge. The chapel was accessible from the upper end of the hall and appears to have been housed in the north wing; like the hall, the chapel may have had a raised ceiling internally.[38]

Fig. 15/6: Oak screen in the Great Hall by Duckett, 1622.

Fig: 15/7: Jacobean panelling, ceiling and chimney piece on the Oak Parlour (Source: Gilbert 1965).

To the south of the central passage lay the pantry, servants' dining room, a lodging chamber, a withdrawing room, a nursery and other rooms. Some of these must have been accommodated in the ground floor of the south wing, which has the characteristics of a service wing. There is likely to have been access from some of the service rooms to the basement kitchen, set beneath the central block and reached from steps descending from the central entrance passage. The massive fireplace arch surviving at the south end of the kitchen is at least 17th century in date and may well be earlier, perhaps having been acquired from the castle. The kitchen had two adjoining cellars and other rooms, one of which contained a range which was used for cooking until c.1945.[39]

The existing staircase ascending from the entrance passage is an 18th century replacement of the 17th century original, which Gilbert thought would have resembled that still surviving at New Park, near Easingwold, another 17th century lodge built by Ingram;[40] Pevsner also noted a 17th century back stair at Sheriff Hutton in 1966.[41] At the top of the existing staircase, there is a curious feature, a very wide four-centred rusticated arch with masks to the responds and keystones.[42] Mrs Edgerton thought that this had originally come from the castle and that the masks, representing Sir Arthur and Lady Ingram, were later additions, although others felt that it was entirely 17th century work.[43] Its detailing bears some broad resemblance to the main doorway of Ingram's York Palace (built 1623-5; see below) as it was illustrated in 1807.[44]

The arch led into another passage, which Pevsner thought might once have overlooked one end of the open hall to the north.[45] In c.1650, the staircase appears to have risen to a first floor landing, giving access to the rooms to either side. To the north, in the central block and the north wing, there were five lodging chambers. Two of these survive in the central block, known as the Bird and Baby Room and the Heraldic Room in 1965,[46] both retaining high quality 17th century interiors, in particular the superb plaster ceilings. To the south, the landing opened into a dining room (equivalent to the space described in other contemporary houses as the great chamber), a lodging chamber and a long gallery with a balcony. The latter would have occupied most of the south wing and was a private space, reserved for the few, in contrast to the more public hall. The dining room or great chamber was remodelled as a drawing room during the 18th century (see below).

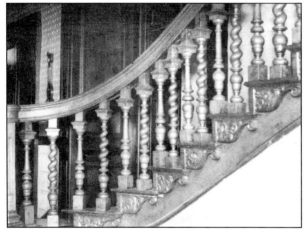

Fig. 15/8: 18th century staircase in the main hall.

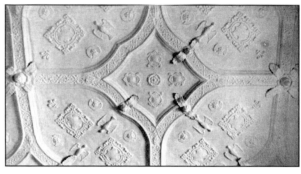

Fig. 15/9: Plaster ceiling in the Bird and Baby Room by John Burridge (Source: Gilbert 1965).

From the first floor, the main staircase rose to the second floor, where there were two great lodging chambers and seven smaller rooms; again some of these rooms must have been contained in the wings. The 1625 survey suggests that the angle turrets to the garden front rose from the second floor, and might have contained belvederes or banqueting rooms.[47] It is uncertain what happened to the second floor when the house was remodelled; a detailed building survey might reveal if it was incorporated into the existing Hall or removed completely.

The surviving Jacobean furnishings within the Hall are testament to the former lavish appearance of the Lodge's interior, and there is no reason to doubt that the wings, especially the chapel and long gallery, were not equally richly treated; indeed, some of the chapel fittings were of sufficient quality to be removed to Temple Newsam during the 1640s (see below). Some of the surviving furnishings are in fact doubly valuable because there were originally set within the castle and were subsequently taken to the Lodge. The account books of Arthur Ingram's steward, John Mattison, record the removal of stone, timber and interior fittings from the castle, taking up the suggestion made by Dinninghof in 1618 that much useful material could be found within.[48] Panelling had been removed from the castle as early as 1598 and another substantial amount, together with lead, was removed in 1617.[49] The panelling in the Oak Parlour on the Hall's ground floor was almost certainly obtained from the castle; Mrs Egerton seems to have been the originator of the theory that the unusual 'H' design of the panelling relates to Henry Fitzroy.[50] It is likely that Ingram would have concentrated on removing only the surviving higher status Tudor furnishings from the castle, as he is hardly likely to have wanted to install old 14th century items into an early 17th century house.

The New Lodge: the forerunner of Temple Newsam?

The substantial size and expensive interior decoration of the Lodge is all the more remarkable when one considers what else Ingram was building at the same time. In addition to the numerous smaller houses he owned, Ingram built or remodelled three major residences, Sheriff Hutton Lodge, York Palace and Temple Newsam house.

In 1613, Ingram leased a former prebendary house belonging to South Cave close to the Minster in York, and in 1618 an adjacent long range which had formerly been part of the Archbishop's Palace. In 1623-25 a new building was erected, linking the two older properties and in the next few years Ingram acquired other surrounding land, in which he created extensive gardens. Due to the incorporation of earlier buildings into its plan, this York house did not have the same symmetry or formal arrangement as at Sheriff Hutton or Temple Newsam, but it was no less richly furnished; the same group of craftsmen worked on all three houses. The gardens, with their orchard, fish ponds, ornaments in the shape of beasts (again by Ventris, as at Sheriff Hutton), bowling green and tennis court were much admired by contemporaries, and it is clear that the whole complex was conceived by Ingram to rival the King's Manor; tax was paid on 33 hearths in both 1662 and 1678.[51] Much like at Temple Newsam (see below), material appears to have been removed from Sheriff Hutton Lodge to furnish the York Palace, including a pair of organs in 1640.[52]

The Temple Newsam estate was bought by Ingram in 1622. He then demolished the east wing of an earlier courtyard house on the site, built by Lord Darcy of Temple Hurst, and remodelled the north and south wings, to create a half-H plan, one of the last uses of such a plan for a large house in the county; the west wing may incorporate parts of the earlier residence.[53] The body of the house was virtually complete by 1634 and the last additions, made in 1636, were a walled forecourt with twin lodges and gateway, and a garden banqueting house, both built in the fashionable Italian manner.[54] The interior was not completed until at least 1637, and made use of many items from Sheriff Hutton. For example, the great organ in the chapel, made in 1625 by George Brownless of York for £40, was removed from the Lodge to Temple Newsam, and in 1635 a glazier, Thomas Elwes, was paid £3 for taking down the coloured glass in the Lodge chapel and re-setting it in Ingram's new chapel; some of this glass was probably originally designed by Barnard Dinninghof.[55] When Temple Newsam was completed, Ingram did not actually live there, preferring to reside at York, but he settled his oldest son at the house, much as he placed Thomas Ingram at Sheriff Hutton Lodge in c.1637.[56]

Sheriff Hutton Lodge stands midway between Ingram's two other large houses, both chronologically and in terms of architectural development. Work at the York Palace commenced slightly earlier but, although the resulting residence was undoubtedly magnificent, Ingram was hampered by having to incorporate parts of a much earlier structure. At Sheriff Hutton, he had a virtual 'greenfield' site - even if the New Lodge did stand on the same site as or close to an earlier building, there is currently no convincing evidence that any part was incorporated within it. Without these constraints, Ingram was able to raise a far more ordered and integrated house than at York. The broad similarities of scale, plan form, internal layout, furnishings and probable appearance of the Lodge to Temple Newsam are notable. It is therefore difficult to avoid the conclusion that Temple Newsam was at the very least heavily influenced by the Lodge, and perhaps even modelled on it; in effect, the Lodge functioned as a very costly 'trial run' for the larger house. Given that Dinninghof may have had a hand in the design of the Lodge, either directly or indirectly (see above), this raises the interesting possibility that in some small way he also indirectly influenced the appearance of Temple Newsam.

The Garden Landscape of the New Lodge

Gardens, and a wider designed landscape, played an important part in creating the appropriate setting for York Palace and Temple Newsam. There is also some evidence that the same theory was applied to Sheriff Hutton, where fragments of the 17th century designed landscape accompanying the house still survive.

The principal approach to the Lodge always appears to have been from the west along what is now known as the Coach Road. However, the alignment of this road may well have differed slightly in the past. Although it is difficult to interpret, the 1624 survey appears to show that the entrance into the park was further to the south than at present, and that the road took a more direct east-west route to the Lodge, eventually turning south-east to enter the forecourt (see plate 37). This would mean that the eastern section of the present Coach Road, to the east of the turning to Oaks Farm, would have been straighter with a more direct east-north-east route.

The 1624 survey also shows a sinuous feature running towards the Lodge from the north but apparently continuing as a footpath west towards the castle. It has been suggested that this feature, together with other aerial photographic evidence, shows that Ingram initially intended the house to be approached from the north, rather than the west, along a formal avenue (see below).[57] There *was* once a trackway approaching the lodge from the north (marked as 'Road to ye Lodge' in 1765,[58]) but this is set further to the west, curving around the original eastern churchyard boundary and running south as an existing footpath. The feature shown on Norden's survey might be no more than a temporary trackway made to move materials from the castle to the Lodge, or it might also be a watercourse, although it is difficult to see in what direction it would have flowed and what purpose it would have served.

There were good reasons why the New Lodge should always have been approached from the west rather than the north. Even today, the existing Coach Road provides superb views towards the ruins of the stone castle. Sir Arthur may have wished visitors to view the decaying ruins as they approached his splendid new building, thus contrasting the passing glory of the Nevilles with the nascent power of the Ingrams.

As described above, the road to the Lodge performed a sharp turn in front of the building to approach the walled forecourt. Norden depicts a central archway, or more probably a large pair of ornate gates in the north side of the forecourt (see figure 15/5 above), described in 1650 as:

> *"on the left side of the Court are sevall out offices, the said Court is encompassed with a strong and high brick wall, with, a faire gate or entrance thereinto".*[59]

The forecourt was swept away during the 18th century alterations, but its former position is preserved as a series of slight earthworks in the paddock to the north of the Hall. The south wall of the forecourt is marked by a shallow linear depression, set approximately 45m to the north of the existing north side of the Hall, behind which the ground surface is slightly raised. Allowing for the demolished wings of the Lodge to project forward, this gives a forecourt of the approximate shape and size of that shown in 1624. The northern returns of the forecourt wall at either end are now difficult to discern, but a sub-rectangular platform to the east end is probably one of the 'out offices' noted in 1650.

After passing through the forecourt gates, the house was approached along a central pathway leading through the forecourt to the entrance in the central block. As described above, this entrance seems to have taken the form of a passage, running through the width of the block and communicating with the gardens in the other side. In 1624, Norden depicted a large rectangular parterre here, laid out on a four-plot plan, perhaps surrounded by a low wall or fence, and then an outer wall which is assumed to correspond with those still surviving within the garden (see figure 15/5 above). He described the garden as 'a fair garden enclosed with a brick wall with mount walks and fair ornaments'.[60] This description was echoed in 1650, when it was noted that:

> "on the Southeast side of the said house is a very faire garden surrounded with a brick wall like unto the Court, wherein are seval litle Monmts with Statues theron placed, at the corner whereof towards the south is a very hansome arbour or place for pleasure coved with leade, and railed about, with seavall stepps to ascende by. Without the said garden, and adioyninge to the wall on the easts and south easte pts are two litle kithen gardens".[61]

It should come as no surprise that the later survey mentions several features, such as the arbour (perhaps a banqueting house) and kitchen gardens, not noted by Norden. Norden's plan was made in 1624, when the house had only just been completed and the wider designed landscape still had to be laid out in full. The gardens and landscape would have continued to develop throughout the 17th century and of course, after Thomas Ingram and his family moved into the Lodge in c.1637, domestic considerations would have required the laying out of items such as the kitchen gardens.

The gardens had once been equipped with a paved terrace, as in 1623 John Lumley was paid to take down the 'tarries' (terrace) at Sheriff Hutton and transport it to York Palace where it paved the area around Ingram's fishponds.[62] 'Stony walks' that needed weeding remained in 1632, but in 1638 Ingram made a contract with William Butler to rebuild the terrace at the Lodge in the same manner as the new garden terrace at York and to carry out other alterations for the sum of £11.[63] Mrs Egerton saw letters showing that there had once been a terrace on the north side of the house as well,[64] but nothing of this remains. However, there are discrete earthworks surrounding those of the forecourt noted above that might be the remnants of a more extensive formal layout. The Lodge was also equipped with a bowling alley or green by 1639, as the same feature at the York Palace was to be made like the one at Sheriff Hutton; the York green had painted seats, wooden railings and a surrounding wall 5-6 feet in height.[65] The year before, Thomas Ventris was employed to carve 20 garden ornaments in the form of heraldic beasts and the German sculptor Andrew Karne was casting lead flowerpots at the Lodge.[66] Finally, Ingram often sent shrubs and fruit trees up from London for the gardens, on one occasion 20 rose trees arrived with the instructions to "have Drew set them at every corner of the knots and cut the privet into beasts and set the court walls with honeysuckle".[67]

Parts of these gardens can still be seen around the Hall. A terrace runs along the south side of the Hall, extending beyond either end of both the house and the parterre walls. At the east end are a flight of steps which Gilbert thought led down into a sunken garden,[68] while to the west there is a large sub-rectangular pond, the date of which is uncertain; the Ordnance Survey 1855 1st edition 6" map shows an avenue of trees here, between the pond and the parterre walls. To the south-east of the Hall, the principal surviving features are the brick walls which once enclosed the parterre. The walls terminate in pedestals, surmounted by statues in the form of heraldic beasts carved by Ventris in 1638 and two groups of *amorini* (figures of infants), perhaps done by Karne at the same time as he was casting the flowerpots. There are further terraces to the east and west of the parterre walls and at the south end, which is now open (see plate 73).

Fig. 15/10: Two amorini, probably by Andrew Karne, c.1638.

Fig. 15/11: Heraldic lion carved by Thomas Ventris in 1638 (Source: Gilbert 1965).

It is therefore clear that substantial improvements were carried out to the gardens of the Lodge from c.1637 onwards. During the later 17th century, the gardens and surrounding landscapes of many country houses underwent a complete transformation, with a new emphasis of formality and symmetry, and making greater use of features such as raised terraces, avenues, statuary, canals, pools and fountains.[69] These were partly used to integrate the house with the surrounding countryside, but also as deliberate assertions of ownership. Indeed, during the early to mid 17th century an avenue of lime, elm or horse chestnut became a recognised aristocratic symbol, and tree planting became as great an aristocratic obsession as dogs and horses.[70] A good example of the landscapes created by these changes can be seen on Kip and Knyff's 1699 view of Temple Newsam, which shows the full range of features deemed to be desirable and also the scale on which they were laid out.[71]

An attempt was made to provide Sheriff Hutton Lodge with a similar landscape, but it appears to have been unsuccessful or at least never carried to completion. In 1946, Mrs Egerton remarked that "The original drive went out in two arms straight towards the village, and these joined together up in the high park, at what, to judge by the mound that remains, must have been a gate-house".[72] These 'arms' were not a drive but the remnants of an avenue and they remained visible as earthworks right up until the High Park was bulldozed in 1982 and subsequently ploughed. We are fortunate that a number of aerial photographs were taken prior to this event, on which the line of the avenue can be seen (see figures 4/2 and 4/7 above). The western side still survives today as a slight parallel linear depressions, set c.5m apart, which run within 50m of the Hall, apparently fading out in line with the forecourt earthworks.

The avenue ran to the north-west of the Hall for over 500m, and is formed by two sets of parallel lines, with a total width of c.30m. Previous aerial photographic survey work shows it to terminate at the possible Roman enclosure in the High Park (see Chapter 4),[73] but on several photographs the outer lines of each side can be seen to continue through the enclosure for a further c.150m, splaying outwards slightly and fading out only at the field boundary to the north; an adjacent angled field boundary may be on the line of the avenue's west side.[74] The relationship between the avenue and the possible Roman enclosure here is intriguing; although one is not properly aligned on the other, it is quite possible that Mrs Egerton saw the remains of a 17th century building within the enclosure, not a gatehouse but a folly or eye-catcher of some kind. If ever such was built, then it did better than the avenue, which was laid out but apparently not completed, as there is no cartographic, documentary or physical evidence that trees were ever planted along the lines. However, it is noticeable that the area in the front of the Hall, in line with the avenue, has been cleared of any of the c.500 year old oak trees which still remain to either side. It therefore appears that what were then c.100 year old trees were to be retained on either side of the new avenue, a pattern noted on other estates where similar landscaping was undertaken during the 17th century.[75]

A possible date for the laying out of the avenue would be the mid to later 17th century, when either Thomas Ingram and his family, or Sir Roger Langley, were in residence, although comparison with other houses suggests that such alterations could also be attributed to Edward Thompson (1676-1701); it is perhaps most likely that the Lodge's garden landscape evolved steadily during the residence of all three owners. If the long axis of the avenue, Lodge and parterre are projected to the south-east, then further parts of a formal 17th century landscape emerge. It is often suggested that the south wall of the parterre, shown as closed in 1624, was demolished in the early 18th century when the Hall was remodelled, in order to open out views to the south-east (see below). However, it is quite likely that the wall was fitted with a central gateway during the later 17th century, like those shown in the Kip and Knyff engraving of Temple Newsam; steps leading down the terrace marking the former southern end of the parterre still survive in this position.

A short distance beyond the terrace, there is a boundary fence incorporating a gateway, which is once again centrally positioned to the former parterre and flanked by the pedestals bearing the stone animals carved by Ventris. The gateway stands at the north end of a large rectangular field on the same axis as the former avenue to the north of the Hall (see plate 73); the field was once much longer, stretching almost as far as Lodge Farm in 1855 and it is named as 'Avenue' on the 1848 tithe map[76] (field 110 on figure 5/7). This field contains a statue of a Roman soldier, traditionally known as 'Alexander' and carved by John Ashbie in 1638,[77] now standing on a plinth some distance from the Hall (see plate 71). As with the south parterre wall, it is sometimes suggested that Alexander was positioned here during the 18th century, but he is again aligned on the same axis as the other features noted above; a c.1700 painting of the late 17th century gardens at Sudbury Hall in Derbyshire shows a very similar arrangement, with a view leading from the garden front of the Hall through a parterre, gateways and terraces towards a statue.[78] Approximately half way between Alexander and the northern end of the field, aerial photographs show a square enclosure overlying earlier ridge and furrow[79] - this is probably too far from the Hall to represent the bowling green but it may well be a 17th century garden feature. As with the paddock to the front of the Hall, in 1855 the central strip of the field appears to be clear of trees, and in 1911 one might even imagine that the remains of an avenue are shown here.[80]

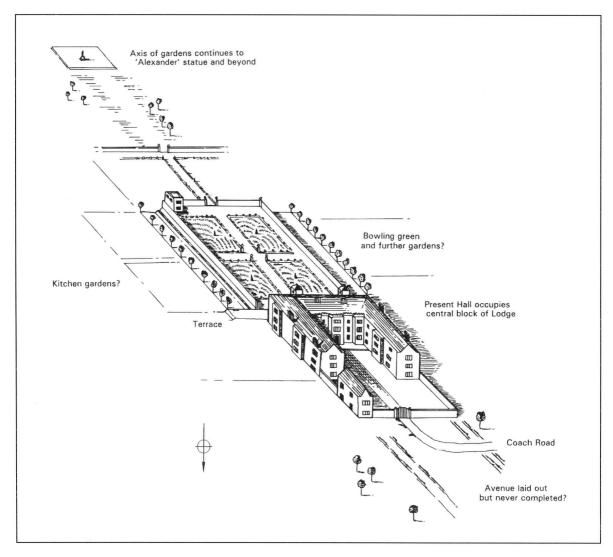

Fig. 15/12: Reconstruction of the Lodge and its gardens in the 17th century.

Any 17th century planned formal landscape at Sheriff Hutton might have been completed by the bowling green, orchards, ponds and further avenues positioned at right angles to the main north-east/south-west axis, as depicted at Temple Newsam by Kip and Knyff. If the Temple Newsam comparison is continued, the most likely location for the bowling green and any further enclosed gardens is to the west of the Hall, in the area to the south of The Rangers

House complex, but nothing now survives in this area. Nevertheless, those parts that do remain, however fragmentary, suggest an ambitious scheme; the total length from the north-east end of the avenue to the south-west end of the field close to Lodge Farm is some 1.2km.

On balance, it seems most likely that the landscape was planned but never realised, although, like at Temple Newsam, mid 18th century works could have removed almost all above-ground traces of an earlier formal layout. Unfortunately, unlike Temple Newsam, no detailed views of the Lodge and its setting other than the 1624 survey have yet come to light - it seems curious that such a significant house was omitted by people like Samuel Buck, particularly as he sketched the castle ruins in 1719-21 (see Chapter 7); perhaps the Thompsons discouraged visitors. Recent work at a house which Buck did sketch, Beningbrough Hall in North Yorkshire, has demonstrated that the orientation and placing of the existing hall was determined by an earlier designed landscape established during the 16th and 17th centuries.[81] However, this does not seem to have been the case at Sheriff Hutton. Although Arthur Ingram may well have wished visitors to contemplate the castle ruins as they approached the Lodge, the designed landscape of the mid to later 17th century was conceived to stamp the authority of the house and its owner on the park, with far less emphasis on any earlier landscape boundaries and features.

The Rangers House

As part of his works at the Lodge, Thomas Ingram undertook the construction of the adjacent complex, now known as 'The Rangers House'. In 1639, work started on a stable block and brewhouse, paving the stable court with cobbles and digging a new well. The new buildings were constructed with some 940 loads of stone taken from the castle[82] although, as stated above, Mrs Egerton had heard a theory that some materials had come from the Launde House which had formerly stood on the same site.

The buildings were described in 1650 as follows:

> *"Alsoe about 20 yardes southweste of the said howse there is a hansome large stable newly builte with a hay lofte and the Groomes chamber over it, at the end whereof is a Brewhouse and on the backside a Coach howse".*[83]

The only part of the existing complex that clearly survives from the 17th century is the east range. It is two storeys in height, nine bays in length and is built from castle stone. The east elevation incorporates four tall, six-light mullioned and transomed windows on the ground floor, flanking a flat-headed doorway with chamfered jambs and lintels (see plate 77). These windows are clearly re-used; their scale is ill-suited to the building and they have been fitted rather haphazardly into the elevation. The first floor fenestration is all modern, and a slight change in the masonry hints that the existing first floor may be a later addition or alteration. A four-light mullioned window survives high up in the north gable, whilst in the west elevation there is a four-centred doorway with a chamfered surround. The re-used features in the east range are unlikely to be any earlier than the 16th century, once again emphasising how the Ingrams preferred to take Tudor, rather than late medieval items, from the castle. The single storey north range of the complex, although also clearly built from castle stone, may be a later remodelling of a 17th century structure, as may be a free-standing two-storey building to the south.

227

It is assumed that The Rangers House complex was remodelled again during the 18th century at the same time as the Hall (see below), although as yet no information has come to light. The 1848 tithe map[84] (see figure 5/7) shows a symmetrical layout, with two opposed L-shaped ranges set about a central entrance in the north side and a further free-standing building to the south-east. By the time the Ordnance Survey 1st edition 6" map had been published in 1855, the complex had apparently been substantially expanded, with the addition of central and southern ranges, creating a double yard plan much like that created at Lodge Farm in the same period (see Chapter 16). Given that a new wing was also added to the Hall in 1848 (see below), the improvements to The Rangers House may have formed part of the same scheme. However, any such improvement was short-lived, as the complex actually decreased in size in the second half of the 19th century, most likely because some of its functions were transferred to Park Farm (see Chapter 16).

By 1880 the western courtyard had gone, whilst the larger courtyard had also been altered. The 1880 sale catalogue describes the complex as follows:

> *"THE STABLING Is placed at an agreeable distance from the Mansion WELL SCREENED BY A PLANTATION OF TREES, &C., And comprises a Stone and Slated Building with 6 Stalls, Washing Room, Saddle and harness Room, Coach House, with 4 Bedrooms over for Coachman and Grooms, Bacon Room and Brew House and Cart Shed adjoining; IN THE BACK YARD A RANGE OF STONE AND TILED BUILDINGS Comprising 4-Stall Stable, 3 Loose Boxes, Gun Room, Store Room, Curing House, Wood House, Cart Shed, Carpenters' Shop with Granary over Near thereto is a COTTAGE, with 3 Bedrooms, Sitting Room, Kitchen, Scullery, Yard and Coal Shed".*[85]

Fig. 15/13: East elevation of The Rangers House showing re-used windows.

Fig. 15/14: West elevation of The Rangers House.

The complex expanded again during the late 19th and early 20th centuries, and by 1911 a small group of buildings had occupied the ground where the second courtyard had been in 1855.[86] Some of the older buildings were presumably demolished during the 1960s when Colonel Ledgard erected a new stable block.[87] In the late 1960s the 17th century east range was converted to residential use and it eventually became a country house hotel (see Chapter 14). It was during this time that a very fine chimney piece and overmantel were brought from Stillington Hall following its demolition and installed in the east range.[88] The Rangers House has stood empty since the late 1990s, although some of the farm buildings to the west remain in use.

The Thompson Remodelling

The Hall owes its existing well-proportioned 'Queen Anne' appearance (see plate 72) to a comprehensive remodelling that took place during the first half of the 18th century. This remodelling is traditionally dated to c.1730 and is ascribed to Leonard Thompson on the basis of an early Sun Fire Insurance plaque affixed over a side doorway. The plaque relates to a policy dated 17th October 1732, taken out by Leonard Thompson:

> *"On his dwelling house only, brick and tiled at Sheriff Hutton aforesaid, exclusive of all manner of outhouses or other adjoining buildings, not exceeding five hundred pounds".[89]*

Stylistically, the house could easily be 30 years earlier but, on the basis of current evidence, there seems little reason to doubt that Leonard Thompson was insuring the house as it had been only recently completed; a significantly earlier date would also require the re-assessment of elements of the garden landscape described above. The architect of the c.1730 remodelling is unknown, although John Etty and his son William are sometimes mentioned as possible candidates. John Etty (c.1634-1708) was a leading architect-craftsmen in York who undertook work on many houses in the region, including the nearby Strensall Hall in 1695.[90] However, he died in 1708 and so to have been designed by him the Hall would have to be significantly earlier than the insurance policy suggests. William Etty (c.1675-1734) is perhaps more likely, although the country-house work definitely attributable to him is limited to Barrowby Hall in West Yorkshire, refronted for the Ingram family between 1718-20, and Baldersby Park in North Yorkshire; he was also probably responsible for the Palladian façade of the York Mansion House.[91]

Whoever was responsible for the remodelling, they clearly had instructions from Leonard Thompson to undertake radical alterations to the existing Lodge. By the early 18th century, the Lodge was not only unfashionable but also unwieldy, and probably too large for the Thompsons' needs. As Pevsner remarked in 1966, the canny visitor to the Hall will note that the main entrance in the west front is not centrally placed, but offset to the north.[92] This perhaps indicates that the central block and part of the eastern end of the south wing were retained but that the north wing was completely demolished. The central block was probably also reduced in height, and the angle turrets to the garden front were certainly demolished. The whole was encased in brickwork about a foot thick, fitted with tall sash windows and given a hipped roof rising from a wooden dentilled cornice, with dormers lighting the attic rooms within. There were evidently some difficulties tieing the 18th century brickwork case into the older house, necessitating the use of spectacular wrought-iron ties, particularly to the south elevation. Internally, many of the Jacobean interiors were retained, although it is not certain to what extent they were covered up during the 18th century. The staircase was replaced and some of the rooms remodelled in early Georgian style.[93]

The earliest depiction of the remodelled house appears on the 1765 plan of Sheriff Hutton, at which date it still went by its old name of The Lodge.[94] This depiction is rather schematic, and it shows a three bay, three storey structure with dormer windows to the hipped roof and three chimneys with plumes of smoke. It is curious that three storeys and dormer windows are shown, rather than the existing two but, as there is no evidence that the post c.1730 Hall has been reduced in height; for the present this must be ascribed to an error on the cartographer's part.

It is unfortunate that the map does not show more of the park landscape surrounding the Hall, as this had no doubt undergone similar radical alterations. The forecourt would have been demolished at the same time as the Hall was remodelled, and Gilbert proposes that the southern parterre wall was taken away to open out the views in this direction[95] although, as argued above, alterations may have taken place here significantly earlier than c.1730. Gilbert also notes that an ice house was built in the grounds near the Hall in c.1730, but it is not clear if this is the same ice house which survives within the eastern service wing of the house (see below). Any elements of a planned formal 17th century landscape that did survive beyond the forecourt would have been swept away in an effort to give the park landscape a more 'natural' appearance. It is possible that part of the L-shaped fishpond to the north of the Hall and some of the belts and copses of woodland around it were first created as part of this 'naturalising' process.

Fig. 15/15: Wrought-iron ties on south side of the Hall.

Fig. 15/16: Lodge at west entrance to the park, taken c.1975 (Source: Sheriff Hutton WI 1975).

The route of the Coach Road may have been modified at the same time to take into account the demolition of the forecourt, and provided with a new entrance lodge. The surviving entrance lodge, which has been substantially extended, was originally a small two storey building with two rooms on the ground floor and two rooms over. The pitched gabled roof has a tall central stack and the Thompsons' arms of three falcons are placed over the porch entrance (see figure 13/3). It has been suggested that the building dates to c.1740 and that it was originally provided with a thatched rather than slated roof.[96] The latter, in conjunction with the mullioned lattice-glazed windows, suggests rustic simplicity and is reminiscent of the Regency fashion for *cottage orné* lodges,[97] perhaps indicating that the building is of the 1790s to 1820s, rather than c.1740.

Nineteenth and Twentieth Century Developments

The Ordnance Survey 1855 1st edition 6" map[98] shows a number of changes to the Hall and its surroundings. Most prominent amongst these was the addition of a new wing to its east side in 1848 by a later Leonard Thompson (see figure 5/9). This wing was created in order to give the Hall a new drawing room with a projecting bay and additional bedrooms on the first floor. Possibly at the same time, an eastern service wing was built to the north of the new drawing room. The service wing incorporates a very impressive ice house, perhaps that suggested by Gilbert to have been built in c.1730.

In the immediate vicinity of the Hall, a short avenue is shown to the north-east in 1855. Known as 'Lady Mary's Walk', this avenue of horse-chestnuts still survives and has a pair of wrought-iron gates at the north end. The plan accompanying the 1880 sale catalogue shows another short avenue to the south-west of the Hall, leading to a small rectangular building below the pond. This had disappeared by 1911, to be replaced by two glasshouses. A much larger conservatory stood at the east end of the east wing and can be seen on the engraving of the garden front included in the 1880 sale catalogue.

Further afield, the 1855 map shows a 'Dog Kennel' some distance to the south-west of the Hall, but all that now survives of this is an area of rubble overgrown with scrub. To the north-east, within Sawtry Plantation, are two rectangular ponds. These ponds still survive in modified form, but the adjacent structures depicted in 1855 have gone.

No major additions have been made to the Hall since the building of the east wing in 1848. Probably the most extensive repairs of recent years were carried out by Rear Admiral and Mrs Egerton, starting in 1937 and continuing after 1946. Substantial parts of the early 18th century brick case were taken down, exposing the remains of the 17th century Lodge behind.[99] Since then, successive owners have been engaged in the ongoing repairs and renovations necessary to keep a property of this size habitable.

Given that she has featured so prominently in this chapter, it is perhaps fitting to leave the last word on the subject to Mrs Egerton:

> *"I once remarked to someone that there constantly seemed to be so much to do to the house that it was somewhat of a 'pig in a poke' that we had got: she replied 'Yes, but it is such a very nice pig.' I hope that you will agree with her – I must confess that I do myself."*[100]

Footnotes

1   Gilbert 1966a, p.548; Field Archaeology Specialists 2003, p.31.
2   Moorhouse 2003c, pp.346-347.
3   West Yorkshire Archive Service (WYAS) Leeds WYL100/SH/A3/2/1-3.
4   Brighton 1978, pp.9.xxii.1 – 9.xxii.9; Kitson 1929; Colvin 1995, p.305.
5   Brighton 1978, pp.9.xxii.4.
6   Girouard 1983, p.314.
7   Brighton 1978, pp.9.xxii.1 – 9.xxii.9; Kitson 1929; Colvin 1995, p.305.
8   WYAS Leeds WYL100/SH/A3/2/4.

9   WYAS Leeds WYL100/SHA3/1.
10   Egerton 1946, p.6.
11   Brighton 1978.
12   WYAS Leeds WYL100/SH/A3/1/1, 2 & 3.
13   WYAS Leeds WYL100/SH/A3/1/4 & 5.
14   WYAS Leeds WYL100/SH/A3/1/6, 7, 8, 9 & 10.
15   WYAS Leeds WYL100/SH/A3/1/6.
16   WYAS Leeds WYL100/SH/A3/1/7.
17   Brighton 1978, p.9.xxii.5.
18   e.g. Colvin 1995.
19   Butler 1988, p.42.
20   Field Archaeology Specialists 2003, p.30.
21   RCHME 1986, pp.50-54.
22   WYAS Leeds WYL100/SH/A3/1/1, 2 & 3.
23   Gilbert 1965; Gilbert 1966a, pp.549-550.
24   Gilbert 1966a, p.551; British Library Harleian MSS no. 6288.
25   Gilbert 1965.
26   Tony Wright, *pers. comm.*
27   National Archives E317/York S/54.
28   British Library Harleian MSS no. 6288; Ordnance Survey 1911 25" sheet 141/5; Tony Wright, *pers. comm.*
29   RCHME 1986, p.50.
30   Ripon Historical Society 1991; National Archives E179/216/481.
31   Harrison & Hutton 1984, p.210.
32   RCHME 1986, p.50; Linstrum 1978, pp.54-55.
33   Tony Wright, *pers. comm.*
34   Egerton 1946, p.6.
35   ibid., p.9; Pevsner 1966, p.341.
36   RCHME 1986, p.50.
37   ibid., pp.50-54.
38   ibid.; Gilbert 1965; Pevsner 1966, pp.340-341.
39   Gilbert 1965.
40   ibid.
41   Pevsner 1966, pp.340-341.
42   ibid.
43   Egerton 1946, p.10; Gilbert 1965.
44   Butler 1988, p.28.
45   Pevsner 1966, pp.340-341.
46   Gilbert 1965.
47   RCHME 1986, p.53.
48   Gilbert 1966a, p.549; WYAS Leeds WYL100/SH/A3/2/4.
49   National Archives E178/2792; WYAS Leeds WYL100/SH/G/4.
50   Egerton 1946, p.10.
51   Butler 1988.
52   ibid., p.37.
53   Linstrum 1978, pp.52-53; Gilbert 1963, p.6.
54   Gilbert 1963, pp.6-7.
55   ibid., pp.9-10; Robertson 1975, pp.21-23.
56   Butler 1988, p.30.
57   Vivien Swan *pers. comm.*
58   WYAS Leeds WYL100/SH/B4/2.
59   National Archives E317/YorkS/54.
60   Gilbert 1966a, p.551.
61   National Archives E317/YorkS/54.
62   Butler 1988, p.38.
63   Egerton 1946, p.6.
64   ibid., p.13.
65   Butler 1988, p.39.
66   Gilbert 1966b, p.631.
67   ibid.

68   ibid.
69   Cliffe 1999, p.61; Taylor 1998, p.65-69.
70   Thomas 1983, pp.206-209.
71   Hill 1981, p.23.
72   Egerton 1946, p.13.
73   Winton 1993, Site 2.
74   Tony Wright, *pers comm.*
75   Rackham 2004.
76   Ordnance Survey 1855 1st edition 6" map sheet 141, surveyed 1854; Borthwick Institute TA411S.
77   Gilbert 1966b, p.631.
78   Cliffe 1999, p.61.
79   Vivien Swann, *pers. comm.*
80   Ordnance Survey 1855 6" map sheet 141 and 1911 25" map sheet 141/5.
81   Dennison & Richardson 2005.
82   Gilbert 1966b, p.628.
83   National Archives E317/YorkS/54.
84   Borthwick Institute TA411S.
85   Sedgwick, Son & Weall 1880 "The Sheriff Hutton Park Estate". Copies held within the village and at the Borthwick Institute (PR/SH/80).
86   Ordnance Survey 1911 25" map sheet 141/5.
87   Gilbert 1966b, p.631.
88   Nancy Megginson, *pers. comm.*
89   Egerton 1946, p.8.
90   Colvin 1995, pp.353-354.
91   ibid., pp.354-355; Pevsner & Neave 1995, pp.195 & 216.
92   Pevsner 1966, p.340.
93   Gilbert 1966b, pp.629-630.
94   WYAS Leeds WYL100/SH/B4/2.
95   Gilbert 1966b, p.631.
96   Sheriff Hutton WI 1975, p.14.
97   Mowl & Earnshaw 1985, pp.137-145.
98   Ordnance Survey 1855 1st edition 6" map sheet 141.
99   Egerton 1946, p.9.
100   ibid., p.13.

CHAPTER 16: THE FARMS IN THE PARK

by Shaun Richardson

with contributions by Robin Barker, Georgina Ratcliff, David and John Armitage, and Mike Rickatson

Introduction

The area of historic park is now subdivided between numerous owners and tenants, but four main centres remain, the Hall, Oaks Farm, Lodge Farm and Park Farm. The buildings associated with the Hall are described in Chapter 15; this chapter deals with the history and surviving buildings of the three farms.[1]

The existing buildings or ranges at the various farms have been assigned a unique number reference code, and these are shown on the sketch plans below. The historic buildings which are discussed below are cross-hatched on the plans, while large modern farm buildings have either been omitted or left blank.

Oaks Farm

Oaks Farm is located on the west side of the park, and is tenanted by Mr Robin Barker (see plate 74). The farm buildings are essentially formed by two quadrangles arranged around rectangular yards; the eastern yard is now covered/infilled, whilst the western yard remains open. The farm holding now comprises approximately 110 acres (44 hectares) growing spring and winter sown cereals, oilseed rape and field beans.

Historical background

In 1841, William Wright, the Park Bailiff, was living at Oaks Farm (see Chapter 13). In 1848, the award accompanying the tithe map shows that the farm was owned by Leonard Thompson of Sheriff Hutton Park and was still occupied by William Wright.[2] Wright also occupied the majority of the land to the west of the farm as far as the park boundary, and to the east as far as the earthwork remains of East Lilling village, confirming a suggestion that much of what is now Park Farm's land was originally farmed from Oaks Farm. Wright's land was divided almost equally between grass and arable, and included two small areas of plantation. At this date, the farm itself apparently consisted of the farmhouse, with isolated structures/ranges to the south and east.

The general layout of the farm is first depicted in detail on the Ordnance Survey 1856 1st edition 6" map.[3] The farmhouse appears with connected ranges running to the west and south-east, and with further isolated buildings/ranges to the east and north-east. In the sale catalogue of 1880,[4] Oaks Farm was described as follows:

> *"THE OAKS FARM in the Parish of Sheriff Hutton and Township of West Lilling, comprising a COMFORTABLE FARM HOUSE, with farm buildings, yards, gardens and lands, containing altogether 108a 2r. 34p., (little more or less).*
>
> *THE HOUSE (Brick and Tiled) Contains 4 Attics, 4 Bedrooms, 2 Men's Rooms, 3 Sitting Rooms, Schoolroom, Kitchen, Dairy, Pantry, Scullery and Cellar; a Range of*

Buildings containing Churning House, Boiling Ditto, Poultry House, Coal House & c.; Pleasant Flower and Kitchen Garden.

THE FARM BUILDINGS comprise Farm Yard, with Cart Horse Stables and Granary over, Harness Room, Barn, Piggeries, Open Sheds, a Range of Bullock Sheds with Cart and Root Houses, 2 Loose Boxes and Cart Sheds, all Brick Built and Tiled".

The buildings described in 1880 are shown on the sale plan in a similar manner to 1856; the easternmost building of the farm complex has a pond at its north end. The farm is depicted in much greater detail on the Ordnance Survey 1911 25" map.[5] The farmhouse is an L-shaped structure, located in the north-east corner of a small enclosure. A range of buildings runs to the west, with another set at an angle to the south-east. There are two parallel north-south aligned ranges to the east of the farmhouse, with an open-sided structure between. An east-west aligned range stands to the north-east of the farmhouse.

The Buildings

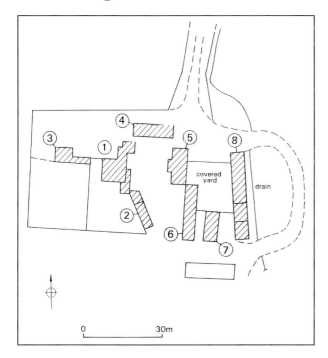

Fig. 16/1: Sketch plan of buildings at Oaks Farm.

Fig. 16/2: The farmhouse (Building 1) at Oaks Farm, looking north-west.

Farmhouse (Building 1)

The farmhouse is L-shaped in plan, with lean-to additions to the south-west and north-east corners, and it has clearly developed in a number of phases. The earliest part is represented by a rectangular double-pile house, of two storeys and an attic, with corbelled brick eaves, a pitched Welsh slate roof and end ridge stacks (see plate 74). The house is built of buff hand-moulded bricks laid in no particular bonding pattern and set with a lime mortar; there is tumbled-in brickwork to the gables. The south elevation has been rendered and provided with projecting ground floor bays and modern UPVC glazing. However, several late 18th/early 19th century unhorned 16-pane (8 over 8) sashes survive in the north elevation, as well as a number of mid 19th century 4-pane (2 over 2) sashes elsewhere. When a small garden and patio area was created on the immediate west side of the west gable, a small cellar was discovered, presumably that noted in the 1880 sale catalogue and shown with a building above in 1911. The cellar appeared to be secondary to the farmhouse.[6]

Internally, as stated above, the earliest part of the farmhouse has a double-pile plan with a central north-south aligned cross-passage. All four ground floor rooms were originally heated and some retain late 18th/early 19th century doors with four raised and fielded panels. The main staircase rises from the east side of the cross passage; it is of an open-string form, with stick balusters and a partly turned newel post. The first floor rooms have a similar layout to those on the ground floor, each retaining a late 18th century cast-iron hob grate with decorative panels. A plain narrow staircase rises to the attic storey, formed by a central passageway flanked by unheated rooms to either side. The roof trusses are exposed within the attic rooms; these are of principal rafter and raised collar form, and pegged throughout. The principals support tusk-tenoned purlins.

The earliest addition to the original house is a short wing projecting from the east end of the north elevation, which was in place by 1856, and which may have contained the schoolroom and men's rooms noted in 1880. The wing is of two storeys (but lower than the main house), with a pitched pantiled roof and no stacks. It is built of red hand-moulded bricks laid in what approximates to a rough English Garden Wall bond (one course of headers to three courses of stretchers) and with modern repointing. Internally, the ground floor is formed by a single room, with doorways in the south and east walls; the first floor was not examined. A well formerly lay just to the north-west of the wing's north-west corner, and a pump is shown here in 1911.

At some point between 1856 and 1911, a two storey aisle/outshut with a catslide roof was added to the east side of the later wing. This aisle is built of similar brickwork to the main house and has a horizontal sliding sash at first floor level. Later still, two single storey pantiled lean-to structures were erected against the north end of the wing. The eastern lean-to is now used as a utility room, whilst the small western lean-to may originally have been an outside WC. There is a further single storey lean-to attached to the south-east corner of the main house, built in two phases.

Garden wall / cart shed (Building 2)

A tall garden wall runs south-east from the south-east corner of the farmhouse. It is built from neatly hand-moulded red bricks, laid in a variation of English Garden Wall bond (five stretcher courses to each header course) and set with a lime mortar. The wall is surmounted by flat stone coping and is truncated at the south end. A four bay single storey open-fronted cart shed, shown in 1856, was built against the east face of the garden wall. It was originally constructed of similar brick to the adjacent garden wall, but it has been substantially altered in machine-made brick, including the conversion of the northernmost bay to a closed structure.

West range (Building 3)

The west range runs west from the north-west corner of the farmhouse. The earliest element appears to be a tall garden wall, built from neatly hand-moulded red bricks, laid in a variation of English Garden Wall bond (four stretcher courses to each header course) and set with a lime mortar. The west end terminates in a short ramped southern return. Within one of the lean-to structures built against the north face of the wall (see below), there is a remnant of free-standing wall which may pre-date the existing garden wall but which also contains a fragment of either a ramped section, or a decorative circular opening, now largely obscured by later additions and alterations.

Fig. 16/3: The west range and garden wall (Building 3) at Oaks Farm, looking north-west.

Fig. 16/4: The stable (Building 4) at Oaks Farm, looking north.

A number of small lean-to structures are built against the north face of the garden wall, none of which are shown in 1848. The largest is at the west end, and has a brick paved floor internally, above which run roof trusses comprising principal rafters supporting tusk-tenoned purlins. To the east, the lean-to structures are of similar construction but smaller. All were in existence by 1856, and formerly comprised the churning house, poultry house, boiling house and coal house noted in 1880.

Stables (Building 4)

A two storey rectangular building with a pitched pantiled roof, clearly built in two separate phases, stands on the north side of the west yard. The western half is built of hand-moulded buff bricks laid in a similar manner to those of the earliest part of the farmhouse, with tumbled-in brickwork and fish-tailed wall-ties to the west gable. There are two rows of evenly spaced slit ventilators in the north wall, apparently with a blocked window above on the first floor. Internally, the ground floor retains wooden mangers and stall partitions. The eastern half is built of similar brickwork to the western half, but slightly better laid, with a very rough bonding pattern of five or six stretcher courses to each header course. The brickwork to the east gable is tumbled-in with fish-tailed wall-ties similar to those noted on the farmhouse and the adjacent threshing barn (see building 5 below). There is a first floor doorway in the east gable above inserted ground floor garage doors. In the south wall, there is a central ground floor doorway with two blocked windows above on the first floor, and two further blocked windows to the north wall's first floor. Internally, none of the roof trusses were clearly visible but there appears to be a blocked first floor window in the west wall, suggesting that the eastern half is the earlier part of the building.

The building is not shown in 1848, but both parts of the building were complete by 1856 and it is shown as a single structure in 1911. The eastern half may be the earlier part, and it had a flight of steps leading to the first floor doorway in 1911, although the brickwork of the western half closely resembles that in the original farmhouse. The ground floor of the western half formed the carthorse stables of 1880 and so presumably the first floor was the granary; the east half may have been the harness room. The blocked first floor windows of both parts of the building suggest that they may initially have comprised lodgings for grooms and/or labourers.

Threshing barn (Building 5)

A two storey threshing barn, shown in 1848 and on the Ordnance Survey 1856 1st edition 6" map, stands on the east side of the west yard. It is rectangular in plan, of five bays internally, with a pitched pantiled roof, and is built of similar brickwork to the earliest part of the farmhouse. There is tumbled-in brickwork and fish-tailed wall-ties to both gables. The north gable retains the remnants of two rows of slit breathers, interrupted modern ground floor garage doors and a 19th century first floor window, both later insertions; the window also disturbed a much smaller original window. The central bays of the east and west elevations break forward slightly and originally housed tall opposed harr-hung doors at either end of the central threshing bay; both have since been blocked and the doorways much reduced in scale. Both elevations have three rows of breathers to the north of the doorways but only two, at first floor level, to the south - the uppermost row are formed by cruciform rather than slit breathers.

Fig. 16/5: Threshing barn (Building 5) at Oaks Farm, looking east.

Fig: 16/6: Sheds to the south of Oaks Farm, looking north-east.

Internally, the barn is floored with concrete and is open to roof height; the original flagstone flooring survives only towards the south end. The southernmost two bays of the interior have been separated from the rest by a modern timber partition wall, although the pattern of the breathers in the external walls indicates that there was originally a raised floor here. The interior of the barn is crossed by four neatly-constructed pegged trusses, all of tie-beam, principal rafter and collar form; the end trusses are supported by wall piers. Each principal rafter supports a pair of staggered tusk-tenoned purlins and the roof retains its original common rafters.

East range of west yard (Building 6)

A long single storey building forms the east range of the west yard. It is shown in both 1848 and 1856, and it butts the south-east corner of the threshing barn at its north end. The range is built of hand-moulded red bricks laid in a variation of English Garden Wall bond and the pitched roof is covered with corrugated sheeting. There is a series of blocked doorways and windows in the west elevation, some retaining sliding ventilators, whilst the east elevation is largely blank. Internally, the building is divided into cow stalls/loose boxes by breeze-block partitions, and is crossed by king-post roof trusses. There is some slight structural evidence to suggest that the range comprises two different phases, although it was clearly all present by 1856. It probably represents the bullock sheds and root house of the 1880 sale catalogue.

Hay barn (Building 7)

A large hay barn stands on the south side of the east yard. The barn is not shown in 1856 but it could be the 'barn' noted in the 1880 sale catalogue, although this could equally refer to the older threshing barn in the west yard. It was definitely present by 1911.

The barn is three bays in length, two storeys in height and has a pitched Welsh slate roof. It is open to the east and west sides, and both the side piers and end gables are built of neatly hand-moulded red bricks laid in a form of English Garden Wall bond; the bricks are rubbed to all corners. Internally, the barn is open to roof height and the interior is crossed by bolted roof trusses of tie-beam and principal rafter form, with raking struts and staggered purlins to the principal rafters.

East range of east yard (Building 8)

A long single storey building forms the east range of the east yard, backing onto a wide drainage ditch. Three separate structures are shown here in 1856, a longer angled structure flanked by a pond and a smaller building to the north and south respectively. In 1880, only the angled structure and pond are shown, but by 1911 the structure had been replaced by the existing building.

The range is built of similar brickwork to the east range of the west yard and has a pitched pantiled roof. The southernmost eight bays are open to the west into the yard, whilst the east elevation is almost completely blank. Internally, the majority of the cross walls between the bays are of brick but rise only to waist height, except at the north end where they reach to the roof ridge. The interior is crossed by a number of softwood bolted king-post trusses. The range probably represents the loose boxes and cart sheds noted in the 1880 sale catalogue, although it may have been adapted for use as a shelter shed at a later date.

To the west of the range, between it and building 6, the west yard is now covered by a 20th century roof utilising angle-steel trusses. To the south, beyond the older hay barn, there is a similarly modern hay barn, five bays in length, with a corrugated sheet roof supported on steel stanchions.

Other buildings

The drainage ditch running to the rear of the east range of the east yard continues south as far as the southern boundary of the park. Approximately half way along, the deep ditch is

239

crossed by a track supported on a c.2.20m tall 19th century brick arch. Further south, there is a pair of mid 19th century opposed single storey sheds on the east side of the ditch. The south shed is the least altered and is divided into three bays beneath a formerly tiled roof supported by softwood king-post trusses. The north shed is divided into five bays and has been re-roofed with pantiles.

Lodge Farm

Lodge Farm is located in the east part of the park and is rented by the Rickatson family. The farm buildings comprise a large quadrangle of older buildings around a covered yard, with large modern sheds to the north and east. The farm holding now comprises 250 acres (101 hectares) and is managed mainly as a dairy farm, although there are some areas of arable.

Historical background

The 1848 tithe map shows that Lodge Farm was owned by Leonard Thompson of Sheriff Hutton Park and was occupied by John Flawith.[7] Flawith occupied all of the land to the north and south of the farm as far as the park boundary, whilst to the east it reached to Moor Lane. The majority of Flawith's land was given over to arable but with areas of grass immediately around the farm and on the former site of East Lilling village. The farm ranges were U-shaped in plan, with the farmhouse standing to the south-west.

The general layout of the farm is depicted in more detail on the Ordnance Survey 1855 1st edition 6" map.[8] Some major improvements had apparently been undertaken since 1848, as by 1855 the farm comprised two conjoined yards, consisting of a large E-plan arrangement with parallel ranges on the south side running east from the farmhouse; a single isolated building stood further to the west. Lodge Farm has a very similar layout on the 1880 sale plan and is described as follows in the accompanying catalogue:[9]

> "THE LODGE FARM In the Parish of Sheriff Hutton and Townships of East Lilling and Thornton-Le-Clay, comprises a CAPITAL FARM RESIDENCE considerably enlarged and improved some few years ago, with convenient Farm Buildings, Yards, Gardens, Cottages and Lands Containing together 283a 1r 18p., (Little more or less)
>
> THE HOUSE, Which is Brick and Slate, contains, on the Upper Floor, 8 Bedrooms, Housemaid's Closet and W.C; on the Ground Floor, 2 Sitting Rooms, Entrance, Large Kitchen, Scullery, Dairy, Larder, Pantry, Store Room, Cellar, Kitchen Yard with Knife House, Coal House, &c., Hard and Soft Water, Kitchen and Flower Gardens.
>
> THE FARM BUILDINGS, with good Yards, comprise Range of Loose Boxes for Cattle, Piggeries, open Sheds for Pigs, Engine House, large Meal House and Loft over for Grinding Mill and Chaff Cutter; Barn, Cart Shed and Granary over, Waggon Lodge, Bullock Houses and Root House, Loose Box, Double Cart Horse Stable, Harness Place, 3-Stall Nag Stable, 2 Loose Boxes; Cow House and Large Root House, Rick Yard, & c.; at a convenient distance a BRICK AND SLATED COTTAGE, with 3 Bedrooms, Living Room and Kitchen, Men's Room and Bedroom over; Implement Shed and Chaise House adjoining".

By 1911, the west yard had been completely roofed over, whilst the east yard was half covered.[10] The east range of the east yard had been extended since 1880 and two long open-sided structures, most probably hay barns, had been added to the north side of the farm complex.

The Buildings

Farmhouse (Building 1)

The existing farmhouse is approximately square in plan, with a later range projecting from the north side, and it stands at the south-west corner of the farm complex. The main house has a double-pile plan (with a somewhat altered circulation pattern) and is of two storeys with attics and cellar, a pitched concrete tiled roof and end ridge stacks (see plate 75). The house is brick-built but all of the exterior is now rendered, preventing any detailed inspection of the original construction. The south elevation has been much modernised by the addition of bay windows to the ground floor, flanking an earlier porch shown in 1911, with three 19th century 16-pane (8 over 8) horned sashes to the first floor above. Elsewhere, much of the other fenestration is modern, and there is a mid 20th century lean-to extension abutting the west gable of the farmhouse which now forms the kitchen.

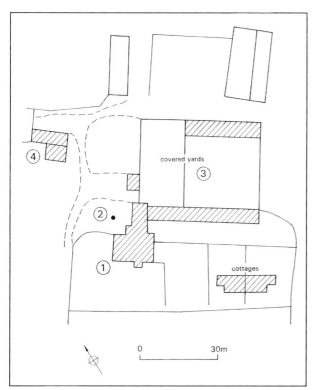

Fig. 16/7: Sketch plan of buildings at Lodge Farm.

Fig. 16/8: The farmhouse (Building 1) at Lodge Farm, looking east.

The main access to the interior of the house is via the back door, which opens into the north-west room of the ground floor. This room gives access to the kitchen in the lean-to to the west, and a tiled pantry and the central stair hall to the east; all doorways retain late 18th/early 19th century doors with six wide raised and fielded panels. The room formerly contained the back stairs of the house but these have since been removed.[12] The principal surviving feature is a projecting chimney breast in the centre of the west wall flanked by a semi-circular headed niche to the south, suggesting that this room was the 'large kitchen' noted in 1880.

Moving into the central stair hall, this also retains panelled doors similar to those noted above, set in early 19th century surrounds with fluted architraves and corner blocks. Approximately half way along its length, the hall is crossed by an arch raised on shallow pilasters surmounted by imposts, and at the south end has the four-panelled front door with a simple geometrically patterned light of early 19th century appearance over. A flight of steps adjacent to the front door leads down into the cellar, which lies beneath the south-west ground floor room. The hall staircase itself is open-string with scrolled decoration to the tread ends and panelling beneath. The ramped handrail is supported by slender turned balusters and slopes down to a turned newel post. On the south side of the house, the stair hall is flanked by the '2 sitting rooms' of 1880. Both are fitted with stylish 1930s/1940s fireplaces; the south-east room also retains contemporary (or perhaps slightly earlier?) rail and muntin wall-panelling incorporating an integral picture-shelf supported by plain quarter-circle brackets.

Fig. 16/9: Doorway in the hall of Lodge Farm farmhouse (Building 1).   *Fig. 16/10: Hall staircase in Lodge Farm farmhouse (Building 1).*

The hall staircase rises up to an L-shaped landing, top-lit by a large ceiling light retaining coloured margin glazing and painted star motifs to the corners, possibly a late 19th century insertion. There is a modern bathroom on the north side of the landing and five bedrooms. Three of the bedrooms have fireplaces with plain pilaster and lintel chimney pieces, and all the rooms are accessed by doorways retaining six-panelled doors similar to those on the ground floor. A hatch over the landing leads up into the attic space, where the slender king-post roof trusses can be seen. The king-posts have raking struts to the principal rafters, each of which supports a pair of slightly trenched staggered tusk-tenoned purlins.

As stated above, a later range was added to the north elevation of the main farmhouse. The south half of this range was in place by 1855, and the north half by 1880. Both are of two storeys, with a pitched concrete tiled roof and a central ridge stack. The south half is built of red hand-moulded bricks, laid in English Garden Wall bond and set with a lime mortar. The brickwork of the north half is similar but laid in Flemish Bond. Almost all of the surviving fenestration is modern. The interior of the range is now accessed through the main house. It has been much altered internally, but the ground floor was originally divided into a kitchen and a room, with a passage to the west, and with stairs at the north and south ends. The north stairs led to a single room at the north end of the first floor, not connected to the other rooms at this level and with a floor set slightly below their floor level. The south stairs rose to a passage with three rooms on its west side;[12] these, taken together with the bedrooms in the main house, must account for the '8 Bedrooms' described in 1880, suggesting that the range had reached its current size by this date.

Game larder or water tank (Building 2)

All traces of the kitchen yard noted in 1880, with its knife and coal houses, appear to have been removed. However, another structure survives beneath the grassed area to the north-west of the farmhouse (see plate 11). It is accessed by lifting a stone slab in the centre of the grass, revealing a circular brick-lined opening some 0.62m in diameter. The opening narrows slightly towards its bottom and opens out into a large circular brick-lined chamber with a broad circular brick vault over. The bricks used in the construction are all buff-coloured, hand-moulded and laid in a header bond, apparently without any mortar. The base of the chamber is lined with stone slabs and brickwork, and contains no drain; it was filled by water 0.25m deep at the time of inspection. The chamber itself is 2.44m in diameter and 1.80m in height from the floor to the underside of the opening in the vault. In addition to the main opening, the vault has five much smaller openings in its east side. These openings are all 0.10m square and appear to be later insertions into the vault. One contains a small diameter metal pipe, whilst another two lead into larger diameter ceramic pipes; all three pipes appear to radiate out towards the north range of the farmhouse.

It is presumed that the structure was used as an underground larder for the storage of meat. Around the turn of the 19th century, the notable Revd Sydney Smith was advising the Earl of Carlisle to build an underground chamber to keep his deer meat fresh for the table, as Smith had noticed that his carcasses kept longer when they were hung in his well at Foston Rectory.[13] The size of the opening at the top is curious, as it is difficult to get into the chamber, but the impression is that the meat was hung from the top and so constant access was not a necessity. However, the metal pipes running into the chamber might also suggest that the larder was later adapted for use as a soft water storage tank, taking rain water from the guttering about the farmhouse's north range. A soft water tank survives at Park Farm (see below) and the 1880 sale catalogue highlighted the fact that both hard and soft water was available at Lodge Farm.

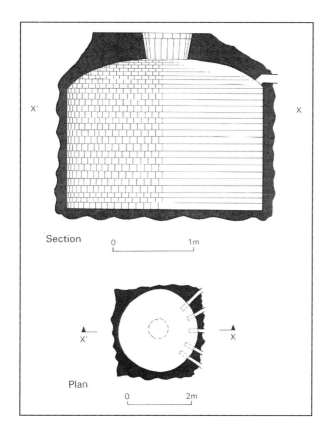

Section

0   1m

Plan

0   2m

Fig. 16/11: Plan and section of game larder (Building 2) at Lodge Farm.

Fig. 16/12: Cottages (Building 4) at Lodge Farm, looking north.

The farmyards (Building 3)

The farmyards have been extensively altered since 1911 and the ranges shown at that date now only survive in a fragmentary form. The west range of the west yard is represented by a single storey lean-to structure, built of hand-moulded red bricks, laid in a variation of English Garden Wall bond and set with a lime mortar. There were formerly stables to the north of the lean-to, perhaps the carthorse stables noted in 1880. The north range of the west yard has been demolished entirely whilst the east range, shared between it and the east yard, survives only as a brick wall, built of similar brickwork to the lean-to described above. At its southern end, the wall contains a number of low blocked openings with wooden lintels, almost certainly for feeding pigs, indicating the location of one of the 1880 piggeries. The floor level of the west yard is set below that of the surrounding ranges and, although the roofing structure over is entirely modern, an older feeding passage and associated troughs survived along the west side of the yard until relatively recently.

The north range of the east yard is formed by a single storey brick building of indeterminate purpose, but formerly with a cart shed at the east end. The east range has now entirely gone, but it once had a two storey granary at the north end, with a return at the south end forming a cart shed. It was most recently used as a tractor shed prior to its demolition.

There are two parallel closely-spaced ranges shown to the east of the farmhouse in 1911, but only the northern one survives, and it now forms the south side of the covered yards. It is of a single storey throughout, and built of red hand-moulded brick laid in a neat form of English Garden Wall bond. There is only a single window in the north elevation, set to the west of a centrally placed cart entrance. There is a much smaller doorway opposite the cart entrance in the south elevation, with several similar doorways to the east retaining stable-type doors.

244

Internally, the west end of the range is divided into several smaller cells, two of which have the remains of flues. None of the flues appear large enough to have served the engine house mentioned in 1880, but they may be the remains of preparation areas for pig and cattle food.

The large open-sided structures shown to the north of the farm yards in 1911 have also disappeared, to be replaced by modern sheds and former Dutch barns. There are also a pair of modern semi-detached houses to the south-east of the farm, built during the 1950s.[14]

The Cottage (Building 4)

The cottage mentioned in the 1880 sale catalogue stands to the west of the farm. It is not shown in 1848 but is depicted in the north-east corner of a small orchard in 1855, and it had been enlarged by 1880 with the addition of an implement shed and chaise house. In 1911, part of the earlier orchard had been cleared, leaving a narrow rectangular enclosure to the west of the cottage; smaller structures are shown adjoining the north and east sides.

The cottage has not been inhabited since the 1950s, and is currently used to store farm implements. It is a rectangular two storey house with a pitched slated roof, built of red hand-moulded bricks laid in a variation of English Garden Wall bond. The principal elevation faces south and contains four boarded-up windows with cambered heads flanking the original central doorway, now blocked. A large doorway has been inserted at the base of the east gable, giving access to the interior, which is divided into two rooms of equal size. The east room was heated by a fireplace in the north wall, with a staircase in the west room leading to the first floor. The remains of the adjoining structures shown in 1911 survive on the north and east sides of the house.

Park Farm

Park Farm is located in the southern part of the park and is farmed by Messrs David and Michael Armitage. The farm buildings comprise three ranges, forming a U-shape in plan, set to the west of the farmhouse. The farm holding now comprises approximately 100 acres (40 hectares) under a mixed arable/dairy regime.

Historical background

Park Farm is the most recently established of the three farms within the park. It does not appear in either 1848 or 1855 and, as stated above, at the former date most of its land was farmed from Oaks Farm. It was certainly present by 1871 when George Wright, the Park Bailiff, was living there together with his wife, two farm servants and a joiner (see Chapter 13). Park Farm (then known as Home Farm) is first shown on the plan accompanying the 1880 sale catalogue, where an irregularly shaped farmhouse stood to the east of three narrow ranges forming a U-shape in plan and partly enclosing a central courtyard.[15] It was described thus in the sale catalogue:

> "*THE HOME FARM with Well-Arranged Buildings, Orchard and Garden, at a convenient distance from the Mansion.*
>
> *Comprising a Bailiff's or Keeper's House, Brick and Slated, with 4 Bedrooms, 2 Attics, Sitting Room, Kitchen, Scullery and capital Dairy, Poultry Houses, Coal House, and W.C., Farm Yard with range of Buildings, consisting of 6-Stall Stable, 3 Loose Boxes,*

Cow House, Root Houses, Cart Shed with Granary over, Barn, Bullock House, Calf House, Piggeries, Boiling and Meal House, Slaughter House, Poultry and Duck House, with Lands, comprising 102a 1r 25p. (Little more or less)".

The farm was leased by the Armitage family until 1886, when David Armitage bought the property and undertook a number of alterations, most notably the addition of a cross-wing to the south end of the existing farmhouse. The development of the farm in the period after 1886 is shown by the changes visible on the Ordnance Survey 1911 25" map. By this date, in addition to the south cross-wing of the farmhouse, the south and west ranges of the farmyard had been doubled in width since 1880.[16] A small timber-built trap shed had also appeared to the north of the farmhouse, whilst to the south-west there was a former rhubarb shed brought to the farm from the West Riding and put to general use.

Surviving account and cash books held by the family and covering the period 1912-14 provide a detailed picture of the farm's business in the period immediately prior to the First World War. Both men and women appear in the entries for wages paid, with Sarah Hawkesby, Tom Russill and Barbara Walker being listed frequently between March to July 1912; wages varied between 4s to £1 per week. During the same period, both stock and milk were being sold, with most of the milk (up to 24 gallons a day) going by rail to the Rowntrees chocolate factory at York via Flaxton station. A valuation undertaken in March 1914 lists all the equipment and stock present at the farm, and this includes items such as a cream separator, cow chains, a scalding tub, hen huts, a binder and cultivator, three ploughs, various harrows, five pairs of blinders, two traps and two carts. There were also 15 ewes and one tup, several pigs, four horses, 29 cattle (including a bull and nine calves) and 80 head of poultry, together with two geese, two ducks and six game birds.[17]

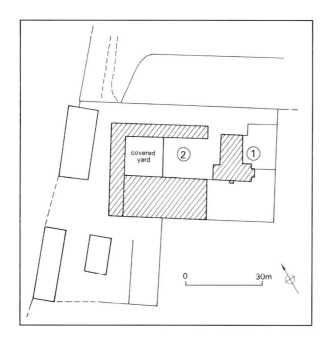

Fig. 16/14: South cross-wing of the farmhouse (Building 1) at Park Farm, looking north.

Fig. 16/13: Sketch plan of buildings at Park Farm.

From the time that the farm was purchased by David Armitage in 1886 right up until the outbreak of the Second World War, a crop rotation system was used on the farm's arable fields in conjunction with permanent pasture for grazing and hay-making. The account books described above show that at least four horses (listed as Darling, Jet, Bob and a 'young horse') were used on the farm in 1914 and the last two, Dolly and Prince, did not leave until the late 1950s/early 1960s. The number of men employed on the farm varied but as recently as the 1940s a man 'lived in', with a couple of other regular labourers in addition to the many seasonal workers. Poultry, raised for meat and eggs, formed an important part of the farm's income during the agricultural depressions of the 1920s and 1930s. In contrast to the widespread ploughing up of former permanent pasture during the Second World War seen elsewhere, Park Farm retained much of its permanent pasture into the 1960s and still has two fields of traditional permanent grassland. Following the war, the farm moved from a traditional mixed regime to a specialised intensive dairy unit, with barley/wheat having assumed a greater importance since 2004.

The Buildings

The Farmhouse (Building 1)

The farmhouse is T-shaped in plan and stands at the east end of the farm complex. In terms of its external appearance, it has received far less alteration than the other two farmhouses in the park. Although the house is modest in scale, the use of features such as the large projecting bay to the southern cross wing also produce a proportionally greater impact in the immediate landscape than the other farmhouses.

The two-phase development of the house indicated by documentary sources is reflected in the standing fabric. The earliest part of the building now forms the north part of the T-shaped plan and may be datable to 1856 from a pencilled inscription formerly existing on the internal staircase.[18] It is three bays in length, of three storeys internally with attics and has a pitched Welsh slate roof and end ridge stacks; the stacks are tall and have dentilled brickwork detailing (see plate 76). This part of the house is built from buff hand-moulded bricks (average dimensions 0.22m by 0.115m by 0.07m) laid in a form of English Garden Wall bond to the north gable but Flemish bond to the east elevation. All the brickwork is set with a lime mortar, slightly understruck to the north gable and with a recessed central line to the horizontal joints surviving in some places.

Prior to the addition of the southern cross wing, the east elevation formed the principal elevation of the house. It is symmetrically arranged, having a central doorway flanked by windows and with three windows above on the first floor. All the windows have cambered heads and modern glazing. There are two similar but smaller windows at attic level in the east gable. The west elevation is partly obscured by the former dairy at the north end, comprising a single storey projection with a pitched slated roof and a large window, and by a two storey projection at the south end. The ground floor of the latter is contemporary with the earliest part of the house, but the first floor was added at the same date as the south cross-wing. The gap between the two projections has been recently infilled but there is a well beneath, over 30m deep; there is also a underground soft water storage tank in the vicinity of the house, fed by rainwater.[19] The roof of the earliest part of the house overhangs both elevations and the north gable, and is supported on the projecting moulded feet of the common rafters.

The main access to the interior of the earliest part of the house is through the back door, which opens into the former dairy (now the kitchen). The ground, first and second floors all have the same arrangement, with rooms flanking a central stair hall entered from the doorway in the east elevation. The open-string staircase rises through all floors and into the attic space through a series of sharp dog-legs around a central well. The staircase has stick balusters, a ramped handrail and a turned newel.

The south cross-wing of the farmhouse was built in 1886,[20] requiring the demolition of the projection at the south end of the earlier house shown in 1880; the walls of this earlier projection survive beneath the floor of the cross-wing. The cross-wing is rectangular in plan, three bays in length and of two storeys with a pitched Welsh slate roof. Both stacks are positioned at the base of either end of the north roof slope and have cogged brickwork bands with yellow pots. The cross-wing is built of neatly hand-moulded buff bricks, laid in a variation of English Garden Wall bond and set with a lime mortar. The principal elevation faces south and has a central doorway obscured by a later porch (built c.1990 and replacing a more ornate Victorian example), flanked by paired windows. Above, on the first floor, there is a single window with coloured glass over the doorway, again flanked by paired windows. All windows have chamfered stone sills and slightly shouldered heads, and are fitted with 2-pane (1/1) sashes. A two storey rectangular bay window breaks forward from the east gable. The east face has three windows at ground and first floor levels; a continuous sill at each floor level effectively forms a stringcourse running across the face. At either end, the sill incorporates a projecting block, an unusual decorative feature. The sills continue around the sides of the bay beneath the single windows here. Like the earlier part of the house, the roof overhangs all sides of the cross-wing and is supported on the moulded feet of the common rafters.

The interior of the cross-wing was not accessible at the time of inspection, but it appears to have the same plan form as the earlier house, with two rooms to each floor placed to either side of a central staircase hall. The rooms were heated by fireplaces in the north wall.

The farm ranges (Building 2)

Fig. 16/15: North range of farm buildings (part of Building 2) at Park Farm, looking north.

Fig. 16/16: West range of farm buildings (part of Building 2) at Park Farm, looking south.

The farm ranges are grouped around a yard to the west of the house; the yard is now grassed but was formerly cobbled. Of the three ranges, only the north range retains the same width as that shown in 1880. It is of a single storey, with a pitched pantiled roof, and is built of similar brickwork to the older part of the farmhouse. The north elevation is largely blank, apart from a section of later disturbance and infilling towards the west of centre, blocking an entrance shown here in 1880. The south elevation, facing into the yard, has five doorways retaining plank and batten stable doors set on spearhead strap hinges; the westernmost door is flanked by windows. Internally, the east end of the range is divided into four smaller rooms or cells, each with separate access from the yard. The first cell from the east is most likely the slaughterhouse noted in 1880. The second cell from the east retains both a fireplace and tack pegs around the walls, whilst those to the west are probably the root house/cow house noted in 1880. The west end of the north range was formerly used as a cow house but is now a calf pen. There was once a feeding passage running along the north side of the interior, which is crossed by softwood king-post trusses.

The west range was much enlarged between 1880 and 1911, and has been much altered again since. However, at the south end of the range, the barn is relatively well preserved. It is a large two storey rectangular brick structure with a pair of cartsheds to the south side. The west elevation has a large doorway with a timber lintel and relieving arch over, flanked by breathers made from ceramic pipes arranged in a diamond pattern to the ground floor and a pair of small openings to the first floor; there is a much smaller doorway in the east elevation opposite the large western doorway. Internally, the barn is open to roof height and divided into five bays by large bolted king-post roof trusses, the only ones within the farm complex to retain rough-sawn oak common rafters, some of which appear to be re-used. At the south end, wooden steps lead up to the first floor over the cart sheds. The remains of a pigeon loft survive within, formerly fitted out with nesting boxes.[21]

Fig. 16/17: West range of farm buildings (part of Building 2) at Park Farm, c.1890.

A superb photograph of this part of the farm, taken in about c.1890, shows a three-storey pigeon cote with a pyramidal roof surmounting the roof ridge here.[22] This photograph also depicts the stackyard beyond the barn, with wood sawing going on in the foreground. Some activities within the barn had clearly been mechanised, as evidenced by the horse gin in the left hand corner of the photograph and a stationary steam engine positioned against the barn's west wall.

249

There are two modern hay barns to the west of the west range and a breeze block structure with a corrugated sheet roof.

The south range is actually formed by two parallel ranges, of which the northern is a replacement of the structure shown here in 1880. It has been much altered, but a number of low blocked openings with arched heads in the yard elevation suggest that it was formerly used as a piggery. The interior of the range is now open and is crossed by king-post roof trusses. These are a later addition, part of a raising of the roof using five short pillars built on top of the earlier yard elevation. The existing roof is covered with slates laid in an unusual overlapping pattern. The south-eastern part of the south range is contemporary with the original parts of the farm, and comprises the stable and two loose boxes referred to in 1880. The stable has been much altered but retains its original plan. The south-western part of the south range had originally comprised a cow house, and was demolished in 1993 to make way for a new milking parlour. During demolition, it was noted that walls of the earlier building rose from footings of large stones similar to those used at the castle, and that parts of the internal brickwork were of re-used narrow bricks. These could well have come from the Hall, and may have been a remnant of Ingram's early 17th century lodge (see Chapter 15).

Discussion and Conclusions

None of the three farms within the park preserves any structural evidence for buildings earlier than the late 18th century. However, as described in Chapter 5, it is probable that the placing of both Oaks Farm and Lodge Farm relates to a tripartite division of the park which dates back to at least the late 16th century. For example, the western boundary of the Lodge Farm holding in 1848 appears to be the same as the division between the central and east parts of the park as described in 1650. Lodge Farm itself may have replaced an earlier, perhaps medieval, complex located a short distance away to the north-west, which now survives only as earthworks (see Chapter 4). It is not yet certain how the park was farmed in the period between c.1600 to 1800, or from where. It is assumed that much continued to be farmed 'in hand' from the Hall itself, with other areas let to tenants who had farm buildings outside the park boundaries, perhaps within either West Lilling or Sheriff Hutton.

On balance, the structural evidence suggests that, in its existing form, Oaks Farm is probably slightly earlier than Lodge Farm, with the main body of the farmhouse built between perhaps c.1790-1800. The other early buildings within this farm complex are the threshing barn and one part of the stables (even though the latter does not appear on the tithe map of 1848). Together with the farmhouse, these buildings were loosely arranged around three sides of a space probably once used as stackyard, and which later became the west yard. The combination of farmhouse, barn and stables suggests that, in its existing form, Oaks Farm was created as an arable holding to take advantage of rising grain prices during the Napoleonic Wars;[23] when first created, it included the land now farmed from Park Farm.

Most of the buildings associated with either housing, feeding or fattening cattle at Oaks Farm are significantly later; one had been built by 1848 and some more by 1855, but others, such as the hay barn did not appear until the later 19th century. It is probable that the construction of these buildings marked a change to a mixed arable/dairy regime. The impetus for this change could have been the construction of the York to Scarborough branch of the York and North Midlands Railway, opened in 1845, the nearest station to Sheriff Hutton being Flaxton, about a mile away.[24] The presence of the railway may have made it profitable to supply markets in York with milk for the first time, although by 1913 Flaxton station's principal traffic was hay and clover, followed by barley and livestock;[25] clover was highly valued as a fodder for horses and may also have been used to feed cattle in urban dairies. The farmhouse was probably expanded at about the same time to accommodate the increased numbers of labourers and seasonal workers who would have been employed on the farm. The ramped garden walls at Oaks Farm are also interesting features, and perhaps indicate a period when the farmhouse was more of a residence than part of a working farm.

The interior fittings of the farmhouse at Lodge Farm show that it dates from the Regency period, and it was probably built some time between c.1800 and 1820. Like Oaks Farm farmhouse, it has a true double-pile plan, still relatively uncommon in the northern Vale of York at this date.[26] On the whole, the surviving fittings are of a higher standard than those at Oaks Farm, which may indicate that it was originally furnished more elaborately. Unlike Oaks Farm however, with the possible exception of the game larder, no buildings of contemporary date to the farmhouse survive. Although the 1880 sale catalogue suggested rather disingenuously that Lodge Farm had been 'considerably enlarged and improved some few years ago', the two large yards were apparently created out of the earlier U-plan yard between 1848 and 1855, perhaps removing or rebuilding much of the earlier structure. The rebuilding apparently formed part of widespread improvements to the estate at this time, including the addition of a new wing to the Hall and changes to The Rangers House (see Chapter 15).

The rebuilding of Lodge Farm between 1848 and 1855 forms part of a mid 19th century change in farming practices that have been recognised right across the country. The recovery of grain prices following the slump in the immediate aftermath of the Battle of Waterloo in 1815, coupled with an increasing population and a steadier market, provided an incentive for farms to raise their output. This was primarily achieved by increasing the numbers of cattle kept at the farmstead and by better conservation of their manure, as, in the absence of artificial fertilisers, the manure provided the main source of fertiliser for the fields.[27] In some cases, the production of manure was deemed to be one of the most important functions of these new farmsteads, leading to the term 'manure factories'.[28] The need to keep increasing numbers of cattle led to changes in the design of the farms themselves, with more yards and accommodation being provided. The range of specific building types accommodated within the farm also continued to increase, and more attention was paid to both mechanisation and the improved flow of feedstuffs and manure through the farm complex.[29]

The buildings of Park Farm (or Home Farm as it was originally known), as the most recent farm to be established in the park, naturally reflect some of the agricultural developments that had taken place during the mid 19th century. There is little reason to doubt that the date '1856' pencilled on the staircase of the earliest part of the farmhouse is when the farm was first established. The farm was created out of land mostly belonging to Oaks Farm and by 1880 it was described as a bailiff's or keeper's house. It is probable that Park Farm was created to fulfil some of the functions formerly carried out at The Rangers House complex adjacent to the Hall, which appears to have been substantially reduced in size between 1855 and 1880 (see Chapter 15). As well as selling produce externally, the farm would have supplied the Hall with foodstuffs and indeed Lady Mary Thompson made the short trip between the two to select milk, cream and cheeses personally. The addition of the cross-wing to the south side of the farmhouse in 1886 marked the point at which the Armitage family bought the farm, rather than continuing to lease it.

The negotiations between Leonard Thompson and George Hudson regarding the possible route of the York to Scarborough railway line over land at Strensall and East Lilling have been noted in Chapter 13. In this context, the intriguing resemblance of the farmhouse at Park Farm to several smaller railways stations in the region is often remarked upon, and sometimes the name of the architect George Townsend Andrews is raised. Andrews (1805-1855) practised at York, and is best known for his work on railway stations in North and East Yorkshire, principally on the York and North Midland Railway.[30] It is certainly true that both parts of the house have the overhanging roof and plan form favoured by Andrews for his smaller railway stations, such as, for example at Haxby.[31] Is it too much of a coincidence - perhaps. However, dates raise greater problems than styling. The York to Scarborough line, along with Flaxton station, was opened in 1845, whilst the farmhouse was built no earlier than 1851 and perhaps as late as 1856, long after the line of the route had been established. Therefore, whilst clearly not designed as a small railway station, its form may well still have been influenced by Andrews, as can be seen in other farmhouses in the York area with similar overhanging roofs. Park Farm farmhouse lacks the Italianate detailing that Andrews so often used on his smaller railway stations, such as the small stone porticos at Nafferton, Lockington and Bempton,[32] but the removal of such unnecessary (and costly) features is exactly what might be expected if someone was adapting one of his designs for use as a house.

Footnotes

1. Thanks are due to Mr Robin Barker and Georgina Ratcliff (Oaks Farm), Mr Mike Rickatson (Lodge Farm) and Messrs David and John Armitage (Park Farm) for their help and co-operation during the building inspections, and for providing information about the farms and the most recent use of the various buildings.
2. Borthwick Institute TA411S.
3. Ordnance Survey 1856 1st edition 6" map sheet 140, surveyed 1851-2.
4. Sedgwick, Son & Weall 1880 "The Sheriff Hutton Park Estate". Copies held within the village and at the Borthwick Institute (PR/SH/80).
5. Ordnance Survey 1911 25" map sheet 140/8.
6. Mr Robin Barker, *pers comm.*
7. Borthwick Institute TA411S.
8. Ordnance Survey 1855 1st edition 6" map sheet 141, surveyed 1854.
9. Sedgwick, Son & Weall 1880 "The Sheriff Hutton Park Estate". Copies held within the village and at the Borthwick Institute (PR/SH/80).
10. Ordnance Survey 1911 25" map sheet 141/5.
11. Mr Mike Rickatson, *pers comm.*
12. ibid.
13. Virgin 1994, p.188; I am grateful to Sam Taylor for this information.
14. Mr Mike Rickatson, *pers comm.*
15. Sedgwick, Son & Weall 1880 "The Sheriff Hutton Park Estate". Copies held within the village and at the Borthwick Institute (PR/SH/80).
16. Ordnance Survey 1911 25" map sheet 141/5.
17. Documents provided by John Armitage.
18. Mr John Armitage, *pers comm.*
19. ibid.
20. ibid.
21. ibid.
22. I am grateful to Mr John Armitage for permission to reproduce this photograph.
23. Mr Robin Barker, *pers comm.*
24. Allen 1974, pp.98-99; Hoole 1985, p.85.
25. Hoole 1985, p.164.
26. Harrison & Hutton 1984, p.211.
27. Wade Martins 2002, p.75.
28. e.g. Hayfield 1991.
29. Wade Martins 2002, pp.75-76; Barnwell & Giles 1997, pp.4-5.
30. Buck 1992, pp.33-39; Hoole 1985, pp.85-106; Felstead *et al* 1993, pp.43-44.
31. Hoole 1985, p.87.
32. Buck 1992, p.37.

CHAPTER 17: EAST LILLING HALL AND THE PLUMERS
by Barbara Foreman

As has been noted in Chapter 4, the medieval village of East Lilling was destroyed and the site taken into the deer park in 1471-85. The detailed survey of the village earthworks showed that the medieval manor house did not lie within the main body of the settlement, and it is likely that it lay further away outside the deer park and perhaps under or close to the present house.[1] A document of 1315 records a house with servants belonging to Roger de Nunwick,[2] and this is presumed to be the manor house. The present Hall is a 19th century Victorian-style residence built by the then owners, the Holtby family.[3]

Details relating to the early ownership of the Hall have been summarised elsewhere.[4] In the early 16th century the lease of the original house and farm was held by the Clapham family. In 1519 a John Clapham was described as a 'gentleman', and he may have been a relative of the previous lessee Christopher Clapham. When John Clapham died in 1537, one of his heirs was another Christopher Clapham, and he married Alice Pacock, the widowed daughter of Alderman George Gale, Sheriff of York. Finding himself heavily in debt, Christopher Clapham mortgaged the lease to Alderman Gale, and it appears that he was never in a position to redeem it, for it passed to the Hall family following the marriage of Alice's sister Isabel to Alderman Robert Hall. In 1586 the lease was alienated to their son Alderman Henry Hall, who later became Lord Mayor of York. Henry married Alice Mary Birkbie, the daughter of James Birkbie, another Alderman of York, and their son Henry was born in 1589.

Fig. 17/1: The east front of East Lilling Hall.

The earliest clear record of East Lilling Hall appears in 1607-08 when Alderman Henry Hall held a 'capital messuage' and a 'mansion house', followed by his son from 1620-22. The house with its grounds are depicted on Norden's plan of East Lilling, where it is shown to lie just outside the bounds of Sheriff Hutton deer park (see plate 38); this house appears to be sited just to the south of the present Hall in an area where possible building foundations have been found in the past.[5]

Henry Hall married Marian Towrie, the daughter and heiress of Wil Towrie of Kirby Grindalythe, and so the manors of Dunnington and Cowden were added to the Hall family estate. Henry and Marian had a son also called Henry, born in 1612, and he married Katherine Baumsfielde. Henry and Katherine had a son, another Henry, who married Mary Elizabeth Hobson, daughter of Wil Hobson of Sigston in Lancashire. Mary Hall died on 1st September 1657 and is buried with her infant son in Sheriff Hutton church. There is a brass plate on the chancel floor on which is the following inscription:

> *"Here lyeth the body of Mary the late and most deare wife of Henry Hall of this parish deceased with their Little son buried the first of Sept. 1657".*

Another son Francis married Mary Rokeby on 10th June 1658 at St Michael le Belfry church in York. Mary was the daughter of Thomas Rokeby and Elizabeth Burey. She was born in 1634, and died on 11th June 1706 at East Lilling. Francis and Mary had a daughter, Alice, who was born on 30th June 1678 at Lilling. Alice married Thomas Plumer of Bedale on 14th December 1710. This caused the Plumers to settle at Lilling, and several memorials to the family may be seen on the walls of the church at Sheriff Hutton.

Their son Thomas Plumer married Mary Ann Thompson (known as Ann) at The British Factory Chaplaincy in Oporto, Portugal, on 15th January 1750. Thomas had inherited East Lilling Hall from his parents Thomas and Alice. It was an elegant two-storey house of rose-coloured brick, sheltered by a belt of trees and surrounded by farmland which extended along the Plain of York to the Castle Howard estate. Adjoining the house were stables, a dairy, a brewhouse and a laundry.

Thomas Plumer was one of a number of English gentlemen with business interests in the port wine trade in Oporto. In 1703 Queen Anne went to war with France, and in an attempt to stifle French wine profits, the English Ambassador John Methuen negotiated a significant tax advantage for Portuguese wines over others coming into England. Subsequently, enterprising British businessmen bought controlling interests in the port trade. They opened trading stations in Portugal which they called 'factories'. The British Factory in Oporto is still standing. It is an elegant building with wood panelled meeting rooms, Waterford chandeliers and large mahogany dining tables at which the port wine shippers (still largely British) meet for lunch every Wednesday.[6] As a result of their investments, many English families settled in Portugal for several generations. The Thompson family of Sheriff Hutton Park were also involved in the trade, and intermarried with the Plumers.[7]

Thomas Plumer kept a memoranda book, in which he recorded many domestic details, and this gives us an interesting insight into 18th century life. He was a devoted father, and frequently records the progress of his children. For example, at his home in London one day he decided to measure the height of his children. The eldest, Hall Plumer, was "aged 17 years 7 months and 24 days" and had reached 5ft 5ins in height. Thomas, Lucy, Catherine and Ann were also measured, Ann being "aged 7 years 10 months and 10 days" and a diminutive 3ft 9ins.[8]

Thomas and his son Hall both had health problems, of which indigestion and dyspepsia seemed to occur frequently. He lists the cost of sundry drugs he bought for his family, and he shopped around to get the best prices. Among the cures he mentioned are Spirits of Lavender, Powdered Peruvian Bark, Salts of Wormwood and Hartshorn Spirits. Other cures used on Hall were blood-letting and blistering.

Thomas Plumer was a Director of the Bank of England, and on fine days he would walk there from his London home in John Street. On 9th April 1769 he wrote:

> *"Walked to and from the City for several days. Cold NE wind blowing. Catched cold. Somewhat anxious about the Election".*

His concern was probably due to the fact that in 1768 he had noted "Bank Stock Capital £10,780,000. Government owes the Bank £11,600,000 Exchequer Bills".

An entry for 1769 says:

> *"Danced much the night before, supped heartily. Took more snuff than ordinary, went into the study. Sat up until 4.30, was perplexed about HP".*

The 'HP' was presumably his son, Hall Plumer. Hall had been sent to Madras at the age of 17 to join the East India Company, in order to further his business education. Thomas always worried when Hall was on one of his voyages overseas, and often accompanied him, both to India and to Portugal.

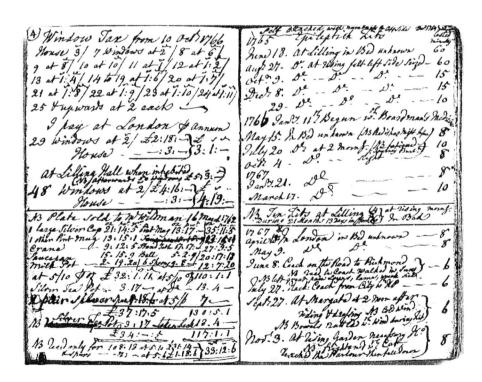

Fig. 17/2: Illustration from Thomas Plumer's 18th century Memoranda Book (Source: NYCRO Z1001).

Thomas also recorded an account of Hall's wedding day, on 15th January 1769 when the reception was held at the Plumer's London home:

255

"Self, wife, 2 sons and 3 daughters enjoyed together a comfortable and affectionate day. Sung hymns. Parting advice to Hall, serious yet cheerful".

Only a few weeks later, Hall had to leave his new wife and set out for Madras on another business trip. Hall seems to have prospered in India, because he eventually owned property in Madras, described as the Pantheon. In 1793 he is reported to have assigned it to a committee appointed to run the Government Museum. He was then described as a Civil Servant and Public Works Contractor.[9]

Thomas kept meticulous accounts for the wine consumed at his homes in London and Lilling. The family got through considerable amounts of White Port, Red Port, Madeira and Malmsey wine.

In his memoranda book, Thomas also complained bitterly about the Window Tax, which had replaced the Hearth Tax in 1696. East Lilling Hall had many more windows than his London home, and, despite some being blocked up, the taxes were considerably higher. His book also contains an inventory of furniture and fittings at Lilling, as well as wages paid to his staff. It is interesting to note that he paid 3d. each for "three coarse chamber pots" but 8d. for "one flowered one".

Despite living so close to the deer park, Thomas appears to have had no interest in hunting. He was solely concerned with his business interests, and Lilling to him was his country home - the farms on his land were just an additional source of income. Timber from his land also provided fuel for brewing, baking and laundering, making East Lilling Hall almost self-sufficient.

One day Thomas noted that "Catherine Thompson died Sunday July 24th 1768. Her fortune is in Mr. Thompson's hands (£1,800)". Catherine left no will and the money was divided equally amongst 'all brothers and sisters'. The beneficiaries were named as John Thompson, H. Thompson, Mary Thompson, Mrs. Seward, Stephen Croft, R. Dingley, Thomas Croft, and Thomas Plumer himself. They each received £238 8s. 8d., being one-eighth of the final total of £1,907 10s. 0d. The Crofts and Dingleys had intermarried with the Thompsons, as had Thomas Plumer. Robert Dingley's wife was Elizabeth Thompson, and their address was given as Somerset House, London.

Thomas died on 17th March 1781 in his 70th year. His son Hall inherited East Lilling Hall, and his mother Ann resided there until her death on 10th March 1795, in her 75th year. According to her memorial in Sheriff Hutton church, she "closed with becoming fortitude and resignation A life she had adorned with every female virtue". With Ann gone, the Plumers seem to have severed their connection with Lilling, as Hall is later noted as living at Stockton Hall at Stockton-on-Forest.

It is interesting to note that the Croft family were in partnership in the port wine trade with the Thompsons, trading at one time as Tilden, Thompson and Croft. Later the firm became well known as the famous House of Croft. The Croft family lived at Stillington Hall, and one of their number, John Croft, born in 1732, became Sheriff of York and travelled regularly between York and Oporto.[10]

Fig. 17/3: Portrait of the Rt. Hon.
Sir Thomas Plumer (Source: National
Portrait Gallery, London).

Fig. 17/4: Portrait of Henry Plumer, 1st
Viscount Plumer by Sir Leslie Ward ('Spy')
1902 (Source: National Portrait Gallery,
London).

Apart from Hall, the children of Thomas and Ann were Thomas (later Sir Thomas) Lucy, Catherine and Ann. Lucy and Catherine married two brothers named Anderson, in a double wedding on 11th September 1784. Lucy married George William Anderson and Catherine married Edmund Anderson. Ann never married, and died at Lilling on the 11th August 1806, aged 45. She must have been a strong-minded lady because she insisted on being buried on the north side of the church, against the custom of that time. Her memorial on the outer chancel wall reads:

> "This stone is in memorial that the Remains of ANN PLUMER Were deposited at Her own request near this spot. The Benevolence that directed all Her Actions prompted a wish to hold out by her example opposition to that idle prejudice which objects to Burial on the north side of a Church but which is neither justified by Reason nor Religion."

Thomas and Ann Plumer's second son Thomas (later Sir Thomas) was born in 1753, and was educated at Eton, then at Oxford. He entered Lincoln's Inn on 6th April 1769. Called to the Bar in 1778, he later defended Warren Hastings, and gained his acquittal. He became a judge

257

and politician, and was made Attorney General on 26th April 1812 and Master of the Rolls in 1818. In 1811 he purchased an estate at Canons in Stanmore, Middlesex, and on his death in 1824 his wealth was described as 'substantial'. He left a wife Marianne, five sons and two daughters.[11]

His great grandson Herbert Charles Onslow Plumer, born at Sussex Place in Kensington in 1857, had a distinguished career in the Army. He was at the Siege of Mafeking, where his commanding officer was Baden-Powell. He fought in the First World War and was a contemporary of Field Marshall Earl Haigh. Because of his character and appearance he is thought to have been the model for Colonel Blimp. He eventually became Field Marshall Lord Plumer of Messines and Bilton (after Bilton-in-Ainsty, where his family had had property). He was an honorary Freeman of the City of York.[12]

On his death in 1932, Lord Plumer was given a State Funeral at Westminster Abbey. His only son was Thomas Hall Rokeby Plumer (2nd Viscount Plumer).

By the time Herbert was born, the Plumers had left East Lilling Hall, and the owner in 1840 is shown in White's Trade Directory as the Revd S. D. Shaftoe. In 1890 the Hall was in the possession of Robert Holtby, who transformed the house into the Victorian home it is today.

Footnotes

1   Swan *et al* 1990, p.100.
2   Calendar of Patent Rolls 1313-1317, p.320 (5 May 1315).
3   Bell 1963.
4   Swan *et al* 1990, pp.100-101.
5   ibid., p.101 note 67.
6   Kincaid, J "Port Wine Revealed" (*www.vino.com/explore/article.asp*).
7   see Chapter 13.
8   North Yorkshire County Record Office (NYCRO) Z1001: Thomas Plumer's Memoranda Book.
9   *Government Museum, Chennai (www.chennaimuseum.org).*
10   "The House of Croft" (*www.kobrandwine.com/prodbook/cft000.html*).
11   Matthew & Harrison 2004 vol 4, p.609-610.
12   Matthew & Harrison 2004 vol 4, p.606-609.
Other Sources:
The International Genealogical Index (*www.familysearch.com*).
Miss Lascelles Green Book (unpublished scrap book held in Sheriff Hutton Village Hall).

CHAPTER 18: CONCLUDING REMARKS

By Barbara Foreman
Co-ordinator, Sheriff Hutton Women's Institute Community Pale Project

At the first meeting of the Pale Project Committee, some members had reservations as to whether we would find enough material on the park to fill a book. It very quickly became clear that there was going to be enough to produce several books, and the main problem was then became what to leave out, rather than what to include.

More than 25 people from the local community have contributed towards the content of this book, each with their own particular knowledge, skills and area of interest. Although they may not all have written text, they have provided vital information such as oral history, old photographs, details of archaeological finds and so on, and many have assisted with the historical research and the site survey work. One of the strengths of such a varied input is that a photographer, farmer, historian, rambler, archaeologist, villager, landowner and ecologist will look at the same feature in entirely different ways, and more than likely come up with entirely different interpretations! During the course of writing this book, each has learned from the other and the resulting text is much improved as a result.

As any proper study should, the work undertaken by the Pale Project has answered some questions, but raised many more. For example, a minor Roman road may have been discovered, but where did it go, or is it actually no more than an early post-medieval boundary? Is the enclosure in the High Park really Roman in date, or is it a medieval hunting lodge or a 17th century garden feature? The existence of the park may have been projected backwards nearly 100 years earlier than previously thought, but we still do not know precisely when it was created and by whom, and what area it actually covered. The first castle appears to have been downgraded from a castle to perhaps a detached lodge in its later phases, but from this has arisen the possibility that the Nevilles had a long term plan for the development of Sheriff Hutton long before John and Ralph Neville in the later 14th century. A 'Lady Bridge' has emerged from the documents and earthworks of the second castle's gardens, but could it really have been built for a planned visit by Elizabeth I, and how did it fit with the earlier designed landscape? A plethora of lodges (or perhaps only one!) and numerous associated structures have been listed within the park, but we still do not know where most of them were. Finally, Arthur Ingram's New Lodge of 1619-24 has been revealed as a house that both rivalled and perhaps inspired Temple Newsam in Leeds, with a formal garden landscape once planned on the same scale but probably never realised.

The voices of ordinary people from the past have remained elusive throughout the project, although those speaking through the 1598 depositions contribute marvellous local colour. Nevertheless, much human interest has emerged, varying from a six year old boy so important that he required some 245 people to look after him, an earl arriving on a rainy day to watch water pouring through the holes in the castle roof, and a young man so burdened with debt that he hung himself.

It is hoped that the results of this Pale Project will act as a stimulus to further research and investigation within the park and the surrounding areas, and who knows, perhaps another book in the future!

CHAPTER 19: BIBLIOGRAPHY

Alexander, A 1993 "Perambulations and Boundary Descriptions". In Le Patourel, H E J, Long, M & Pickles, M F (eds) *Yorkshire Boundaries*, 39-51 (Yorkshire Archaeological Society, Leeds).

Allen, C 1974 *The North-Eastern Railway* (Ian Allan Ltd, Rochester).

Almond, R 2003 *Medieval Hunting* (Sutton Publishing, Stroud).

Armitage, E S & Montgomerie, D H 1912 "Ancient Earthworks". In Page, W (ed) *Victoria County History of the County of York* vol 2, 1-73 (Constable & Co. Ltd, London).

Arvanigian, M 2003 "Henry IV, the Northern Nobility and the Consolidation of the Regime". In Dodd, G & Biggs, D (eds) *Henry IV: The Establishment of the Regime, 1399-1406*, 117-138 (York Medieval Press, York).

Atkinson, J C (ed) 1889 *Quarter Sessions Records 1677-1716*. North Riding Record Series (Old Series) vol 7.

Aveling, H 1966 *Northern Catholics: the Catholic Recusants of the North Riding of Yorkshire 1558-1790* (G Chapman, London).

Baillie-Grohman, W A & F (eds) 1909 *The Master of Game by Edward, 2nd Duke of York: The Oldest Book on Hunting* (Ballantyne, London; reprint AMS, New York 1974).

Bain, J (ed) 1890 *The Hamilton Papers: Letters and Papers Illustrating the Political Relations of England and Scotland in the XVIth Century* (2 vols) (Registrar House, Edinburgh).

Barnet, R C 1980 "The Lord Presidency of the North and the Succession of James I". *York Historian* vol 3, 16-21.

Barnwell, P & Giles, C 1997 *English Farmsteads 1750-1914* (Alden Press, Oxford).

Bell, J 1963 "Lilling Hall". *York Times vol3(1)* Spring 1963, 26-28.

Beresford, M W 1954 "The Lost Villages of Yorkshire Part IV". *Yorkshire Archaeological Journal* vol 38, 280-309.

Beresford, M W 1957 *History on the Ground: Six Studies in Maps and Landscapes* (Lutterworth Press, London, reprinted 1984 by Alan Sutton Ltd, Gloucester).

Beresford, M W & St Joseph, J K S 1979 *Medieval England: An Aerial Survey* (Cambridge University Press, Cambridge - 2nd edition).

Bernard-Wood, G 1959 "Cornbrough Villa. Sheriff Hutton". *Yorkshire Life Illustrated* vol 12(10), 35-37.

Birrell, J 1982 "Who Poached the King's Deer? A Study in 13th Century Crime". *Midland History* vol 7, 9-25.

Birrell, J 1992 "Deer and Deer Farming in Medieval England". *Agricultural History Review* vol 40, 112-126.

Birrell, J 1996a "Peasant Deer Poachers in the Medieval Forest". In Britnell, R & Hatcher, J (eds) *Progress and Problems in Medieval England* (Cambridge University Press, Cambridge).

Birrell, J 1996b "Hunting and the Royal Forest". In Cavaciocchi, S (ed) *L'Uomo e la Foresta, secc. XIIIe-XVIIe*, 437-457. Atti delle "Settimane di Studi" e altri Convegni 27. Istituto Internazionale di Storia Economica "F Datini" (Prato, Italy).

Bise, G (no date) *The Hunting Book by Gaston Phoebus*. Translated by J Peter Tallon (Regent Books, London).

Black, M 1985 *Food and Cooking in Medieval Britain: History and Recipes* (English Heritage, London).

Blackett-Ord, M 1986 "Lord Wharton's Deer Park Walls". *Transactions of the Cumberland and Westmoreland Antiquarian and Archaeological Society* (New Series) vol 86, 133-139.

Boland, B 1977 *Gardener's Magic and other Old Wives' Lore* (Bodley Head, London).

Bond, C J 1981 "Woodstock Park under the Plantagenet Kings: the Exploitation and Use of Wood and Timber in a Medieval Deer Park". *Arboricultural Journal* vol 5, 201-213.

Bond, C J 1988 "Rabbits: the Case for their Medieval Introduction into Britain". *Local Historian* vol 18(2), 53-57.

Bond, C J 1994 "Forests, Chases, Warrens and Parks". In Aston, M & Lewis, C (eds) *The Medieval Landscape of Wessex*, 115-150 (Oxbow Monograph 46; Oxbow Books, Oxford).

Bond, C J 1998 *Somerset Parks and Gardens* (Somerset Books, Taunton).

Boxer, A & Black, P 1980 *The History of Herbs* (Octopus Books Ltd, London).

Brayshaw, T (ed) 1889 "The Yorkshire Portion of Leland's Itinerary". *Yorkshire Archaeological Journal* vol 10, 312-344.

Brighton, J 1978 *The Enamel Glass-Painters of York: 1585-1795* vol 1 (unpublished D. Phil Thesis, University of York).

Brookes, F W 1954 *York and the Council of the North* (St Anthony's Press, London).

Brown, A E & Taylor, C C 1977 "Cambridgeshire Earthwork Surveys, II". *Proceedings of the Cambridge Antiquarian Society* vol 64, 85-102.

Brown, W (ed) 1896 *Yorkshire Lay Subsidy .. 1301*. Yorkshire Archaeological Society Record Series vol 21.

Brownlow, F W (ed) 1999 *The Book of the Laurel* (Associated University Presses, London).

Brunskill, R 1999 *Traditional Farm Buildings of Britain and their Conservation* (Victor Gollancz Ltd, London).

Buck, G 1992 *A Pictorial Survey of Railway Stations* (Oxford Publishing Company, Oxford).

Burton, J 1758 *Monasticon Eboracense* (York).

Burton, T 1888 *The History and Antiquities of the Parish of Hemmingbrough .. edited and enlarged by J Raine.* Yorkshire Archaeological & Topographical Association, Extra Volume 1 (Sampson, York).

Butler, L 1988 "York Palace, a Vanished Jacobean Mansion". *York Historian* vol 8, 25-45.

Butlin, R A 2003 "Historical Maps". In Butlin, R A (ed) *Historical Atlas of North Yorkshire*, 242-252 (Westbury Publishing, Otley).

Calthrop, C 1923 "Sheriff Hutton". In Page, W (ed) *Victoria County History: A History of Yorkshire North Riding* vol 2, 172-186 (St Catherine Press, London – reprinted 1968).

Camden Society 1855 *The Camden Miscellany volume 3* (Camden Society, London).

Cantor, L M 1982 "Forests, Chases, Park and Warrens". In Cantor, L (ed) *The English Medieval Landscape*, 56-85 (Croom Helm, London).

Cantor, L M 1983 *The Medieval Parks of England: a Gazetteer* (Dept of Education, Loughborough University of Technology).

Cantor, L M & Hatherley, J 1979 "The Medieval Parks of England". *Geography* vol 64(2), 71-85.

Capern, A 2004 "In Search of Andrew Marvell". *Paragon Review*, Issue 5 (*www.hull.ac.uk/oldlib/archives/paragon.1996/mvell.html*).

Cash, A H 1975 *Laurence Sterne: the Early and Middle Years* (Methuen, London).

Clark, M K 1935 *Gazetteer of Roman Remains in East Yorkshire.* Roman Malton and District Report No 5.

Clay, J W (ed) 1895 *Yorkshire Royalist Composition Papers or the Proceedings of the Committee for Compounding with Delinquents during the Commonwealth, vol 2.* Yorkshire Archaeological Society Record Series vol 18.

Clay, J W (ed) 1899 *Dugdale's Visitation of Yorkshire.* Surtees Society vol 36.

Cliffe, J 1999 *The World of the Country House in Seventeenth Century England* (Yale University Press, New Haven and London).

Clinch, G 1907 "Early Man". In Page, W (ed) *Victoria County History of Yorkshire* vol 1, 357-414 (Archibald Constable & Co. Ltd, London).

Colvin, H 1995 *A Biographical Dictionary of British Architects 1600-1840* (Yale University Press, New Haven and London).

Colvin, H M, Ransome, D R & Summerson, J 1975 *The History of the King's Works* vol 3 (1485-1660) (H.M.S.O., London).

Cowling, G C 1967 *The History of Easingwold and the Forest of Galtres* (Advertiser Press, Huddersfield).

Cox, J C 1907 "Forestry". In Page, W (ed) *Victoria County History of the County of York* vol 1, 501-523 (Archibald Constable & Co. Ltd, London).

Creighton, O 2002 *Castles and Landscapes* (Continuum, London).

Cross, C 1987 *The Puritan Earl: The Life of Henry Hastings, 3rd Earl of Huntingdon 1536-1595* (McMillan, London).

Cross, W L 1909 *The Life and Times of Lawrence Sterne* (McMillan, New York).

Cummins, J 1988 *The Hound and The Hawk: the Art of Medieval Hunting* (Weidenfeld & Nicholson, London).

Cummins, J 2002 "Veneurs s'en vont en Paradis: Medieval Hunting and the 'Natural' Landscape". In Howe, J & Wolfe, M (eds) *Inventing Medieval Landscapes: Senses of Place in Western Europe*, 33-56 (University Press of Florida, Florida).

Davies, R 1843 *Extracts from the Municipal Records of the City of York* (York).

Davies, R 1863 *The Life of Marmaduke Rawdon of York*. Camden Society Publications vol 85.

Davies, R 1873 "A Memoir of Dr John Burton MD FSA …" *Yorkshire Archaeological Journal* vol 2, 403-440.

Dennison, E 1997 "Sheriff Hutton Castle". *Archaeological Journal* vol 154, 291-296.

Dennison, E 1998a *Sheriff Hutton Castle, North Yorkshire: An Archaeological and Architectural Survey* (unpublished EDAS report 1996/10R.01 for English Heritage and Dr R Howarth).

Dennison, E 1998b "Recent Work at Sheriff Hutton Castle". *CBA Forum: The Annual Newsletter of CBA Yorkshire*, 7-12.

Dennison, E 1999 "Stile House, Sheriff Hutton, North Yorkshire: Archaeological Watching Brief" (unpublished EDAS report 1998/55R.01).

Dennison, E 2004 "Woodhall Rabbit Warren, Carperby". In White, R F & Wilson, P R (eds) *Archaeology and Historic Landscapes of the Yorkshire Dales*, 137-144. Yorkshire Archaeological Society Occasional Paper No 2. (Smith Settle, Otley).

Dennison, E & Richardson, S 2005 "Beningbrough Hall, North Yorkshire: Historic Landscape Survey" (unpublished EDAS Ltd report 2003/223R.01 for National Trust).

Dickens, A G 1955 *Robert Holgate, Archbishop of York and President of the King's Council in the North*. Borthwick Papers No. 8.

Dormer, I 2003 "Medieval Forests and Parks". In Butlin, R A (eds) *Historical Atlas of North Yorkshire*, 78-82 (Westbury Publishing, Otley).

Drake, F 1736 *Eboracum or The History and Antiquities of the City of York* (Reprinted by E P Publishing, Wakefield, 1978).

Duckett, G 1877 "Harwood Evidences: Redman of Harwood and Levens". *Yorkshire Archaeological Journal* vol 4, 84-113.

Dugdale, W (ed. Caley, J, Ellis, H & Bardinel, B) 1846 *Monasticon Anglicanum* (London).

Dyer, C 1994 *Everyday Life in Medieval England* (Hambleton Press, London).

Egerton, J 1946 "Sheriff Hutton Park". *York Georgian Society Occasional Papers* No 2, 5-13.

Emery, A 1996 *Greater Medieval Houses of England and Wales Volume 1: Northern England* (Cambridge University Press, Cambridge).

English, B (ed) 1996 *Yorkshire Hundred and Quo Warrento Rolls.* Yorkshire Archaeological Society Record Series vol 151.

Everson, P 1996 "Bodiam Castle, East Sussex: Castle and its Designed Landscape". *Chateau Gaillard* vol 17, 79-84.

Everson, P 1998 "Delightfully Surrounded with Woods and Ponds: Field Evidence for Medieval Gardens in England". In Pattinson, P (ed) *There By Design: Field Archaeology in Parks and Gardens*, 32-38 (Royal Commission on the Historical Monuments of England, Swindon).

Everson, P 2003 "Medieval Gardens and Designed Landscapes". In Wilson-North, R (ed) *The Lie of the Land: Aspects of the Archaeology and History of the Designed Landscape in the South West of England*, 24-33 (The Mint Press and Devon Gardens Trust, Exeter).

Everson, P, Taylor, C C & Dunn, C J 1991 *Change and Continuity: Rural Settlement in North-west Lincolnshire* (H.M.S.O., London).

Fallow, T M 1913 "Priory of Marton". In Page, W (ed) *Victoria County History of the County of York* vol 3, 223-226 (Constable & Co. Ltd, London).

Farrer, W (ed) 1914 *Early Yorkshire Charters vol 1* (Ballantyne Hanson & Co., Edinburgh).

Farrer, W 1915a "The Sheriffs of Lincolnshire and Yorkshire, 1066-1130". *Economic History Review* vol 30, 277-285.

Farrer, W 1915b *Early Yorkshire Charters vol 2* (Ballantyne Hanson & Co., Edinburgh).

Faull, M L & Stinson, M 1986 *Domesday Book 30: Yorkshire* (Phillimore, Chichester).

Felstead, A, Francis, A & Pinfield, L 1993 *Directory of British Architects 1834-1900* (Mansell, London).

Field, J 1972 *English Field Names: A Dictionary* (David & Charles, Newton Abbot).

Field Archaeology Specialists Ltd 2003 "Conservation Plan: Sheriff Hutton Castle, North Yorkshire: Volume 1" (unpublished FAS report for Dr R Howarth).

Foster, J (no date) "Pedigrees of Yorkshire Families Vol 3: The North and East Ridings" (manuscript in York Reference Library Y.929.2Fos).

Franks, T (no date) "What's in a Name?". In Pomfret, D (ed) *Sheriff Hutton: Impressions of History*, 22-27.

Fretwell, K 1995 "Lodge Park, Gloucestershire". *Garden History* vol 23(2), 133-144.

Friar, S 2001 *The Local History Companion* (Sutton Publishing Limited, Stroud).

Gelling, M 1984 *Place-names in the Landscape* (J M Dent & Sons, London).

Gilbert, C 1963 "Light on Sir Arthur Ingram's Reconstruction of Temple Newsam 1622-1638". *Leeds Art Calendar* no 51, 6-12.

Gilbert, C 1965 *A Short Historical Guide to Sheriff Hutton Park* (the Author, Leeds).

Gilbert, C 1966a "Sheriff Hutton Hall, Yorkshire - I". *Country Life* vol 140, no 3627 (8th September 1966), 548-551.

Gilbert, C 1966b "Sheriff Hutton Hall, Yorkshire - II". *Country Life* vol 140, no 3628 (15th September 1966), 628-631.

Gilbert, C 1973 "New Park, Huby – an Early 17th Century Hunting Lodge". *Yorkshire Archaeological Journal* vol 45, 185-188.

Girouard M 1983 *Robert Smythson and the Elizabethan Country House* (Yale University Press, New Haven and London).

Gledhill, T 1998 "Medieval Woodland in North Yorkshire". In Atherden, M A & Butlin, R A (eds) *Woodland in the Landscape: Past and Future Perspectives*, 103-119 (Leeds University Press, Leeds).

Grainge, W 1855 *The Castles and Abbeys of Yorkshire* (Whitaker, London).

Grieve, M 1931 *A Modern Herbal: the Medicinal, Culinary, Cosmetic and Economic Properties, Cultivation and Folklore of Herbs, Grasses, Fungi, Shrubs and Trees with all their Modern Scientific Uses* (Jonathon Cape Ltd, Kent).

GSB Prospection Ltd 2004 "Sheriff Hutton, North Yorkshire" (unpublished GSB report 2004/89 for Ed Dennison Archaeological Services Ltd).

Harley, J 1928 *Report on the Manuscripts of the Late Reginald Rawdon Hastings Esq. of the Manor House, Ashby De la Zouche*. Historic Monuments Commission vol 78 (H.M.S.O., London).

Harrison, B 1984 "Evidence for Main Roads in the Vale of York during the Medieval Period". *Sciant Presentes: Newsletter of the Medieval Section of the Yorkshire Archaeological Society* no 13, 3-8.

Harrison, B 1998 "William Gossip's House in Ogleforth". *York Historian* vol 15, 53-61.

Harrison, B & Hutton, B 1984 *Vernacular Houses in North Yorkshire and Cleveland* (John Donald Publishers Ltd, Edinburgh).

Harvey, J 1972 *The Mediaeval Architect* (Wayland, London).

Harvey, J 1981 *Mediaeval Gardens* (B T Batsford Ltd, London).

Harvey, J 1983 *English Mediaeval Architects* (Alan Sutton, Gloucester).

Hayfield, C 1991 "Manure Factories? The Post-enclosure High Barns of the Yorkshire Wolds". *Landscape History* vol 13, 33-46.

Henderson, P (ed) 1948 *The Complete Poems of John Skelton, Laureate* (J M Dent and Sons, London - 2nd edition).

Heritage House Group Ltd 2001 *Raby Castle* (Heritage House Group Ltd, Derby).

Hicks, M 2002 *Warwick the Kingmaker* (Blackwell Publishers Ltd, London).

Higham, M C 2003 "Take it with a Pinch of Salt". *Landscape History* vol 25, 59-65.

Hill, D 1981 "Archives and Archaeology at Temple Newsam House". *Leeds Art Calendar* no 89, 22-32.

Hislop, M 1998 "John Lewyn of Durham: A North Country Master Mason of the Fourteenth Century". *Journal of the British Archaeological Association* vol 151, 170-189.

H.M.S.O. 1967 *Maps and Plans in the Public Record Office* (H.M.S.O., London).

Hoole, K 1985 *Railway Stations of the North-East* (David & Charles, Newton Abbot).

Horne, P 2003 "Case Study 2: Rural Settlement in Roman North Yorkshire, an Aerial View". In Butlin, R A (eds) *Historical Atlas of North Yorkshire*, 58-61 (Westbury Publishing, Otley).

I'Anson, W M 1913 "The Castles of the North Riding". *Yorkshire Archaeological Journal* vol 22, 303-399.

Illingworth, J L 1938 *Yorkshire's Ruined Castles* (reprinted 1970 by S R Publications, Wakefield).

Jackson, G 1973 *Hull in the Eighteenth Century* (University of Hull, Hull).

Jamison, C 1966 *A Catalogue of the Shrewsbury and Talbot Papers in Lambeth Palace Library ...* Historic Monuments Commission Joint Publications vol 6 (H.M.S.O. London).

Johnson, M 2002 *Behind the Castle Gate: From Medieval to Renaissance* (Routledge, London).

Jones, R F J 1988 "The Hinterland of Roman York". In Price, J & Wilson, P R (eds) *Recent Research in Roman Yorkshire*, 161-170. British Archaeological Reports (British Series) 193 (BAR, Oxford).

Kaner, J 1998 "Historic Woodland in the Vale of York". In Atherden, M A & Butlin, R A (eds) *Woodland in the Landscape: Past and Future Perspectives*, 120-139 (Leeds University Press, Leeds).

Kendall, P M 1987 *Richard III* (Unwin Paperbacks, London).

Kent, G H R 2002 "Hilston". In Kent, G H R (ed) *A History of the County of York, East Riding: Volume VII Holderness Wapentake Middle and North Divisions*, 50-55 (Oxford University Press, Oxford).

King, D J C 1983 *Castellarium Anglicanum* (2 vols) (Kraus, London)

Kitson, S 1929 "Barnard Dinninghof". *Journal of the British Society of Master-Glass Painters* vol 3(2), 55-58

Lascelles, U M (no date) "Sheriff Hutton 'Posy Ring'". In Pomfret, D (ed) *Sheriff Hutton: Impressions of History*, 44.

Lascelles, U M 1929 "Sheriff Hutton 'Posy Ring'". *Yorkshire Archaeological Journal* vol 29, 352-352.

Lawrence, H & Hoyle, R 1981 "New Maps and Surveys by Christopher Saxton". *Yorkshire Archaeological Journal* vol 53, 51-56.

Le Patourel, H E J 1973 *The Moated Sites of Yorkshire.* Society for Medieval Archaeology Monograph Series vol 5.

Leech, A F 1898 *Memorials of Beverley Minster ...* Surtees Society vol 98.

Leech, P E 1988 *English Heritage Monument Protection Programme Single Monument Description: Ringworks* (unpublished EH publication).

Liddiard, R 2003 "The Deer Parks of Domesday Book". *Landscapes* vol 4(1), 4-23.

Linstrum, D 1978 *West Yorkshire: Architects and Architecture* (Lund Humphries Publishers Ltd, London).

Mabey, R 1996 *Flora Britannica* (Sinclair-Stevenson, London).

Malden, J 1976 "The Walker Iron Foundry, York, c1825-1923". *York Historian* vol 1, 37-52.

Markham, C 1973 *Richard III* (Chivers, Bath).

Margary, I D 1973 *Roman Roads in Britain*. (John Baker, London - 3rd edition).

Matthew, H G & Harrison, B (eds) 2004 *Oxford Dictionary of National Biography* (60 vols) (Oxford University Press, Oxford).

Miller, J 2000 *James II* (New Haven, London).

Mitchell, A F 1966 "Dating the 'Ancient Oaks'". *Quarterly Journal of Forestry* vol 60, 271-276.

Moorhouse, S 1981 "Demesne Farming". In Faull, M L & Moorhouse, S A (eds) *West Yorkshire: An Archaeological Survey to AD 1500, Volume 3 The Rural Medieval Landscape*, 758-767 (West Yorkshire Metropolitan County Council, Wakefield).

Moorhouse, S 2003a "Review Article". *Newsletter of the Medieval Section of the Yorkshire Archaeological Society* vol 32, 32-38.

Moorhouse, S 2003b "Medieval Yorkshire: A Rural Landscape for the Future". In Manby, T G, Moorhouse, S & Ottaway, P (eds) *The Archaeology of Yorkshire. An Assessment at the Beginning of the 21st Century*, 181-214. Yorkshire Archaeological Society Occasional Paper No 3 (Charlesworth Group, Huddersfield).

Moorhouse, S 2003c "Anatomy of the Yorkshire Dales: Decoding the Medieval Landscape". In Manby, T G, Moorhouse, S & Ottaway, P (eds) *The Archaeology of Yorkshire. An Assessment at the Beginning of the 21st Century*, 293-362. Yorkshire Archaeological Society Occasional Paper No 3 (Charlesworth Group, Huddersfield).

Morris, J S J (ed) 1872 *The Troubles of Our Catholic Forefathers Related by Themselves* (3 volumes) (London).

Mowl, T & Earnshaw, B 1985 *Trumpet at a Distant Gate: The Lodge as Prelude to the Country House* (Waterstone, London).

Muir, R 1997 *The Yorkshire Countryside: A Landscape History* (Keele University Press, Edinburgh).

Muir, R 2000 "Pollards in Nidderdale: A Landscape History". *Rural History* vol 11(1), 95-111.

Murphy, B A 2003 *Bastard Prince: Henry VIII's Lost Son* (Sutton Press, Stroud).

Murphy, P & Scaife, G 1991 "The Environmental Archaeology of Gardens". In Brown, A E (ed) *Garden Archaeology*, 83-99. Council for British Archaeology Research Report 78 (Council for British Archaeology, London).

Musee Conde 1969 *The Tres Riches Heures of Jean, Duke of Berry* (Wellfleet Press, Secaucus, New Jersey).

Myerscough, R D 2003 "Sheriff Hutton Castle and Mowthorpe Quarries: Field Report". *Rydedale Vernacular Building Materials Research Group.*

Myerscough, R D 2005 "The Geology of Sheriff Hutton Castle" (unpublished mss for EDAS Ltd).

Neave, S 1991 *Medieval Parks of East Yorkshire* (Hutton Press, Beverley).

Neville, C 1994 "Keeping the Peace on the Northern Marches in the Later Middle Ages". *English Historical Review* vol 109, 1-25.

Nichols, J G 1855 *Inventories of the Wardrobes, Plate, Chapel Stuff etc of H. Fitzroy, Duke of Richmond ...* The Camden Miscellany vol 3 (Camden Society, London).

Oates, J 2001 "Independent Volunteer Forces in Yorkshire during the Forty-Five". *Yorkshire Archaeological Journal* vol 73, 123-131.

Oldfield, E 1867 "On some Roman Bronze Vessels discovered on the Castle Howard Estate, Yorkshire". *Archaeologia* vol 41, 325-332.

Orme, N 2003 *Medieval Children* (New Haven, London).

Ormrod, W 2000 "Competing Capitals? York and London in the Fourteenth Century". In Rees Jones, S, Marks, R & Minnis, A (eds) *Courts and Regions in Medieval Europe*, 75-98 (York Medieval Press, York).

Ottaway, P 2003 "The Archaeology of the Roman Period in the Yorkshire Region: A Rapid Resource Assessment". In Manby, T G, Moorhouse, S & Ottaway, P (eds) *The Archaeology of Yorkshire. An Assessment at the Beginning of the 21st Century*, 125-149. Yorkshire Archaeological Society Occasional Paper No 3 (Charlesworth Group, Huddersfield).

Packenham, T 1996 *Meetings with Remarkable Trees* (O. Weidenfield & Nicholson Ltd, London).

Palaiseul, J 1976 *Grandma's Secrets: Her Green Guide to Health from Plants* (Penguin).

Parker, C B 1929 *Lay Subsidy Rolls I Edward III North Riding and the City of York.* Yorkshire Archaeological Society Record Series vol 74, 104-171.

Parsons, D (ed) 1836 *The Diary of Sir Henry Slingsby of Scriven, Bart.* (Longmans, London and G. Todd, York)

Paterson, J M 1996 *Tree Wisdom* (Thorsons/Harper Collins, London).

Payne, A 2003 "The Beauchamps and the Nevilles". In Marks, R & Williamson, P (eds) *Gothic: Art for England 1400-1547*, 219-223 (V & A Publications, London).

Pevsner, N 1966 *The Buildings of England: Yorkshire The North Riding* (Penguin Books, London).

Pevsner, N & Neave, D 1995 *The Buildings of England: Yorkshire: York and the East Riding* (Penguin Books, London).

Podlech, D 1996 *Herbs and Healing Plants of Britain and Europe* (Harper Collins, London).

Pollet, M 1971 *John Skelton: Poet of Tudor England* (J M Dent & Sons, London).

Pressley, I 1946 "The Thompsons of Sheriff Hutton Park". *York Georgian Society Occasional Papers* No 2, 14-19.

Pritchett, J P 1887 "The Works of the Nevilles round Darlington". *Journal of the British Archaeological Association* vol 43, 217-237.

Purdy, J D 1991 *Yorkshire Hearth Tax Returns* (University of Hull, Hull).

Purvis, J S (ed) 1949 *Select XVI Century Causes in Tithe from the York Diocesan Registry*. Yorkshire Archaeological Society Record Series vol 114.

Rackham, O 1980 *Ancient Woodland: its History, Vegetation and Uses in England* (Edward Arnold, London).

Rackham, O 1986 *The History of the Countryside* (J M Dent & Sons, London).

Rackham, O 1989 *The Last Forest: The Story of Hatfield Forest* (J M Dent & Sons, London).

Rackham, O 2004 "Pre-Existing Trees and Woods in Country-House Parks". *Landscapes* vol 5(2), 1-16.

Radley, J 1974 "The Prehistory of the Vale of York". *Yorkshire Archaeological Journal* vol 46, 10-22.

Raine, A 1939 *York Civic Records I*. Yorkshire Archaeological Society Record Series vol 98.

Raine, J & Clay, J (eds) 1854 *Testamenta Eboracensia vol 2*. Surtees Society vol 30.

Rawcliffe, C 1997 *Medicine and Society in Later Medieval England* (Sutton Publishing Ltd, Stroud).

RCHME 1972 *North-East Cambridgeshire* (H.M.S.O., London).

RCHME 1986 *Rural Houses of West Yorkshire 1400-1830* (H.M.S.O., London).

Reid, R R 1975 *The Kings Council in the North* (EP Publishing, Wakefield).

Richardson, S & Dennison, E forthcoming (a) "North-East Tower, Sheriff Hutton Castle, North Yorkshire: Architectural and Archaeological Survey Work" (unpublished EDAS Ltd report).

Richardson, S & Dennison, E forthcoming (b) "Harewood Castle, West Yorkshire: Architectural and Archaeological Survey Work" (unpublished EDAS Ltd report).

Richardson, S & Dennison, E forthcoming (c) "Castle Farm, Sheriff Hutton: Architectural Survey and Archaeological Watching Brief" (unpublished EDAS Ltd report).

Ridsdill Smith, G 1978 *In Well Beware: the Story of Newburgh Priory and the Belasyse Family 1145-1971* (Roundwood Press, Kineton).

Ripon Historical Society 1991 *The Hearth Tax List for the North Riding of Yorkshire Michaelmas 1673: Part III, Birdforth & Bulmer Wapentakes.*

Roberts, E 1988 "The Bishop of Winchester's Deer Parks in Hampshire, 1200-1400". *Proceedings of the Hampshire Field Club and Archaeological Society* vol 44, 67-86.

Robertson, A 1975 "The Jacobean Chapel at Temple Newsam". *Leeds Arts Calendar* no 76, 21-23.

Robinson, D 1970 *Beneficed Clergy in Cleveland and the East Riding, 1305-40.* Borthwick Papers no. 37.

Robinson, D (ed) 1978 *The Register of William Melton, Archbishop of York 1317-1340, volume 2.* Canterbury & York Society vol 71.

Rogers, A 1992 "The Civil War and Its Aftermath". In Husthwaite Local History Society *Coxwoldshire, Historical Aspects* (Sessions, York).

Ross, C D 1981 *Richard III* (Methuen, London).

Rowe, F E S 1966 "The Battle Axe Series in Britain". *Proceedings of the Prehistoric Society* vol 32, 199-245.

Rushton, J 1986 *The Ryedale Story* (Ryedale District Council, Malton).

Rushton, J 2003 *The History of Ryedale From Earliest Times to the Year 2003* (Blackthorn Press, Pickering).

Saul, N 1999 *Richard II and Chivalric Kingship* (University of London, London).

Scarisbrick, J J 1983 *Henry VIII* (Methuen English Monarchs Series, London).

Sheppard, J A 1974 "Metrological Analysis of Regular Village Plans in Yorkshire". *Agricultural History Review* vol 22, 118-135.

Sheppard, J A 1976 "Medieval Village Planning in Northern England: Some Evidence from Yorkshire". *Journal of Historical Geography* vol 2(1), 3-20.

Sheriff Hutton Women's Institute 1975 *Treasure Survey* (Sheriff Hutton Women's Institute, York).

Shirley, E P 1867 *Some Account of English Deer Parks, with Notes on the Management of Deer* (John Murray, London).

Skaife, R H 1870 "The Register of Burials in the York Minster, Accompanied by Monumental Inscriptions and Illustrated with Biographical Notices". *Yorkshire Archaeological Journal* vol 1, 225-330.

Skaife, R H 1873 "The Register of Marriages in York Minster". *Yorkshire Archaeological Journal*, vol 3, 81-146.

Skaife, R H 1881 "The Register of Baptisms in York Minster". *Yorkshire Archaeological Journal* vol 6, 384-395.

Skaife, R H (no date – 19th century) "Civic Officials and Parliamentary Representatives of the City of York" (manuscript held in York Library, 3 vols).

Smith, A H 1928 *Place-names of the North Riding of Yorkshire*. English Place Name Society vol 5 (Cambridge University Press, Cambridge).

Spray, M 1981 "Holly as a Fodder in England". *Agricultural History Review* vol 29, 97-110.

Stamper, P 1988 "Woods and Parks". In Astill, G & Grant, A (eds) *The Countryside of Medieval England*, 128-148 (Basil Blackwell, Oxford).

Steane, J M 1975 "The Medieval Parks of Northamptonshire". *Northamptonshire Past and Present* vol 5(3), 211-233.

Storey, R L 1966 *The End of the House of Lancaster* (Barrie & Rockliffe, London).

Swan, V G, Jones, B E A & Grady, D 1993 "Bolesford, North Riding of Yorkshire: a Lost Wapentake Centre and its Landscape". *Landscape History* vol 15, 13-28.

Swan, V G, Mackay, D A & Jones, B E A 1990 "East Lilling, North Yorkshire: The Deserted Medieval Village Reconsidered". *Yorkshire Archaeological Journal* vol 62, 91-109.

Taylor, C 1982 "Medieval Market Grants and Village Morphology". *Landscape History* vol 4, 21-27.

Taylor, C 1998 *Parks and Gardens of Britain: A Landscape History from the Air* (Edinburgh University Press, Edinburgh).

Taylor, C 2000 "Medieval Ornamental Landscapes". *Landscapes* vol 1(1), 38-55.

Taylor, C 2004 "Ravensdale Park, Derbyshire, and Medieval Deer Coursing". *Landscape History* vol 26, 37-57.

Telesko, W 2001 *The Wisdom of Nature: The Healing Powers and Symbolism of Plants and Animals in the Middle Ages* (Prestel Verlag, Munich).

Tempest, S 1875 *The History of Sheriff Hutton and District* (S Tempest, Sheriff Hutton).

Thiébaux, M 1967 "The Medieval Chase". *Speculum* vol 42, 260-273.

Thomas, K 1983 *Man and the Natural World: Changing Attitudes in England 1500-1800* (Penguin Books Ltd, London).

Todd, G 1824 *Castellum Huttonicum: Some Account of Sheriff Hutton Castle* .. (George Todd, York).

Tuck, J 1968 "Richard II and the Border Magnates". *Northern History* vol 3, 27-52.

Tucker, M J 1962 *The Life of Thomas Howard, Earl of Surrey, 1443-1522* (Maqnton & Co., The Hague).

Turnbull, S 1985 *The Book of the Medieval Knight* (Arms & Armour Press, London).

University of York (Department of History) 2000 "The Lord Lieutenants and High Sheriffs of Yorkshire 1066-2000" (unpublished mss).

Upton, A F 1961 *Sir Arthur Ingram c.1565-1642: A Study of the Origins of an English Landed Family* (Oxford University Press, Oxford).

Veale, E M 1957 "The Rabbit in England". *Agricultural History Review* vol 5(2), 85-90.

Venn, J & J A 1922-54a *Alumni Cantabrigiensis: Part I from Earliest Times to 1751* (Cambridge University Press, Cambridge).

Venn, J & J A 1922-54b *Alumni Cantabrigiensis: Part II from 1752 to 1900* (Cambridge University Press, Cambridge).

Virgin, P 1994 *Sydney Smith* (Harper Collins, London).

Wade-Martins, S 2002 *The English Model Farm: Building the Agricultural Ideal 1700-1914* (Windgather Press, Cheshire).

Wakefield Historical Publications 1979 *Samuel Buck's Yorkshire Sketchbook* (Wakefield Historical Publications, Wakefield).

Watkin, J R 1987 "Three Finds of Bronze Age Metalwork from the Vale of York". *Proceedings of the Prehistoric Society* vol 53, 493-498.

Weaver, J 1998 *Middleham Castle, North Yorkshire* (English Heritage guidebook).

Wheater, W 1888 *Some Historic Mansions of York and their Associations, volume 2* (Richard Jackson, Leeds).

Whitaker, J 1892 *A Descriptive List of Deer Parks and Paddocks of England* (Hanson & Co, Ballantyne).

White, T H 1963 *The Age of Scandal* (Penguin, London).

White, T H 1998 *The Sword in the Stone* (Harper Collins, London - reprint of 1938 original).

Wilkinson, D 2003 *Early Horse Racing in Yorkshire and the Origins of the Thoroughbred* (Old Bald Peg Publications, Byland).

Williams, J 2003 "Hunting, Hawking and the Early Tudor Gentleman". *History Today* vol 53(8), 21-27.

Winton, H L 1993 "Sheriff Hutton Air Photographic Transcription" (unpublished mss held by English Heritage NMR).

Woodward, E 1982 *Oxfordshire Parks* (Oxford Museums Service, Woodstock).

Woodward, G W O 1966 *The Dissolution of the Monasteries* (Blandford Press, London).

Woolgar, C M 1999 *The Great Household in Late Medieval England* (Yale University Press, New Haven & London).

Wragg, B 2000 *The Life and Works of John Carr of York* (Oblong Press, York).

Young, C R 1979 *The Royal Forests of Medieval England* (Leicester University Press).